The Telemann Compendium

The Boydell Composer Compendium Series

The aim of the Composer Compendium series is to provide up-to-date reference works on major composers and their music that can both provide instant information and act as a gateway to further reading. The authors are all leading authorities on the composers in question who have been given the remit not only to assemble and present already existing data but also, where appropriate, to make personal interpretations, to introduce new facts and arguments and to shed light on the many discourses surrounding the chosen musicians from their lifetime up to the present day.

The core of each volume is a dictionary section with entries for people, institutions and places connected with the composer; musical, analytical and historical terminology of particular relevance to them; significant events in the reception history of their music; the genres in which they composed; individual compositions or groups of compositions – in short, anyone and anything judged to be pertinent. Entries in the dictionary section are carefully cross-referenced to each other and also to a very comprehensive bibliography section at the end of the volume. Between the dictionary and the bibliography there is a work list based on the latest information, and the volume is prefaced by a concise biography of the composer. Numerous music examples and illustrations are included. By means of this simple formula, the series aims to provide handbooks of wide and durable interest responding to the needs of scholars, performers and music-lovers alike.

Michael Talbot
Series editor

Proposals are welcomed and should be sent in the first instance to the publisher at the address below. All submissions will receive prompt and informed consideration.

email: editorial@boydellandbrewer.com

Previous volumes in this series:

The Vivaldi Compendium, Michael Talbot, 2011
Also available in paperback
The Rameau Compendium, Graham Sadler, 2014
Also available in paperback
The Janáček Compendium, Nigel Simeone, 2019
Also available in paperback
The Telemann Compendium, Steven Zohn, 2020
The Purcell Compendium, Peter Holman and Bryan White, 2025

The Telemann Compendium

Steven Zohn

THE BOYDELL PRESS

First published 2020
The Boydell Press, Woodbridge
Paperback edition 2026

ISBN 978 1 78327 446 8 (hardback)
ISBN 978 1 83765 321 8 (paperback)

The Boydell Press is an imprint of Boydell & Brewer Ltd
and of Boydell & Brewer Inc.
website: www.boydellandbrewer.com

Our Authorised Representative for product safety in the EU is Easy Access System Europe – Mustamäe tee 50, 10621 Tallinn, Estonia, gpsr.requests@easproject.com

A catalogue record for this book is available from the British Library

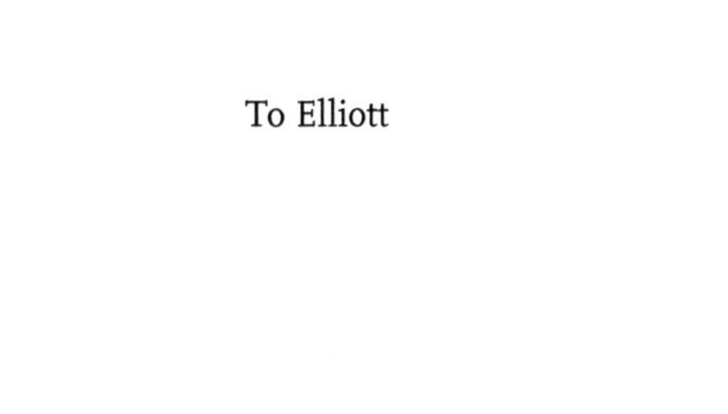

To Elliott

Contents

Illustrations

The author and publisher are grateful to all the institutions and individuals listed for permission to reproduce the materials in which they hold copyright. Every effort has been made to trace the copyright holders; apologies are offered for any omission, and the publisher will be pleased to add any necessary acknowledgement in subsequent editions.

Introduction

This Compendium appears between two significant Telemann commemorations: the 250th anniversary of his death in 1767 and the 300th anniversary of his 1721 arrival in Hamburg, where he spent nearly half a century. That the former commemoration was marked by concert festivals and scholarly conferences worldwide is one indication of the steady rise in popularity Telemann has enjoyed since the middle of the twentieth century. No longer regarded merely as a giant among *Kleinmeister*, the composer has emerged from the shadows of his friends Johann Sebastian Bach and George Frideric Handel to reclaim his rightful place as one of the most significant musicians of the eighteenth century. If Telemann's instrumental works have long been mainstays of the baroque repertory, then his vocal works – comparatively unfamiliar to performers and audiences – are fast becoming better known. All of the surviving operas have been revived, in some cases multiple times, and the passions, cantatas and songs are increasingly programmed in live performances and recordings. This renewed appreciation of Telemann has been supported by growing scholarly attention to all aspects of his biography and music. Yet the resulting critical editions, books and articles have been mainly in German, to the disadvantage of English speakers, and some are difficult to come by. Thus there has long been a need for a guide to Telemann's life and works that can also function as a gateway for exploring the rapidly expanding literature on the composer.

As with previous volumes in this series, the Compendium's first section is devoted to a stage-setting Biography. This is based on a combination of Telemann's own autobiographical essays and the latest research, and in large measure distils information in the following Dictionary. Because the Biography is intended to be both self-contained and accessible, I have left it uncluttered by footnotes. Readers wishing to follow up on certain aspects should easily locate more detailed information in the relevant Dictionary entries.

The Dictionary itself, despite being the book's longest section, can only begin to suggest something of the fullness of Telemann's life and the richness of his musical legacy. Deciding who and what to include presented a special challenge, given the composer's exceptionally vast and varied output and his interactions with countless musicians, writers and patrons over a seven-decade career. One gets the sense that Telemann knew everyone of consequence in his musical world. I have therefore chosen to include only people with close connections to him (and even by this standard, not everyone could be granted entry). Also included are a number of scholars, both living and deceased, who have had an important impact on the field of Telemann studies.

In order to limit the number of entries for individual musical works, I discuss many noteworthy pieces in the context of published collections, coherent groups of works and genres. Thus the famous solo concertos for viola and trumpet are mentioned in the entry for 'Concerto', and the serenata on the death of Friedrich August I (Augustus the Strong) is discussed under 'Funeral music'. Yet many of the best known and most important vocal works, including all the extant operas and the late oratorios, odes and cantatas, receive their own entries, as do several popular overture-suites with characteristic titles. Because so many of Telemann's own publications of instrumental music have entries, providing more general discussions under the headings of 'Sonata', 'Trio' or 'Quartet' would have been redundant. An exception in this respect is 'Keyboard music', which encompasses most of the published keyboard works. Instrumental ensemble music is also discussed in entries devoted to instruments that are closely associated with Telemann, including the calchedon, chalumeau, flute, oboe, recorder, viola and viola da gamba. Thanks to recent research on the church cantatas, I have been able to give attention to each of the known annual cycles, retaining the German titles by which they are commonly identified. There are no entries for places where Telemann lived, as these would largely duplicate material found in the Biography. But I do provide entries for other significant locations (for example, Berlin, Darmstadt, Dresden and Paris).

Although the Dictionary is not intended to be read from start to finish, discoveries via browsing are encouraged by the cross-references indicated by asterisks. (When keywords are more than one word long, the asterisk is placed after the final word, as with Collegium musicum* or Telemann selective critical edition*.) I have also tried to redirect readers to the appropriate place when they search for a person, place or work that is discussed under a different title or in a related entry. Definite and indefinite articles in German titles are skipped in the alphabetical ordering, so that *Die Kleine Cammer-Music* appears under 'K' and *Ein Lämmlein geht und trägt die Schuld* at 'L'. Quotations from German texts are given only in English translation, but the originals may be found in one or more items cited at the end of the entry. Musical examples, which can be useful for underscoring certain points, are omitted because they would benefit only some of the book's potential readers. The illustrations, on the other hand, should prove both informative and entertaining for all readers.

By virtue of its extended length and variable format, the List of Works departs from those in previous volumes of this series. The immensity of Telemann's output discouraged a tabular presentation, except in the case of genres for which I found it especially advantageous, such as the church cantatas, operas, sonatas, concertos and overture-suites. A special feature of the list of church cantatas is a column indicating the annual cycle to which each work belongs (when known); this information draws on some of the latest scholarship. For reasons of space, I have decided to omit most of the lost compositions, opting instead to provide an overview of what is missing. Likewise, works of questionable authenticity and those misattributed to Telemann are, with few exceptions, not accounted for. Although I have made every effort to ensure that this list is as accurate and up-to-date as possible, it is in the nature of such exercises to be provisional.

The Bibliography is necessarily selective and places an emphasis on literature from the past few decades. Readers will quickly notice the preponderance of German-language items, the majority consisting of essays in conference reports and other multi-authored books. This reflects the past and present nature of Telemann research. But I have made every effort to include as many relevant English-language items as possible. In order to keep the Bibliography from becoming too unwieldy, I have omitted articles in standard reference works, prefaces in critical editions of music and, for the most part, writings that do not focus primarily on Telemann. Most items are identified by a code consisting of the first three letters of the author's or editor's surname plus the first three letters of the title (or a significant word within it). Thus *KleDok* is the code for Christine Klein, *Dokumente zur Telemann-Rezeption, 1767 bis 1907*, and *SteFrü* stands for Wolfram Steude, 'Zum kirchenmusikalischen Frühschaffen Georg Philipp Telemanns'. These codes function as literature references at the end of entries in the Dictionary.

This book could not have been completed (or even started, for that matter) without the assistance and encouragement of numerous colleagues and friends. I am grateful to Ralph-Jürgen Reipsch for allowing me to read his work prior to publication. He and his colleagues at the Zentrum für Telemann-Pflege und -Forschung in Magdeburg, Carsten Lange, Ute Poetzsch and Brit Reipsch, also furnished me with essential information at various points during my work. Wolfgang Hirschmann was kind enough to provide me with copies of published and unpublished research by himself and others. Ellen Exner's close reading of drafts of the Biography and Dictionary improved both their content and readability. I owe a great debt of gratitude to Michael Middeke, my commissioning editor at Boydell, and his assistant editor Megan Milan for their unflagging encouragement and patience. And I have benefited enormously from the support, advice and careful eye of the series editor, Michael Talbot, whose own work continues to serve as an inspiration to me.

Steven Zohn
Philadelphia
August 2019

Biography

Georg Philipp Telemann lived one of the longest and most extraordinary musical lives of the eighteenth century, and we are fortunate that he was only too happy to tell us about it in the form of two lengthy autobiographical essays. A musical prodigy before reaching his teens, a force to be reckoned with by his early twenties, the most highly respected German-speaking composer by his thirties and a tireless seeker of new musical paths even in his ninth decade, Telemann was much more than the creator of an unknowably vast amount of music. His compositional fluency, in fact, is arguably the least impressive among his many accomplishments.

There was little in Telemann's family background to augur his career as a musician. His father Heinrich Telemann (1646–85) was born in Cochstedt and educated in various towns in Saxony-Anhalt and Lower Saxony. Heinrich's theology studies at the university in Helmstedt prepared him to become a pastor in Hakeborn in 1668 and deacon at the Heiligen-Geist-Kirche in Magdeburg in 1676. Probably in 1669 he married Johanna Maria Haltmeier (1642–1711), daughter of a pastor in Markt Alvensleben near Magdeburg. Heinrich and Johanna Maria had seven children together, only two of whom would survive childhood. When Heinrich died in January 1685, just short of his thirty-ninth birthday, Johanna Maria was left with four children: twelve-year-old Heinrich Matthias (who became a pastor in Wormstedt near Weimar), ten-year-old Anna Margarethe (who died at thirteen), the nearly four-year-old Georg Philipp and two-year-old Johann Gerhard (who died less than two months later). Telemann recalled helping to support his mother financially through his singing while studying the catechism, Latin and Greek at Magdeburg's Altstädtisches Gymnasium and German poetry at the cathedral school.

In all of his autobiographical writings Telemann stresses how little formal musical training he received as a boy. Here there may be an element of exaggeration in the service of demonstrating his early independence and genius, as with similar stories told about Johann Sebastian Bach, George Frideric Handel and others. At nine or ten Telemann took singing lessons from the Gymnasium's cantor, Benedikt Christiani, studied keyboard with an organist for a mere two weeks (being repelled by having to learn German organ tablature and hearing his teacher's stiff playing) and taught himself recorder and violin ('nature was my teacher', as he claimed). Studying the scores of Christiani and others inspired him to try his own hand at composing arias, motets, instrumental pieces and, at age twelve, a setting of the Hamburg opera libretto *Sigismundus* by C.H. Postel. All this mobilised the 'enemies of music' to persuade Johanna Maria that her son's musical activities could only lead to his ruin, and so she forbade him to compose any more music and confiscated his instruments. Yet in an act of 'innocent disobedience', Telemann continued to compose under cover of darkness and spend 'many hours in secluded places with hidden instruments'.

Johanna Maria renewed her efforts to separate her son from music – in vain, as it turned out – by sending him to boarding school in Zellerfeld in the Harz mountains in 1693 or 1694. There Telemann studied with the Superintendent Caspar Calvör (1650–1725), a pastor, theologian, historian, mathematician and writer who encouraged the boy's musical gifts (having heard his composition for a mountain festival) and most likely exposed him to the theological, classical and baroque literature in his extensive library. Telemann taught himself thoroughbass and continued to compose, providing church music almost every Sunday (including motets for the choir) and writing instrumental pieces for the town musicians. He intensified his musical activities while attending the Andreanum Gymnasium in Hildesheim (1697–1701), where he was successful enough at his studies to graduate third in a class of 150. The school's rector, J.C. Losius, had Telemann write arias for the school plays, and the young composer also provided German cantatas for the Catholic church at the monastery of St Godehard. Telemann was now playing the keyboard again, and he also took up the oboe, flute, chalumeau, viola da gamba, contrabass and bass trombone in response to hearing gifted instrumentalists during his frequent visits to the courts at Hanover and Brunswick, where he also became better acquainted with the French, Italian and theatrical styles. He modelled his church and instrumental works on the music of Antonio Caldara, Arcangelo Corelli, Johann Rosenmüller and Agostino Steffani, and indeed his earliest extant compositions, including sacred concertos and ensemble music for strings apparently composed during the period 1697–1702, reveal his mastery of these mid-baroque idioms.

Back in Magdeburg after graduating from the Gymnasium, Telemann resolved to give up music again, now in favour of studying law (in 1718 he claimed that this was his own choice; in 1740 he recalled following the results of an examination – both stories perhaps intended to deflect any blame from Johanna Maria). Leaving his music and instruments behind with the intent of sacrificing them to 'eternal oblivion', he decided to attend Leipzig University. On his way he passed through Halle, where he 'nearly imbibed the poison of music again through making the acquaintance of the already consequential' George Frideric Handel, then sixteen years old (Telemann was twenty). Over the next several years, as Telemann recalled, he and Handel 'had a steady engagement in melodic matters and their exploration through frequent visits' in both Halle and Leipzig 'and by letter'.

Immediately after matriculating at Leipzig University in October 1701, Telemann was once again confronted with musical temptation, this time in the form of a roommate who owned numerous musical instruments (which he couldn't play very well). This anonymous young man in effect launched Telemann's professional career in music, as the story goes, by uncovering a setting of Psalm 6 in his suitcase (probably *Ach Herr, strafe mich nicht in deinem Zorn*, TVWV 7:3) and arranging to have it performed in the Thomaskirche. Hearing the piece, mayor Franz Conrad Romanus commissioned the twenty-year-old Telemann to compose music for the city's two principal churches, the Thomaskirche and Nikolaikirche, every two weeks – this despite the fact that Johann Kuhnau, longtime organist at the Thomaskirche, had just been appointed the city's music director and Thomaskantor months earlier. Once again impelled to pursue a career in music, Telemann sent back his allowance to his mother as a sign of his newfound autonomy, and in return she gave him her blessing.

Just over a year later, Telemann became director of the Leipzig Opera, contributing at least four works (and probably more) to the company, starting with *Ferdinand und Isabella* (TVWV 21:2) during the 1703 New Year's Fair. He sang minor tenor roles in two of his three operas for 1704, *Der lachende Democritus* (21:1) and *Cajus Caligula* (21:3). Nearly all of this music has been lost, though most of the arias for the third opera of that year, *Germanicus* (21:*deest*) have survived. Telemann also revived the city's Collegium musicum around this time (the dates 1701 or 1702 are often given but cannot be confirmed). As the composer reported in 1718, the ensemble performed with up to forty instrumentalists and singers, often entertained Elector Friedrich August I of Dresden and other 'great rulers' and included more than a few students who went on to have significant careers in music. The Collegium's repertory is difficult to reconstruct, but among the works likely to have been intended for the ensemble are six quintets for two violins, two violas and continuo (TWV 44:5, 11 and 32–35), modelled on the sonatas of Tomaso Albinoni's Op. 2 (Venice, 1700), and the B-flat violin concerto TWV 51:B2, which was evidently known to Handel by 1706.

In August 1704 Telemann was appointed organist and music director of Leipzig's Neue Kirche (so named because extensive renovations had been completed just five years earlier, in 1699). The Collegium immediately became the church's 'house band' and was pressed into service the following month when Telemann provided a colourful setting of the Magnificat (almost certainly TVWV 9:17) to celebrate the consecration of the rebuilt organ. Kuhnau, who had formerly overseen the church's music, can only have viewed this development as a further assault on his authority, and he openly resented the siphoning off of his church musicians by the Collegium and Opera. He may also have known that Leipzig's city council had begun considering Telemann as his potential successor as early as 1703. For his part, Telemann had only kind things to say about Kuhnau, admiring his considerable erudition and claiming to have learned much about fugue and counterpoint generally from the older musician's music.

Some time in 1704 Telemann was offered the position of *Kapellmeister* at the court of Count Balthasar Erdmann von Promnitz (1683–1745) in the Lower Lusatian town of Sorau (now Żary). He had previously experienced court life at Brunswick and Hanover, and twice during his Leipzig years he visited the Berlin court, hearing Giovanni Bononcini's opera *Poliphemo* and meeting a number of famous musicians. Telemann also provided four operas for the Weißenfels court (all lost), and his music received 'the approval of the virtuosos' in the Dresden *Hofkapelle*. Based upon these experiences, he idealised the life of a court musician. As he wrote in 1718:

> If there is anything in the world to encourage a person's spirit, to make him ever more skilful at what he has learned, then it is surely the court. One seeks to gain the grace of great lords, the courtesy of nobles, and the love and deep respect of other servants, sparing no effort to reach one's goal, especially when one is still young enough to have the necessary fire for such undertakings.

Telemann left Leipzig by the middle of 1705, having tendered his resignation from the Neue Kirche position on 12 June. At Sorau he took a deep dive into the French instrumental style, turning to the music of Jean-Baptiste Lully, André Campra 'and other good masters' as models for the two hundred 'Ouvertüren' (ensemble suites) he composed in just two years. In one of his formative musical experiences, Telemann heard tavern musicians in the Polish countryside and in Cracow when the court removed to its residence in Pleß (Pszczyna) in Upper Silesia for six months. He marvelled at the richness of the musicians' improvisations and later adapted the style to concertos, trios and other works. From this point onward, Telemann regarded the Polish and Moravian styles (or at least his version of them) as nearly on a par with the French and Italian idioms when it came to the 'mixed taste' characteristic of German music. He was evidently highly valued by the Francophile Count Promnitz, who retained his *Kapellmeister* during two large-scale dismissals of court musicians. Telemann visited Berlin twice more while at Sorau, in June 1705 and November 1706; he also fled the town for Frankfurt an der Oder between January or February and June 1706 in order to avoid an invasion led by King Charles XII of Sweden.

Telemann's intellectual sparring partner at Sorau was the 'famous music theorist' Wolfgang Caspar Printz, who held the positions of cantor and *Capell-Director* (a lesser post than *Kapellmeister*). Printz was four decades Telemann's senior and had a history of entering into disputes with his colleagues. Taking the role of the 'weeping philosopher' Heraclitus, Printz 'wailed bitterly about the melodic excesses of contemporary composers', while Telemann, playing the 'laughing philosopher' Democritus, 'laughed at the unmelodic artificiality of the old composers'. Another important contact at Sorau was the court dean and preacher Erdmann Neumeister (1671–1756), appointed just months after Telemann's arrival. The composer may already have set texts from Neumeister's *Geistliche Cantaten* (1702), significant for being the first annual cycle of church cantata librettos in the new madrigalian style (with recitatives and arias); the eight known settings by Telemann, scored for solo voice, one or two obbligato instruments and continuo, are the earliest surviving works of their kind. Also most likely dating from Telemann's Leipzig or Sorau years are a dozen settings of biblical verses from Neumeister's earlier cycle of strophic odes (the *Poetische Früchte der Lippen, in Geistlichen Arien* of 1700) for two voices, two violins and continuo (TVWV 1:100 and 10:21–31). In later years, Neumeister would become Telemann's librettist of choice for church music, and in 1711 he became a godfather to the composer's first child, Maria Wilhelmina Eleonora (1711–42).

Telemann's second and, as it turned out, last full-time court position was in the service of Duke Johann Wilhelm in Eisenach. Having previously placed various pots in the fire, only to allow tastes from some of them (as he put it), the composer now endeavoured to show everything he had learned 'with all my instruments, with singing and with the pen', as he remarked in 1740. Eisenach was, he recalled, his 'finishing school' in composition and a place where he became 'a completely different person' in terms of his Christian faith.

The duke had engaged the violinist, dulcimer virtuoso and dancing master Pantaleon Hebenstreit (1667–1750) to begin assembling instrumentalists for a new *Hofkapelle* in October 1707, and Telemann was appointed *Konzertmeister* on 24 December 1708 not only to play violin, but also to write church cantatas after hiring singer-violinists. Among these musicians was Johann Friedrich Helbig (1680–1722), who later succeeded Telemann as *Kapellmeister* and provided librettos to three of his annual cycles of church cantatas. Having filled out the *Hofkapelle's* personnel, Telemann added the position of *Kapellmeister* to his portfolio in August 1709, also becoming court Secretary. The Eisenach orchestra had been set up in the French manner, and Telemann later considered it to be superior to the Paris Opera orchestra, which he heard in 1737–38.

In his capacity as *Konzertmeister*, Telemann performed solos with Hebenstreit, whose superior ability as a violinist caused Telemann to lock himself in the practice room with a rolled-up left shirt sleeve and strong oil for his nerves. It is probable that most or all of Telemann's double violin concertos were composed for him to play with Hebenstreit on these occasions. One of these works, TWV 52:G1, was copied out by Johann Sebastian Bach in nearby Weimar around 1708–9, and thus constitutes the earliest known evidence of contact between the two composers. Telemann recalled in 1718 that he initially found concertos difficult to warm up to, but nevertheless composed a quantity of them at Eisenach and Frankfurt. 'At least', he observed, 'they smell of France.' He also wrote a quantity of sonatas in two to nine parts, winning special praise for his trios.

But vocal music, especially that for the church, was Telemann's first priority. He composed four or five annual cycles of church cantatas for the Eisenach court, along with two incomplete cycles for afternoon services. At least one of the full cycles, the *Geistliches Singen und Spielen* (1710–11, to librettos by Neumeister), was composed at Eisenach, whereas the others may have been sent by Telemann from Frankfurt beginning in 1714. The composer also wrote masses, Communion pieces, psalms, about twenty serenatas for birthdays and namedays (to his own librettos) and fifty secular cantatas, mostly to German texts. It was apparently around 1712 that Telemann's literary inclinations inspired him to adopt his anagrammatic pseudonym 'Melante', which remained in occasional use until the 1730s. Such pseudonyms were not uncommon among musicians, dancers and writers in early eighteenth-century Germany.

Soon after receiving the titles of *Kapellmeister* and Secretary, Telemann wed Amalie Louise Juliane Eberlin (1681–1711), lady-in-waiting to Countess Anna Maria in Sorau, and daughter of the composer and violinist Daniel Eberlin (1647–c. 1715), who had served as *Kapellmeister* in Eisenach during the 1670s and 1680s but was now apparently no longer active as a musician (though Telemann praised him as a 'strong violinist' and 'learned contrapuntist'). The couple were married on 13 October 1709, but tragically, Amalie Louise died on 21 January 1711 during the birth of their daughter, Maria Wilhelmina Eleonora. Telemann's mourning process included writing a lengthy poem memorialising his late wife, and it seems possible that this event, surely the most traumatic he had experienced to that point in his life, contributed to his decision to leave Eisenach by the end of that year. (In December Telemann also learned of the death of his mother, who had been living with his brother Heinrich Matthias.)

In his letter of application for the position of Frankfurt 'Directoris Musices', written between early December 1711 and early February 1712, Telemann expressed a wish to 'quit court life and take up a quieter one'. Shortly before his official appointment to the position on 21 March 1712, he admitted to Johann Georg Ochs, a member of a prominent Frankfurt family, that prior to coming to the city he had turned down a lucrative offer from Elector Friedrich August I of Dresden because, as the composer explained, at court the workload is too heavy, one's employers are not all appreciative of music and it is too easy to fall into disfavour. Later, in his autobiographical essays, Telemann recalled that he 'considered the hoped-for calm of an [imperial] free city conducive to the prolongation of my life' and endeavoured to follow the maxim 'whoever wishes to have lifelong security must settle in a republic'.

Telemann's resolve to leave behind the life of a *Kapellmeister* – at least as far as residing at a court was concerned – was again tested in 1717 (he recalled 'about 1716'), when he travelled through Gotha and was asked to stay as the successor to the recently deceased Christian Friedrich Witt. Not only this, but Duke Ernst August of Weimar proposed making Telemann general *Kapellmeister* to all the courts in the Ernestine line (Eisenach, Gotha and Weimar), 'at least by sending certain compositions' to them. The composer was hardly an unknown quantity in Weimar. In 1715 he had dedicated his first publication, the *Six sonates à violon seul*, to the teenaged Prince Johann Ernst, who was to die just five months later (in 1718 Telemann published Johann Ernst's *Six concerts à violon concertant*). And his relationship to the Weimar court organist and concertmaster Bach must have become close by 1714, for in March of that year he stood godfather to Bach's second son, Carl Philipp Emanuel. A journey by Telemann to Weimar in order to raise the infant out of the baptismal font (as was customary for godparents, and as Emanuel later claimed occurred) seems probable. Nothing came of the general *Kapellmeister* proposal, but Telemann remained in personal contact with Ernst August, sending him instrumental music and secular cantatas from Frankfurt and Hamburg in 1720–21. And in 1717 the composer became *Kapellmeister* in absentia ('Kapellmeister von Haus aus') to the Eisenach court, which required him to send a new annual cantata cycle every two years. He had already been sending cycles to Eisenach, but now he was required to use texts provided by the court. The arrangement, which involved at least five cycles in addition to music for birthdays and other celebrations, remained in effect until Duke Johann Wilhelm's death in 1729.

At Frankfurt Telemann entered a situation very similar to what he had encountered in Leipzig. He directed music at the city's main church, the Barfüßerkirche, and taught music to six to eight boys at the Latin school. He soon added the music directorship of the city's secondary church, the Katharinenkirche, as well as various administrative and musical duties for the Gesellschaft Frauenstein (a society made up of men from the city's patrician families), including the direction of its Collegium musicum. One member of this society, Zacharias Conrad von Uffenbach (1683–1734), may have been responsible for recommending Telemann for the Frankfurt position, but it was his younger brother, Johann Friedrich Armand (1687–1769), who would maintain a long-standing friendship with the composer and provide him with librettos and accompanying copper-plate engravings for a cantata cycle (the *Emblematischer Jahrgang* of 1727–28).

Telemann composed five new annual cycles of church cantatas while at Frankfurt. One was a second setting of Neumeister's *Geistliches Singen und Spielen* (1717–18), but the first of them set new texts by the poet: the so-called *Französischer Jahrgang* (1714–15), known as such for its emphasis on style features common in French opera (including syllabic declamation in arias, frequent arioso passages in recitatives, homophonic choruses alternating smaller and larger groups of singers, and forms such as rondeaus, French overtures and chaconnes). This was followed by the first *Concerten-Jahrgang* (1716–17/1719–20; with librettos by Neumeister and Paul Gottfried Simonis), the *Sicilianischer Jahrgang* (1718–19; librettos by Johann Friedrich Helbig) and the second *Concerten-Jahrgang* (1720–21; librettos by Simonis). The 'Concerto' (or 'Italian') cycles emphasise the concertante interaction of vocal and instrumental forces, whereas the 'Sicilian' cycle (performed first in Eisenach, then years later in Frankfurt) is named for its 'pastoral' scoring (with oboes or recorders frequently playing in thirds) and prevalence of style features associated with the siciliana dance. Telemann's significant innovation in each of his Frankfurt cycles was to conceive them as a group of works unified textually and musically, something that has been misleadingly credited to Johann Sebastian Bach, who wrote his famous 'chorale' cantata cycle a full decade later.

The Frauenstein Collegium musicum gave concerts every Thursday and, later, every other Thursday. Although none of its programmes survive, the ensemble's repertory most likely included instrumental music along with secular and sacred vocal works. One piece surely intended for the collegium is the overture-suite TWV 55:B11 (known today as 'La Bourse'), which offers ironic commentary on the growth and eventual bursting of the Mississippi Company stock bubble in 1719–20. This financial drama would have had special resonance for members of the Gesellschaft Frauenstein, as Haus Braunfels, the building that housed the society (and served as Telemann's residence), was also home to Frankfurt's stock exchange.

But the real highlight of Telemann's association with the collegium was the performance, on 2 and 3 April 1716, of his setting of the famous passion libretto by Barthold Heinrich Brockes, *Der für die Sünde der Welt gemarterte und sterbende Jesus* (TVWV 5:1), known as the *Brockes-Passion*. These events, held in the Barfüßerkirche in order to accommodate larger-than-usual audiences, were public concerts at which one gained entrance by purchasing a printed libretto – quite an innovation for the time. Participating was the entire Darmstadt *Hofkapelle*, and in attendance were various high-born persons. This was Telemann's first passion setting, and its brilliantly theatrical music reflects all that he had learned in nearly two decades of composing music for the church and stage. The success of this venture encouraged him to compose and publicly perform a series of passion oratorios (as distinct from liturgical passions that follow one of the four Gospel narratives) in Frankfurt and Hamburg into the 1760s.

In addition to his ties with the Eisenach and Weimar courts, Telemann established or maintained connections with other courts while at Frankfurt. He visited the Stuttgart court in August 1720 and the Dresden court in September and October 1719, during the wedding festivities for the Habsburg archduchess Maria Josepha and the electoral prince Friedrich August II. At Dresden he would have renewed his friendships with the violinist Johann Georg Pisendel (for whom he wrote a violin concerto during his visit) and Handel, who was there recruiting singers for his London operas. Telemann also continued to provide operas for Leipzig, though only two new works (1715–19) can at present be assigned to his Frankfurt years. He did, however, write other dramatic works for Frankfurt, including a recently discovered wedding serenata, the *Pastorelle en Musique oder Musikalisches Hirtenspiel* (TVWV 11:*deest*; c. 1713–16). This is the earliest dramatic work by the composer to survive intact, and is presumably one of the 'twenty-odd fully scored *Dramata* for the most illustrious weddings both here and abroad, and for the attendance of great lords' that Telemann wrote to his own librettos.

In a publishing venture that foreshadowed his later activities in Hamburg, Telemann followed up his 1715 set of violin sonatas with four more instrumental collections, again issued at his own expense. Noteworthy among them are *Die Kleine Cammer-Music* (1716), suites for melody instrument and continuo dedicated to four oboists, and the *Six Trio* (1718), trio sonatas featuring violin partnered with six different instruments. Five published collections of music in three years (six, if one counts Prince Johann Ernst's concertos) was an output practically unheard of in early eighteenth-century Germany.

Telemann remarried in August 1714, to the sixteen-year-old Maria Catharina Textor (1697–1775), who was seventeen years his junior and hailed from a middle-class Frankfurt family. The couple had nine children, though not all of them survived past childhood. When they left Frankfurt in 1721, Telemann was able to maintain life-long citizenship in the city for himself and his family by sending an annual cycle of church cantatas every two or three years (which he continued to do until 1761). Thus his music remained a staple in the Barfüßerkirche and Katharinenkirche repertories until the last quarter of the eighteenth century.

In September 1718 Telemann wrote the first of two autobiographical essays at the request of Johann Mattheson, who was then soliciting contributions for a book on the lives of musicians. The essay was published only in 1731, as a model for other contributors, and when Mattheson finally completed his book in 1740 it included an entirely new essay by Telemann. The 1718 essay includes a number of the composer's own poems, and additional poems by him were published in anthologies during the 1720s. In later years Telemann wrote and published memorial poems on the deaths of his friends and colleagues Johann Sebastian Bach, Reinhard Keiser and Johann Georg Pisendel.

There are signs that Telemann was being groomed for a 'lateral' move to Hamburg already in 1720, many months before Joachim Gerstenbüttel, director of music at the five principal churches and cantor of the Johanneum school, died in April 1721. The *Brockes-Passion* was performed in Hamburg in 1718, 1719 and 1720, the year that Brockes himself joined the city's senate. Also in 1720, Brockes provided Telemann with librettos for the secular cantatas *Alles redet itzt und singet* (TVWV 20:10) and *Das Wasser im Frühlinge* (20:1; lost), both of which were performed in Hamburg later that year. Further, Telemann's opera *Der geduldige Socrates* (21:9) premiered at the city's Gänsemarkt Opera on 5 February 1721 (with at least five more performances that month), and he contributed a duet to J.G. Vogler's opera *Ulysses*, heard in Hamburg on 7 July. If Brockes helped paved the way for Telemann to succeed Gerstenbüttel, it was the composer's long-time collaborator, Erdmann Neumeister, then head pastor at Hamburg's Jacobikirche, who actively supported his application. An offer was extended to Telemann on 10 July 1721, he petitioned the Frankfurt city council for his release on 21 July and he was installed as Hamburg's music director on 17 September and as cantor of the Johanneum on 16 October.

The demands of Telemann's new position were considerable. As cantor he taught voice lessons, music theory and music history to the boys (he hired others to teach Latin for him). As city music director he was responsible for approximately 120 annual performances of large-scale vocal works between the city's five principal churches (St Petri, St Nikolai, St Katharinen, St Jakobi and St Michaelis): ninety of 'Grosse Musik' (with trumpets and drums) and thirty of 'Kleine Musik' (without trumpets and drums). The annual liturgical Passion (cycling through the accounts of the four Evangelists in the order Matthew, Mark, Luke and John every four years) was heard no fewer than thirteen times. Almost every year he had to provide an oratorio-serenata pair for the celebration of the captains of Hamburg's militia, the so-called *Kapitänsmusik*. There was also a steady call for music to celebrate the installation of preachers and the inauguration of churches in Hamburg and environs, and works had to be provided for political functions and school examinations.

On regular Sundays, Telemann provided concerted music that was heard at three points during the morning service: before the sermon (a full-length cantata, usually a new work), after the sermon (a shorter or less-fully scored cantata heard during Communion, often from an older cycle) and at the end of the service (a one- or two-movement piece that might be a psalm setting or from one of the cantatas performed earlier, generally followed by a chorale). On a given Sunday, a new cantata was heard in one of the five principal churches, rotating in a continuous cycle from oldest to newest church (starting with St Petri and ending with St Michaelis).

Telemann lost little time in reviving Hamburg's Collegium musicum. Starting on 15 November 1721 he instituted a weekly public concert series in his apartment in the Johanneum that ran from late October or early November until the spring, with no concerts offered during the Christmas season and relatively few in the summer. Concerts started to be offered in public venues during the Collegium's second season, and in March 1724 the series expanded to two concerts per week and moved to the Drillhaus, a military exercise facility that doubled as one of Hamburg's main concert halls.

Whatever his expectations were for the new position, Telemann's first year in Hamburg did not quite go according to plan. He was reprimanded in July 1722 for performing his music publicly and charging admission, as he had done without resistance in Frankfurt, and in that year he clashed with the city printer over who had the right to print librettos for his annual liturgical passions – the beginning of a dispute that was periodically renewed over the next thirty-five years. Telemann also discovered that his overall compensation was lower than expected: an ordinance prevented him from writing wedding music on commission, the number of funerals for which he could furnish music was down and his salary and benefits lagged far behind those he had left at Frankfurt. Moreover, he found his teaching duties onerous and the church choirs acceptable only because he hired 'many accessory virtuosos' at his own expense. Telemann was therefore no doubt intrigued to learn that the position of Leipzig city music director and Thomaskantor had become vacant following the death of Johann Kuhnau on 9 June 1722. The city council's first choice for a replacement was in fact not the eventual appointee, Bach, but Telemann, whom they remembered from his university years and, as they noted, had become 'world famous on account of his compositions'.

Telemann performed two test cantatas in the Thomaskirche on 9 August (apparently *Ich muß auf den Bergen weinen und heulen*, TVWV 1:851, and the lost *Wenn du es wüßtest, so würdest du auch bedenken*, TVWV 1:*deest*), and was elected to succeed Kuhnau two days later. After signing a letter of intent, he returned to Hamburg, where on 3 September he wrote a terse letter informing the senate of the Leipzig offer and asking for his dismissal, noting the healthy state of music there, his responsibility to provide for his family and his present unfavourable circumstances in Hamburg. On 15 October he wrote a more extensive 'Memorial' to the Collegium Scholarchale, the school board that oversaw Hamburg's cantorate, in which he again outlined the difficulties of his present position and noted that at Leipzig he could better support his household of eleven or twelve people. The response was swift, with the senate deciding that this 'famous man and virtuoso' was to be retained at all costs. Telemann turned down the Leipzig offer on 6 November.

Meanwhile, he had just assumed the directorship of the Gänsemarkt Opera, and what appears to have been his first contribution to the company in his new role, *Der Sieg der Schönheit* (TVWV 21:10, which premiered shortly before he travelled to Leipzig), proved to be one of his greatest operatic successes. With his Hamburg prospects now enhanced, Telemann embarked on an ambitious programme of composition. He wrote fourteen full-length operas between 1722 and 1730 (including two for the Bayreuth court), in addition to four intermezzos and a dozen operatic prologues. During the same period he composed at least eight complete annual cycles of church cantatas for Hamburg, Frankfurt and Eisenach. Liturgical passions, *Kapitänsmusiken* and various occasional vocal works were repeated in public performances following their initial presentation in the city's principal churches or private venues. Telemann also revived his Frankfurt practice of writing non-liturgical oratorios; his first Hamburg effort, the *Seliges Erwägen* of 1722 (TVWV 5:2), became one of his most successful compositions in any genre, and it sometimes replaced the annual liturgical passion in the city's secondary churches.

Although there were eight paid positions for church singers in Hamburg, Telemann appears not to have had them available together consistently (often there was only one tenor, even when the other parts could be doubled). These were adult professionals, not choir boys, which meant that both concertists and ripienists (doubling singers) could be given solo numbers. Some of these singers, in fact, were active at the Opera, and might appear in church and theatre on the same day. Only from the 1740s did Telemann use boy sopranos instead of male falsettists. His core group of instrumentalists included eight *Ratsmusikanten* plus two adjunct musicians (*Exspektanten*) and ten to thirteen *Chormusikanten* drawn from various other groups of municipal musicians (*Rollbrüder, Grünrollmusikanten, Türmer, Garnisonshautboisten* and *Ratstrompeter*), for a maximum total of eighteen to twenty-one instrumentalists. Telemann hired extra players as needed, especially when music had to be performed simultaneously in several locations.

The mid-1720s through the 1730s were years of great professional success for Telemann in the face of personal challenges. By 1723 he had begun laying plans to print his own music, as he had done earlier in Frankfurt. Between 1725 and 1739 he brought out forty-two new publications containing his own music (several more were second editions or issued by other publishers). The first of these was also among the most ambitious: the *Harmonischer Gottes-Dienst* (1725–27), an annual cycle of seventy-two church cantatas for voice, melody instrument and continuo. This and a few other early Hamburg publications were set in moveable type by professional printers, but already in 1726 Telemann began experimenting with engraving copper plates with hammer-driven punches himself. The first, rather imperfect, product of his efforts was the *Essercizii musici*, containing twenty-four solo and trio sonatas. Telemann continued to engrave his publications from 1727 onward, eventually switching to pewter plates in emulation of London publishers. He aimed in part to edify and educate consumers of printed music through instrumental and vocal works in a variety of scorings and styles, from fantasias for unaccompanied melody instrument and songs for voice and continuo, to more fully scored instrumental and vocal chamber music, to concertos and suites for orchestra (as in the ambitious *Musique de table*), to an opera (the intermezzo *Pimpinone oder Die ungleiche Heyrath*, TVWV 21:15).

It is worth stressing that the extent of Telemann's efforts to engrave and publish his own music was without parallel in the eighteenth century. He also marketed and distributed his products through advertisements of various kinds, including printed catalogues (which sometimes listed forthcoming works), notices in the press and correspondence with prospective customers. His broad network of booksellers and musicians who collected subscriptions and sold copies on commission extended across German-speaking lands as well as to foreign centres such as Amsterdam, London and Paris. Some idea of the audience for Telemann's publications may be gained from the printed lists of subscribers included with the *Musique de table* (Hamburg, 1733) and *Nouveaux quatuors en six suites* (Paris, 1738).

As he had been in Frankfurt, Telemann was still sought after as a *Kapellmeister* during his Hamburg years. He declined an offer from the St Petersburg court in 1729 but nevertheless took on ancillary court appointments as *Kapellmeister* in absentia for Bayreuth (1723–26) and corresponding agent for Eisenach (1725–30). This last post required him to supply news from across northern Europe via ambassadors in Hamburg and his contacts in Berlin, Copenhagen, Denmark, The Hague, Hanover, London, Moscow, Paris, Poland and Vienna; Telemann claimed to correspond with his London and Paris contacts in their native tongues. No doubt he also used these contacts to explore opportunities for selling his publications.

By 1726 Telemann's marriage to Maria Catharina had deteriorated, apparently because of her spendthrift habits. She had been running up a considerable debt that grew to 5,000 Reichstalers – several times her husband's annual income. Telemann had repaid 3,000 Reichstalers by September 1736 (a figure that may include 600 Reichstalers collected by Hamburg citizens), at which time he reported that his wife was 'away from me'. He further remarked that he had no idea where all this money had come from, but it may be that his intensive publishing activities during the late 1720s and 1730s were intended in large measure to offset Maria Catharina's debt. One also wonders whether Telemann's periodic reports of illness during the 1730s – a 'severe paroxysm' required him to dictate a letter to his fifteen-year-old son Andreas in 1730, he was again ill in 1736 and visited the curative mineral baths in Bad Pyrmont at least several times during the decade – were brought on by the stress of overwork. Telemann and Maria Catharina may have reconciled in the late 1730s, for she took care of the book-keeping for a 1738 performance of the *Seliges Erwägen* while he was in Paris, and she adopted a daughter in Hamburg three years later. We lose track of her from this point on, but learn from burial notices that she died in her native Frankfurt in 1775. The long-standing claim that Maria Catharina left her husband for a Swedish military officer, first advanced in the early nineteenth century, appears to have no basis in fact.

The trip to Paris is described in Telemann's 1740 autobiographical essay in almost triumphal terms, and he may well have regarded it as a kind of capstone to his career. One is tempted to compare the trip with those made to London a half century later by Joseph Haydn, another sixtyish German-speaking composer who, then at the top of his game, enjoyed considerable success in a foreign capital. Telemann's 'long-anticipated' visit to Paris commenced in October 1737 and lasted until May 1738. He had been invited by several unnamed musicians, perhaps the same ones who premiered the *Nouveaux quatuors*: flautist Michel Blavet, violinist Pierre Guignon, gambist Jean-Baptiste Antoine Forqueray and cellist Eduoard (whose first name is unknown). Telemann already appears to have enlisted Blavet as his Parisian publishing agent for the *Musique de table*, and publishing concerns – specifically, the halting of unauthorised Parisian reprints of the composer's music – were no doubt a motivating factor behind the trip. Telemann received a twenty-year royal publishing privilege on 3 February 1738, and with it he issued two sets of instrumental works in addition to the *Nouveaux quatuors*. But he was evidently most proud of his motet *Deus judicium tuum regi da* (TVWV 7:7), which was performed twice at the Paris Concert Spirituel in March 1738. This was a singular honour, for few other foreign composers before or after Telemann participated in the French grand motet tradition. Unfortunately, much of what Telemann wrote in Paris has been lost, including two psalm settings, concertos, a French cantata and a comic symphony.

Telemann arrived back in Hamburg to find that the failing Gänsemarkt Opera had at last closed its doors for good. Shortly before or after his arrival, his sixteen-year-old son, Augustus Bernhard, died. Now fifty-seven, Telemann may well have considered these events, following upon those of recent years, as marking a crossroads in his personal and professional life. He had, after all, weathered the twin storms of marital trouble and a serious financial crisis, operated an unprecedented publishing venture, seen a thirty-year career as an opera composer come to an end and made a highly successful visit to Paris. He could expect that his career might last only another decade, and this realisation may have prompted him to adjust his priorities. He issued a few more publications of his own music and then, on 14 October 1740, announced in a local newspaper that he was selling the engraved plates to his publications, which he stipulated must be purchased together or divided into no more than two groups. It is not known who, if anyone, purchased the plates. But Telemann's career as a publisher of his own music was now at an end.

Some commentators have regarded this step as indicative of a creative crisis on Telemann's part, or at least as initiating a fifteen-year 'retirement' period, during which the composer drastically scaled back his professional activities to the point of fulfilling his official duties and not much else. The fact that he now took up gardening as a hobby – throwing himself into the task with characteristic vigour – has only added to this impression. The garden, just outside the city gates, was set up by the spring of 1741. Over the next few decades Telemann mobilised his extensive network of friends and colleagues to help him stock it with rare specimens of flora from all over Europe. Handel and Pisendel personally sent him shipments of plants in the years 1749–54, and a visitor to the garden in 1753 reported seeing 'many strange and beautiful plants'.

Yet aside from closing his publishing business, moving away from writing instrumental music and no longer composing operas (in fact, no new stage works had been written since 1733), Telemann was hardly resting on his laurels or contentedly sniffing the sweet blooms of past successes. For one thing, he continued to issue his music through a new generation of German music publishers: the 1740s saw the publications of two more annual cycles of church cantatas, the *Musicalisches Lob Gottes* and the *Engel-Jahrgang*, alongside the 1745 St John Passion and a few smaller ventures. Only after 1750, as he approached seventy, did Telemann start limiting his production of new church cantatas.

He also re-dedicated himself to producing theoretical works during this period, as was announced in a presumably authorised biographical essay published in 1744. His main theoretical project was a book, first mentioned in 1735, entitled *Theoretisch-practischer Tractat vom Componiren* (Theoretical-Practical Treatise on Composition), a distillation of writings by Johann Joseph Fux and Johann David Heinichen combined with Telemann's 'own ideas and discoveries'. But like several writings proposed in earlier years, this book never saw the light of day. However, Telemann's election in 1739 to Lorenz Christoph Mizler's Correspondierende Societät der musikalischen Wissenschaften (Corresponding Society of Musical Science) resulted in his *Neues musikalisches System* (1742/43, published in 1752 and revised in 1767), a system of tuning intervals enharmonically so that non-keyboard instruments 'will be able to play purely, or nearly so'. These kinds of adjustments, the composer claimed, would increase the sonority of harmonies. Telemann's system was praised by some writers on music theory and criticised by others, but he appears to have been content to remain above the fray.

The year 1755 saw two events that would profoundly shape Telemann's last years. First, his seven-year-old grandson Georg Michael came to live with him following the death of his father, Andreas, at the age of forty. Andreas was the eldest child of Telemann and Maria Catharina, and had been serving as pastor in Ahrensbök. Telemann gave his grandson a thorough musical education, and Georg Michael would assist and deputise for him in church performances during the 1760s before serving as interim director of Hamburg's five principal churches in 1767–68 (ahead of the appointment of Telemann's godson, Carl Philipp Emanuel Bach). From 1773 Georg Michael served as cantor in Riga, performing and promoting his grandfather's music well into the nineteenth century.

The second event of 1755 was Telemann's concert performance in March of two new lyric passion oratorios (with contemplative texts including little or no narrative), the *Betrachtung der neunten Stunde an dem Todestag Jesu* (TVWV 5:5) and *Der Tod Jesu* (5:6). Telemann had received Karl Wilhelm Ramler's libretto for *Der Tod Jesu* from Berlin, where it was simultaneously set by Carl Heinrich Graun. The two settings were heard in the opposite cities (Graun's in Hamburg and Telemann's in Berlin) in the following year, and these performances initiated a series of lyric passion oratorios, odes and secular cantatas written by Telemann during his last decade. The librettos were provided by a group of young poets (two generations younger than Telemann, in fact) that included, in addition to Ramler, Christian Wilhelm Alers, Friedrich Gottlieb Klopstock, Daniel Schiebeler and Friedrich Wilhelm Zachariae. This late musical flowering kept the elderly Telemann at the forefront of literary and musical developments into the late 1750s and early 1760s, a remarkable achievement, especially considering that two of the best pieces among the lot – the oratorio *Der Tag des Gerichts* (Alers; 1762) and the cantata *Ino* (Ramler; c. 1765) – were composed when he was past eighty.

Telemann appears to have corresponded enthusiastically with friends, colleagues and employers throughout his life, and the ninety surviving letters from his pen (along with thirty-nine more written to him) provide both important biographical information and revealing glimpses at his personality. Particularly significant are his epistolary exchanges with other musicians during the 1740s and 1750s, as preserved in letters to the composer from the Berlin court musicians Johann Friedrich Agricola, Carl Philipp Emanuel Bach, Franz Benda, Christoph Nichelmann, Carl Heinrich Graun and Johann Joachim Quantz, as well as from friends such as George Frideric Handel, Johann Georg Pisendel and Johann Adolph Scheibe. Telemann's connection to Berlin became especially strong during the 1750s, due to the influence of his songs on the so-called First Berlin Lieder School, to Berlin performances of his music and to his work as the Hamburg publishing agent for treatises by Agricola, Bach and Quantz.

Three letters between Telemann and Graun from 1751–52 encapsulate the older composer's rigorous thought regarding text declamation and musical style while illustrating the wit and irony often found in his correspondence. Whereas Graun could not understand why the French recitatives of Rameau used so much arioso and shifted between metres, Telemann not only demonstrated the advantages of these practices, but showed how they could be applied with profit to Italianate recitative. Writing on 15 May 1756, Graun referred to a lost letter from Telemann as well as to their earlier exchange on recitative:

> The delay in my reply is due in part to your apparently dubious praises, in particular to the conclusion: 'I shall consider whether I have meant everything seriously'.
>
> The dear, somewhat satirical Telemann has already played such a joke on me when, regarding recitative, he partly took Rameau's side and partly didn't. I have turned over your letter in my mind more than twenty times, in order to savour the bitter and the sweet; however, I still haven't quite found [the latter], aside from the sweet name by which you call me your dear friend.

As Telemann entered his seventies, he abandoned the practice of composing complete annual cycles of church cantatas and began repeating a single work for each five-church cycle of performances, rather than compose a new cantata weekly. In another instance of economising, the annual liturgical passions from the 1760s often include borrowed or recomposed music from earlier works. Weakness in Telemann's legs prevented him from directing performances of his music after 1762 (Georg Michael and other students regularly filled in for him), but for the most part he reacted to his increasing physical infirmity with characteristic humour. On a composing score containing alternative aria settings for the 1762 St Matthew Passion, Telemann penned a short poem making light of his struggles: 'With ink that is all backed up, / With pens that only [write] gooily, / With feeble eyes and gloomy weather, / With a lamp producing little light, / I composed these tidy sheets; / Don't chide me on account of it.' In fact, his mental acuity appears to have remained undiminished, as witnessed not only by the music he produced, but also by his interactions with others. When the musician Johann Wilhelm Hertel (1727–89) visited the eighty-four-year-old Telemann at his Hamburg home in 1765, he was surprised to find the 'old musical hero' engaging him 'so deeply in a discussion about compositional theory'.

Telemann had outlived his time, for most of his contemporaries – Bach, Handel, Mattheson, Rameau, Scarlatti and Vivaldi, to name just the most famous – were long gone. Composers young enough to be his grandchildren, such as J.C. Bach and Haydn, were by now well established in their careers, and the Mozart family was already touring. Yet this figure from the past had somehow managed to remain in the consciousness of the present, and it would take a few decades before posterity, largely ignorant of his music and informed by shifting aesthetic priorities, began to judge Telemann's achievements with unwarranted harshness.

His death around 9 p.m. on 25 June 1767 at the hands of a 'severe chest ailment' was followed by numerous laudatory obituaries in Hamburg, Leipzig and Berlin. Memorial poems were contributed by two of his former students and librettists, Christian Wilhelm Alers and Johann Joachim Eschenburg. Georg Michael received letters of condolence from Telemann's friend Johann Heinrich Rolle, his godson Carl Philipp Emanuel Bach and his Berlin colleague Christian Gottfried Krause. Rolle recalled that during a visit to Telemann in early 1767, the composer confided to him that he would surely die in the present year. Among the many moving sentiments in his letter, Rolle asked 'for how many years would music in Germany perchance have remained miserable and pathetic had there arisen no Telemann, who by his divine genius and through his exceedingly great industry lifted music out of darkness and gave it a completely different and new impetus?'

Dictionary

Note to Readers

Telemann wrote several autobiographical essays (see Autobiographies below), the most significant of which are cited in the Dictionary as follows:

AB 1718 'Lebens-Lauff mein Georg Philipp Telemanns; Entworffen In Frankfurth am Mayn d.10.[-14.] Sept. A. 1718', in Johann Mattheson, *Grosse General-Baß-Schule. Oder: Der exemplarischen Organisten-Probe* (Hamburg: Johann Christoph Kißner, 1731; repr. Hildesheim: Georg Olms, 1968), 168–80.

AB 1738 Autobiographical sketch, transcribed in Ralph-Jürgen Reipsch, 'Unbekannte Biographien Georg Philipp Telemanns: Eine autobiographische Skizze und ein zweiter deutsch-französischer Lebenslauf', *Die Musikforschung* 67/4 (2014), 318–40.

AB 1740 'Telemann', in Johann Mattheson, *Grundlage einer Ehren-Pforte* (Hamburg: Mattheson, 1740; repr. Kassel: Bärenreiter, 1969), 354–69.

***Adelheid oder die ungezwungene Liebe*, TVWV 21:17** From 1723 to 1726 Telemann served as *Kapellmeister* 'von Haus aus' (in absentia) for the Bayreuth court, whereby he provided occasional instrumental works and an opera once a year for a salary of 100 Reichstalers. His first opera for Bayreuth, the lost *Alarich oder Die Straf-Ruthe des verfallenen Roms* (1723; TVWV 21:12), was followed the next year by *Adelheid*, the music of which is mostly lost as well. The libretto for *Adelheid*, by Johann Philipp Praetorius*, revolves around the conquest of Italy by the German king Otto I (Otto the Great, 912–73) in 951. Otto's invasion of Lombardy results in his falling in love with Adelaide, widow of the previous king of Italy, through a series of intrigues involving disguises and imprisonments. Telemann revived the opera in Hamburg on 17 February 1727, and within a year he published eleven arias and two duets from the comic scenes in reduced scoring as the *Lustige Arien aus der Opera Adelheid* (the publication has been lost, but a 1733 reprinting survives). This is the only extant music from the opera, apart from a twelfth aria preserved in manuscript, and Telemann's print followed a tradition of published excerpts from Hamburg Opera productions that went back to the 1680s. Among these excerpts are some frivolous texts that were criticised as 'shameless' by Johann Mattheson* and others. *HobAdh, TayCan.*

Admiralitätsmusik Telemann composed this allegorical serenata, *Unschätzbarer Vorwurf erkenntlicher Sinnen* (TVWV 24:1) with text by Michael Richey*, for a festive meal on 6 April 1723 celebrating the centennial of the Hamburg Admiralty, an organisation that oversaw all naval concerns of the port city. It is therefore related to the annual *Kapitänsmusik** Telemann composed for the same organisation. According to an eyewitness account of the meal, 'the large hall of the Niederbaumhaus was beautifully decorated, a dinner well prepared, a stage erected and hung with tapestries for the vocal and instrumental musicians, and a lieutenant with petty officers and forty grenadiers placed on guard before the house. In front of the tree lay the admiralty yacht, which fired its cannons during toasts. All of the ships present were decked out in their finest with pennants and flags, and those ships with cannons boldly let themselves be heard. . . . During the dinner Herr Telemann performed a very pleasant piece of music and, separately, an excellent serenata for which the popular Herr Professor Richey had written exceptionally beautiful verses. The festivities lasted until morning.' The 'very pleasant piece of music' was the *Wasser-Ouverture** (TWV 55:C3) and the so-called *Admiralitätsmusik* subsequently enjoyed great success as a concert work, being heard multiple times in Hamburg's Drillhaus in 1723. *MaeAdm.*

Agricola, Johann Friedrich Agricola (1720–74), who studied with Johann Sebastian Bach* and Johann Joachim Quantz*, succeeded Carl Heinrich Graun* as *Kapellmeister* of the Berlin *Hofkapelle* of Friedrich II, King of Prussia (Frederick the Great)* in 1759. In the first of three letters* Agricola wrote to Telemann (1752, 1755 and 1757), he recalled that six of the composer's cantatas had served him as models of writing for the voice, and that these works (possibly the *Sechs Cantaten** of 1731), along with Telemann's church pieces, had been the first musical works to 'touch his heart'. A manuscript copy of the *Sechs Cantaten* in Agricola's early hand belongs to the music collection of the Sing-Akademie zu Berlin*, as do his copies of selected Telemann quartets, concertos and sacred cantatas. Telemann acted as a publishing agent for Agricola's treatise on singing, the *Anleitung zur Singkunst* (1757), apparently receiving six free copies of the book in exchange for collecting thirty subscriptions by October 1755. Agricola and Telemann both set Karl Wilhelm Ramler's* cantata libretto *Die Hirten bei der Krippe zu Bethlehem* (in 1757 and 1759, respectively), and it seems possible that Agricola shared his setting, or at least Ramler's poetry, with Telemann. *HenSin, ReiSin, TelBri.*

Albinoni, Tomaso The early published instrumental works of Albinoni (1671–1751), especially Op. 2 (*Sinfonie e concerti a cinque*; Venice, 1700), Op. 5 (*Concerti a cinque*; Venice, 1707) and Op. 6 (*Trattenimenti armonici per camera*; Amsterdam, c. 1712), exerted a demonstrable influence on the concertos and sonatas Telemann composed in Leipzig, Sorau and Eisenach. In particular, Telemann modelled his six string quintets (TWV 44:5, 11 and 32–35) on Albinoni's Op. 2, most likely while at Leipzig (1701–05). Many years later, a Hamburg performance of Telemann's comic intermezzo *Pimpinone** (the libretto of which was based on that of Pietro Pariati, set by Albinoni in 1708) featured Italian concertos between the acts, including the eighth and tenth concertos of Albinoni's Op. 9 (*Concerti a cinque*; Amsterdam, 1722). *SwaSol, TalAlb, ZohMix.*

Alers, Christian Wilhelm Alers (1737–1806), who first came into contact with Telemann as a student at Hamburg's Johanneum, worked as a pastor and preacher in Rellingen and Ütersen near Hamburg. In 1762 he provided the libretto to Telemann's last oratorio, *Der Tag des Gerichts**, TVWV 6:8. Three years later he wrote the words to a strophic serenata set by Telemann in honour of the centennial celebration of Hamburg's Handlungs-Deputation (Commerce Deputation), the lost *Hamburgs Flor*, TVWV 24:4; the work's sinfonia was published in 1765 in keyboard reduction as the *Symphonie zur Serenate auf die erste hundertjährige Jubelfeyer der Hamburgischen Löblichen Handlungs=Deputation*, TWV Anh. 50:1. *RatAle.*

***Alster-Ouverture*, TWV 55:F11** Like the better known *Wasser-Ouverture**, to which it may have been conceived as a kind of 'water music' sequel, this overture-suite* has been associated with a festive Hamburg dinner held on 4 June 1725 in honour of the visiting Duke August Wilhelm of Braunschweig-Wolfenbüttel. The event featured Telemann's lost serenata *Auf zur Freude, zum Scherzen, zum Klingen*, TVWV 13:6, and took place in Uhlenhorst (now a district of Hamburg) following a boat ride on the Alster lake. There is, however, no documentary evidence connecting the suite to this occasion. Regardless, the *Alster-Ouverture* (a modern appellation; Telemann left the work untitled) appears to have been heard publicly in Hamburg several times in December 1725 and offers a remarkably vivid and ingenious sound portrait of life in and around the Alster. Scored for two oboes, four horns and strings, the suite follows an overture with eight movements bearing characteristic titles: 'Die canonierende Pallas' (The Can[n]oning Pallas Athena; featuring both imitation 'cannon' blasts and musical canons), 'Das Alster Echo' (Echo of the Alster; featuring antiphonal double-echoes), 'Die Hamburgische Glockenspiele' (The Hamburg Carillon), 'Der Schwanen Gesang' (The Swan Song; another punning title referring to the Alster's water fowl and the musical lament tradition), 'Der Alster Schäffer Dorff Music' (Village Music of the Alster Shepherds; appropriately rustic and naive), 'Die concertierenden Frösche und Krähen' (The Concertizing Frogs and Crows; full of outrageously chromatic sighs and unresolved dissonances), 'Der ruhende Pan' (Resting Pan) and 'Der Schäfer und Nymphen eilfertiger Abzug' (Hurried Departure of the Shepherds and Nymphs). Two additional movements scored for horns and bassoon, 'Der jauchzende Pan' (Rejoicing Pan) and 'Der frohlockende Peleus' (Jubilant Peleus) are inserted (but crossed out) before 'Der ruhende Pan' in a set of manuscript parts apparently sent by Telemann to the Dresden *Hofkapelle*; these movements may belong to an early or alternative version of the piece, perhaps performed in the open air as *Harmoniemusik**. *MaeOrc, SchGlo, ZohMix.*

Arolsen *See* **Bad Pyrmont** and **Polon, Maria Domenica**

***Die Auferstehung*, TVWV 6:7** Telemann's second oratorio on the resurrection of Jesus premiered on 13 April 1761, almost exactly a year after *Die Auferstehung und Himmelfahrt Jesu**. The libretto, by Justus Friedrich Wilhelm Zachariae*, is more lyrical than its predecessor: in the absence of a designated narrator, several unnamed personages both relate the events (from the earthquake at the resurrection of Jesus to his ascension) and react to them. The work's form is also unconventional, with a predominance of accompanied recitatives (featuring orchestra in addition to solo violin, flute and trumpet) and choruses, the two often paired. Aside from a substantial soprano aria, this thirty-minute work includes only two additional arias, both brief, one paired with chorus. Telemann's music is noteworthy for his vivid word-painting and expressive (and often surprising) harmonies and modulations in the accompanied recitatives. These last effects recall the composer's advice to Carl Heinrich Graun* a decade earlier: 'If there is nothing new to find in melody, then one must seek it in harmony.'

***Die Auferstehung und Himmelfahrt Jesu*, TVWV 6:6** This oratorio to a libretto by Karl Wilhelm Ramler* was first performed in Hamburg's Drillhaus, a combination of military exercise space and concert hall, on 28 April 1760. In February of that year Ramler wrote to the poet Johann Wilhelm Ludwig Gleim in Halberstadt that Telemann 'wishes to sing his swan song, and I am to submit the words for him'. The libretto, which covers events from the earthquake at the resurrection of Jesus to his ascension, does not feature a typical Evangelist and close dialogue between biblical characters, but rather a narrating Christian who reacts sensitively to events and quotes dialogue. Telemann, however, divided some of Ramler's recitatives between multiple singers to make it more apparent which character is speaking at a given moment. Balancing the arias and duets are a number of choruses, including a triumphal one in cantional style that is heard three times during the oratorio. It has been suggested that the sarabanda-like instrumental sinfonia, marked 'sombre' (*Finster*), and the following fugal chorus were intended by Telemann as a remembrance of his friend George Frideric Handel*, who had died almost exactly a year before the oratorio's premiere (the fugal chorus appears to have been modelled on the chorus 'He smote all the first born in Egypt' from *Israel in Egypt*). Writing to Ramler about the oratorio in 1760, Christian Gottfried Krause* in Berlin considered the oratorio 'absolutely incomparable. Telemann has shown that, in his eightieth year, he can do anything.' *Die Auferstehung und Himmelfahrt Jesu* has been published in volume 32 (1997) of the Telemann selected critical edition*. *HobTom, ReiBea.*

Auszug der jenigen musicalischen . . . Arien *See* ***Harmonisches Lob Gottes***

Autobiographies Telemann wrote no fewer than four autobiographical essays between 1718 and 1740, and these are of vital importance for establishing the basic facts of his first six decades. In fact, no other major composer of the eighteenth century took as much care, over so many years, in recounting his life experiences. The first essay (AB 1718) was written at the request of Johann Mattheson*, who was then assembling composers' autobiographies for a projected book. Telemann completed it on 10 September 1718, recounting his first thirty-seven years while peppering the text with his own poetry and quotations in foreign languages; he added supplementary information in a letter* to Mattheson of 14 September. Mattheson eventually published the essay in his *Grosse General-Baß-Schule. Oder: Der exemplarischen Organisten-Probe* (Hamburg, 1731) as a model for other composers who might contribute biographies. The second autobiographical essay takes the form of a brief vita with covering letter, dated 20 December 1729, sent by Telemann to Johann Gottfried Walther*, who published the information in his *Musicalisches Lexicon* (Leipzig, 1732). Much briefer than AB 1718, this dictionary entry nevertheless incorporates new material, including a list of Telemann's publications up to 1728 and a statement about his stylistic development; it was the basis for several subsequent dictionary and encyclopaedia articles on the composer. A

366 T

„darauf, nach vorhergegangenem Einladungs-Programmate, mittelst einer
„Rede, de Musica in Ecclesia, feierlich eingeführet.

„Ohngefehr ein Jahr hernach wurden die in Abnehmen gerathene
„Opern, durch einige Ministers und hochadeliche Personen, in einen verbes-
„serten und prächtigen Stand gesetzet, und mir dabey die Aufsicht über die
„Musik, nebst der Verfassung neuer Schauspiele, gegen 300. Rthlr. jähr-
„lichen Einkommens, aufgetragen.

„Anno 1723. berief mich Leipzig an die Stelle weiland Herrn **Johann**
„**Kuhnau**, Musikdirectoris und Cantoris daselbst, welche Ehre der Nachfolge
„mir bereits vor 20. Jahren zugedacht war: weil jenes Schwächlichkeit dessen
„baldigen Tod vermuthen ließ; allein es beliebte der Stadt Hamburg, diesen
„Ruf, durch ansehnliche Verbesserung meines Unterhalts, abzulehnen.

„Der eisenachische Hof, dem ich annoch, als Capellmeister, mit
„einer Besoldung von 100. Rthlr., bedient war, ernannte mich 1724. zum Cor-
„respondenten, mit Beilage von ebenmäßiger Summe: in welcher Ver-
„waltung ich die merckwürdigsten Neuigkeiten im Norden wöchentlich zwei-
„mahl zu berichten hatte.

„Ferner erhielt ich 1726. von Bayreuth eine Bestallung, als Capell-
„meister, lieferte von Zeit zu Zeit einige Instrumental-Musik, und jährlich eine
„Oper: wofür mir 100. Rthlr. Besoldung angediehen.

„Im 1729ten Jahre wurde mir aus Rusland gewincket, um eine deut-
„sche Capelle zu errichten, die sich hernach in eine welsche verwandelt hat. Ham-
„burgs Annehmlichkeit aber, und der Vorsatz, nach vorhergegangenem viermah-
„ligen Rücken, endlich stille zu sitzen, überwogen die Begierde nach einer ausser-
„ordentlichen Ehre.

„Meine längst-abgezielte Reise *) nach Paris, wohin ich schon von
„verschiedenen Jahren her, durch einige der dortigen Virtuosen, die an etlichen
„meiner gedruckten Wercke Geschmack gefunden hatten, war eingeladen wor-
„den, erfolgte um **Michaelis**, 1737. und wurde in 8. Monathen zurück geleget.

Da-

*) Hier kann ich nicht umhin, dem Verfasser, der aus Bescheidenheit von seiner grossen Stär-
cke in den lebenden Sprachen stilleschweiget, ins Wort zu fallen, und ihm Gerechtigkeit
wiederfahren zu lassen, mit dem Geständnis, daß er schon längst vor seiner Pariser Reise,
und ohne Deutschlands Gräntzen weit zu überschreiten, nicht nur für einen Meister
im Frantzösischen, und Italiänischen, sondern auch so gar einiger maassen im Eng-
ländischen hat gehalten werden können: wie mir solches aus unserm Briefwechsel bekannt ist. Ach! es ist ein schönes, nützliches Ding um diese Sprachen. Lieben Leute,
lernet sie, wo ihr in der Welt fort kommen, und zuletzt in eurer Einsamkeit, unter den
todten Lehrmeistern, ein vergnügtes Leben führen wollet.

1. An excerpt from Telemann's autobiographical essay in Johann Mattheson's *Grundlage einer Ehren-Pforte* (Hamburg, 1740), in which he recalls becoming director of the Hamburg Opera, turning down the position of Leipzig Thomaskantor, becoming correspondent to the Eisenach court and *Kapellmeister* in absentia to the Bayreuth court, declining the position of *Kapellmeister* to the St Petersburg court and visiting Paris (Staatsbibliothek zu Berlin – Preußischer Kulturbesitz, Music Department and Mendelssohn Archive, Mus. D 1082). Image courtesy of Art Resources, NY. Reproduced by permission.

c. 1738 autobiographical sketch in Telemann's own hand recently came to light in Riga (AB 1738). It was inherited by Georg Michael Telemann* and appears to have been intended as a draft of the longer autobiographical essay written for Mattheson in 1739 or 1740 (AB 1740), essentially updating AB 1718; this last autobiography appeared in the *Grundlage einer Ehren-Pforte* (Hamburg, 1740), the book on musicians' lives that Mattheson had been planning since 1715. Telemann's willingness to communicate the details of his life may have been inspired by his father, Heinrich Telemann*, who sketched a family tree and exhorted following generations to contribute to the Telemann genealogy; this material passed to Heinrich Matthias Telemann* (the composer's older brother), then to Andreas Telemann* (the composer's eldest son, who wrote an autobiographical essay shortly before his death) and finally to Georg Michael (whose own autobiographical essay was published in 1831). *ChaCou, ReiBio, SieLeb, VieAut, ZohRef.*

Bach, Carl Philipp Emanuel Telemann stood as godfather to Carl Philipp Emanuel Bach, lending his middle name to his godson, and was probably present in Weimar to raise the infant out of the baptismal font on 10 March 1714, as was later claimed by Bach. He appears to have taken seriously his responsibility as a spiritual and professional guide/role model for his godson, especially after the death of Johann Sebastian*, for his Hamburg performances of the younger Bach's Easter cantata *Gott hat den Herrn auferwecket*, Wq 244, in April and May 1756 were most likely intended to pave the way for his godson to succeed him as the city's music director, which in fact occurred in 1768. There is further evidence that the two were in close contact during the 1750s: Telemann acted as Bach's publishing agent for the first part of the *Versuch über die wahre Art das Clavier zu spielen* (1753), wrote a letter of recommendation in support of Bach's 1755 application for the vacant post of Leipzig Thomaskantor and received two friendly letters from his godson in December 1756 and July 1759 (probably the remnants of a once extensive correspondence). Bach had visited Mattheson in Hamburg in June 1751, and it seems reasonable to assume that he also called upon his godfather at this time. During his Hamburg years, Bach borrowed settings of biblical recitatives, turba choruses and chorales from Telemann's 1745 St John Passion, *Ein Lämmlein geht und trägt die Schuld** (TVWV 5:30), for his own St John Passion pasticcios of 1772, 1776, 1780, 1784 and 1788; additionally, Telemann's 1760 St Luke Passion provided models for Bach's passions in 1771, 1779 and 1787. Bach also performed a number of Telemann's vocal works throughout his tenure at Hamburg. His evident familiarity with the 'Heilig' chorus from Telemann's inauguration music* for the Heilige Dreieinigkeitskirche in St Georg (TVWV 2:6; 1747), and with another chorus from the inauguration music for the Great St Michaeliskirche (2:12; 1762), can be heard in his own famous *Heilig* (Wq 217; 1776). Among the music Bach owned by his godfather were four annual cantata cycles, including the *Musicalisches Lob Gottes in der Gemeine des Herrn** and the *Engel-Jahrgang**. *ExnGod, HirHei, HirKom, KnoHam, RatDon, ReiAuf, SatRez, SchTel, TelBri, WolOst, WolPas.*

Bach, Johann Sebastian Despite many points of contact between Telemann and Bach, the precise nature of their relationship remains unclear, not least because of a conspicuous lack of correspondence between them (though they surely exchanged letters). The two composers must have met no later than Telemann's years in Eisenach (1708–12), when Bach was employed at the nearby ducal court in Weimar. A set of manuscript parts to Telemann's double violin concerto TWV 52:G1, copied by Bach c. 1708–09, provides the earliest evidence of contact between the two, and their relationship must have become close by the time Carl Philipp Emanuel Bach* was born on 8 March 1714, for Telemann stood godfather to the infant and was probably present at the baptism two days later. In 1775 Emanuel wrote of his father that 'in his younger days he saw a good deal of Telemann, who also raised me out of the baptismal font. [crossed out:] He esteemed him, particularly in his instrumental things, very highly.' This statement helps explain not only Bach's copy of Telemann's double violin concerto, but also his c. 1713–14 solo keyboard transcription of the violin concerto TWV 51:g1 (BWV 985) and his borrowing of a theme from the concerto for oboe or flute TWV 51:G2 (in the second movement of the concerto BWV 1056, refashioned as the sinfonia to the cantata BWV 156). In 1722 Telemann probably visited the Bach family as he passed through Cöthen on the way to and from Leipzig, and by this time the young Wilhelm Friedemann Bach* had learned Telemann's keyboard suite TWV 32:14. As Leipzig Thomaskantor, Bach performed at least several of Telemann's church cantatas, and the two appear to have kept in touch during the late 1720s and 1730s: Telemann published Bach's 'Hudemann' puzzle canon, BWV 1074, in *Der getreue Music-Meister** (1729), and Bach subscribed to Telemann's *Nouveaux quatuors en six suites* (Paris, 1738). In 1751 Telemann wrote a memorial sonnet for Bach (one of only three memorials he is known to have written, the others being for George Frideric Handel* and Reinhard Keiser*). In this poem, published by Friedrich Wilhelm Marpurg* in 1755, he praises Bach's organ playing and compositions (the latter 'regarded with great pleasure, and also often with envy'), and notes that his students and sons will immortalise his name, singling out Emanuel in this regard ('But what we most cherish about you, / Berlin shows us in a worthy son'). *ExnGod, HirInd, HobBer, LanBac, LanHer, PayBac, RacSin, RatSon, ReiAnn, SchBac, SchTel, ZohImi.*

Bach, Wilhelm Friedemann The eldest son of Johann Sebastian Bach* performed two of Telemann's annual cantata cycles, the *Französischer Jahrgang** and *Engel-Jahrgang**, while music director at Halle (1746–64). He also modelled at least one of his own cantatas on a work by Telemann. His contact with the older composer's keyboard music* went back to his pre-teen years, as the *Clavierbüchlein für Wilhelm Friedemann* includes the three-movement Suite in A major, TWV 32:14. Although Telemann most likely first met Friedemann as a small boy in Weimar, there is no evidence of a personal relationship between the two in later years. *TayBac, WolFle.*

Bad Pyrmont This town near Hamelin in Lower Saxony was popular for its mineral springs and baths, and it was the summer residence of the Prince of Waldeck, for whose court in Arolsen Telemann supplied music from 1726. The composer mentioned having visited Bad Pyrmont three times by 1734, and he continued to return in later years (his presence is documented in 1731, 1736, 1742 and 1751). Visitors to this spa relaxed by taking strolls, playing games of billiards and cards, dancing, listening to oboe bands and attending performances at the opera house and theatre. In 1734 Telemann published a set of trios that both reflects and promotes the carefree atmosphere of spa life. The *Scherzi melodichi* (the full title of which may be translated as 'Melodic scherzos for the entertainment of those who drink the mineral water in Pyrmont, with simple and easy ariettes for violin, viola and continuo') include seven suites of seven movements each – one work for each day of the week. Two more instalments were planned by Telemann but never materialised; together they would have provided daily music for a full cure, which typically lasted three to four weeks. *BruAro, ZohMix.*

Bartels, Heinrich Remigius A Frankfurt banker, city councilman and musician, Bartels (1686–1735) underwrote and was a founding member of the Frauenstein Society's Collegium musicum* that Telemann directed from 1713. In AB 1718 the composer devoted a laudatory poem to Bartels and described him as an 'extraordinary music lover and connoisseur' who was not only well versed in both French and Italian music, as well as in a 'mixed taste'* (*gemischter Goût*) that combined them, but was also a singer and player of several instruments, particularly the violin. Bartels hosted private performances of Telemann's *Brockes-Passion** in his home, and directed the first public performances of the work on 2–3 April 1716 in Frankfurt's Barfüßerkirche. He may have played a role in Telemann's decision to leave Eisenach for Frankfurt in 1711–12, and in August 1718 stood godfather to Telemann's son Heinrich Matthias. *FisDok.*

Bayreuth *See* ***Adelheid oder die ungezwungene Liebe*, TVWV 21:17**

Beck, Heinrich Valentin Beck (1698–1758) was cantor in Lauterbach and Hanau before moving to Frankfurt in 1738 to sing as a bass and serve as 'Vice-Capell-Director'. He assumed musical direction of the city's Peterskirche from 1743, and from 1750 served as Vice-Music Director of the Barfüßerkirche and Katharinenkirche. More than 300 scores and sets of performing parts to Telemann's cantatas at the Universitätsbibliothek Johann Christian Senckenberg Frankfurt am Main are in Beck's hand. His scores, and some parts, predate his arrival in Frankfurt and were apparently copied from Eisenach* sources authorised by the composer. *JunKan, KerKan, KerRez, PoeKir, SchKat.*

***Das befreite Israel*, TVWV 6:5** This oratorio, to a libretto by Friedrich Wilhelm Zachariae*, was first performed at a public concert in Hamburg's Drillhaus, a combination of military exercise facility and concert hall, on 29 March 1759. Zachariae's text draws on the Book of Exodus in recounting the parting of the Red Sea, and mixes narration of and reflection upon that event with an extended song of praise to God. Telemann's setting is not divided in the conventional manner between arias, recitatives and chorales; rather, ariosos and arias alternate freely with choruses, with scarcely any recitative. Regarding this quality, Zachariae noted that Telemann had 'demonstrated that poetry can be musical even when there are no recitatives or arias'. The oratorio has been published in volume 22 (1971) of the Telemann selected critical edition*.

Behrndt-Jahrgang *See* ***Stolbergischer Jahrgang***

Berlin Telemann's contact with Berlin's musical life spanned much of his career. As he recalled in AB 1740, he visited the city twice while at Leipzig (1701–05) and twice more while at Sorau (in 1705 and 1708). Three decades later, Telemann was in contact with musicians connected with the Prussian crown prince and eventual king, Friedrich II (Frederick the Great)*. Letters* between Telemann and Berlin musicians, including Johann Friedrich Agricola*, Carl Philipp Emanuel Bach*, Franz Benda, Carl Heinrich Graun*, Christoph Nichelmann (the composer's former student*), and Johann Joachim Quantz*, span the years 1739–59. During this period Telemann acted as a publishing agent for books by Agricola, Bach, Friedrich Wilhelm Marpurg* and Quantz; he must also have been in contact with other Berlin musicians and literary figures such as Christian Gottfried Krause* and Karl Wilhelm Ramler*, several of whose texts he set during the 1750s and 1760s. That Telemann's music was well known and frequently heard in Berlin from at least the 1740s onward is clear from Quantz's *Versuch* and pedagogical materials, Marpurg's *Abhandlung von der Fuge*, the inclusion of three songs* in the *Oden mit Melodien* (edited by Krause and Ramler), the music archive of the Sing-Akademie zu Berlin* (which reflects musical repertories heard in churches, concerts, salons and other venues) and public performances of *Die Donnerode**, *Ino**, *Der Messias**, *Seliges Erwägen** and *Der Tod Jesu**. It has been suggested that Telemann may have visited Graun and other Berlin musicians sometime in 1751, for his relationship with them appears to have deepened from this date. It is also possible that one set of Telemann's duets*, the *Sei duetti* (TWV 40:130–35), was written for Frederick the Great and Quantz around this time. *CzoGra, TelBri, ZohMix.*

Beschreibung der Augen-Orgel During his 1737–38 trip to Paris* Telemann encountered the as yet incomplete 'clavecin pour les yeux' (keyboard for the eyes) or 'clavecin oculaire' (ocular keyboard) of Louis Bertrand Castel (1688–1757), a Jesuit priest who taught mathematics, physics and other topics at the Collège Louis-le-Grand, and whose 'wit and courtesy' Telemann experienced at first hand. The instrument was designed so that when a key was depressed, a silk string, iron wire or wooden lever pulled or pushed a colourful little box, panel, plate or lightly painted lantern, so that one would both hear a tone and see a colour. Upon returning to Germany, Telemann published his own German translation of an anonymous French letter describing Castel's keyboard as the *Beschreibung der Augen-Orgel* (Description of the eye-organ; Hamburg, 1739). According to the letter's author, 'the colours are as varied as the sounds and have certain correspondences [with them]. The eye can merge them, facilitate their comparison and perceive their order and disorder. This perception causes pleasure and stimulation in all things, and the real musical pleasure consists in repeatedly observing such a distinction [both] instantly and gradually over a short period of time.' In his brief preface, Telemann remarks that he will honour a request by 'not a few' friends to publish his impressions of musical life in Paris: 'Up to now, time constraints alone have placed limitations on my intentions, but have not prevented a good many of them to be set down onto paper.' Regrettably, he never published his Parisian impressions. Castel himself published Telemann's *Beschreibung* (in French translation) in his book *L'optique des coulers* (Paris, 1740), and Lorenz Christoph Mizler* reprinted the original German version (*Musikalische Bibliothek*, 1742) in association with his Correspondierende Societät der musikalischen Wissenschaften (Corresponding Society of Musical Science), of which Telemann was a member. *WolBes.*

***Betrachtung der neunten Stunde an dem Todestag Jesu*, TVWV 5:5** This brief oratorio, to a libretto by Joachim Johann Daniel Zimmermann*, was first performed on 19 March 1755 during a concert in Hamburg's Drillhaus, a double-bill with *Der Tod Jesu** (Telemann performed the two works together at least five times). Along with *Der Tod Jesu*, the *Betrachtung* initiated a series of concert oratorios, odes and cantatas written by Telemann during his last decade. In describing the ninth hour on the day of Jesus' death, Zimmermann does not depict the eclipse of the sun, earthquake, tearing of the temple curtain or burial and resurrection, but instead provides a meditation on these events by an unnamed poetic figure who has observed them. Telemann assigned these meditations to four solo singers (alto, tenor and two basses) and inserted three well known chorales among the recitatives, arias and a cavata (this last set as a continuous series of contrasting ariosos for three soloists). The oratorio has been published in volume 31 (2006) of the Telemann selected critical edition*.

Bibliography A comparison of published bibliographies devoted to Telemann research from 1963 to the present reveals how remarkably far the field has advanced in just six decades. The bibliography by Wolf Hobohm*, appended to a collection of essays from the first scholarly conference devoted to Telemann (Magdeburg, 1962), includes surprisingly few studies focused mainly on the composer and his music. By the time Hermann Wettstein published his bibliography in 1981 the situation had improved markedly in this respect, and further progress is reflected in Jeanne Swack's 1992 annotated bibliography of Telemann publications since 1975, and in her 2013 online annotated bibliography. Over the past two decades the literature has grown exponentially, with studies of Telemann's sacred vocal works (particularly the cantatas) emerging as a main area of focus. The Zentrum für Telemann-Pflege und -Forschung* maintains extensive online bibliographies devoted to Telemann's life and works and to the annual cycles of church cantatas, in addition to a discography. One might conclude from this increased scholarly activity that Telemann scholarship has now reached an 'early maturity', especially as the field is increasingly international in nature. Yet a glance at the necessarily selective bibliography in this volume reveals that the secondary literature is still predominantly in German, with English-language writings largely the work of a handful of authors. Contributions in other languages remain comparatively rare. It is also apparent that music theorists have been slow to turn their attention to Telemann's music. *BibLeb, HobBib, ReiBib, SwaBib, SwaRes, WetBib.*

Biographies Following Telemann's own autobiographies*, an anonymous but presumably authorised biographical essay was written during the early 1740s. Issued in both German and French (each version taking up two full pages), this accompanied the publication by Balthasar Schmid* in Nuremberg of Telemann's cantata cycle *Musicalisches Lob Gottes** and an engraved portrait* of the composer in 1744. A second version of the biography is much more concise and corrects some errors in the original. Known only from a corrected proof belonging to Telemann, it was written about 1746 but apparently never appeared in print. The Nuremberg biography, along with Telemann's autobiographies, various lexicographical entries derived from them and the criticism of Christoph Daniel Ebeling*, formed the basis for the 1792 entry on the composer in Ernst Ludwig Gerber's *Historisch-Biographisches Lexicon der Tonkünstler*, itself highly influential on nineteenth-century accounts. The first substantial modern biography was Max Seiffert's* extensive preface to his edition of *Der Tag des Gerichts** and *Ino** for volume 28 (1907) of the Denkmäler Deutscher Tonkunst series, which set a new standard for Telemann scholarship. Romain Rolland's 1919 essay on Telemann as a 'forgotten master' (translated into German and English) brought the composer's life and achievements to a broader audience during the first half of the twentieth century. Since then Telemann has remained underserved by book-length biographies. Those by Erich Valentin (1931), Richard Petzoldt (1967; English translation, 1974), Karl Grebe (1970), Walther Siegmund-Schultze (1980) and Eckart Kleßmann (1980 and 2004) provide overviews of Telemann's life and works for a general audience. But even the most expansive among them, by Petzoldt, stops well short of treating its subject comprehensively. Useful supplements to these studies are the documentary biography by Werner Rackwitz (1981) and the pictorial biography by Werner Menke* (1987). Siegbert Rampe's more recent biography includes reprints of the autobiographies, a detailed works list and an extensive bibliography. It draws heavily on scholarly work relating to Telemann's life and music but emphasises raw information (lists, tables and source quotations) at the expense of interpretation. *GreBio, HobDru, HobÜbe, KleHam, KleTel, KreCan, KreRol, MenBil, PetBio, RacSin, RamBio, ReiBio, RolFor, SeiBio, SieTel, SteHam, ValBio.*

Blavet, Michel As the leading French flautist of his time, Blavet (1700–68) held principal positions in Paris' Concert Spirituel, the Musique du Roi and the Opéra while publishing three books of flute sonatas. He ordered twelve copies of Telemann's *Musique de table** (Hamburg, 1733), which suggests he was acting as the composer's publishing agent in Paris. Later he participated in the first performances of Telemann's *Nouveaux quatuors* (Paris, 1738) at the French court and in Paris. He was presumably among the 'leading Paris virtuosos' (AB 1740) who invited Telemann to visit the city. In 1752 Blavet published Telemann's six duets* for violins, flutes or oboes as the *Second Livre de Duo* (TWV 40:124–29).

Bodinus, Johann Christoph In July 1721 Bodinus (1690–1727) succeeded Telemann as city music director in Frankfurt*. During the next six years he made over three hundred sets of performing parts for Telemann cantatas (now at the Universitätsbibliothek Johann Christian Senckenberg Frankfurt am Main), some of which were sent directly by the composer to Bodinus in fulfilment of Telemann's obligation to provide Frankfurt with cantatas every two years in order to maintain citizenship for himself and his family. Telemann's comment in a 1723 letter to his Frankfurt friend Johann Friedrich Armand von Uffenbach* that music in the city had gone downhill since his departure may reflect his negative impression of Bodinus' direction of the church music. *JunKan, KerKan, KerRez, SchKat.*

Böhm, Johann Michael Böhm (c. 1685–1755 or later) was an important member of the Darmstadt* *Hofkapelle*, playing the oboe, flute and recorder and directing some of the instrumental music between 1711 and 1729. Upon his 1720 marriage to Susanna Elisabetha Textor, sister of Telemann's second wife Maria Catharina, he became the composer's brother-in-law. In 1716 Böhm was one of four oboists to whom the composer dedicated *Die Kleine Cammer-Music** (Frankfurt, 1716). In April and May of that year he accompanied the *Hofkapelle* to Frankfurt for performances of Telemann's *Brockes-Passion** and birthday music for Archduke Leopold. He left Darmstadt in 1729 for a position at the Württemberg ducal court at Ludwigsburg, near Stuttgart*, claiming mistreatment at the hands of his employer. In response, he was charged with stealing music and instruments, but claimed that he had taken only his 'own Telemann things', of which there were 'nearly as many' as the violinist Johann Samuel Endler* owned – thus at least a hundred manuscripts. Böhm's Telemann collection has not been identified, though it is possible that he owned several Darmstadt manuscripts of Telemann trios and quartets bearing the possessor mark 'C.B.' (= 'Concertmeister Böhm'?) on their title pages. He remained at the Württemberg court for the rest of his career, eventually rising to the position of concertmaster. Telemann probably composed some of his solo wind music for Böhm, such as the well known overture-suite* in A minor for recorder and strings, TWV 55:a2 (transmitted only in a Darmstadt manuscript), and the elaborate oboe solo in the *Brockes-Passion* sinfonia. In 1733 Böhm was a subscriber to Telemann's *Musique de table**. *BilGra, HayKle, NoaDar, ZohMix.*

Brandenburg-Jahrgang Telemann's annual cycle of church cantatas for the 1723–24 liturgical year in Hamburg* (repeated in 1724–25, both times after the sermon) is preserved as a fragment, with twenty-nine librettos and twenty-two musical settings extant. It was his first cantata cycle written specifically for Hamburg, previous cycles having been written originally for Eisenach and Frankfurt. The librettos were furnished by Michael Christoph Brandenburg (1694–1766). Telemann announced plans to publish this cycle in December 1723, and its design and modest scoring (two solo arias, two solo recitatives and a concluding duet, all requiring two voices, two violins and continuo) was apparently intended to facilitate publication. In the end, however, the cycle remained unpublished because Brandenburg failed to provide all the required librettos; Telemann then turned to Matthäus Arnold Wilkens* for librettos to what would become his first published cantata cycle, the *Harmonischer Gottesdienst** (Hamburg, 1725–27). *ReiCan.*

Breitkopf, Johann Gottlob Immanuel In his seventies Telemann corresponded with Breitkopf (1719–94) about publishing music with the Leipzig firm. In a letter* of 20 November 1755 the composer inquired about the costs associated with Breitkopf's new method of letterpress printing using 'mosaic' type. Telemann wrote to him again on 27 May 1759, offering one of his 'current works' (thirty-five pages in score), to which he proposed to add 'a discourse of several pages on the numerous points that a composer should observe in the descriptive manner of writing'. He also suggested that Breitkopf might publish his 1759 St Mark Passion (TVWV 5:44) by instalment (including a discussion of 'the advantages in composing vocal music that I have gained through experience, especially a correct use of the German language, which is often disfigured by the constraints of Italianate melodies'), as well as an annual cycle of feast day cantatas. None of these works was published by the firm, which did, however, offer numerous vocal and instrumental works by Telemann in its three series of printed catalogues (books and printed music, 1760–80; handwritten music, 1761–80; and handwritten music, 1762–87, including thematic incipits). Among these offerings were fifteen printed editions of music in addition to the biography* and portrait* published by Balthasar Schmid*. To judge from the catalogues, most of the firm's Telemanniana was acquired during the period 1763–66. The firm still owned a number of its master or 'house' copies of Telemann's music when it held its 'Grosse Musikalien-Auction' of manuscript and printed music in Leipzig beginning on 1 June 1836. Some of the Telemann manuscript sources now at the Staatsbibliothek zu Berlin – Preußischer Kulturbesitz bear the Breitkopf firm's blue-grey paper wrappers. *FleBre, TelBri, ZohMix.*

Brockes, Barthold Heinrich A poet and member of the Hamburg senate from 1720, Brockes (1680–1747) was a founding member of the city's Teutsch-Übende Gesellschaft and Patriotische Gesellschaft, which published the moral weekly *Der Patriot* (1724–26). As a poet, Brockes is best known for his didactic poems published as the *Irdisches Vergnügen in Gott* (1721–48), set in part by Telemann, and for his passion libretto *Der für die Sünde der Welt gemarterte und sterbende Jesus* (known as the *Brockes-Passion**), set by Telemann in 1716. Several years later, Telemann set Brockes' cantata *Alles redet itzt und singet* (entitled *Die uns im Frühling zur Andacht reitzende Vergnügung des Gehörs*; TVWV 20:10), receiving the poet's text prior to its publication in the *Irdisches Vergnügen in Gott*. This cantata and another with a libretto by Brockes, *Das Wasser im Frühlinge* (20:1; lost), were performed in Hamburg in 1720, that is, a year before Telemann moved to the city. Two further Brockes cantatas set by Telemann in 1721 and 1722, *Der Herbst* (20:11) and *Der Winter* (20:12), have been lost. In summer 1722 the composer programmed *Alles redet itzt und singet* and *Das Wasser im Frühlinge* on the inaugural concert of his Hamburg Collegium musicum*. Telemann also set three of Brockes' poems in his collection of songs*, the *Singe-, Spiel- und Generalbass-Übungen* (1733–34). The two were on friendly terms: Brockes stood godfather to Telemann's son Johann Barthold Joachim in 1723, and in a letter of 3 July 1738 to Telemann, Brockes referred to his colleague as 'my very dear friend'. The two may have known each other since 1701–02, when Telemann was a university student in Leipzig and Brockes was finishing his studies in nearby Halle. And it is probable that Brockes, together with Erdmann Neumeister*, supported Telemann's application for the position of Hamburg city music director in 1721. *PoeBro, SchBro, TelBri.*

***Brockes-Passion* (*Der für die Sünde der Welt gemarterte und sterbende Jesus*), TVWV 5:1** The famous passion libretto by Barthold Heinrich Brockes* (1712) was set by a dozen composers, including Reinhard Keiser* (1712), Telemann (1716), Johann Mattheson* (1718), George Frideric Handel* (HWV 48; by 1719), Johann Friedrich Fasch* (1723) and Gottfried Heinrich Stölzel (1725); Johann Sebastian Bach* used some of Brockes' aria texts in his St John Passion (BWV 245; 1724). Brockes drew on the Gospel narratives of all four Evangelists (principally that of St Matthew), structuring his libretto around ten cantata-like soliloquies for the principal characters, some of them allegorical: Jesus, Judas and Maria each have one soliloquy, Peter and the Faithful Soul each have two, and the Daughter of Zion has three. The result is less narration from the Evangelist and more reflective movements as compared to most other passion librettos. Telemann's setting is arguably the outstanding masterpiece of his early career, and was first heard publicly in concerts on 2–3 April 1716 with the Darmstadt *Hofkapelle* in Frankfurt's Barfüßerkirche. On these occasions the printed libretto served as an admission ticket. The concerts were apparently sponsored by the Frauenstein Society's Collegium musicum*, which gave concerts every other Thursday under Telemann's direction. Directing the work was the banker and musician Heinrich Remigius Bartels*. The *Brockes-Passion* was performed frequently in Hamburg concerts during the 1720s, and between 1730 and 1747 excerpts were heard in a pasticcio that also included music from the settings by Keiser, Handel and Mattheson. Among Telemann's passion oratorios, only the *Seliges Erwägen** (1722) was performed more often during his lifetime.

The music of Telemann's *Brockes-Passion* reflects his considerable experience with works for both church and theatre (Judas' soliloquy, Nos. 35–37, is especially operatic), and takes full advantage of his expert performers through writing that is demanding of both vocalists and instrumentalists. Noteworthy as well are Telemann's efforts at enhancing musico-dramatic coherence over the course of such a lengthy work through the gradual move from flat to sharp tonalities (an arc spanning C minor and E-flat major in the opening movements to E major in No. 51), the musico-rhetorical connection of successive arias through the use of 'sighing' figures (Nos. 11, 14 and 16) and a double recollection of Jesus' melody to the words 'Es ist vollbracht' (Nos. 73–75). The *Brockes-Passion* has been published in volume 34 (2008) of the Telemann selective critical edition*. *FreBro, LanBro.*

Bürgerkapitänsmusik *See* **Kapitänsmusik**

Burme(i)ster Members of a patrician family in Hamburg, the four Burmester (or Burmeister) brothers were patrons of Telemann during the 1730s. Telemann dedicated his second set of methodical sonatas* (1732) to the amateur violinists Rudolph (1699–1755), a *Bürgerkapitän* (captain of the city militia), and Hieronymus (1700–73), a merchant who was later president of the city's *Commerz-Deputation* (Commercial Deputation) and an alderman. Rudolph, Hieronymus, Johann Wilhelm and Henricus appear in the printed list of subscribers to the *Musique de table** (1733); the first three brothers were also dedicatees of the *Douze Solos à violon ou traversière** (1734).

Burney, Charles (Dr) The historian and lexicographer (1726–1814) played an important role in defining Telemann's posthumous reputation in the English-speaking world. His knowledge of the composer's music must have deepened during a 1772 trip through the Low Countries, Germany and Austria, which resulted in his second published travelogue, *The Present State of Music in Germany, The Netherlands, and United Provinces* (London, 1773) and furnished material for his monumental *A General History of Music* (London, 1776–89). In his discussion of Telemann in *The Present State*, Burney noted that 'this composer, like Raphael and some other great painters, had a first and second manner, which were extremely different from each other; in the first he was hard, stiff, dry, and inelegant; in the second, pleasing, graceful, and refined'. Burney repeated material from *The Present State* in his 1804–05 article on Telemann for Abraham Rees' forty-five-volume *Cyclopædia; or, Universal Dictionary of Arts, Sciences, and Literature* (London, 1802–20), but also referenced the 1770 discussion by Christian Daniel Ebeling* of Telemann's vocal works; Ebeling had offered in 1771 to send Burney 'many pieces of Telemann'. How much of the composer's music Burney actually knew is unclear, but the 1814 auction catalogue of his estate includes copies of *Der Tod Jesu**, *Deus judicium tuum regi da**, the *Quadri** (in the first, Hamburg edition) and the *Fugirende und veraendernde Choraele** (a manuscript copy of the 1735 Hamburg publication). *EveEng, ZohRec.*

Calchedon This instrument, also known as the calichon (and sporting a number of variant spellings), is a bass lute usually with six strings (five double courses and a chanterelle) and commonly tuned D-G-c-f-a-d'. The calchedon was sometimes also known by the term 'mandora' in eighteenth-century Germany. Telemann specified the 'calc[h]edon' on autograph scores and parts for works he wrote in Leipzig (1701–05) and Frankfurt (1712–21), and played the instrument himself: in his letter of application for the position of city music director at Frankfurt, written in late 1711, he claims to be proficient on the violin, his principal instrument, in addition to keyboard, 'Flaute', chalumeau, cello and 'Calchedon'. The instrument appears in two works Telemann wrote for the Leipzig Neukirche about 1705: a Sanctus setting (TVWV 9:*deest*) and the *Missa* in B minor (Kyrie and Gloria), TVWV 9:14. Johann Kuhnau*, who used the calchedon for performances in the city's Thomaskirche and Nikolaikirche at this time and later, described it as having a 'penetrating' tone. The instrument appears frequently in the cantatas Telemann wrote while in Frankfurt, and appears generally to have played only bass lines; in exceptional cases, including recitatives and obbligato passages, it provided a chordal realisation of the bass. Six double flute concertos Telemann composed c. 1719–21 (TWV 52:e2 and 53:D1, G1, A1, a1 and h1) also include the instrument in the continuo group, sometimes with bassoon indicated as an alternative. *ReiCal.*

Calvör, Caspar A pastor, theologian, historian, mathematician and writer, Calvör (1650–1725) held the position of Superintendent in Zellerfeld when Telemann was sent by his mother to study there from 1693/94 to 1697. Telemann called him his 'Latin keeper' (AB 1740), and Calvör supervised the boy's education while encouraging his musical interests. Calvör's personal library, which survives mostly intact and had grown to eight thousand items by his death, is rich in Protestant theology, classical Greek and Roman authors, and baroque humanist literature. But he would appear to have had little to teach Telemann about modern, *galant* literature, something that the composer would encounter later in his studies. *ChaCou.*

Canary cantata *See* ***Trauer-Musik eines Kunsterfahrenen Canarienvogels***

Canon Telemann took a special interest in canons, especially during the 1720s and 1730s. In response to a question posed by Johann Mattheson* in his journal

Critica Musica (1722), Telemann noted that 'even simple canons at the unison with two, three or four voices produce an effect that is agreeable to the ear and delights the faculty of the intellect. . . . But just as insufficiently fiery minds thereby sink all too easily into pedantry, there are those who are far too *galant* to engage in such cerebral composition. . . . In short, canons deserve praise; but they are to be compared to individual trees in a great forest or, alternatively, to a room in a spacious palace.' Telemann's own journal, *Der getreue Music-Meister**, includes a *galant* sonata for viola or viola da gamba and continuo (TWV 41:B3; also playable as a duet* with various instrumental combinations) that is strictly canonic in each of its four movements; the same is true of another one of his trios, for recorder, treble viol and continuo, TWV 42:C2. For *Der getreue Music-Meister* he also commissioned canons by several other composers, including Johann Sebastian Bach* and Jan Dismas Zelenka*. During the following decade Telemann issued two 'canonic' publications: six vocal canons in two to four parts as *Telemanns Canones à 2, 3, 4* (Hamburg, 1735) and six instrumental duets* as the *XIIX Canons mélodieux* (Paris, 1738). Further evidence of Telemann's fascination with canons is his entry of the six-voice canon TVWV 25:114 into the visitor book of Conrad Arnold Schmid in Lüneburg on 23 June 1735. Canonic writing figures prominently in Telemann's other duet collections, including the *Sonates sans basse* (Hamburg, 1726), *Sei Duetti* and the recently rediscovered set of flute duets belonging to the Sing-Akademie zu Berlin*. There are also canonic arias among his church cantatas, such as *Bekehret euch zu mir* (TVWV 1:121) and *Kündlich gross ist das gottselige Geheimnis* (TVWV 1:1020), both published in the *Fortsetzung des harmonischen Gottesdienstes* (which derives from the *Schubart-Jahrgang**). *ZohMix.*

XIIX Canons mélodieux *See* **Canon** and **Duet**

Cantata The approximately 1,400 extant church cantatas by Telemann represent the most substantial and diverse contribution to the genre by a single composer. He also made an important contribution to the German secular cantata, though these are much fewer in number. Writing of Telemann's church cantatas in 1758, Johann Ernst Bach (nephew of Johann Sebastian Bach*) claimed that 'his church pieces have thence found such universal acclaim that one can barely find a Protestant church in Germany where Telemann's annual cantata cycles are not performed'. In fact, Telemann's church cantatas were performed across German-speaking lands from the first decade of the eighteenth century until the 1770s, and even later in Hamburg* (under the composer's godson and successor, Carl Philipp Emanuel Bach*) and Riga (under the composer's grandson, Georg Michael Telemann*). Telemann's high productivity as a composer of church cantatas is partly due to the nature of his professional obligations. From 1717 to 1730 he provided annual cycles to the Eisenach* court every other year as *Kapellmeister* in absentia, and following his departure from Frankfurt* in 1721 he maintained citizenship for himself and his family by sending a cycle to the city every two or three years. Unusually, in Hamburg cantatas were heard both before and after the sermon in the city's five main churches, with the pre-sermon cantata usually from a new cycle and the post-sermon cantata from an older cycle. The service concluded with another piece that was generally an opening or closing movement from one of the previously heard cantatas. The new cantata for each Sunday and feast day was heard only in one principal church at a time, with the other four churches taking their turns in succeeding weeks (the usual order was St Petri, St Nikolai, St Katharinen, St Jakobi and St Michaelis). If, as a result of this scheme, the new cantata did not align with the day's readings, then the old cantata rectified this situation. Telemann also devised alternation patterns for the re-performance of his old cantata cycles.

The earliest among Telemann's surviving church pieces are inspired by the seventeenth-century sacred concerto, and consequently lack the madrigalistic movement types (recitatives and arias) associated with the sacred cantata after 1700. These works appear to have been composed in Hildesheim (1697–1701) or possibly soon after Telemann's move to Leipzig in 1701. A number of them have been published in volume 36 (2003) of the Telemann selective critical edition*. By the early 1710s Telemann began conceiving his church cantatas as self-contained annual cycles (each known as a *Jahrgang*) that are often unified musically through scoring and style, and textually by standardising movement types and order. Whenever possible, he set librettos by a single author, with Erdmann Neumeister* being his most frequent collaborator. Following the standard practice of his time, Telemann used the word 'cantata' to describe madrigalistic works consisting only of arias and recitatives, with apparent reference to the Italian secular cantata. Works also including settings of chorales and biblical verses (dicta) were more often called 'Musik', 'Haupt-Musik' or 'Concerto'. The term 'oratorio' was applied to pieces in which singers are assigned names of allegorical or biblical characters, as is the case with cycles for the 1730–31 and 1731–32 liturgical years.

Recent research has established that Telemann composed at least twenty-one annual cycles of church pieces up to 1750, thirteen of which survive more or less complete. These are identified by the titles of published librettos, by nicknames given to them during the eighteenth-century, or by the name of the librettos' author, and include the *Geistliche Cantaten** (c. 1702–06), *Geistliches Singen und Spielen** (1710–11; second setting, 1717–18), *Französischer Jahrgang** (1714–15), *Concerten-Jahrgang** (1716–17/1719–20; second cycle, 1720–21), *Sicilianischer Jahrgang** (1718–19), first *Lingen-Jahrgang** (1722–23), *Brandenburg-Jahrgang** (1722–23), *Jahrgang ohne Recitativ** (1724–25), *Harmonischer Gottes-Dienst** (1725–27), *Harmonisches Lob Gottes** (by 1726–27), *Emblematischer Jahrgang** (1727–28), second *Lingen-Jahrgang** (1728–29), *Oratorischer Jahrgang** (1730–31), *Schubart-Jahrgang** (1731–32), *Stolbergischer Jahrgang* (1736–37), *Horn-Jahrgang** (1739–40), *Musicalisches Lob Gottes in der Gemeine des Herrn** (1742–44), *Lied-Jahrgang** (1743–44) and *Engel-Jahrgang** (1748–49). Ongoing work with surviving musical and textual sources (including Hamburg librettos printed under the title *Texte zur Music*) suggests that Telemann may have composed additional cycles in 1725–26, 1733–34 and 1749–50. In a feat without parallel during the eighteenth century, he published five complete cycles of seventy-two works apiece: the *Harmonischer Gottes-Dienst*, *Auszug derjenigen musicalischen und auf die gewöhnlichen Evangelien gerichteten Arien* (arias from the *Harmonisches Lob Gottes*; Hamburg, 1727), *Fortsetzung des Harmonischen Gottesdienstes** (arrangements of movements from the *Schubart-Jahrgang*; Hamburg, 1731–32), *Musicalisches Lob Gottes in der Gemeine des Herrn* and *Engel-Jahrgang*. The possibility of publishing a 'feast day annual cycle' (perhaps the 1749–50 cycle referred to above) was suggested by Telemann to Johann Gottlob Immanuel Breitkopf* in 1759, though nothing came of it (the composer had planned, but failed to realise, another such cycle in 1728).

Between 1750 and 1755 Telemann appears to have performed few new cantatas by himself; more start to appear with the 1755–56 church year, about the time he began composing a series of sacred vocal works for the concert hall, starting with *Der Tod Jesu**. Like these concert works, the church cantatas from Telemann's last decade (now called 'cantata' no matter what movement types they contain) include settings of librettos by prominent young poets who studied in Hamburg, such as Daniel Schiebeler* and Johann Joachim Eschenburg, and many of them are for feast days. What appear to be the last newly composed cantatas by Telemann date from the 1763–64 church year, and by this time he increasingly entrusted the composition and performance of cantatas to his students (for example, Georg Michael Telemann wrote at least six cantatas in 1764–66). Though it is unknown how often Telemann performed cantatas by other composers in earlier years, an annual cycle by Johann Friedrich Fasch* was heard in Hamburg in 1732–33.

Of Telemann's approximately seventy-five extant or documented secular cantatas, most are 'chamber' works for solo voice and continuo, with or without an obbligato instrument, to German texts – itself remarkable given that most German composers of chamber cantatas set Italian texts. Those transmitted in manuscript may have been composed principally during Telemann's Eisenach period (1708–12); in AB 1718 and AB 1740 he recalled having composed about fifty works to mostly German texts at this time. None of these works indicates the librettist's name, and it is reasonable to suppose that Telemann either wrote or compiled many of the texts himself. Two decades later at Hamburg, he published nineteen German cantatas: one for voice and continuo in *Der getreue Music-Meister** and six apiece in the *Sechs Cantaten** (1731; solo voice and strings with an occasional obbligato wind instrument) and the two sets of *Moralische Cantaten** (1735 and 1736; the first for voice and continuo, the second for voice with obbligato flute/violin and continuo). The subjects of Telemann's chamber cantatas are often amorous, but many are instead (or also) moralising, that is, they promote an ethical world view in which one strives for moderation in one's pleasures, seeks happiness and fortune in one's faith, is satisfied with what one has and aims to be a good friend. In keeping with the pastoral-mythological personages that populate many librettos, the music of Telemann's arias often has a song- or dance-like quality. Finally, among Telemann's late concert works is a cycle of four cantatas, *Die Tageszeiten** (1757; each with solo voice, chorus and orchestra), and the extraordinary *Ino** (c. 1765) for soprano and orchestra. *See also* **Choir**. *EicInn, EicKan, EicSpä, FleMor, HobJah, HobKan, JunKan, KerKan, LebCan, MauTho, MenVok, NeuKir, PoeKir, ReiBeo, ReiJah, ReiSpä, RetTro, SteFrü, SwaOuv, TayCan, ZohMor.*

Capriccio Telemann used the title 'capriccio' for compound instrumental movements that alternate sections with contrasting tempos and affects. The inspiration for such movements may have been the Grave/Adagio – Allegro alternations in the opening movement of Arcangelo Corelli's* violin sonata Op. 5, No. 1. Telemann introduces three alternating elements in the 'Capriccio' for flute and continuo (TWV 41:G5) in *Der getreue Music-Meister**. Two or three alternating elements are found in movements of other published works from the 1720s and 1730s, including the sixth and tenth solos of the *Essercizii musici**, the first 'Concerto' of the *Quadri**, the eighth of the *Douze Solos à violin ou traversière**, and several unaccompanied fantasias* for flute (Nos. 3, 5 and 12), violin (No. 5) and viola da gamba (Nos. 1 and 10). The more common usage of the word 'capriccio' is to indicate a cadenza-like passage that does not elaborate a cadence. A brief example of this type of capriccio occurs before the concluding ritornello in the first movement of the early violin concerto TWV 51:E3. *ZohMix.*

Castel, Louis-Bertand *See* ***Beschreibung einer Augen-Orgel***

Chalumeau Telemann composed for the chalumeau (a single-reed woodwind instrument related to its younger cousin, the clarinet) over the course of half a century, and he recalled playing it during his Gymnasium years in Hildesheim (AB 1740). He composed almost exclusively for the alto and tenor sizes of the instrument, sometimes using them in an unequal pairing. The earliest of several church cantatas calling for two chalumeaux is *Danket dem Herrn Zebaoth*, TVWV 1:163 (from the *Geistliches Singen und Spielen**, 1710–11), and the instrument appears in a few Frankfurt-period cantatas as well. In Hamburg Telemann used the chalumeau in a number of vocal works, including the oratorio *Seliges Erwägen des bittern Leidens und Sterbens Jesu Christi** (1722), the opera *Der Sieg der Schönheit** (1722) and the *Kapitänsmusik** for 1728, 1742 and 1760. Among his instrumental works for chalumeau are two double concertos (TWV 52:C1 and d1), a 'sonata' for two chalumeaux and unison violins (TWV 43:F2/52:F5), a concerto-suite in F major (TWV 54:F1, though the chalumeau parts do not survive), an overture-suite for two chalumeaux and two violette (TWV 55:F2/44:6) and the late *Concert à 9 Parties* (TWV 50:1, c. 1758–66). Telemann's music journal *Der getreue Music-Meister** (1729) includes a characteristic piece entitled 'Carillon' for two chalumeaux. The instrument may also substitute for solo voice in the composer's first published annual cycle of church cantatas, the *Harmonischer Gottes-Dienst** (1725–27). *BecCha, LawCha, StaCha.*

Characteristic music *See* **Overture-suite**

Choir The size and disposition of the church choirs that sang Telemann's cantatas* in Frankfurt (1712–21) and Hamburg (1721–67) were variable, but the basic pool of four singers (concertists) was, whenever possible, supplemented by up to four doubling singers (ripienists) who performed only chorales and choruses, or portions thereof. Following an offer to become *Kapellmeister* at the court of Sachsen-Gotha, Telemann wrote to the Frankfurt city council on 5 October 1717 requesting additional singers and instrumentalists for the Barfüßerkirche and Katharinenkirche, noting that 'formerly the vocal parts were set *in duplo*', presumably meaning that he had been able to perform with one ripieno singer doubling each concertist singer. This practice, and its deterioration over time, is confirmed by surviving Frankfurt sets of parts that appear to reflect the original disposition of singers. But it is also clear that the number of available ripieno singers varied greatly in the years after Telemann left Frankfurt.

We are far better informed about Telemann's Hamburg choir (the *Chorus musicus*), and here there are important parallels with Johann Sebastian Bach's* ensemble in Leipzig, as well as some significant differences. In Hamburg there were eight paid positions for church singers, and Telemann seems to have preferred to have all eight whenever possible. Yet circumstances probably made this impossible on a consistent basis, and many works were heard with only four singers; in 1728 Johann Mattheson* noted that seventeen Hamburg churches had just five or six singers. Although normally paid at different rates, concertists and ripienists sometimes received the same amount. When this occurred, it was because they shared solo duties. Thus it would appear that Telemann was starting to conceive of his vocal ensemble as a true double quartet, which was possible because all eight singers were highly proficient; unlike Bach in Leipzig, Telemann did not use choirboys for concerted music (they sang only chorales), but relied mostly on adult professionals, some of whom also sang at the Hamburg Opera (including the bass Johann Gottfried Riemschneider*). His use of ripienists as soloists was facilitated by what seems to have been a frequent practice of part-sharing (for which there is little evidence from elsewhere in eighteenth-century Germany).

Unusually, concerted vocal music in Hamburg's principal churches, with the exception of the large Michaeliskirche, was not heard from the organ gallery or altar, but from a choir gallery placed at the nave's centre. This arrangement appears to have de-emphasised the bass register, which explains why Telemann often added a ripieno vocal bass part to the basic ensemble of four or eight singers. Because good tenors were in short supply, however, Telemann was often forced to use a single tenor even when all the other parts were doubled. For alto parts, Telemann favoured adult falsettists over boys; his most accomplished alto was Otto Ernst Gregorius Schieferlein*, who not only sang in church and at the Opera, but also became Telemann's principal copyist. Male falsettists were used for soprano parts as well until the early 1740s, when Telemann turned to a succession of boy sopranos. Female singers were famously not permitted to sing in Hamburg's principal churches and cathedral, although this rule was occasionally relaxed for the performance of passion oratorios in secondary churches or when music was heard simultaneously in all five principal churches. On such occasions, Telemann could sometimes count on the participation of the celebrated soprano Margaretha Susanna Kayser*. Finally, it was Hamburg practice for cantional chorale settings to be sung by the congregation, sometimes in alternation with the professional choir. *FisDok, NeuLie, NeuKir, ReiOde, SwaCho, SwaPer, TayCan.*

Collegium musicum Telemann established or re-established Collegia musica in Leipzig (c. 1702–04), Frankfurt (1713) and Hamburg (1721) soon after arriving in these cities. No concert programmes for any of these organisations survive, making it difficult to say much about their repertories. In AB 1718 Telemann noted that his Leipzig collegium performed with up to forty musicians, entertained the Saxon Elector Friedrich August I (Friedrich August II, King of Poland) and 'other great rulers', included many talented musicians who went on to achieve considerable fame and performed at the Neukirche. Following the composer's departure from Leipzig in 1705, the collegium was directed by Melchior Hoffmann (with Johann Georg Pisendel* briefly acting as a substitute), Johann Gottfried Vogler, Georg Balthasar Schott and Johann Sebastian Bach*. The Frankfurt collegium held its concerts in the Frauenstein Society's Haus

2. Frankfurt's Haus Braunfels on the Liebfrauenberg in a photograph from c. 1933. The building formerly housed the city's stock exchange (*Börse*) and the Frauenstein Society, which maintained a Collegium musicum that Telemann directed from 1713. The composer also served as secretary and treasurer for the society while living in Haus Braunfels (Historisches Museum Frankfurt, Inv. C31394; © Staatliche Bildstelle Berlin). Reproduced by permission.

Braunfels, at first every Thursday and later every other Thursday. However, the premiere of Telemann's *Brockes-Passion** on 2–3 April 1716 was moved to the Barfüßerkirche in view of the unusually large and distinguished audience. Only a few months after arriving in Hamburg, Telemann revived the city's Collegium musicum with a weekly concert series held in his apartment between the end of October or beginning of November and some time in the spring; the ensemble went silent during the Christmas season and offered relatively few performances in the summer. Telemann's move in 1722 to a larger apartment may reflect the early success of his concert series. At that time he began holding performances in public venues, including the Drillhaus, a combination of military exercise hall and concert venue that became the collegium's home in March 1724, when the series expanded to twice weekly. Concerts may have typically begun with an instrumental work, for those attending the opening performance of the collegium's third season on 30 October 1723 were advised that 'the symphony begins at four o'clock'. *CloHam, ZohMix.*

Concerten-Jahrgang Telemann's *Concerten-Jahrgang* (also known during the eighteenth century as the *Italienischer Jahrgang*) is actually two annual cycles of church cantatas with overlapping content and a complicated genesis. The first cycle, performed during the 1716–17 church year in Eisenach and Frankfurt, began with texts by Erdmann Neumeister*, who supplied Telemann with librettos for the first Sunday in Advent through the third day of Pentecost. Librettos for the remainder of the church year (Trinity Sunday through the twenty-sixth Sunday after Trinity) were provided by Paul Gottfried Simonis* in the style of Neumeister. The complete Neumeister/Simonis texts were eventually published together under the title *Das Harmonische Zion*. Telemann repeated the Neumeister portion of his first *Concerten-Jahrgang* in Frankfurt in 1719–20, but as Neumeister had by this time completed librettos for Trinity Sunday through the fourteenth Sunday after Trinity, Telemann provided new settings of these. For the end of the church year (the fifteenth through twenty-sixth Sundays after Trinity), Telemann set librettos by himself, Simonis and an anonymous poet. (Neumeister finally completed his cycle in 1726, but these new librettos were apparently never set by Telemann.) A second *Concerten-Jahrgang* was heard in Frankfurt during the 1720–21 church year, now with texts entirely by Simonis. Repeated were the Simonis-Telemann cantatas from the first *Concerten-Jahrgang*, but Telemann now set Simonis' new librettos for the first Sunday in Advent to the third day of Pentecost (published as *Herrn Gottfried Simonis . . . neues Lied*).

Both Neumeister's and Simonis' librettos surround varied configurations of arias and recitatives with an opening biblical verse (dictum) and concluding chorale – a blueprint that would prove highly influential for later church cantatas by Telemann and other composers, but which was far from standard in works before 1720. In musical terms, both 'concerto' or 'Italian' cycles derived their names during the eighteenth century not only from an emphasis on the Italian style (itself not unusual in cantatas from the time), but also from the concertante interaction of vocal and instrumental forces. Another feature of the cycles is the prevalence of arioso passages in recitatives. Aside from performances in Eisenach, Frankfurt and (later) Hamburg, cantatas from one or both cycles were also performed in Berlin, Rudolstadt, Weißenfels and Zerbst (under

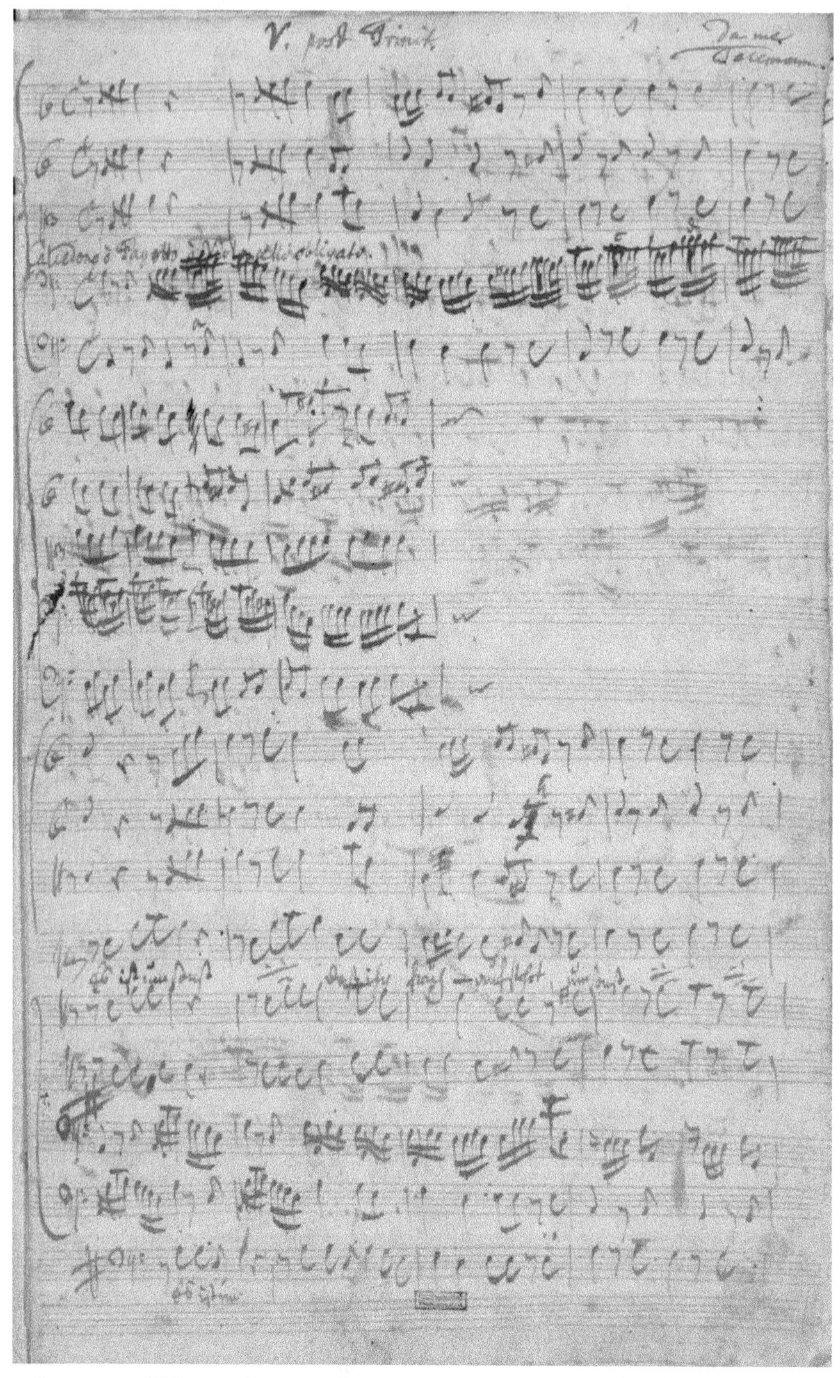

3. First page of Telemann's composing score to *Es ist umsonst, daß ihr früh aufsteht*, TVWV 1:1753, for the fifth Sunday after Trinity in 1720 (part of the first *Concerten-Jahrgang*) to a libretto by Erdmann Neumeister (Frankfurt am Main, Universitätsbibliothek Johann Christian Senckenberg, Music and Theatre Department, Ms. Ff. Mus. 994). Reproduced by permission.

Johann Friedrich Fasch*); the complete first *Concerten-Jahrgang* was owned by the Thomasschule library in Leipzig.

The cantatas from the first *Concerten-Jahrgang* for the fifth Sunday after Easter (Rogate Sunday) through the third day of Pentecost (Whit Tuesday), as well as the cantatas from the second *Concerten-Jahrgang* for Trinity Sunday through the sixth Sunday after Trinity, have been published in volume 51 (2015) of the Telemann selective critical edition*. Further selections from the second *Concerten-Jahrgang*, from the twenty-first through the twenty-sixth Sundays after Trinity, and from the first Sunday in Advent through the third day of Christmas, have been published in volume 53 (2019). In addition, the Frankfurter Telemann-Ausgaben series of editions has published most of the second *Concerten-Jahrgang* cantatas. *HobKan, HobNeu, JunKan, PoeKir, SawSim.*

Concertos In an infamous passage from AB 1718, Telemann said of his concertos, 'I must confess that they have never really come from my heart, although I have already written a considerable quantity of them. . . . At least it is true that they mostly smell of France.' Despite his apparent ambivalence toward the genre, Telemann was among the first German composers to write instrumental concertos, and he may have already started doing so at Leipzig (1701–05): a borrowing by George Frideric Handel* from the violin concerto TWV 51:B2 dates this work to c. 1705–06. At Eisenach (1708–12) Telemann probably composed most or all of his double violin concertos, including TWV 52:G1 (copied out in parts by Johann Sebastian Bach* c. 1708–09) and TWV 52:e2 (performed at the Dresden court in 1710–11); these works were most likely intended for Telemann, whose principal instrument was the violin, to perform with his Eisenach colleague Pantaleon Hebenstreit*. Bach also made a keyboard transcription in 1713–14 of the violin concerto TWV 51:g1 (BWV 985). Another work from this period is the famous trumpet concerto, TWV 51:D7. None of these early concertos 'smell of France', but are instead modelled on the first wave of Italian solo concertos by Giuseppe Torelli, Tomaso Albinoni* and others – works that predate the introduction into Germany of concertos by Antonio Vivaldi*. Among their salient features are modest dimensions, sonata-like motivic interplay between the soloist and accompanying strings (often at the expense of soloistic 'display' passages), and the generation of rhythmic contrast between solo and tutti (rather than within each group). Already evident is Telemann's long-standing preference for the four-movement, da chiesa formal scheme (slow–fast–slow–fast).

Two further groups of concertos may be placed with some confidence during the late Eisenach and Frankfurt years (c. 1710–21). Telemann's eight oboe concertos (TWV 51:c1, c2, D5, d1, d2, e1, f1 and G2), which number among his most effective works with a wind soloist, explore the 'vocality' of the instrument through a number of slow movements in recitative, arioso and aria style. As with the early string concertos, their fast movements often involve close dialogues between solo and tutti. The concertos that Telemann claimed 'smell of France' surely include a group of ten works written around the time of AB 1718: six concertos for two flutes (TWV 52:e2; TWV 53:D1, G1, A1, a1 and h1), two for two recorders (TWV 52:a2 and B1), one for two oboes (TWV 53:C1) and one for two flutes and violin (TWV 53:e1). These mixed taste* works are effective blends of the Italian and French styles. For example, the double oboe concerto (which tellingly bears the bilingual title 'Concerto à la francese' in one scribal copy) begins with a rondeau and includes a sarabande and minuet. At least some of the double flute concertos were probably composed in 1718–19 for the Dresden* court orchestra, an ensemble that was famous for its expertise in both the Italian and French styles. While in Dresden in September 1719 Telemann composed a flashy violin concerto for his friend Johann Georg Pisendel* (TWV 51:B1).

Telemann also made an important contribution to the history of the *concerto a quattro* or, as Vivaldi sometimes called it, the *concerto ripieno*, scored for four-part strings without independent parts for soloists. This is a genre that few German composers cultivated to any great extent (though Bach's Third Brandenburg Concerto and Handel's Grand Concerto Op. 6, No. 7 are firmly within its orbit), and generally did not survive past the 1720s. Telemann's nineteen examples (TWV 40:200, 43:D5, Es1, E2, e5, F3–5, G7–9, A5–6, a4–5, B1–3; and TWV 44:1) are the most significant body of ripieno concertos by a non-Italian composer, and appear to date from before 1720. His most original contribution to the type are two works in the Polish style* (TWV 43:G7 and B3) and three for the apparently unique combination of four violins without accompaniment (TWV 40:201–03).

Telemann's solo concertos from the later Frankfurt and early Hamburg years – he appears to have stopped regularly composing concertos by the late 1730s – reveal the influence of Vivaldi's music, though this is assimilated into an already highly individual concerto style. The well known viola concerto, TWV 51:G9, features Vivaldian ritornello forms in each of its four movements (an unusual experiment for Telemann). Violin concertos served as overtures for two of Telemann's Hamburg operas: *Der neumodische Liebhaber Damon** of 1724 (51:C3) and *Die Last-tragende Liebe, oder Emma und Eginhard** of 1728 (51:a2). Dating from this period as well may be the two concertos for recorder (51:C1 and F1) and the seven for flute (51:D1–4, E1, G1 and h1); some of these works may have been composed for the Darmstadt wind player Johann Michael Böhm*. Among Telemann's best known double concertos are the works for flute and recorder (TWV 52:e1) and for recorder and viola da gamba (52:a1). Both of these solo combinations appear to be unique in the concerto literature, and both works conclude with vigorous Polish rondeaus; the *galant* rhythmic language of the concerto for recorder and viola da gamba places it slightly later, perhaps around 1730. Among Telemann's most mature concertos are two belonging to the 'group' type, with three or four soloists: the concerto for flute, oboe d'amore and viola d'amore (TWV 53:E1) and the concerto for two flutes, violin and cello (54:D1). Both are excellent demonstrations of Telemann's mastery of instrumental colour and texture, and the latter is one of the most *galant* and symphonic of his orchestral works. Telemann's last concerto, evidently composed in the 1740s or 1750s, is another work that 'smells like France': the concerto-suite* TWV 51:F4.

Virtually all of Telemann's concertos have appeared in at least one modern edition. Selections of violin concertos, concertos for several instruments and ripieno concertos have been published in volumes 23 (1973), 26 (1989) and 28 (1995) of the Telemann selective critical edition*; the three concertos for four violins are included in volume 6 (1955). *DruCon, HirCon, HirFra, KroCon, ZohMix.*

Concerto-suite Telemann wrote at least three works in the mixed taste* that follow a concerto-allegro in ritornello form with a suite-like series of dance-based movements; hence the hyphenated genre name 'concerto-suite' (a similar work by Johann Melchior Molter bears the title 'concerto en suite'). The slightest of these three works, the 'Concerto di camera' for solo recorder, two violins and continuo, TWV 43:g3, commences with a concerto-allegro movement and continues with a siciliana, bourrée and minuet. More ambitious is the colourful TWV 54:F1, which might be described as a cross between an overture-suite* and a 'concerto con molti istromenti' (a term coined by Antonio Vivaldi* for the concerto RV 558, with eleven concertante instruments). Scored for oboe doubling on recorder, two chalumeaux, two horns, two concertante violins, two concertante cellos, strings and continuo, this work features a different combination of soloists in each movement. What appears to have been Telemann's last concerto of any kind is the concerto-suite TWV 51:F4, which was probably composed for Johann Georg Pisendel* during the decade 1745–55 and first appeared in print in 1907. Although the violin soloist is featured prominently in most movements, secondary soloists are drawn from pairs of flutes, oboes and horns, which are often granted a 'symphonic' independence from the string ensemble. *FleAna, HutSui, KleSch, ZohMix.*

Continuation des sonates méthodiques *See* **Methodical sonatas**

Corelli, Arcangelo The Opp. 1–4 trio sonatas and Op. 5 solo sonatas of Corelli (1653–1713) loomed large as avatars of the Italian instrumental style, and their influence is palpable in the earliest among Telemann's Italianate sonatas in two and three parts, probably composed at Leipzig, Sorau or Eisenach before 1710, and in his first publication, the *Six sonates à violon seul** (Frankfurt, 1715). Two decades later, Telemann reimagined the Corellian trio sonata in his *Sonates corellisantes* (Hamburg, 1735), three *da chiesa* and three *da camera* sonatas for two flutes or violins with continuo that imbue the by then 'classic' Corellian idiom with elements of the modern *galant* style. Thus old-fashioned elements such as walking-bass lines, conservative thematic material, chains of suspensions, close imitation between the upper voices and melodic echoes are heard alongside newfangled effects such as syncopated rhythms, drum basses and heightened motivic contrast. The publication therefore does more than cash in on Corelli's posthumous fame by being 'compos'd in imitation' of him (as many others of the time did), but achieves a novel mixed taste* of the old and new Italian styles even as it introduces a contrapuntal rigour – especially in the fast-movement fugues – that is more German than Italian. The *Sonates corellisantes* has been published in volume 24 (1974) of the Telemann selective critical edition*. *FinCor, ZohMix.*

Danzig The eastern Prussian city of Danzig (now Gdańsk, Poland) was, like Hamburg, a member of the former Hanseatic League, an alliance between cities in the North Sea and Baltic regions. Resident in the city from 1739 was Telemann's former student* Johann Jeremias Du Grain, who performed music by his former teacher and became organist at the reformed church of St Elisabeth. In 1754 Telemann reworked his 1750 St Matthew Passion for performance in the city (TVWV 5:53), following local liturgical practice by omitting the work's poetic portions (arias, choruses and reflective recitatives) and including thirty-four chorales for congregational singing. Also in 1754, Telemann wrote the church cantata* *Ich bin ja, Herr, in deiner Macht* (TVWV 1:822) for Danzig. This cantata is built around cantus-firmus or cantional settings of every verse of a chorale. Four similar works (TVWV 1:138, 394, 970 and 984) have also been connected with Danzig, although they may have originated in Hamburg between the mid-1740s and 1754. All five cantatas have been edited in volume 60 (2013) of the Telemann selective critical edition*. *AndOst, FecDan, KeiDan, LanDan, ReiOde.*

Darmstadt Telemann's music appears to have played an important role in the repertory of the *Hofkapelle* of Ernst Ludwig, Landgrave of Hessen-Darmstadt (1667–1739; reigned from 1688), and his successor, Ludwig VIII (1691–1768; reigned from 1739). The remnants of this collection contain 350 manuscript sources* of Telemann's sonatas, concertos and overture-suites, some dating from Telemann's years at nearby Frankfurt (1712–21) and many copied by the *Kapellmeister* Christoph Graupner* and the violinist and eventual Vice-*Kapellmeister* Johann Samuel Endler*. The wind player Johann Michael Böhm*, who became Telemann's brother-in-law in 1720 and owned a large collection of the composer's music, must have been the inspiration of numerous works now in the Darmstadt collection. The entire Darmstadt *Hofkapelle* performed in Frankfurt performances of Telemann's *Brockes-Passion** on 2–3 April 1716 (in the presence of Landgrave Ernst Ludwig), and the composer recalled the 'incomparable execution of the Darmstadt orchestra' (AB 1718) in Frankfurt performances of his cantata *Auf Christenheit! Begeh ein Freudenfest* (TVWV 12:1ab) and serenata *Deutschland grünt und blüht in Friede* (TVWV 12:1c) celebrating the birth of Archduke Leopold on 17 May 1716. In the 1760s Telemann wrote a series of nine orchestral works for Ludwig VIII (TWV 50:2 and 21–23, 55:D21–23, F16 and g9); four of these are inscribed to the landgrave on the composing scores. *Auf Christenheit! Begeh ein Freudenfest* has been published in volume 16 (1994) and *Deutschland grünt und blüht in Friede* in volume 17 (1992) of the Telemann selective critical edition*. *BilGra, HirSer, SieLeb, ZohEns, ZohMix.*

Dedications The dedicatees of Telemann's Frankfurt and Hamburg publications reflect his transition from courtly employment to a career in the free imperial cities of Frankfurt and Hamburg. He dedicated three of four Frankfurt publications containing his own music to aristocratic patrons, no doubt in part because during this period (1715–18) he was still being pursued by courtly *Hofkapellen*. These dedicatees include Prince Johann Ernst of Sachsen-Weimar* (*Six sonates à violon seul**, 1715), the oboists Johann Michael Böhm, Peter Glösch, François La Riche and Johann Christian Richter (*Die Kleine Cammer-Music**, 1716), Duke Friedrich II of Sachsen-Gotha (*Six trio*, 1718) and Count Heinrich XI Reuß zu Schleiz (*Sei suonatine per violino e cembalo*, 1718). By contrast, of the eleven Hamburg publications bearing dedications, the majority were inscribed to members of patrician families, merchants, and musicians (both amateur and professional): George Behrmann and Pierre Diteric Toennies (*Sonates sans basse*, 1727), Andreas Plumejon (*Sept fois sept et un menuet*, 1728), Count Friedrich Carl von Erbach* (*Zweytes Sieben mal Sieben und ein Menuet*, 1730), Joachim Erasmus von Moldenit* (*Quadri**, 1730), Benedetto Marcello* (*XX Kleine Fugen*, 1731), brothers of the Burme[i]ster* family (*Continuation des sonates méthodiques*, 1732; *Douze Solos à violon ou traversière**, 1734), Johann Christian Pichel (*Moralische Cantaten**, 1735), Pierre Chaunel (*Fantaisies pour la basse de violle*) and Johann Adolph Scheibe* (*Vier und zwanzig, theils ernsthafte, theils scherzende, Oden*, 1741). *LanAlt, ReiMol, ZohMix.*

***Deus judicium tuum regi da*, TVWV 7:7** This motet was first performed on 25 March 1738 in Paris* as part of the Concert Spirituel public concert series held in the central pavilion of the Tuileries palace, and was evidently repeated two days later. That the music was performed by 'nearly a hundred select people' (AB 1740) was clearly a point of pride for Telemann, as such large performing groups were virtually unknown in German-speaking lands. Conceived in the venerable French grand motet tradition, *Deus, judicium tuum regi da* is virtually the only such work composed by a non-Frenchman. In Hamburg, Telemann publicly performed the motet in the Drillhaus at least ten times between 1740 and 1757, making a number of revisions along the way. The work also appears to have been well known in central and northern Germany, and was subject to at least one anonymous arrangement. Telemann's concise setting of Psalm 72 (known to the composer as Psalm 71) includes a series of brief solo and duet arias – each scored differently, and together offering a varied palette of vocal and instrumental colour – separated by three substantial fugal choruses functioning as the work's structural pillars. Of particular interest is the solo bass' accompanied recitative in the Italian style, an emblem of the French-Italian *goût réunis* that was highly prized in Paris during the 1730s and a reflection of the enharmonic style of singing that impressed Telemann during his visit. The following tenor aria ('Descendit sicut pluvia in vellus') features two obbligato bassoons accompanying the voice while violins provide cascading rain drops (which turn into heavier showers once the bassoons get into the meteorological act). In a scoring recalling Telemann's *Nouveaux quatuors en six suites** (published in Paris at this time), the sarabande-like soprano aria 'Et adorabunt eum omnes reges terrae' treats the voice, flute and solo violin as equal partners in a quartet texture. Both the Parisian and Hamburg versions of the motet have been published in volume 45 (2007) of the Telemann selective critical edition*. *See also* **Neues musikalisches System**. *LesCon, HirInn, HirPsa.*

***Die Donner-Ode*, TVWV 6:3** This title encompasses two distinct works first written for Hamburg's principal churches and later performed at public concerts. The first, performed on 10 October 1756 (the seventeenth Sunday after Trinity) after the sermon in the Katharinenkirche, and again on 17 October (the eighteenth Sunday after Trinity) before the sermon in the Jacobikirche, is *Wie ist dein Name so groß*, TVWV 6:3a, to verses from Psalms 8 and 29 as translated by Johann Andreas Cramer (*Poetischer Uebersetzung der Psalmen*, 1755) and arranged by Karl Wilhelm Ramler* and Christian Gottfried Krause*. A public performance of excerpts from the work was given on 15 November 1756 in Hamburg's Drillhaus, and a complete performance in the Drillhaus followed on 20 October 1757. The second work, *Mein Herz ist voll vom Geiste Gottes*, TVWV 6:3b, is based on Cramer's translation of Psalm 45 and was first heard before the sermon in the Katharinenkirche on New Year's Day 1760; it was first performed publicly on 26 April 1762 in the new concert hall 'auf dem Kamp' (in the field). Telemann himself performed the two works under the collective title *Der große Name Gottes*, considering the 1756 setting of Psalm 29 to be the *Donner-Ode* proper and the rousing choral aria on Psalm 8 (*Wie ist dein Name so groß*) that both precedes and follows the ode as a separate entity that could also be performed with the second ode (*Mein Herz ist voll vom Geiste Gottes*). The 'thunder' in the first ode's informal title refers to the duet for two basses with a prominent timpani accompaniment, 'Er donnert, dass er verherrlichet werde' (He thunders, that He shall be exalted). Thanks to research by Ralph-Jürgen Reipsch*, we may dismiss the long-standing assumption, based solely on a casual remark in a December 1757 letter from Ramler to Johann Wilhelm Ludwig Gleim, that this work was commissioned by the Hamburg town council for a special day of prayer and repentance on 11 March 1756 in commemoration of the Lisbon earthquake of 1 November 1755. Nor are the two works oratorios, despite their designation as such in the Telemann thematic catalogue*. Both have been edited in volume 22 (1971) of the Telemann selective critical edition*. *KirErh, LütDon, LütMon, RatDon, SchAuf.*

***Don Quichotte auf der Hochzeit des Comacho*, TVWV 21:32** Written when Telemann was eighty years old, this one-act comic serenata (comprising five scenes with ballet) was first performed at a public concert at Hamburg's recently opened concert hall 'auf dem Kamp' (in the field) on 5 November 1761. Telemann adapted a libretto provided by the twenty-year-old Daniel Schiebeler* entitled *Basilio und Quiteria* and based upon the episode of Comacho's wedding from the second book of Miguel de Cervantes Saavedra's famous novel *El ingenioso hidalgo Don Quijote de la Mancha* (The Ingenious Gentleman Sir Quixote of La Mancha; Madrid, 1615). In this episode Don Quixote and Sancho Panza are squabbling over their latest misadventures when they encounter a wedding celebration for the prosperous shepherd Comacho and the beautiful shepherdess Quiteria. They learn that Quiteria's father has promised her hand to Comacho, even though she is in love with another shepherd named Basilio. Before the ceremony begins, Basilio appears with a bloody dagger in his breast and pleads with Quiteria (in the serenata's only accompanied recitative) to grant him his dying wish and marry him. Comacho figures his rival will soon expire, so he willingly gives his consent. But Basilio has feigned his impending death and harmlessly pulls out the dagger. Camacho threatens vengeance before storming out, and the happy couple are left to celebrate. Don Quixote and Sancho Panza are mostly observers of these events, yet they receive the lion's share of the arias (three apiece, plus a duet).

The serenata was apparently Telemann's last dramatic work, and possibly the first since the Hamburg Opera had closed more than two decades earlier. (It is unrelated to the much earlier characteristic overture-suite* illustrating various scenes from Cervantes' novel, the *Ouverture Burlesque de Quixotte**.) Its music, though stylistically far removed from that of his earlier surviving stage works, reveals the elderly composer's flair for the comic to be undiminished. In fact, the score is exceptionally rich in invention. Arias for the delusional Don Quixote feature an appropriate blending of seria and buffa elements, whereas Sancho's arias are more firmly in buffa mode. These contrast with the more naïve style of the shepherds' song- or dance-like arias, an exception being the heart-rending lament for the shepherd Grisostomo ('Kein Schlaf besucht die starren Augenlider'). *BasDon, JahDon, RuhDon.*

Don Quixote *See* ***Ouverture Burlesque de Quixotte*****, TWV 55:G10**

Douze Solos à violin ou traversière Telemann's last published collections of solos (1734) is scored, like the earlier sets of methodical sonatas*, for flute or violin and continuo (though here there are twelve, rather than six, works). Besides examples of the *Sonate auf Concertenart**, the collection is especially rich in cross-genre movement types familiar from his earlier collections: fast movements in da capo form; slow movements with ostinato basses, aria-like double motto openings or a ritornello frame; and a capriccio*. *SwaSol, ZohMix.*

Dresden The Dresden electoral court of Friedrich August I (Augustus the Strong; 1670–1733) unsuccessfully attempted to hire Telemann as *Kapellmeister* in 1711, just before the composer accepted the position of civic music director in Frankfurt. Telemann was in Dresden in September and October 1719, during wedding festivities for the Habsburg archduchess Maria Josepha and the electoral prince Friedrich August II (1696–1763; reigned from 1733), and would then have renewed his friendships with George Frideric Handel* (who was recruiting opera singers for London) and the court violinist Johann Georg Pisendel*, for whom he composed a violin concerto during the visit (TWV 51:B1; titled 'Concerto grosso, per il Sig.ʳ Pisendel' on the composing score). Telemann would also have met other members of the *Hofkapelle*, which was among the best and largest organisations of its kind in Europe; in later years he was in contact with Christian Pezold, Johann Joachim Quantz* (then in Berlin), Johann Christoph Schmidt, Sylvius Leopold Weiss* and Jan Dismas Zelenka*. The *Hofkapelle* performed many of Telemann's sonatas, concertos and overture-suites* from about 1710 until at least the 1750s, and it is most likely that more than a few of these works were written specifically for the Dresden musicians. Many of the 170 manuscript sources* containing Telemann's instrumental music now in the Sächsische Landes- und Hochschulbibliothek (including several composing scores) originally belonged to Pisendel and were subsequently purchased by the court. *FecPis, FecStu, FisDok, LanQue, ZohMix.*

Du aber, Daniel, gehe hin, **TVWV 4:17** This well known funeral music* was composed at an indeterminate time for an unknown, but evidently prominent, person. Yet its mixture of madrigalistic movements (recitatives and arias) associated with the cantata* and movements recalling the sacred concerto suggests that it dates from the early years of the eighteenth century. The work is scored for four voices, oboe, violin, bassoon, continuo and the 'soft' instrumentation of recorder and two violas da gamba often associated with funeral music (as in the *Actus Tragicus*, BWV 106, of Johann Sebastian Bach*). Its anonymous libretto is based on the Old Testament Book of Daniel (chapter 12, verse 13) and illustrates important themes of Lutheran pietism: distrust of the world, ardent longing for death and trusting hope in eternal bliss. Perhaps the most extraordinary movement is the soprano aria 'Brecht, ihr müden Augenlieder', in which the heartrending vocal melody interacts with solo oboe over an undulating accompaniment of unison violas da gamba, all supported by short notes in the recorder and violin (no doubt an evocation of funeral bells). *Du aber, Daniel, gehe hin* is preserved only in a manuscript score and set of performing parts belonging to the musical archive of the Sing-Akademie zu Berlin* and copied primarily by the Berlin cantor of the Nikolaikirche, Jakob Ditmar (1702–81); some of the parts and an associated libretto were prepared for a priest's funeral in 1757. The return of the Sing-Akademie archive to Berlin in 2001 enabled a new critical edition of the work, published by Carus. *ReiDan.*

Duets Telemann's duets are among his most popular works today, and they were just as highly regarded during his lifetime. He wrote at least five sets of them, each containing six works, and also published a further duet for flute and violin in *Der getreue Music-Meister**. His first set, the *Sonates sans basse* for flutes, violins or recorders (Hamburg, 1726; TVWV 40:101–06), is perhaps the best known duet collection from the eighteenth century. Friedrich Wilhelm Marpurg* cited movements from these works as models of double fugues, and Johann Joachim Quantz* was no doubt thinking of them when he listed the qualities of good duets in his *Versuch einer Anweisung die Flöte traversiere zu spielen* and wrote his own flute duets. Printed from moveable type but reissued in engraved editions in Amsterdam (1729), Paris (1736–37) and London (1746), the *Sonates sans basse* were dedicated by Telemann to the Hamburg patrician amateurs George Behrmann and Pierre Diteric Toennies. The four-movement duets are notable for the equality of the two instrumental parts, and each work includes a lively fugue as its second movement. A dozen years later, Telemann published his *XIIX Canons mélodieux* for flutes, violins or 'basses de viol' (TWV 40:118–23) during his 1737–38 visit to Paris*. Each of the three movements in these duets is canonic at the unison, with the distance between the first voice (*dux*) and second voice (*comes*) varying from movement to movement. Like many of Telemann's other canons* from the 1720s and 1730s, these duets combine strict counterpoint with the *galant* style. The collection was reprinted in London in the same year as the *Sonates sans basse* and seems to have enjoyed great popularity in Berlin; it was still available in Paris as late as 1775.

The last three duet collections are less well known today. Michel Blavet* published Telemann's *Second Livre de Duo* for violins, flutes or oboes (TWV 40:124–29) in Paris in 1752. These are relatively brief, uncomplicated works in three movements that emphasise homophonic textures (just two fugal movements are included), but are nevertheless well-crafted sequels to the first two published duet collections. Two more sets of duets are preserved only in manuscript copies. An untitled set of nine flute duets (TWV 40:141–49) preserved in a late eighteenth-century manuscript resurfaced in the music collection of the Sing-Akademie zu Berlin* in 2001. This manuscript originally belonged to Sara Levy (1761–1854), a virtuoso harpsichordist, music collector and great-aunt of Felix Mendelssohn. The first six works may date from the 1730s or 1740s and are worthy successors to the *Sonates sans basse* and *XIIX Canons mélodieux*. However, the sharp drop-off in quality in the last three duets suggests that they were not written by Telemann (who in any case never wrote another set of nine works). Finally, the *Sei Duetti* for flutes (TWV 40:130–35), also known from a scribal copy, stand apart from Telemann's other duets in their unforgiving tonalities for the flute (up to four flats and four sharps), unusual technical challenges and extreme expressivity. Such qualities were especially prized at the Berlin court, where the two most prominent flautists were Quantz and his royal pupil, Friedrich II, King of Prussia (Frederick the Great)*, and it is therefore possible that Telemann wrote the *Sei Duetti* expressly for them in the prevailing 'Berlin style'. The *Second Livre de Duo* and *Sei Duetti* have been published in volume 7 (1955) and the *Sonates sans basse* and *XIIX Canons mélodieux* in volume 8 (1955) of the Telemann selective critical edition*. Bärenreiter has also published a separate critical edition of the Sing-Akademie duets. *ReiQua, ReiUnb, ZohMix.*

Ebeling, Christoph Daniel Educated in Lüneburg, Göttingen and Leipzig, Ebeling (1741–1817) moved permanently to Hamburg in 1769, teaching trade and economics and later, at the academic Gymnasium, history and Greek. He eventually became director of Hamburg's municipal library. Ebeling published in the fields of geography, history, classical philology and the fine arts. He was also an early Americanist and translated the travelogues of Charles Burney* (to whom Ebeling offered to send 'many pieces of Telemann'). The posthumous reception* history of Telemann's music may be said to begin in earnest with Ebeling's 1770 'Versuch einer auserlesenen musikalischen Bibliothek' (Essay on a choice musical library), published in Hamburg's monthly periodical *Unterhaltungen.* Ebeling's essay deals only with vocal music (his planned sequel on instrumental music never appeared) and gives pride of place to the works of Carl Heinrich Graun*, George Frideric Handel*, Johann Adolf Hasse and Telemann. His extensive discussion of Telemann's vocal works focuses on the period after 1740, and it is unsurprising that he criticises some of the older, unfashionable texts as well as Telemann's use of musical word-painting – something that Ebeling's generation found distasteful. For example, he remarked of *Die Donnerode** that it 'must be judged one of the most sublime compositions of [Telemann], which has no fault other than some too common depictions of thunder and the like'. Overall, Ebeling had much good to say about Telemann's music. But later writers tended to focus exclusively on his criticisms: the quip that 'polygraphs seldom produce masterpieces' (though untrue in Telemann's case) proved especially fateful for the composer's posthumous reputation, being repeated many times in reference works for over a century. *KleDok, RacSin, ReiEbe.*

Editions Modern editions of Telemann's music began to appear at the turn of the twentieth century and were an important impetus for a revival of interest in the composer. Landmark publications in this respect were four volumes in the Denkmäler deutscher Tonkunst series: *Der Tag des Gerichts** and *Ino** (vol. 28, 1907; edited by Max Schneider* with an important biography* of the composer), the concerto-suite* TWV 51:F4 (vols. 29–30, 1907; edited by Arnold Schering), the *Vier und zwanzig, theils ernsthafte, theils scherzende, Oden* (vol. 57, 1917; edited by Wilhelm Krabbe and Joseph Kromolicki) and the *Musique de table** (vols. 61–62, 1927; edited by Max Seiffert*). These early efforts were followed by a flood of practical editions, especially of the sonatas and concertos, so that by the turn of the twenty-first century most of Telemann's instrumental works had appeared in print (though many still lack critical editions). In the 1940s Seiffert conceived a plan for a selective critical edition of Telemann's works, which became Georg Philipp Telemann:

Musikalische Werke, published by Bärenreiter. The first volume, containing both sets of methodical sonatas* and edited by Seiffert, was prepared in 1944 but appeared only in 1950 (not 1955, as is often stated). Progress on the edition was initially slow: only twenty-two volumes were published by 1974, and the following fifteen years saw the appearance of just two additional volumes. The emphasis during this period was on the instrumental works, notable exceptions including the complete *Harmonischer Gottes-Dienst** and *Der geduldige Socrates**. Since 1992, however, another thirty-five volumes have appeared, devoted almost exclusively to vocal music; a particular focus from 2003 has been a systematic selection of the church cantatas, especially annual cycles (*Jahrgänge*).

Paralleling this focus on the church cantatas is Habsburger Verlag's Frankfurter Telemann-Ausgaben series (1996–), which has published critical editions of over a hundred cantatas preserved in Frankfurt, including most of the second *Concerten-Jahrgang**. Carus has published critical editions of several dozen vocal works, including *Deus judicium tuum**, *Die Donner-Ode**, *Du aber, Daniel, gehe hin**, the Magnificat* in C major and *Die Tageszeiten**, in addition to a number of church cantatas, masses and motets. Most of Telemann's instrumental works that had not yet been published by the 1990s (especially the ripieno concertos and dozens of overture-suites) found their way into print via the 130 numbers of the Severinus Press Urtext Telemann Edition (1995–2006). Further critical editions of note include those of A-R Editions (*Don Quichotte auf der Hochzeit des Comacho**, *Douze Solos à violon ou traversière** and early trios), Ortus (*Germanicus**, *Die wunderbare Beständigkeit der Liebe, oder Orpheus** and the *Six Ouvertures à 4 ou 6**), PRB Productions (*Fortsetzung des Harmonischen Gottesdienstes**) and Edition Walhall (*Singe-, Spiel- und Generalbass-Übungen*, *Vier und zwanzig, theils ernsthafte, theils scherzende, Oden*, cantatas of the *Engel-Jahrgang** and the fantasias* for viola da gamba). *PoeEdi, SchDen.*

Emblematischer Jahrgang This annual cycle of church cantatas to librettos by Johann Friedrich Armand von Uffenbach* (published as the *Poetischer Versuch*; Frankfurt, 1726) was heard in Hamburg during the 1727–28 church year (starting with New Year's Day) and sent to Johann Balthasar König* in Frankfurt. Fifteen settings performed before the sermon by Telemann are documented by Hamburg librettos (*Texte zur Music*), but only two musical sources (of questionable authenticity) survive. The cycle gets its name *Emblematischer Jahrgang* – Telemann's own coinage – from Uffenbach's ornamental copper-plate engravings for the librettos; he sent these to Telemann along with additional engravings for Sundays that had not appeared in the *Poetischer Versuch*. *ReiUff.*

Emma und Eginhard *See* ***Die Last-tragende Liebe oder Emma und Eginhard*, TVWV 21:25**

Endler, Johann Samuel Endler (1694–1762) attended university in Leipzig* from 1716 and directed the Collegium musicum founded there by Johann Friedrich Fasch* from 1721 to 1723, when he joined the Darmstadt* *Hofkapelle* as a singer and violinist. He became Vice-*Kapellmeister* in 1740 and succeeded Christoph Graupner* as *Kapellmeister* in 1760. Among his collection of nearly one hundred manuscripts containing instrumental works by Telemann, about eighteen were copied in Saxony during the decade 1713–23. These last manuscripts, together with others (in various unidentified copying hands) that Endler brought with him to Darmstadt, reveal something of the Leipzig Telemann repertory in the years after the composer's departure from the city in 1705. *BilGra, NoaDar, ZohMix.*

Engel-Jahrgang This annual cycle of church cantatas* to librettos by Daniel Stoppe* and an anonymous poet (who, following Stoppe's death in 1747, wrote the librettos starting with the seventh Sunday after Trinity), may have been Telemann's last complete cycle. It received its first performance in Hamburg during the 1747–48 and 1748–49 church years; Telemann performed individual cantatas from the cycle over the next fifteen years, and Carl Philipp Emanuel Bach* led performances of several works in 1779 and 1788. Telemann published the cycle starting, apparently, at Easter 1748. As with the earlier *Musicalisches Lob Gottes in der Gemeine des Herrn**, Telemann entrusted the engraving, printing, marketing and distribution of this, his fifth and final church cantata cycle to appear in print, to hands other than his own – in this case, the organist Christoph Heinrich Lau in Hermsdorf near Hirschberg. The printed cycle derives its name *Engel-Jahrgang* from the vignette of a kneeling cherub ('Engel' or angel) on the title page to each of the seventy-two cantatas. It was printed in parts, unlike the *Harmonischer Gottes-Dienst**, *Auszug derjenigen musicalischen und auf die gewöhnlichen Evangelien gerichteten Arien* (derived from the *Harmonisches Lob Gottes**) and *Musicalisches Lob Gottes**, most likely with the needs of professional church musicians in mind. Each cantata follows the movement plan chorale–aria–recitative–aria–chorale. The arias, scored for solo voice, two violins and continuo, tend to be longer than in Telemann's earlier cycles and encompass an exceptionally wide range of styles. Five feast-day works replace the opening chorale with a biblical verse (dictum) calling for four voices and adding trumpets and drums to the string ensemble. As in the dicta from the *Musicalisches Lob Gottes*, indications of solo ('Einer') and tutti ('Alle') suggest how one might perform the music with extra (ripieno) singers. Manuscript copies of the *Engel-Jahrgang* show that it was performed widely in German-speaking lands through the 1780s. Two cantatas were performed in 1766 during inauguration ceremonies for the new building of the Holy Trinity Lutheran Church in Lancaster, Pennsylvania – the earliest known performance of Telemann's music in the New World. *ReiVer, NeuEng, PfaNeu, SzéLit, TayCan.*

Essercizii musici This published collection of 'musical exercises' includes twelve solos and twelve trios scored for the most widely used instruments of the time (recorder, flute, oboe, violin, viola da gamba and keyboard), each of which receives two solos and participates in four trios. The keyboard solos are both suites, and the trios include four works for melody instrument and obbligato keyboard – apparently the first such pieces to appear in print. As much as any instrumental publication by Telemann, the *Essercizii musici* illustrates his originality, fluency in the emerging *galant* style and knack for flatteringly idiomatic writing, all of which helps explain its continuing popularity. Martin Ruhnke determined that the *Essercizii musici* must have appeared about 1740, since the collection is not listed among Telemann's publications in AB 1740. But based on an examination of Telemann's engraving practices, together with documentary evidence and a critique of the music's style, the present author reassigned the collection to c. 1727–28, that is, towards the beginning of his activities as an engraver. Kota Sato subsequently refined this dating to late 1726, confirming that the *Essercizii musici* was the first publication that Telemann engraved himself. The composer appears not to have publicly advertised the collection, suggesting that, as an imperfect first effort at engraving, he decided to sell or gift it privately among friends and colleagues. The collection has been published in volume 47 (2009) of the Telemann selective critical edition*. *RuhVer, SatEss, ZohMar, ZohMix.*

Estate Much of what can be reconstructed of Telemann's musical estate is presently at the Staatsbibliothek zu Berlin – Preußischer Kulturbesitz, where 136 composing scores and dozens more scribal copies of vocal works (many including Telemann's handwriting) were once owned by the composer's grandson Georg Michael Telemann*, who inherited them around 1767. Music that did not go to Georg Michael or other heirs was to be auctioned off on 6 September 1769, as announced in the July issue of Hamburg's *Unterhaltungen* and in the August and September issues of the *Relations-Courier*. The announcement notes that 'many of the best musical works of Telemann' will be available in both printed and manuscript form, but makes no mention of books or musical instruments. The vocal works include thirty-nine passion oratorios, thirty-two works for the installation of preachers, thirty-three *Kapitänsmusiken** (some missing either the oratorio or serenata), twenty works for coronations and inaugurations (including 'many sublime pieces'), twelve funeral works (including those for five Hamburg mayors, three emperors and the king of Poland) and fourteen wedding pieces in addition to the *Seliges Erwägen**, *Die Tageszeiten**, *Der Tod Jesu**, *Die Auferstehung und Himmelfahrt Jesu**, *Die Auferstehung*, *Das befreite Israel**, *Der Messias**, *Der Tag des Gerichts**, *Deus judicium tuum regi da**, *Der May** and *Don Quichotte auf der Hochzeit des Comacho**. In 1769 these last-named works would still have been familiar as concert pieces in Hamburg. The announcement pointedly notes that no annual cycles of church cantatas will be included, and that 'the printed things are available singly, in duplicate, or in several exemplars', including 'many quartets', the *Sonates corellisantes* 'and other trios', *Sechs Cantaten**, *Six Ouvertures à 4 ou 6**, *Canons mélodieux* and three sets of keyboard fantasias*. There is also 'an appendix of several old [and] for the most part incomplete things, for example from German operas, concertos, ouverturen, etc., mostly for gambas'. The auctioneer Klefecker was to issue catalogues (*Verzeichnisse*), but no copies of these are known. On 30 September 1816 Georg Michael wrote to his former student Georg Johann Daniel Poelchau that he regretted having lost his grandfather's 1763 St Mark Passion (TVWV 5:48) through lending the score to a Hanoverian musician named Hesse and never getting it back. He also mentioned that the parts had been auctioned off after his grandfather's death ('along with much other music'). This suggests that in 1767–68 Georg Michael received his grandfather's scores, when available, and left the performing parts of the same works to be auctioned off. Although Telemann's library of music and books can be reconstructed in part from letters*, the material that was auctioned off has remained unidentified. Yet one possible exception is a Berlin copy of the second volume of Michael Praetorius' *Syntagma musicum* (1618), which bears the notice 'G.P. Telemann, Frankfurt 1712'. *HobGru, HobMis, KleDok, MaeKap, ZohMix.*

Fantasias Telemann issued six sets of twelve fantasias apiece for unaccompanied solo instrument during the 1730s: three sets for keyboard (1732–33) and one apiece for flute (1731), violin (1735) and viola da gamba (1735). The flute fantasias, long thought to date from 1732, have recently been redated to late 1731, whereas the viola da gamba fantasias were thought lost until 2015, when a copy unexpectedly surfaced in a private collection. The latter were dedicated to Pierre Chaunel (1703–89), a wealthy businessman in the French Huguenot community of Altona (then a suburb of Hamburg, now part of the city). The violin fantasias survive only in an eighteenth-century manuscript copy made from Telemann's lost print. Most of the fantasias for flute, violin and viola da gamba follow one or two movements in contrasting styles and forms with a binary movement that is usually dance-based. Telemann advertised the violin fantasias as containing six works with fugues and six 'Galanterien' and this is also true of the viola da gamba fantasias, which alternate works with and without fugues. But there is also much fugal writing in the flute fantasias, where one might least expect it, alongside unlikely movement types such as the French overture and passacaglia. Similarly, the violin and viola da gamba fantasias include concerto-style movements; there are even a few da capo 'arias' in the latter set. Facing the challenge of writing relatively brief works for a single melody instrument evidently inspired some of Telemann's most imaginative instrumental writing, and he is at his epigrammatic best in these fantasias. Not surprisingly, the three keyboard sets stand somewhat apart from their instrumental counterparts. But they, too, follow a standard formal scheme in which the first movement is repeated, da-capo style, after the second, and the first fantasia in a pair is reprised following the second. The first and third sets are in the 'Italian' style and include two-movement works, whereas the 'French' second set includes three-movement works that are often in a suite-like configuration.

There is some evidence that Telemann regarded the six sets of fantasias as a cycle: the total of seventy-two works correspond to the number of liturgical cantatas* required by Hamburg's church calendar (as represented in Telemann's published annual cantata cycles) and recall the six times twelve of Arcangelo Corelli's* opuses; and the collective scoring of the fantasias closely resembles that of the *Quadri** (1730) and *Nouveaux quatuors** (1738), as if to highlight the quartets' four instruments in turn. Moreover, Telemann adopts a different, yet coherent, tonal scheme for each of the six sets. The fantasias for flute and violin have been published in volume 6 (1955) of the Telemann selective critical edition*. *BraRhe, EppFan, LanAlt, SatNot, ZohFan, ZohMix.*

Fasch, Johann Friedrich Fasch (1688–1758) encountered Telemann's music while attending Gymnasium (and studying with Johann Kuhnau*) in Leipzig during the period 1705–08, and later regarded the older composer as a friend. In his 1757 autobiography Fasch recalled a youthful deception during his Gymnasium years: 'Because Telemann's *Ouverturen* were well known, I was at last bold enough to take a stab at writing such a work. I offered it under his name at a rehearsal of the first-form students' Collegium musicum, and much to my joy, they believed that it was by him. On this occasion I cannot avoid publicly confessing that at that time I learned most everything from the beautiful works of my most esteemed and dearest friend, Herr *Kapellmeister* Telemann, for I constantly took them as my model, especially the *Ouverturen*.' Fasch enrolled at Leipzig University in 1708 and founded his own collegium, which under the later direction of Johann Samuel Endler* (1721–23) appears to have had a number of Telemann's instrumental works in its repertory. As *Kapellmeister* at the Zerbst court from 1722, Fasch performed much music by Telemann, including ninety instrumental works and four annual cantata cycles: the *Geistliches Singen und Spielen**, first *Concerten-Jahrgang**, *Französischer Jahrgang** and *Sicilianischer Jahrgang**. Telemann, in turn, performed one of Fasch's cycles, the *Evangelische Kirchen-Andachten* (1730–31; to librettos by Erdmann Neumeister*), in Hamburg in 1733–34. Also in 1733, Fasch subscribed to Telemann's *Musique de table**. *PoeZer, SawKan.*

Fast allgemeines Evangelisch-Musicalisches Lieder-Buch At almost two hundred pages, Telemann's 'Nearly Universal Protestant-Musical Hymnal' (Hamburg, 1730) was one of his most ambitious publications*. Its materials must have been assembled over a period of many years, and engraving the plates must have taken many weeks. For the text of the index (at the front) and the practical 'lesson' (*Unterricht*) on four-part composition and continuo accompaniment (at the back), Telemann hired the printer Philip Ludwig Stromer (the texts were reset by Jeremias Conrad Piscator for the hymnal's 1751 second edition). An engraved frontispiece showing King David playing the harp within an elaborate architectural cartouche laden with instruments was supplied by Telemann's friend Johann Friedrich Armand von Uffenbach*. According to its lengthy subtitle, the hymnal contains 'very many old chorales gathered together according to their original melodies' and 'indicates a great many variants common today', along with a figured bass 'so that one can play the melodies in four voices throughout'. In all, there are two thousand chorales with over five hundred melodies. The thirty-four-page index allows one to look up a chorale by its text incipit and find the melody or melodies associated with it. When consulting a melody, notes or phrases with variants are marked with a number that leads one to a list of these variants (in small type) at the end of the melody. Many melodies have few or no variants, but others have up to two dozen. Telemann does not explain why he has privileged one version of a melody, nor does he identify his sources for variants. But he acknowledges that he adopted most of the older melodies from Franz Elers' *Cantica sacra* (Hamburg, 1588) and consulted newer printed and manuscript hymnals. Unlike most hymnals of the time, the *Fast allgemeines Evangelisch-Musicalisches Lieder-Buch* does not reflect the repertory of a particular institution, city or region. Thus it is in fact 'nearly universal' in its scope. *KreFre, KreLie.*

Fischer, Johann Christoph Fischer (1717–69) served as city music director in Frankfurt from 1759 until his death, and in this capacity he copied nearly three hundred scores and sets of performing parts to Telemann cantatas that are now preserved at the Universitätsbibliothek Johann Christian Senckenberg Frankfurt am Main. Fischer also reused earlier copies of Telemann cantatas by Johann Christoph Bodinus*, Johann Balthasar König* and Heinrich Valentin Beck*, sometimes marking certain movements for deletion in performance. *JunKan, KerKan, KerRez, SchKat.*

Flavius Bertaridus, König der Longobarden, **TVWV 21:27** This opera seria – Telemann's only surviving Hamburg opera to lack any comic elements – was first performed on 23 November 1729. The libretto is a collaboration between Telemann and Christoph Gottlieb Wend*, and the two based their text upon a 1706 Venetian libretto by Stefano Ghigi (set to music by Carlo Francesco Pollarolo) that concerns the events following the death in 661 of Aripert I, king of the Lombards. (George Frideric Handel's* 1725 opera *Rodelinda*, HWV 19, takes the same historical point of departure but is based on a different literary model.) The action opens with the dictator Grimoaldus ruling over the Lombards, having exiled his brother Flavius Bertaridus and imprisoned Flavius' wife Rodelinda and their son Cunibert (both of whom eventually escape). Grimoaldus has taken Flavia, Flavius' sister, for his wife and she plots for her brother's return. Following a series of reunions and cases of mistaken identity, Grimoaldus is killed by Cunibert and Flavius, who thus wins back his throne while Flavia marries her suitor, the general Orontes. In keeping with an established practice of the Hamburg Opera, the libretto is bilingual: twelve Italian aria texts were adopted from Ghigi's libretto, with the other texts translated into German. Telemann's singers were mostly veterans of the Hamburg Opera, including Maria Domenica Polon* (Flavius) and Margaretha Susanna Kayser* (Flavia). Telemann's music is stylistically and formally diverse, providing finely drawn sound portraits of characters and situations despite an unusual emphasis on the Italian seria style. Many arias take on added colour by featuring obbligato instruments, including recorder, flute, oboe, bassoon, trumpet or horn, violetta and violoncello. *Flavius Bertaridus* has been published in volume 43 (2005) of the Telemann selective critical edition*.

Fleischhauer, Günter A key figure in fostering the growth of Telemann scholarship from the 1960s onward, Fleischhauer (1928–2002) studied and taught at the Martin-Luther Universität Halle-Wittenberg, earning his doctorate there with a dissertation on music in ancient Greece and Rome (and later a habilitation degree with a dissertation on music historiography). Among his students at Halle were a number of important Telemann scholars of the following generation. Fleischhauer's Telemann-related interests were wide-ranging, encompassing instrumentation, style and form in the instrumental works (particularly the concertos), secular cantatas, late vocal works such as *Der May** and issues of reception and dissemination. He also edited several volumes of conference proceedings deriving from the Telemann-Festtage*. *FleAna, FleAnn, FleBre, FleGet, FleIns, FleMar, FleMay, FleMes, FleMor.*

Flute Telemann's contributions to the transverse flute's repertory are among the most significant of any composer, for both their quality and breadth. His writing for the instrument is always highly idiomatic, a quality that probably reflects his own experience as a player. The flute already appears in some of the church cantatas* Telemann wrote in Frankfurt (1714–21), and in the *Brockes-Passion** (1716). Around the same time he published a trio with flute in the *Six Trio* (1718) and composed concertos* for two flutes (TWV 52:e2; TWV 53:D1, G1, A1, a1 and h1) or two flutes and violin (TWV 53:e1), all of which 'smell of France' (AB 1718). In Hamburg Telemann used one or two flutes in his vocal music with increasing frequency, and by the 1740s the instrument is virtually a standard member of the ensemble in large-scale works such as passions and other oratorios, serenatas and occasional pieces. Some particularly fine obbligato flute parts appear in his first published cycle of church cantatas, the *Harmonischer Gottes-Dienst** (1725–27), in the *Schubart-Jahrgang** (1731–32; excerpts published as the *Fortsetzung des Harmonischen Gottes-Dienstes*) and in the *Stolbergischer Jahrgang* (1736–37). Telemann's second set of *Moralische Cantaten** (1736) also includes obbligato flute parts in each work. His first Hamburg publications of instrumental music, the *Essercizii musici** (1726; solos and trios) and *Sonates sans basse* (1726; duets*), contain some of his best known flute music. Four more collections of flute duets followed over the next quarter century: the *XIIX Canons mélodieux* (Paris, 1738), the *Second Livre de Duo* (Paris, 1752) and two sets that Telemann left unpublished. Noteworthy among his other published solos and trios for flute are three sets of methodical sonatas* (solos in 1728 and 1732, trios in 1731) that include ornamented slow movements, the *Six concerts et six suites** (1734), the *Douze Solos à violin ou traversière* (1734) and the *Sonates Corellisantes* (1735). All three sets of quartets published by Telemann – the *Quadri** (1730), *Nouveaux quatuors en six suites** (1738) and *Six quatuors ou trios** (1733) – include a flute part, and the first two sets (known collectively as the 'Paris' quartets) feature some of his best writing for the instrument. Included in the *Musique de table** (1733) are a number of significant flute works: a solo, two quartets and triple concerto with one flute, and a trio, quartet, overture-suite* and 'conclusion' with two flutes. But Telemann's most celebrated published flute works are the twelve unaccompanied fantasias* (1731), regarded as mainstays of the instrument's repertory since their republication in the 1950s. Finally, numerous trios, quartets and concertos that Telemann left unpublished include important works for one or two flutes. Among these are six trios in the French style (the so-called trios *alla francese*), two quartets for flute and two violas da gamba (TWV 43:G10 and G12), seven solo concertos (TWV 51:D1–4, E1 and G1–2) and several more concertos for multiple soloists: flute and recorder (TWV 52:e1), flute and violin (52:e3), flute, oboe d'amore and viola d'amore (TWV 53:E1), two flutes, violin and cello (TWV 54:D1) and two flutes, oboe and violin (54:B1). *TreQua, ZohMix.*

Förster, Christoph Initially engaged as a violinist and then as *Konzertmeister* at the Merseburg court, Förster (1693–1745) became Vice-*Kapellmeister* (1742) and then *Kapellmeister* (1745) at the Rudolstadt court. In a letter* to Telemann dated 14 March 1733 (the composer's fifty-second birthday) Förster reported that he had secured a subscription to the *Musique de table** from the Duke of Sachsen-Weißenfels and enclosed payment for his own copy (both men eventually appeared on the published list of subscribers). Förster also purchased the *Fast allgemeines Evangelisch-Musicalisches Lieder-Buch** from Telemann. Several years later Telemann published Förster's *Sei duetti a due violini e basso ad libitum*, Op. 1, but whether this occurred in Hamburg or Paris remains unclear (the only surviving edition appeared in Paris). In AB 1740 Telemann remarked that he had published music by Förster and others 'to please good friends'. *HobHer, TelBri, ZohMix.*

Fortsetzung des Harmonischen Gottes-Dienstes *See* **Schubart-Jahrgang**

Französischer Jahrgang Telemann's annual cycle of church cantatas for 1714–15 was performed simultaneously in Eisenach* and Frankfurt*, and was the first cycle he composed in the latter city after his move there in early 1712. The librettos by Erdmann Neumeister* were published under the title *Geistliche Poesien mit untermischten Sprüchen und Choralen*. A particularly noteworthy feature of them is the prevalence of chorales, with stanzas often alternating with freely composed poetry (in the form of recitatives and arias) and biblical quotations (dicta); some chorale stanzas function as refrains. Telemann's settings were known during the eighteenth century as 'French' (there is no evidence that the title is his own), presumably due to a number of stylistic features associated with French opera. Arias tend to avoid coloratura writing in favour of syllabic declamation, recitatives contain frequent arioso passages (something Telemann associated specifically with French recitative) and choruses are predominantly homophonic with alternations between smaller and larger groups of singers (recalling the French distinction between 'petit' and 'grand choeur'). Some arias are in rondeau form, and among the cantatas are examples of the French overture and chaconne. Telemann's basic instrumental ensemble for the cycle consists of two oboes and four-part strings, but the cantatas between Easter Sunday and the twenty-third Sunday after Trinity include a second viola part. The cantatas for New Year's Day through Sexagesia Sunday and for the Annunciation of Mary have been published in volume 40 (2006) of the Telemann selective critical edition*. *HerFra, HobNeu, JunKan, KerQue, PoeKir, SatFra.*

French style As a self-styled 'grand partisan de la musique Française' (letter to Johann Mattheson* of 18 November 1717), Telemann maintained a lifelong fascination with the French style, from his visits to the Hanover and Brunswick courts while a Gymnasium student at Hildesheim (1697–1701), to his trip to Paris* in 1737–38, to his advocacy of French recitative in correspondence with Carl Heinrich Graun* during the 1750s, to his late overture-suites* of the 1760s. Music in the French style was a main ingredient of the German mixed taste* that Telemann cultivated to such good effect, but he also wrote many works in which the French style is especially prominent, including much keyboard music* and ensemble works such as trios (including several that Johann Joachim Quantz* considered to be in the 'true French style'), quartets (among which are the *Nouveaux quatuors en six suites**), concertos* (especially those that 'smell like France', as Telemann put it in AB 1718) and overture-suites. He adapted French airs in the *Pastorelle en Musique oder Musikalisches Hirtenspiel** and wrote his own for some of his Hamburg operas, such as *Die wunderbare Beständigkeit der Liebe, oder Orpheus**. *ZohMix.*

Friedrich II, King of Prussia (Frederick the Great) Although there is at present no evidence of direct contact between Telemann and Frederick the Great (1712–86; reigned from 1740), the flute-playing king appears to have owned a number of the composer's solos for flute and continuo, and there is evidence that his flute teacher, Johann Joachim Quantz*, used many of Telemann's duets and trios during lessons. Given that Telemann was in contact with several other members of Frederick's *Hofkapelle*, including Johann Friedrich Agricola*, Carl Philipp Emanuel Bach*, Franz Benda and Carl Heinrich Graun*, it would not be surprising if he visited the Berlin* court at some point during the 1740s or 1750s. In fact, the style of one set of Telemann's duets*, the *Sei duetti* (TWV

40:130–35), suggests that they may have been written for Frederick and Quantz. *SynFri, ZohMix.*

Friedrich Carl, imperial count of Erbach and Limburg An amateur composer and poet, Friedrich Carl (1680–1731) was on friendly terms with both Johann Friedrich Armand von Uffenbach* and Telemann, who met the count by 1720 and visited his home, south of Darmstadt*, for several weeks in September and October 1727 (Uffenbach may also have visited at this time). Telemann is known to have exchanged letters* with Friedrich Carl (lost in World War II), and he set six of the count's French cantata librettos (TVWV 20:4–9; all lost). In 1730 Telemann dedicated a collection of keyboard music*, the *Zweytes sieben mal sieben und ein Menuet*, to Friedrich Carl, noting in a flattering poem that 'you effortlessly combine the French liveliness, melody, and harmony; the Italian flattery, invention, and strange passages; and the British and Polish jesting in a mixture filled with sweetness'. *ReiUff, TelBri, ZohMix.*

Fritzsch, Christian A talented professional engraver, Fritzsch (1695–1769) settled in Hamburg in 1718 and produced over two hundred portraits in addition to a well known depiction of the 1719 *Bürgerkapitäne* celebration and various other illustrations. Telemann hired him between 1728 and 1736 to engrave the lettering for his publications, including the title page and list of subscribers for the *Musique de table**. Fritzsch's son Christian Friedrich (1719–c. 1772) engraved a pastoral scene in the French tradition of the *fête galante* on the title page to Telemann's second published collection of songs*, the *Vier und zwanzig, theils ernsthafte, theils scherzende, Oden. ZohAes, ZohMix.*

Fugirende und veraendernde Choraele *See* **Keyboard music**

Fugues légères et petits jeux *See* **Keyboard music**

Funeral Music Telemann's funeral music ranges from a modest remembrance of a pet canary (the *Trauer-Musik eines Kunsterfahrenen Canarienvogels**) to elaborate tributes for mayors and monarchs – and nearly everything in between. The surviving works also span a wide chronological range, from the composer's teenage years in Hildesheim (1698–1701) to 1766, his eighty-fifth year. Among the earliest examples are two sacred concertos: the *Trauer-Actus über die Nicht- und Flüchtigkeit des menschlichen Lebens* (*Ach, wie nichtig*; TVWV 1:38) and a setting of Psalm 6, *Ach Herr, strafe mich nicht in deinem Zorn* (TVWV 7:3), that may be the one that Telemann's Leipzig University roommate discovered in his trunk (according to AB 1718 and AB 1740). (Another setting of Psalm 6 with the same title, TVWV 7:1, is thought to have been composed in Leipzig, c. 1704–05.). But the best known among Telemann's early funeral music is the cantata *Du aber, Daniel, gehe hin**, written for an unknown occasion sometime in the first decade of the eighteenth century. At Hamburg, Telemann provided funeral music for nine of the city's mayors between 1722 and 1749. This relatively low number – considering the length of Telemann's tenure – is explained by the fact that commissions for such music did not come from the city, but rather from the deceased's relatives, not all of whom were willing to pay for music. Several of Telemann's librettos were provided to him by Michael Richey* and Christian Friedrich Weichmann*, but the text of the operatic funeral music for Hartlieb Sillem (TVWV 4:6; 1733) was provided by the mayor himself. Five more funeral pieces were written for monarchs, including the elector of Dresden and king of Poland, Friedrich August I (Augustus the Strong), *Unsterblicher Nachruhm Friedrich Augusts* (TVWV 4:7; 1733), and the Holy Roman Emperor Charles VII, *Ich hoffete aufs Licht* (TVWV 4:13; 1745).

The *Unsterblicher Nachruhm Friedrich Augusts,* to a libretto by the young Joachim Johann Daniel Zimmermann*, is not so much traditional funeral music as a secular serenata providing reflection on the life of Friedrich August I; among its allegorical personages are Saxony, Majesty, Heroism, Wisdom and a Chorus of Citizens. The score appears to be one of Telemann's first to use German dynamic, tempo and expression indications*, and like the funeral music for Garlieb Sillem, it opens with a lengthy instrumental sinfonia featuring muted trumpets and timpani – in this case with a timpani fanfare for two players, each on one drum, that leads to two antiphonal choirs of three muted trumpets. (Muted trumpets and timpani often figure in aria accompaniments in Telemann's Hamburg funeral music more generally.) Telemann presumably led all four public performances of the serenata in May and June 1733. By contrast, the funeral music for Charles VII was performed simultaneously in all five of Hamburg's principal churches during regular services on 14 March 1745. Considering the significant logistical challenge this represented for Telemann, who had to call in out-of-town singers to fully staff the five musical ensembles, the high quality of the music is even more remarkable. The work was repeated in a public performance in Hamburg's Drillhaus on the following 29 April. *Unsterblicher Nachruhm Friedrich Augusts* has been published in volume 49 (2008) of the Telemann selective critical edition.* *BolBeg, FieTra, KreTra, LeiTra, MaeEng, MaePlä, NeuKir, NeuTra, ReiSer.*

Fux, Johann Joseph *See* **Theory**

Gardening Telemann may have begun gardening soon after moving to Hamburg in 1721, but the first documentation of his beloved hobby comes in the dedicatory letter* (dated 19 June 1741) to Johann Adolph Scheibe* in his second published collection of songs*, the *Vier und zwanzig, theils ernsthafte, theils scherzende, Oden.* In this letter Telemann mentions receiving Scheibe at his garden (probably between April and June 1741) in front of the city's gate. In August 1742 Telemann wrote to his Frankfurt friend Johann Friedrich Armand von Uffenbach* that 'for a few years' he had been indulging his 'love of flowers' ('Bluhmen-Liebe') as a counterpart to his musical activities (my 'field and plough'). Not content to exchange plants only with friends in Hamburg, Telemann used his extensive professional network to acquire rare plants from all over Europe; among the colleagues from whom he requested specimens, or who helped support his efforts, were Carl Heinrich Graun*, George Frideric Handel (who twice sent crates of plants from England), the poet Albrecht von Haller (1708–77), Lorenz Christoph Mizler*, Johann Georg Pisendel* (who also sent Telemann a shipment of plants) and Uffenbach, to whom Telemann inadvertently sent an extensive list of the plants he already owned (the intended, as yet unidentified, recipient of the list lived in Durlach). A visitor to Telemann's garden in 1753 noted the 'many strange and beautiful plants'. This was evidently no modest patch of greenery, for as late as 1843 Karl Gottfried Zimmermann (1796–1876) counted it among the most significant Hamburg gardens of the preceding century. *NeuBot, ReiBlu, ReiDok.*

Gdańsk *See* **Danzig**

***Der geduldige Socrates*, TVWV 21:9** Telemann's initial work for the Hamburg Opera appears to have been first heard on 5 February 1721 (five more performances are documented for February, in addition to one on 12 June and a revival in 1730). The composer, then in Frankfurt, must have been commissioned to write the opera before being offered the job in Hamburg – which in any case did not become available until the cantor there, Joachim Gerstenbüttel, died in April 1721. Yet the oft-repeated claim that Telemann must have travelled from Frankfurt to rehearse and direct the first performance cannot be confirmed. The opera's text was adapted by Johann Ulrich von König* from a libretto by Count Niccolò Minato (Prague, 1680) that was set to music by Antonio Draghi. König followed his model closely, translating the recitatives and leaving most of the arias in Italian (bilingual librettos were common at the Hamburg Opera), but also adding numerous new aria texts in German. The result was a pre-reform, Venetian-style libretto that, unusually for the eighteenth century, emphasises duets (ten in all), ensembles (four) and choruses (three). The duets and ensembles are also a function of the many dramatic conflicts in the plot, which takes place in ancient Athens following a war. The city's senate has decreed that the birthrate should be boosted by each man taking two wives, and although the philosopher Socrates advocates patience, his is sorely tested by his two quarrelling wives, Xantippe and Amitta. One of his former pupils, Prince Melito, struggles with the choice of a second wife: Rodisette and Edronica are equally desirable, but the former is unwilling to share him; both women are pursued by Prince Antippo, who is also indecisive about whom to choose. The impasse is resolved when Socrates encourages Melito to marry Rodisette, who loves him more. Edronica is then free to marry Antippo.

Telemann's brilliantly inventive music makes *Der geduldige Socrates* a landmark in the history of the Hamburg Opera. The libretto's balance of serious and comic characters and situations – the purely comic character of Pitho receives as many arias as Socrates and Antippo – clearly brought out the best in him. The mixture of seria and buffa music is seen not only in the juxtaposition of arias with sharply contrasting affects, but also in the contrapuntal rigour applied to many comic numbers and in the 'mezzo carattere' (middle character) nature of the music for Socrates, whose sage pronouncements are thereby rendered slightly ridiculous. In a mixed-taste* nod toward the French theatrical tradition, Act III opens with a *divertissement* placed at a feast of Adonis. *Der geduldige Socrates* was the first of Telemann's full-length operas to be revived in modern times, starting with a 1934 performance in Krefeld. It was also the first to be published, appearing in volume 20 (1967) of the Telemann selective critical edition*. *CloHam, CloTon, JanGed, LanSoc.*

Geistliche Cantaten The librettos of Erdmann Neumeister's* *Geistliche Cantaten*, first published in 1702, are significant for being the first annual cycle of church cantatas in the new madrigalian style, in which brief arias and recitatives replace the strophic arias and biblical or chorale verses characteristic of seventeenth-century sacred concertos. The librettos were first set by Johann Philipp Krieger, *Kapellmeister* at the Weißenfels court, where the cantatas were first performed in 1703–05. But none of Krieger's settings survive, making the eight extant cantatas by Telemann some of the earliest examples of their type. It is unclear whether Telemann set Neumeister's entire cycle, but documentary evidence indicates that more than eight cantatas once existed. The surviving works' musical style suggests their origin around the time of Neumeister's publication (reprints of which appeared in 1704 and 1705), when the composer was a university student in Leipzig or in his first court position, at Sorau. Each of the cantatas is set for solo voice, one or two obbligato instruments and continuo, underscoring the connection between the Italian chamber cantata and the new madrigalian church cantata. One of them, *Ich weiß, daß mein Erlöser lebt*, TVWV 1:877, was once erroneously considered a work by Johann Sebastian Bach* (BWV 160). *HobNeu, PoeKir, ReiDie.*

Geistliches Singen und Spielen This annual cycle of church cantata librettos, also known during the eighteenth century as the *Eisenacher-Jahrgang*, was the first that Erdmann Neumeister* provided to Telemann, and the composer's settings constitute the earliest cycle of madrigalian church cantatas (containing a mix of recitatives and arias) to survive complete. Here, for the first time, Neumeister combines biblical and chorale verses with newly composed arias and recitatives, and these textual elements are mixed in an extremely varied sequence and number from one work to the next; it appears that Telemann encouraged Neumeister to include stanzas from multiple chorales in some librettos. Most cantatas have one to three arias that may be in strophic or da capo form, sometimes with interspersed recitatives. Telemann's settings were first performed in Eisenach in 1710–11, and Neumeister published the librettos in 1711. After moving to Frankfurt, Telemann set Neumeister's librettos again for the 1717–18 church year, though it is unclear that this was a complete setting (fourteen cantatas survive complete in addition to a few cantata fragments and indications of the one-time existence of several more works). This second cycle may have been repeated in 1718–19. The 1710 cantatas for the first Sunday in Advent through the Sunday after Christmas, and the 1717 cantatas for four of the same occasions, have been published in volume 39 (2004) of the Telemann selective critical edition*. *HobNeu, JunKan, PoeKir.*

Die gekreuzigte Liebe oder Tränen über das Leiden und Sterben unseres Heilandes, **TVWV 5:4** Telemann's passion oratorio *The Crucified Love or Tears on the Suffering and Death of our Saviour*, to a libretto by Johann Ulrich König*, received its first performance in Hamburg's Drillhaus on 22 March 1731. Intended, like the immensely popular *Seliges Erwägen** of 1722, as a non-liturgical concert oratorio, *Die gekreuzigte Liebe* is a 'lyric' work in which the narrative of the Passion and death of Jesus Christ is minimised in favour of reflection upon the events; even the recitatives are mainly reflective in nature. Thus no evangelist tells the story according to one of the four Gospel narratives, and aside from the historical characters (Jesus, Peter, Pilate, John, Mary and Mary Magdalene) there are allegorical roles for the Faithful Soul and the Pious Soul in addition to an unnamed bass. In a notice of the upcoming premiere performance the *Hamburger Relations-Courier* observed that Telemann's music is 'almost consistently sombre and is alternatingly accompanied by various stirring instruments'. Among the work's colourful instrumental accompaniments are pairs of soprano recorders and oboes d'amore (an appropriately pastoral instrumentarium for Jesus' siciliano-style aria 'Aus Liebe lag ich in der Krippe') and pairs of flutes and chalumeaux (for Maria's aria 'Seele meiner Seelen'). The two main characters, Peter and Jesus, each receive extended monologues in the form of two successive recitative–aria pairs. Besides several chorales and turbae, there are two substantial motet-like works for chorus (representing the repentant sinners and women of Jerusalem). In a telling indication of the fluid barrier between Telemann's sacred and secular dramatic works, the A section of the bass aria 'Verfluchte Menschen haltet ein' parodies that of Orasia's rage aria 'Sù, mio core à la vendetta' from the 1726 opera *Die wunderbare Beständigkeit der Liebe, oder Orpheus**; but Zimmermann's text dictated that Telemann provide an entirely new B section for the bass aria.

Gensericus *See* ***Sieg der Schönheit*, TVWV 21:10**

German dynamic, tempo and expression indications From 1733 onward (beginning, perhaps, with the funeral music* for Friedrich August I, Elector of Saxony) Telemann increasingly replaced standard Italian dynamic, tempo and expression indications with German equivalents in his vocal works (but not, significantly, in his instrumental works). Thus, for example, 'piano' became 'gelinde' and 'forte' became 'stark', while 'langsam' replaced 'adagio'. But Telemann went well beyond translating standard Italian indications into German, for many of his markings promote a heightened subtlety of expression: 'gleichgültig' (indifferently), 'sehnlich' (ardently), 'prasselnd' (clattering), 'gebieterisch' (imperiously), 'schläfrig' (sleepily) and 'ehrbahr hirtenmässig' (honourably shepherd-like), to name a few. This innovation, apparently without parallel among Telemann's German contemporaries (though Johann Valentin Görner adopted German expression marks in his *Sammlung Neuer Oden und Lieder* of 1742 in apparent imitation of the songs* in Telemann's *Vier und zwanzig Oden*), may be associated with the composer's broader efforts at placing the German literary and musical languages on a par with the French, Italian and English – a concern that he shared with his colleagues in the Hamburg literary society 'Teutschübende Gesellschaft', and which is on clear display in his music journal, *Der getreue Music Meister**. Nothing suggests that Telemann's practice was motivated by anything other than this type of national pride, along with practicality and a desire for refined, sentimental expression (*Empfindsamkeit*). And yet one of the first detailed descriptions of it, in a 1941 article by Werner Menke*, was couched in terms of a darkly nationalistic 'renewal of German spirit and German culture' and of 'art for the good of the nation' ('Kunst als Nationalgut'). *BasVor, MenFac, MenVok.*

Germanicus*, TVWV 21:*deest This German opera was first performed in Leipzig during the Michaelmas fair of 1704 and repeated there during the Michaelmas fair of 1710, now with at least seventeen new Italian arias and up to six German ones replacing some of the originals. In between these performances, the opera was heard in its original version at the Hamburg Opera in 1706, and the revised version was repeated in Leipzig in 1720. Forty arias and duets (but no recitatives) survive from the opera's 1710 form, along with an additional aria from 1704. *Germanicus* is thus the most completely preserved of the works Telemann wrote as director of the Leipzig Opera. The libretto by Christine Dorothea Lachs (b. 1672), daughter of the composer Nikolaus Adam Strungk (who founded the Leipzig Opera in 1692), is modelled upon Giulio Cesare Corradi's *Germanico sul Reno* (Venice, 1676), set to music by Giovanni Legrenzi. Lachs had already provided librettos for two more Telemann operas earlier in 1704: *Der lachende Democritus* (TVWV 21:1; New Year's fair) and *Cajus Caligula* (TVWV 21:3; Easter fair). The plot is based on the second Germania campaign of the Roman general Nero Claudius Drusus Germanicus in 15–16 CE. Having defeated the Teutons and occupied Cologne, Germanicus believes that his enemy Arminius (Hermann), chieftain of the Germanic Cherusci tribe, has drowned in the Rhine. But Arminius has survived, and makes a failed attempt to abduct Germanicus' wife Agrippina as revenge. He is captured by the Roman captain Florus, who wishes to become emperor by tricking Germanicus into going back to Rome so that Florus can consolidate power. The trick fails, and Arminius avoids execution by escaping from the tower in which he has been imprisoned. A misunderstanding causes Germanicus to believe that Agrippina wishes to betray him, and she is imprisoned. When Florus frees her but fails to convince her to assassinate Germanicus, the general again misunderstands her intentions and decrees that she will be sacrificed in the temple. Agrippina is saved when an oracle confirms her fidelity, and Germanicus avoids assassination at the hands of Florus with help from Arminius, who now swears loyalty to the general. Telemann's music for the 1704 version of the opera (most of the German arias) shows him to have been already highly accomplished as a composer of dramatic music at age twenty-three, as is evident in arias such as Agrippina's Act II lullaby-lament 'Komm, o Schlaf, und laß mein Leid'. Yet the new music he wrote in Eisenach in 1710 (including all the Italian arias) reveals how far he had come in just six years. For example, Agrippina's Act I lamenting aria 'Rimembranza crudel' and Germanicus' Act II aria 'Gelosia, ti sento al core' reveal a depth of expression absent in most of the earlier music. *MauLei.*

Der getreue Music-Meister For a year beginning in November 1728 Telemann issued his 'Faithful Music Master', the first-ever journal consisting solely of printed music. Every two weeks, subscribers received an issue of four pages of music (a 'Lection' or lesson) containing a variety of works – everything from brief dances and contrapuntal exercises to sonatas, suites, arias and a cantata. All the principal national styles and the most common instruments are well represented in the journal's pages. Some works are without parallel in Telemann's output, such as the sonata for unaccompanied viola da gamba (TWV 40:1) and continuo sonatas for bassoon (TWV 41:f1) and cello (TWV 41:D6), and several arias are all that remain from lost operas* by the composer. Subscribers could try their hand at writing serious counterpoint, such as fugues based on subjects that Telemann had given to applicants for a church organist position the previous year, and chuckle at a satirical violin duet (TWV 40:108) illustrating scenes from the recently published *Gulliver's Travels* by Jonathan Swift. Telemann himself supplied most of the journal's music, but a number of others

4. Title page to *Der getreue Music-Meister* (Hamburg, 1728–29) and page 32 (Lection 8) of the journal, including a 'Carillon' for two chalumeaux (TWV 40:109), a menuet for two horns (40:110) and the 'Lilliputsche Chaconne' from the *Intrada, nebst burlesquer Suite* (40:108) for two violins based on Jonathan Swift's *Gulliver's Travels* (Paris, Bibliothèque nationale de France, Music Department, Vm7-3878). Reproduced by permission.

responded to his call for contributions, among them Johann Sebastian Bach*, Johann Georg Pisendel*, Sylvius Leopold Weiss* and Jan Dismas Zelenka*. In a brilliant marketing strategy, Telemann broke up multi-movement works between issues to incentivise consumers to subscribe to the journal rather than purchase individual issues. In his preface, Telemann noted that he had been inspired by the 'moral' periodicals that had become popular in Germany during the 1720s, following their introduction in London during the previous decade. Just as these literary 'weeklies' served their readership a mixture of education and entertainment, Telemann's 'Faithful Music Master' provided his 'readers' with exemplary models that instructed with a distinctly light touch. *ChaCou, FleMus, ZohFai, ZohMix.*

Graf, Johann Graf (1684–1750) was *Konzertmeister* (from 1722) and then *Kapellmeister* (from 1739) at the court of Schwarzburg-Rudolstadt. In 1732 he subscribed to Telemann's *Musique de table** on the court's behalf, and in succeeding years arranged to purchase additional music from him. Telemann later published Graf's *6 Soli* for violin and continuo, Op. 3 (Hamburg, 1737), engraving the music himself. In AB 1740 Telemann remarked that he had published music by Graf and others 'to please good friends'. *HobHer, TelBri, ZohMix.*

Graun, Carl Heinrich Telemann's relationship with Graun (1703–59) may date to the 1720s, when Telemann's operas were performed at the Brunswick court (possibly with Graun singing roles in them), or to the early 1730s, when some of Graun's operas were performed in Hamburg. In any case, they appear to have begun corresponding before the spring of 1735. Nine letters between the two (all but one written by Graun) survive from 1739–56, during which period Graun became director of the Berlin Opera and *Kapellmeister* to Friedrich II, King of Prussia (Frederick the Great)*. It is clear from his earliest extant letters, and those that must have preceded them, that Graun subscribed to Telemann's publications and assisted him in securing subscribers. In later years, the two had high praise for each other's music, and Telemann enlisted Graun's help in procuring plants for his gardening* hobby. It has been suggested that the friendly tone of Graun's later letters may indicate that Telemann visited him and other Berlin musicians around 1751, for after this date Telemann's relationships with his younger colleagues appear to have deepened.

Three letters, from 1751–52, famously address the subject of text setting in French and Italian recitative. (It is surely with these in mind that Georg Michael Telemann*, who inherited his grandfather's correspondence, suggested in 1816 to Georg Johann Daniel Poelchau that the Graun–Telemann letters ought to be published.) For Graun, French recitative was unnatural, used arioso indiscriminately and needlessly shifted between metres. He attempted to illustrate these points with musical examples drawn from *Castor et Pollux* (Paris, 1737) by Jean-Philippe Rameau*, and his own settings of the French texts were designed to show that one could dispense with the characteristic changes of metre. Yet as Telemann pointed out with keen analytical acumen, Graun's versions exhibit poor declamation, misplaced emphasis on less important words, 'sour' harmony and a disregard for textual imagery, among other infelicities. When Graun considered that frequent metrical shifts, though inaudible to listeners, would cause difficulty for the performers, Telemann countered that 'the changes of meter [in recitative] cause no difficulty for the French. Everything flows continuously like champagne.' To prove his point that the metrical shifts, far from bothering performers, foster a natural accentuation of the text, Telemann quoted a German recitative from his 1746 St Matthew Passion in which he alternated meters (as he frequently did in his recitatives from the 1740s onward). Although he admitted to mainly following Italian recitative practice, he found it advantageous to borrow French elements (not just metrical shifts, but also arioso-like melodic writing and more active bass lines) – another instance of his mixed taste*. On the other hand, Graun, who probably had little experience with French music, comes across as closed-minded in claiming the superiority of Italian over French recitative. Telemann and Graun also differed in their opinions of dissonance treatment, with the younger composer advocating restraint in harmonic matters and the older one stating something of a manifesto: 'If there is nothing new to find in melody, then one must seek it in harmony. Yes, it is said: but one should not go too far; as far as the deepest bedrock, I reply, if one wishes to merit the name of a diligent master.' To be sure, Telemann's vocal works of the 1750s and 1760s often display daring harmonies. In 1755, in the wake of their epistolary exchange, Graun and Telemann both composed settings of the passion oratorio *Der Tod Jesu** (to a libretto by Karl Wilhelm Ramler*), apparently in friendly competition with each other. *CalRez, CzoGra, RosRec, TelBri.*

Graupner, Christoph Graupner (1683–1760) attended the Thomasschule in Leipzig, where he studied with Johann Kuhnau* alongside Johann David Heinichen and Johann Friedrich Fasch*. Like Telemann, he studied law at the university and later declined the position of Thomaskantor that eventually went to Johann Sebastian Bach*. Engaged at the Darmstadt* court as Vice-*Kapellmeister* in 1709 and as *Kapellmeister* from 1712 (a position he held until his death), Graupner copied about ninety of Telemann's instrumental works, many as study scores. These can be dated with reference to paper types also found in the composing scores of Graupner's church cantatas at Darmstadt, from which it emerges that his Telemann manuscripts post-date the composer's move to Hamburg. In other words, Graupner and Telemann appear to have had little musical contact during the latter's nine years (1712–21) in nearby Frankfurt, reinforcing an impression that the two did not have a particularly close relationship. Neither composer, for example, mentions the other in his autobiographies, and Graupner appears not to have been a member of Telemann's Leipzig Collegium musicum while the two were both students in the city. *BilGra, NoaDar, ZohMix.*

Grimma Founded in 1550, the Fürstenschule in Grimma (today St Augustin) assembled a rich collection of sacred vocal works that now encompasses about 1,300 manuscripts and prints spanning the late sixteenth to the early nineteenth centuries. Included among these are 150 manuscript copies of sacred concertos and cantatas by Telemann performed under the direction of a succession of cantors through the 1770s (the earliest performance date found on the title pages is 1707). Among these works are some of Telemann's earliest surviving vocal music. In 1961–62 the Telemann manuscripts, along with others from the seventeenth and eighteenth centuries, were transferred to the Sächsiche Landesbibliothek (now the Sächsische Landesbibliothek – Staats- und Universitätsbibliothek) in Dresden. Ortrun Landmann published a catalogue of the Telemann sources* in 1983, and an online compilation of the source entries in RISM Series A/II: Musical manuscripts after 1600 was prepared by Andrea Hartmann in 2009. *HarGri, LanQue, ReiDie.*

Hagedorn, Friedrich von Secretary to the 'English Court' (*Englischer Hof*) in Hamburg from 1733, Hagedorn (1708–54) was among the most significant German poets of his generation. Telemann set six of his poems among the songs* of the *Singe-, Spiel- und Generalbass-Übungen* (1733–34) and *Vier und zwanzig, theils ernsthafte, theils scherzende, Oden* (1741). Hagedorn's poetry fits especially well with the anacreontic orientation of Telemann's second collection, and 'An den Schlaf' inspired one of the loveliest melodies among the composer's songs. *RicHag.*

Haltmeier, Carl Johann Friedrich Haltmeier (c. 1698–1735) was the great nephew of Telemann's mother Johanna Maria Telemann* (née Haltmeier). Born in Verden, where his father Joachim Friedrich Haltmeier (1668–1720) served as cantor from 1696, Carl Johann Friedrich spent his career in Hanover, first as organist at the Marktkirche (1720–25/26) and then as court organist. In 1729 Telemann published one of Haltmeier's keyboard fantasias in *Der getreue Music-Meister**. Haltmeier left two unpublished musical treatises. The first, a brief guide to transposition (*Anleitung: wie man einen General-Baß, oder auch Hand-Stücke, in alle Tone transponieren könne*), was published by Telemann at his own expense in 1737; the composer even engraved the musical examples himself. His plan to publish Haltmeier's second treatise, on the resolution of dissonances, was never realised. *HobDok, HobHer.*

Hamann, Johann Georg Following his move to Hamburg in 1728, Hamann (1697–1733) edited various periodicals, including the newspaper *Hamburger Correspondent* and the moral weekly *Die Matrone* (1728–30), in which he praised Telemann's opera *Sancio, oder die siegende Grossmuth*, TVWV 21:20 (1727). Hamann also provided libretti for a number of Telemann's works, including the operatic prologue *Die Glückseligkeit des Russischen Kayserthums* (TVWV 23:9, 1730), the operas *Margaretha Königen in Castilien* (TVWV 21:29, 1730) and *Der Weiseste in Sidon* (TVWV 21:30, 1733), and the *Kapitänsmusik** for 1730 (TVWV 15:5) and 1731 (TVWV 15:6). *BeiHam, MaeHam, ZohFai.*

Hamburger Ebb und Fluht *See* ***Wasser-Ouverture***

Handel, George Frideric The friendship between Telemann and Handel (1685–1759) lasted over half a century, from 1701, when Telemann passed through Halle on the way to Leipzig ('I nearly imbibed the poison of music again through making the acquaintance of the already consequential Herr Georg Friedrich Händel'; AB 1740), to the next several years ('Handel and I had a steady engagement in melodic matters and their exploration through frequent visits on both sides and by letter'; AB 1740), to their mutual presence in Dresden in 1719 during wedding festivities for the electoral prince Friedrich August II and the Habsburg archduchess Maria Josepha, and to correspondence during the 1750s (in which Handel wrote to Telemann in French). Handel borrowed from Telemann's music over 120 times between 1727 and 1749, especially from *Der Harmonischer Gottesdienst**, the *Sonates sans basse** and the *Musique de table** (Handel subscribed to the latter publication). The earliest known borrowing dates from 1705–06, when Handel drew inspiration for the first movement of his 'Sonata à 5' for violin and strings, HWV 288, from the opening Adagio of Telemann's violin concerto TWV 51:B2. Handel may also have borrowed melodic material from the aria 'Meine Lippen sind voll Lachens' from the opera *Lucius Verus* (composed by Telemann in Leipzig for the 1703 Easter fair; TVWV 21:*deest*) in his cantata *Il delirio amoroso*, HWV 99 (Rome, 1707).

Telemann performed at least ten of Handel's operas in Hamburg, including *Tamerlano* (1725), *Ottone* (1726), *Ricardo I* (1729), *Poro* (1732) and *Almira* (1732). For these he composed new German recitatives and added arias and choruses. Decades later, the anonymous librettist for Telemann's 1759 *Kapitänsmusik** (TVWV 15:22; music lost) based his text on Handel's oratorio *Solomon* (1749). At present there is no evidence to indicate that Handel performed Telemann's music. The two may have renewed their friendship in 1729, when Handel visited Hamburg to engage the singer Johann Gottfried Riemschneider* for his London operas. In December 1750 Telemann sent Handel his *Neues musikalisches System**, to which the latter noted 'it is worthy of your efforts and your learning'. At this time Handel sent Telemann a crate of flowering plants ('the best plants in all of England') in support of his friend's gardening* hobby. Handel wrote to Telemann again in September 1754, promising another shipment of plants and relating how he had been given the false impression that Telemann had recently died. It has been suggested that the sarabanda-like instrumental sinfonia and following fugal chorus of *Die Auferstehung und Himmelfahrt Jesu**, TVWV 6:6 (1760) was intended by Telemann as a remembrance of Handel, who had died almost exactly a year earlier. The chorus appears to have been inspired by Handel's chorus 'He smote all the first born in Egypt' from *Israel in Egypt*. During the 1780s Telemann's former student at the Hamburg Johanneum, Johann Joachim Eschenburg (1743–1820), recalled that Telemann often spoke of his early acquaintance with Handel, and of the esteem he had for Handel's music. Telemann's arrangement of Handel's *Ricardo I* (as *Der misslungene Brautwechsel oder Richardus I, König von England*) has been published in volume 46 (2009) of the Telemann selective critical edition.* *BasBez, BasHän, CumHän, DerHan, HarRic, HirHän, HobTom, KocHän, KocOtt, KreHän, LynOtt, MauLei, PayCap, RamHän, RobHan, SeiMus, TelBri, WilBor.*

Harmoniemusik Telemann wrote some of the earliest known music for wind band (or 'Harmonie') in scorings that are more familiar from the late eighteenth and early nineteenth centuries. In Frankfurt he composed a ceremonial 'Marche' for three oboes, two horns and bassoon (TWV 50:43; 1716), and wrote at least seven overture-suites* for two oboes, two horns and bassoon or continuo (TWV 44:3, 7–8, 12–14 and 16). To these may be added a possible wind-band version of the *Alster-Ouverture**. *HobHau, HofHar, ZohMix.*

Harmonischer Gottes-Dienst, oder geistlichen Cantaten Telemann's first complete annual cycle of church cantatas for Hamburg (the earlier *Brandenburg-Jahrgang**

of 1723–24 remained incomplete) was not only his inaugural musical publication after moving to the city and the first of his five published annual cantata cycles, but also the first-ever cycle of madrigalian church cantatas (with arias and recitatives) to appear in print. Financed largely by subscribers, the *Harmonischer Gottes-Dienst* was typeset in score – something unusual for concerted vocal music at the time – and appeared in regular instalments between December 1725 and January 1727. Part 1 of the collection includes cantatas for New Year's Day and for Sundays through Pentecost; Part 2 contains the cantata for Christmas Day and for Sundays between Trinity and the Sunday after Christmas; and an appendix contains cantatas for seldom-observed Sundays and feast days held on fixed dates or weekdays. Most of the texts were provided by the young lawyer Matthäus Arnold Wilkens*, but five other authors (including Michael Richey*) contributed one or more librettos. Telemann was already planning the cycle's publication by October 1724, when he asked his Frankfurt friend Johann Friedrich Armand von Uffenbach* to supply copper-plate engravings for the print. The delay of publication beyond the start of the 1725–26 liturgical year may have been due to complications in obtaining the requisite number of subscribers, but could also have been part of a marketing strategy to break up cantatas for the most important feast days between the collection's two parts. Each of the cycle's seventy-two cantatas consists of two solo arias separated by a brief recitative. The solo vocal part, for either high (soprano/tenor) or middle (low soprano/high alto/low tenor/high bass) voice, is joined by an instrumental accompaniment of treble instrument (flute, recorder, oboe or violin) and continuo. As noted on the collection's title page, the cantatas were intended for 'private, house and public church devotion', and in fact Telemann performed the works in Hamburg's principal churches between New Year's Day 1726 and the Sunday after Christmas of that year (following the sermon). Manuscript copies made from the print were prepared for use in churches and court chapels throughout northern Europe. In his preface, Telemann offers advice on singing appoggiaturas in recitatives, transposing the continuo line for a high-pitched (*Chorton*) organ and adding extra singers and instrumentalists. Owners of the *Harmonischer Gottes-Dienst* included Johann Gottfried Walther* (organist at Weimar's Stadtkirche) and George Frideric Handel*, who borrowed thematic material from it for use in his oratorio *Solomon*, among other works. Thanks to its complete republication in volumes 2–5 (1953–57) of the Telemann selective critical edition*, the *Harmonischer Gottes-Dienst* has become the composer's best known cantata cycle. *ReiCan, ReiVer, TayCan, ZohMar.*

Harmonisches Lob Gottes This annual cycle of church cantatas to librettos by Johann Friedrich Helbig* (also known as the second *Helbig-Jahrgang*) was first performed in Hamburg (mostly before the sermon) and Frankfurt during the 1726–27 church year. The cycle was heard concurrently, or perhaps earlier, in Eisenach, and was repeated in Roßla near Stolberg in 1729–30. Each of the fifty-four surviving cantatas begins with an instrumental sinfonia followed by a dictum (biblical verse) and a mixture of arias, recitatives and chorales. Twelve cantatas for Sundays and feasts from Ascension Day through the seventh Sunday after Trinity have been published in volume 56 (2017) of the Telemann selective critical edition*. Telemann himself published two arias from each cantata in arrangements for voice and continuo as the *Auszug derjenigen* *musicalischen und auf die gewöhnlichen Evangelien gerichteten Arien* (Hamburg, 1727), issued not by the composer but by the bookseller Johann Christoph Kißner. Although the full cantatas are scored for strings with oboes *ad libitum*, the arias are in two real parts (violins in unison doubling voice, viola in unison with the continuo), indicating that Telemann had conceived them with publication in mind. For the *Auszug*, Telemann not only eliminated the string parts, but also shortened, cut or reworked ritornellos. Publishing only arias in the *Auszug* aligned it with printed collections of arias excerpted from operas and Passion settings, not to mention the many hymnals popular at the time. It also recalls Telemann's earlier *Jahrgang ohne Recitativ* (Hamburg, 1724–25), which included only dicta for solo voice, arias and chorales. In fact, the modest scoring and dimensions of the *Auszug* made it even more suitable for private devotional services than the *Harmonischer Gottes-Dienst** cycle of the previous year (as Telemann noted in his preface). Like the *Harmonischer Gottes-Dienst*, the *Auszug* begins with the cantata for New Year's Day. A number of arias from the *Auszug* were recommended by Johann Mattheson* in his *Große General-Baß-Schule* (Hamburg, 1731) and *Kleine General-Baß-Schule* (Hamburg, 1735) for practising figured bass realisation and as models of church music in the theatrical style. The entire *Auszug* has been published in volume 57 (2012) of the Telemann selective critical edition*. *HirAri, KühAri, ReiHel, ReiJah, TayCan.*

Hebenstreit, Pantaleon An accomplished violinist, keyboardist and dancing master, Hebenstreit (1667–1750) invented the 'Pantaleon', a type of dulcimer on which he toured as a virtuoso. Telemann first met him in Leipzig, and the two were colleagues at the Eisenach court before Hebenstreit (who held the positions of director of music and dancing master) embarked on tours across Europe. Hebenstreit was a court chamber musician in Dresden* from 1714, directed the music in the Catholic court church from 1729 and became Vice-*Kapellmeister* in 1733. In AB 1718 Telemann recalled playing double violin concertos with Hebenstreit while at Eisenach (probably in 1708–09), noting that he had to practise hard and 'oil his nerves' in preparation. In fact, Telemann's surviving double violin concertos all appear to have been written during his Eisenach years. In 1709 Hebenstreit and Telemann collaborated on the opera *Mario*, TVWV 21:6, heard at the Leipzig Opera during the Easter fair of that year. *MauLei.*

Helbig-Jahrgang *See* ***Harmonisches Lob Gottes***

Helbig, Johann Friedrich Helbig (1680–1722) sang tenor in the Leipzig Collegium musicum* under Telemann's successor, Melchior Hoffmann, before joining the Eisenach court (most likely at Telemann's invitation) as a singer in 1709. He was soon appointed court secretary and, following Telemann's departure in 1712, *Kapellmeister*. From 1718 until his death, he was also responsible for providing poetry for the court's church music. Telemann set three of his cantata libretto cycles in whole or in part as the *Sicilianischer Jahrgang**, *Jahrgang ohne Recitativ** and the *Harmonisches Lob Gottes**. *OefEis, OefTex, ReiHel.*

Hirschmann, Wolfgang Following doctoral studies and a post-doctoral research position at the Friedrich-Alexander-Universität Erlangen-Nürnberg, Hirschmann joined the Historical Musicology faculty at Martin-Luther Universität Halle-Wittenberg in 2007. From 2004 he served on the Board of Editorial Advisors for the Telemann selective critical edition*, becoming General Editor (with Carsten Lange*) in 2010; his ten volumes for the edition (by far the most of any contributor to Georg Philipp Telemann: Musikalische Werke) include operas as well as sacred and occasional vocal works. Since his dissertation on Telemann's concertos (published in 1986), Hirschmann has contributed numerous studies on the composer's concertos, sacred and occasional vocal works, operas and passions, with an emphasis on issues surrounding musical style, aesthetics and reception history. *HirAlt, HirAri, HirCon, HirFes, HirFra, HirHän, HirHei, HirInd, HirInn, HirIno, HirJoh, HirKan, HirKom, HirMic, HirNeu, HirPas, HirPol, HirPsa, HirRez, HirSch, HirSer, HirSpä, HirSpu, HirVer.*

***Die Hirten bei der Krippe zu Bethlehem*, TVWV 1:797** Together with *Die Auferstehung und Himmelfahrt Jesu** and *Der May**, this 1759 Christmas cantata forms a trio of works Telemann composed to librettos by Karl Wilhelm Ramler* c. 1760. Ramler had written *Die Hirten bei der Krippe zu Bethlehem* for the Berlin *Kapellmeister* Johann Friedrich Agricola* in 1757, and it is possible that Agricola (who was in touch with Telemann at this time) shared his setting, or at least Ramler's text, with his Hamburg colleague. Since Ramler did not include the four chorale settings found in Telemann's score, it may be that the composer inserted them to enhance the cantata's suitability for liturgical performance. A score of the work by Telemann's principal copyist, Otto Ernst Gregorius Schieferlein*, lacks the chorales and may therefore represent an earlier, concert version of the piece. Both of the cantata's symmetrically structured parts include an aria, two accompanied recitatives (with vividly evocative orchestral writing), two chorales and a concluding chorus that fluently alternates contrapuntal and homophonic passages. The idyll-like character of Ramler's libretto is reflected in Telemann's music by the pastoral style of the solo movements, featuring drones, siciliano rhythms, compound meters and scorings with flutes and recorders. In an invocation of the Polish style*, the instrumental introduction to the shepherds' accompanied recitative ('Hirtenlied', No. 2) is marked – in Schieferlein's score, not in Telemann's composing score – 'Ernsthaft lustig' (serious-funny). This seeming paradox, which is surely Telemann's, echoes his reference in the *Singe-, Spiel- und General-Bass-Übungen* to the Polish style as 'die lustige polnische Ernsthaftigkeit' (the comic Polish seriousness). *Die Hirten bei der Krippe zu Bethlehem* has been published in volume 30 (1997) of the Telemann selected critical edition*.

Hobohm, Wolf A leading figure in Telemann scholarship since the 1960s, Hobohm (b. 1938) became founding director of the study group 'Georg Philipp Telemann' (then belonging to the cultural alliance of the German Democratic Republic) in 1961, and in 1978 joined the staff of the Zentrum für Telemann-Pflege und -Forschung* in Magdeburg, later serving as its director (1985–2003). He earned his doctorate from the Martin-Luther-Universität Halle-Wittenberg in 1982 with a dissertation on musical life in nineteenth-century Magdeburg. Hobohm's published research on Telemann has included studies of biography, reception, dissemination and the genesis and style of both instrumental and vocal works. With Martin Ruhnke*, he served as General Editor of the Telemann selective critical edition* from 1992 to 2004 (also contributing three volumes of vocal music), and thereafter sat on the edition's Board of Editorial Advisors until 2010. He has also edited numerous conference reports deriving from the Telemann-Festtage* in Magdeburg along with volumes in the Magdeburger Telemann-Studien series. *HobBem, HobBer, HobBib, HobBio, HobBog, HobBri, HobDok, HobEmm, HobErb, HobGru, HobHau, HobHer, HobJah, HobKan, HobKle, HobLei, HobLom, HobMar, HobMis, HobNeu, HobRam, HobRei, HobSch, HobTom, HobÜbe, HobVer.*

Hollander, Johann Reinhold Three letters* from Telemann to his friend Hollander (1711–38), a businessman in Riga, survive from the period 1732–36. They are friendly in tone and deal alternately with business and personal matters. Two of the three are written entirely in verse, while the other alternates prose and poetry; this surely reflects Telemann's and Hollander's mutual poetic interests (the latter sent the former a text to be set to music in 1736). Hollander collected subscribers to a number of Telemann's publications, and himself purchased the *Musique de table**, among other collections. *HobBio, KocRig, TelBri.*

Horn-Jahrgang Telemann composed this annual cycle of church cantatas for performance in Hamburg during the 1739–40 church year to librettos by two or more unidentified poets. Eight musical settings are extant, but a total of forty works from the cycle are documented in printed Hamburg librettos (*Texte zur Music*) published through the 1763–64 church year. Most of the extant arias feature a part for horn, lending the cycle its nickname, and each of the cantatas follows an eight-movement scheme in which three chorales alternate with three arias before a concluding recitative and biblical verse (dictum) set for chorus. *ReiBeo.*

Hurlebusch, Conrad Friedrich A talented yet vain keyboardist and composer, the well travelled Hurlebusch (1691–1765) spent several years in Italy before returning to Germany and turning down a number of court positions, including in his native Brunswick. He spent 1722–25 as *Kapellmeister* at the Swedish royal court, then again travelled in Germany. Hurlebusch was the subject of a 1723 epigram by Telemann entitled 'To a famous virtuoso who always played for too long': 'You play incomparably well, but stir only half the senses. He who does more with less will gain ten times as much as you. You ask: how come? I instruct: you don't know when to stop.' Just two years later, in June 1725, Johann Mattheson* entertained both Telemann and Hurlebusch at his Hamburg home, but the trio soon made an 'honourable withdrawal' from each others' company. Hurlebusch moved to Hamburg in 1727, and in 1735 applied for the vacant organist position at the Petrikirche but was turned down, apparently because he refused to play the customary test recital under Telemann's supervision. Also part of the audition process was a set of twelve music-theoretical questions prepared by Telemann. Hurlebusch's bitingly satirical answers, as transmitted in a manuscript copied by Mattheson, reveal that he considered answering these 'naïve' (but in fact deceptively complicated) questions beneath his dignity. Hurlebusch unsuccessfully applied for the position of cantor at Hamburg's cathedral in 1739, and in 1743 settled into the organist post at Amsterdam's Oude Kerk. *ZohJob.*

***Ich hoffete aufs Licht*, TVWV 4:13** *See* **Funeral music**

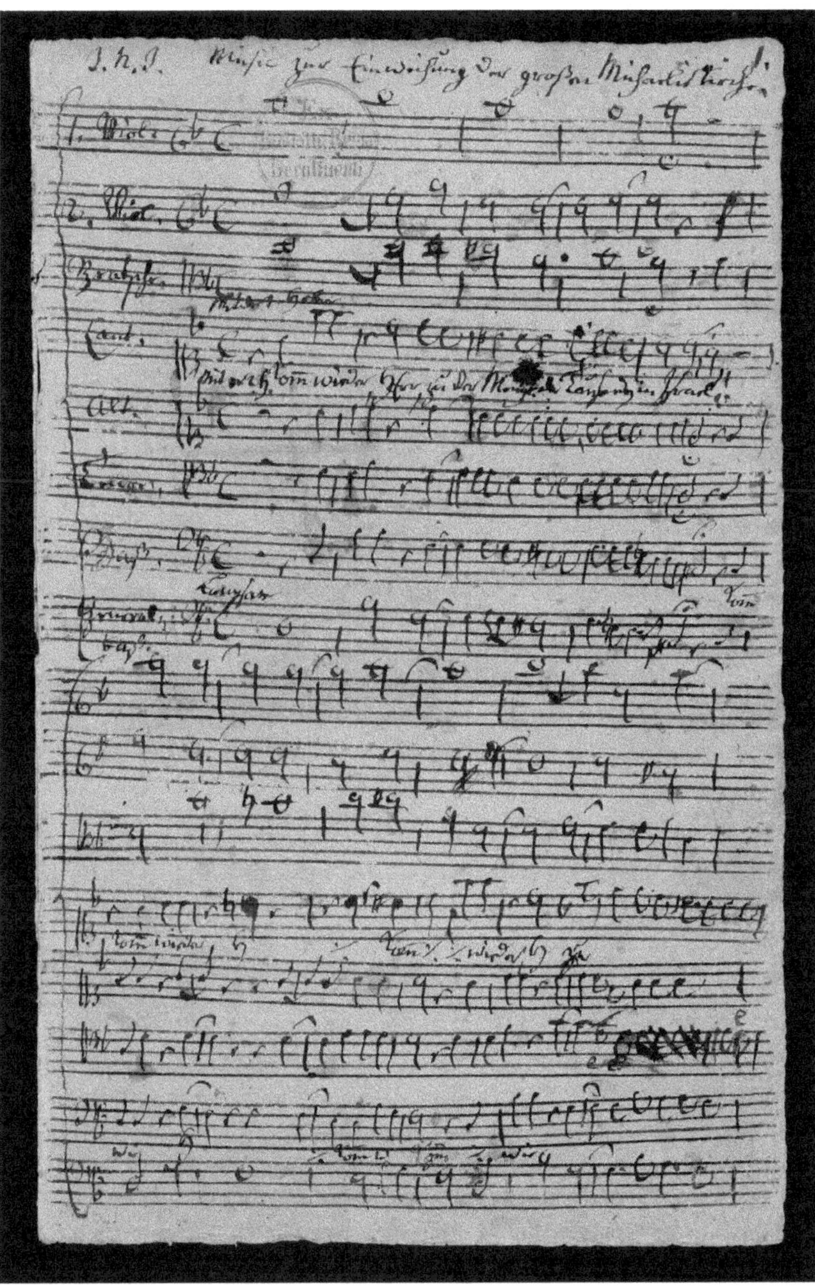

5. First page of Telemann's composing score to *Komm wieder, Herr, zu der Menge der Tausenden in Israel*, TVWV 2:12, music for the inauguration of Hamburg's Great St Michaeliskirche on 19 October 1762 (Staatsbibliothek zu Berlin – Preußischer Kulturbesitz, Music Department and Mendelssohn Archive, Mus. ms. autogr. G. P. Telemann 8). Image courtesy of Art Resources, NY. Reproduced by permission.

Inauguration music Writing festive vocal music for the inaugurations of churches and altars provided Telemann with a supplementary source of income during his later Hamburg years, and some of these works were commissioned from outside the city. The surviving 'outside' inauguration works include those for the St Nicolaikirche in Billwerder (1739; TVWV 2:3), the Heilige Dreieinigkeitskirche in St Georg (1747; 2:6) and churches in Neuenstädten (1751; 2:7) and Rellingen, Holstein (1756; 2:9). Telemann's Hamburg inauguration music includes works for the altar of the St Getrudkirche (1742; TVWV 2:4), for the church in St Hiob-Hospital (1745; 2:5) and for the Great St Michaeliskirche (1762; 2:12). Three additional works are known only from printed librettos. The music for Hamburg's Great St Michaeliskirche belonged to one of the most important eighteenth-century celebrations in the city, attended by more than five thousand people on 19 October 1762. The old Michaeliskirche had been destroyed when its tower caught fire after being struck by lightning on 10 March 1750, and the completion of the new, monumental building had been delayed several times. Telemann's inauguration music is appropriately festive, including two choirs of three trumpets with timpani, and was performed by ten singers and and orchestra of thirty-two instrumentalists. In attendance in 1762 was Johann Mattheson*, who personally financed the church's organ (completed in 1770), and remarked on Telemann's 'excellent oratorio'. The composer repeated the work at a concert given in Hamburg's concert hall 'auf dem Kamp' (in the field) on 10 March 1763. The opening 'Heilig' chorus of TVWV 2:6 enjoyed fame as a separate concert piece in Hamburg during the 1770s and 1780s, and it appears to have exerted a strong influence on the *Heilig* (Wq 217; 1776) of Carl Philipp Emanuel Bach*. All of Telemann's surviving inauguration music has been published in volumes 35 (2004) and 65 (2017) of the Telemann selective critical edition.* *HirAlt, HirFes, HirHei, HirMic, NeuKir, OrtEre, PfaNeu.*

Ino One of the outstanding masterpieces of Telemann's old age, this secular cantata for soprano and orchestra reveals that the composer's dramatic powers and alertness to modern musical idioms remained intact into his mid-eighties. The libretto by Karl Wilhelm Ramler* is based on a story from Ovid's *Metamorphoses*. Ino's sister, Semele, has been killed because she gave birth to Bacchus after a tryst with Jupiter. Bacchus has found a new mother in Ino. But Juno (Saturnia in the cantata), Jupiter's wife, exacts further revenge by afflicting Ino's husband, Athamas, with madness. Athamas consequently kills one of his own sons, and he now pursues Ino in order to kill his other son, Melicertes. As the cantata opens, a desperate Ino throws herself into the sea with her son. They survive, but Melicertes slips from Ino's arms and is rescued by nymphs. Mother and son are made immortal by Neptune as the sea-gods Leukothea and Palaemon. Aside from a da capo aria and a dal segno aria, Telemann's musical forms are relatively fluid: a through-composed aria, recitatives leading to ariosos, instrumental dances thematically linked to following vocal sections and a preponderance of accompanied recitative. Ramler and Telemann divide the story into three sections separated by instrumental dances: Fleeing/Despair (recitative–aria–recitative), Rescue (*scena*: recitative–arioso) and Metamorphosis/Apotheosis (recitative–arioso–aria–recitative–aria). Telemann's settings of the three arias follow a stylistic progression:

'Ungöttliche Saturnia' is a late-baroque rage aria, 'Meint ihr mich' represents the mid-century style of Johann Adolf Hasse or Carl Heinrich Graun*, and the concluding 'Tönt in meinem Lobgesang' is, rather astonishingly, in the early classical style associated with Christoph Willibald Gluck and Joseph Haydn (here immortality is musically underscored by music of the future, as it were). It is no exaggeration to say that with this work Ramler and Telemann redefined the secular cantata as a genre.

Precisely when Telemann composed *Ino*, and where it was first performed, remains unclear. Ramler's libretto was first published in Berlin in 1765, then reprinted in Hamburg the following year with mention that it had been 'set to music' by Christian Gottfried Krause*; in fact, Krause had made an arrangement of Telemann's setting. Thus Telemann must have composed his cantata in 1765 or earlier. *Ino* was performed in Hamburg in 1768 by Carl Philipp Emanuel Bach* and in Berlin the following year, but printed sources fail to mention a composer. The earliest attribution of the cantata to Telemann comes in 1770, when Christoph Daniel Ebeling* mentioned his authorship and Krause's arrangement. It is therefore possible that Telemann never heard a performance of *Ino*, and that his authorship of the work was not recognised in early Berlin and Hamburg performances. The cantata was edited by Max Scheider* in volume 28 (1907) of the series Denkmäler deutscher Tonkunst (a 1958 revision of the edition by Hans Joachim Moser unfortunately introduced errors to the musical text). Schneider's manuscript source, a late eighteenth-century score, contains faulty textual readings that are given in what is presumably their correct (original) form in Krause's arrangement. *HirIno, LütMon, SeiIno.*

Italienischer Jahrgang *See* ***Concerten-Jahrgang***

Jahrgang ohne Recitativ Telemann composed this annual cycle of church cantatas to texts by the Eisenach court secretary and *Kapellmeister* Johann Friedrich Helbig* (who provided librettos for the first Sunday in Advent through Sunday in Ascension Week before his death in April 1722) and the Ansbach court poet Benjamin Neukirch (1665–1729; librettos for Pentecost through the twenty-sixth Sunday after Trinity). Printed librettos and documentary evidence confirm the cycle's simultaneous performance in Eisenach, Frankfurt and Hamburg during the 1724–25 church year (though seven cantatas were already heard in Hamburg in 1723–24). The cantatas, scored mostly for strings without winds, consist of five to seven movements combining arias (in two or three contrapuntal parts and usually not in da capo form), four-part chorale settings and biblical verses or 'dicta' (usually for solo voice). The conspicuous absence of recitatives inspired the title 'Jahrgang ohne Recitativ' on a Frankfurt set of scribal parts to the cantata for the first Sunday in Advent. Twelve cantatas for the third Sunday in Lent through the fourth Sunday after Easter, and for the Visitation of Mary, have been published in volume 55 (2015) of the Telemann selective critical edition*. *ReiRec.*

Johann Ernst, Prince of Sachsen-Weimar Johann Ernst (1696–1715) studied music and later composition with Johann Gottfried Walther*, and in 1713–14 appears to have commissioned the Weimar court organist Johann Sebastian

Bach* to make keyboard arrangements of concertos (BWV 592–96 and 972–87; including Telemann's violin concerto TWV 51:g1, BWV 985), some of which the prince had collected during a two-year study trip to the Netherlands in 1711–13. Months before Johann Ernst's untimely death in Frankfurt in August 1715, Telemann dedicated his first publication, the *Six sonates à violon seul**, to the prince. Three years later Telemann published Johann Ernst's *Six concerts à violon concertant*, which apparently did not sell well despite being the first published collection of solo concertos by a German composer. In his dedicatory preface, Telemann explained that the prince had planned on engraving the collection himself but died before completing it, and before he could embark on a sequel collection. *SwaErn, SwaSol, ZohMix.*

Kapitänsmusik Each year the fifty-seven captains of the Hamburg city militia held a celebration on the first Thursday after St Bartholomäus Day (24 August) in the Drillhaus, with a sacred oratorio preceding a banquet and a secular serenata heard during the banquet as *Tafelmusik**. Telemann produced thirty-six oratorio-serenata pairs between 1723 and 1766 (the celebration was not held in some years). Of these, nine pairs survive intact in addition to three oratorios and serenatas that are missing their companions (librettos for nine more pairs are extant, and fifteen are completely lost). The librettos to both the oratorios and serenatas are populated with allegorical characters and extol Hamburg's virtues in a manner that may have been unique among European cities. In the 1738 oratorio, for example, the characters include Hammonia (Hamburg) and the virtues of Devotion, Justice, Truth and Trust; the vice of Negligence; and the choruses of Hammonia's children and Shepherds of the Elbe. Among the librettists Telemann worked with on his *Kapitänsmusiken* were Johann Georg Hamann*, Johann Philipp Praetorius*, Michael Richey* and Joachim Johann Daniel Zimmermann*. As with other types of occasional vocal works originally intended for private celebrations, Telemann's *Kapitänsmusiken* were subsequently heard in public concerts. The 1730 *Kapitänsmusik* has been published in volume 27 (1995) of the Telemann selected critical edition*. *MaeMar, MaeKap, SchBru.*

Kayser, Margaretha Susanna A celebrated soprano, Kayser (1690–1774) was active in her native Hamburg as a concert and opera singer almost continuously from c. 1708 to 1750, also performing in the city's churches under Telemann and in the cathedral under Johann Mattheson*. She was a member of the Darmstadt* *Hofkapelle* from 1709 until about 1717, in which capacity she would have participated in the first performances of Telemann's *Brockes-Passion** in Frankfurt on 2–3 April 1716 (perhaps singing the part of the Daughter of Zion), and in performances of his cantata and serenata for the birth of Archduke Leopold (TVWV 12:1) on the following 17 May. Between late 1721 and early 1723 she sang operas by Reinhard Keiser* in Copenhagen under the direction of her husband, the instrumentalist Johann Kayser (who worked under Telemann in various capacities, including as director of Hamburg's municipal musicians). Returning to Hamburg, she sang operatic roles regularly from 1724, served as leaseholder of the Hamburg Opera between 1729 and 1737 and thereafter was active as a concert impresario. She was in Stockholm by 1751, becoming a court singer no later than 1754. *MaeInt, MaeKap, NeuKir.*

Keiser, Reinhard Keiser (1674–1739) was the leading composer for the Hamburg Opera between 1693 and 1719, when he left the city to spend two years at the Württemberg-Stuttgart court before becoming the royal Danish *Kapellmeister* in 1722. He returned to Hamburg in 1723, and in 1728 succeeded Johann Mattheson* as cantor of the cathedral. Although the nature of the relationship between Telemann and Keiser remains unclear, the two must have met during the former's visit to Stuttgart* in August 1720, and from 1723 they appear to have worked well with each other in Hamburg. This impression seems to be confirmed by the sonnet Telemann wrote upon Keiser's death. Published by Johann Adolph Scheibe* in 1739, the 'Sonnet on the Death of the Famous Kapellmeister Keiser' includes the lines 'How richly, how new, how beautifully, how perfectly he thought! How he brought song to full adornment, for the world still knew it as something shapeless'. *CloHam, KocKei, KocPim, RacSin.*

Keyboard music If Telemann's keyboard works remain one of the more dimly lit corners of his output, this is perhaps due to the small dimensions and modest technical demands of much of the music. Yet his contributions to the repertory are nevertheless significant, varied and stylistically progressive. The eight suites transmitted in manuscript (TWV 32:11–18), some beginning with a French overture or prelude, are musically substantial works that most likely date from before 1720. One (32:14) was included by Johann Sebastian Bach* in the *Clavierbüchlein* for the ten-year-old Wilhelm Friedemann Bach*, and was consequently once attributed to the elder Bach (as was 32:18). These works contain a mixture of idiomatic keyboard textures and those recalling the overture-suite* for instrumental ensemble. Telemann's published keyboard works, by contrast, were aimed at a broad audience and are therefore more *galant* in style and thinner in texture. He appears to have been the first composer to publish trios with obbligato keyboard, with four works in the *Essercizii musici** (1726), and he published a dozen more in the *Six concerts et six suites** (1734). The *Essercizii* also include two solo keyboard suites, and two more (one in burlesque style) are found in *Der getreue Music-Meister**. Several other publications from the late 1720s and early 1730s are devoted to miniatures: two sets of fifty minuets (*Sept fois sept et un menuet*, 1728; *Zweytes sieben mal sieben und ein Menuet*, 1730), three sets of twelve fantasias* (*Fantaisies pour le clavessin*, 1732–33) in the French and Italian styles, and twenty brief (minute-long) fugues in four voices (*XX Kleine Fugen*, 1731; dedicated to Benedetto Marcello*) intended as preludes to chorales in unusual keys from the *Fast allgemeines Evangelisch-Musikalisches Liederbuch**. The *Fugirende und veraendernde Choraele* (1735) include preludes on twenty-four well known chorale melodies, each of which is first accompanied by two 'fugal' (imitative) voices and is then 'varied' by being placed against a single accompanimental voice, for a total of forty-eight preludes. All of these works may be performed on a single-manual keyboard, suggesting their suitability for both church and home use; in this sense they are keyboard analogues to Telemann's published church cantatas* and arias. Telemann's last two publications of keyboard music offer fresh takes on the suite. The six *Fugues légères et petit jeux* (1738 or 1739) follow a 'light' two-voice fugue with three or four lively movements in binary form (the 'little games' of the collection's title), whereas the lengthier *VI Ouverturen nebst zween Folgesätzen* (1745) introduce two sonata-style movements with a French overture. The music of both sets is by turns profound, witty and playful – and the same might be said of Telemann's keyboard music as a whole. *RuhFug, PayFra, PolLus, RodRet, SchKla, ZohMix.*

Die Kleine Cammer-Music This collection of six partitas (suites) for violin, flute or 'especially' oboe and continuo (also playable on keyboard) was published by Telemann in Frankfurt in September 1716 and dedicated to four oboists: François La Riche (1662–c. 1733), La Riche's former student Johann Christian Richter (1689–1744), Peter Glösch and Johann Michael Böhm* (probably a student of La Riche as well). La Riche and Richter were both members of the Dresden* electoral *Hofkapelle* (Telemann wrote his E-minor oboe concerto, TWV 51:e1, for the latter), Glösch worked in the Berlin *Hofkapelle* and Böhm was *Konzertmeister* at the Darmstadt* court. Telemann had heard La Riche, and perhaps Glösch, perform in Berlin between 1702 and 1706. In May 1716, Glösch participated in the Frankfurt performance of Telemann's serenata *Deutschland grünt und blüht im Friede*, TVWV 12:1c, for the birth of Archduke Leopold, and in this connection the composer referred to him as a 'renowned Berlin virtuoso on the oboe' (AB 1718); Glösch later subscribed to the *Nouveaux quatuors**. In his preface to *Die Kleine Cammer-Music*, Telemann claimed that he had 'endeavoured to present something for everyone's taste'. The first edition was printed in moveable type, but in 1728 Telemann issued an engraved second edition in Hamburg as *La petite musique de chambre; Die Kleine Cammer-Music*. Soon after the Frankfurt publication, Telemann arranged the partitas as overture-suites for two oboes, bassoon and strings (TWV 55:B2, G11, c3, g3, e6 and Es5), composing new French overtures to introduce the original movements. *HayKle, HobKle, SwaSol, ZohMix.*

XX Kleine Fugen *See* **Keyboard music**

Klopstock, Friedrich Gottlieb *See* ***Der Messias*, TVWV 6:4**

König, Johann Balthasar König (1691–1758) was a choirboy and later a bass singer and cellist during church services in Frankfurt before becoming music director at the city's Katharinenkirche in 1718. From 1727 until his death he served as city music director, succeeding Johann Christoph Bodinus*. He made about 650 copies of church cantatas by Telemann from 1716 through the mid-1740s, including scores for five annual cycles and parts for a further seven. König performed certain cantatas as late as 1750, sometimes recomposing recitatives for a different vocal part or expanding the original instrumentation. In a 1728 catalogue of his published works, Telemann listed König as his Frankfurt agent. *JunKan, KerKan, KerRez, PoeKir, SchKat.*

König, Johann Ulrich von König (1688–1744) was a founder, alongside Barthold Heinrich Brockes* and Michael Richey*, of Hamburg's 'Teutsch-übende Gesellschaft' before becoming court poet at Dresden*. He provided Telemann with librettos for the *Davidische Oratorien* (TVWV 6:1, 1718), the operas *Der geduldige Sokrates** (TVWV 21:9, 1721) and *Sancio oder Die siegende Großmuth* (TVWV 21:20, 1727) and the passion oratorio *Die gekreuzigte Liebe** (TVWV 5:4, 1731). In his foreword to the libretto of the *Davidische Oratorien* Telemann praised König as a 'splendid poet . . . who understands the characteristics of music in a quite exceptional way'.

Krause, Christian Gottfried A Berlin jurist, privy councillor, amateur musician and author, Krause (1719–70) ran a musical salon on Wednesdays in his home during the 1750s and 1760s that included musicians from the Berlin *Hofkapelle* (especially Johann Joachim Quantz*) and the city's leading literary figures. These performances included a number of Telemann's late oratorios, odes and cantatas. Along with Karl Wilhelm Ramler*, Krause edited three of Telemann's songs* (TVWV 25:110–12) in the first volume of the *Oden mit Melodien* (Berlin, 1753). This collection was in some respects a practical supplement to Krause's *Von der musikalischen Poesie* (1752), a theoretical tract on texts best suited to musical setting that appears to have been heavily influenced by Telemann's songs. In 1756 Krause worked with Ramler to select and arrange the texts for *Die Donnerode**, and in a 1757 Berlin performance of the work, he played the celebrated timpani part. Writing in 1760 to Ramler regarding the score of *Die Auferstehung und Himmelfahrt Jesu**, Krause gushed, 'I say to you, it is absolutely incomparable. Telemann has shown that, in his eightieth year, he can do anything.' Krause fashioned arrangements of Telemann's *Der Tod Jesu** and *Ino**, the latter significant for preserving presumably original readings in the musical text that are found in corrupted form in the cantata's other manuscript source (which is the basis for the work's only modern edition). *CzoGra, HirIno.*

Kuhnau, Johann Kuhnau (1660–1722) was organist at Leipzig's Thomaskirche from 1684, becoming cantor and university music director in 1701. Among his students were Johann Friedrich Fasch*, Christoph Graupner* and the Dresden* *Kapellmeister* Johann David Heinichen. Kuhnau must have seen Telemann's 1701 commission from mayor Franz Conrad Romanus* to provide music for the Thomaskirche and Nikolaikirche every two weeks as an assault on his authority, whereas Romanus probably considered the younger composer as a possible successor to the sickly Kuhnau. When, in 1704, the Neue Kirche organ was completed, the Leipzig town council named Telemann organist and transferred responsibility for directing the church's music from Kuhnau to Telemann; the older musician scornfully referred to Telemann as an 'Operiste'. Yet Telemann had nothing but praise for Kuhnau in AB 1718: 'I became acquainted with Herr Kuhnau and his music; and as life must be arranged by illustrious examples, the erudition this extraordinary man possessed in music, jurisprudence and many languages (even Hebrew) awakened in me the desire to attain some of these praiseworthy qualities in time.' In AB 1740 Telemann stated more simply that at Leipzig 'the excellent pen of Herr Johann Kuhnau served me as a model in fugue and counterpoint'. *GlöKuh.*

***Ein Lämmlein geht und trägt die Schuld*, TVWV 5:30** Telemann's 1745 St John Passion was published in late 1746 by Balthasar Schmid* in Nuremberg under the title *Music vom Leiden und Sterben des Welt Erlösers* (Music on the Suffering and Death of the World's Saviour). It is the only one of Telemann's liturgical Passions – or oratorio* of any kind, for that matter – to appear in print during his lifetime. Among those who appear to have subscribed to the publication was Carl Heinrich Graun*, which suggests that Telemann's Passion was well known in Berlin*. Joachim Johann Daniel Zimmermann* provided the composer with a rhetorically expressive libretto that immediately breaks with convention through an unusually long poetic introduction or *exordium*:

following the opening chorale is a dramatic soliloquy for Jesus in the form of an arioso, accompanied recitative and aria. Only after this does the narrative of the Passion and death of Jesus begin. Telemann's music for the Passion is not only dramatic, but occasionally explores new stylistic paths, as in the soprano aria 'Soll mir's zu bitter dünken' (No. 15), which represents a mid-century idiom often referred to as the *empfindsamer Stil* ('sentimental style') and associated particularly with Carl Philipp Emanuel Bach*. Bach, in fact, used Telemann's turba choruses, chorale melodies and biblical recitative in his own St John Passion pasticcios in 1772, 1776, 1780, 1784 and 1788. *Ein Lämmlein geht und trägt die Schuld* has been published in volume 29 (1996) of the Telemann selected critical edition*.

Lange, Carsten Following studies at the Martin-Luther-Universität Halle-Wittenberg, Lange joined the research staff of the Zentrum für Telemann-Pflege und -Forschung in Magdeburg in 1986, succeeding Wolf Hobohm* as the centre's director in 2003. He received his PhD from Martin-Luther-Universität with a dissertation on Telemann's *Brockes-Passion** in 2010. Also in that year he became General Editor, along with Wolfgang Hirschmann*, of the Telemann selective critical edition*, to which he contributed the volume containing the *Brockes-Passion**. Lange has also edited a number of volumes in the Magdeburger Telemann-Studien series, conference reports deriving from the Telemann-Festtage*, and the newsletter of the International Telemann Society*. His Telemann research has focused on the passions, chamber music and biographical issues. *LanAlt, LanBac, LanBro, LanDan, LanHer, LanNou, LanPas, LanSoc, LanTra.*

***Die Last-tragende Liebe oder Emma und Eginhard*, TVWV 21:25** This three-act *Singspiel* premiered at the Hamburg Opera on 22 November 1728. Its success is reflected in repeat performances in 1731 and 1732, and by Telemann's publication of five arias and a duet in *Der getreue Music-Meister**. Christoph Gottlieb Wend* fashioned his original libretto from the epic poem *Mandragende Maeght* (1637) by Jacob Cats and the first of the *Heldenbriefe* (1663) by Christian Hofmann von Hofmannswaldau. The plot is set in Aachen around 785, as emperor Charlemagne and his court celebrate the victorious denouement of the Saxon War. Charlemagne's daughter, Princess Emma, is torn between her love for Eginhard, Charlemagne's secretary, and her sense of duty. Eginhard reciprocates Emma's affection despite their class differences. But the Saxon prince Heswin has also fallen in love with Emma, though he realises that her sister, Hildegard, has feelings for him. When Emma and Eginhard's attempt to run off together is foiled, Charlemagne resolves to make an example of them by sentencing them to death. They are first imprisoned and then taken to the scaffold, but are saved at the last minute by a voice coming from the clouds that commands Charlemagne to have mercy. After Hildegard and Heswin prostrate themselves, Charlemagne pardons Emma and Eginhard, elevating the latter to an earldom. The two couples can now pursue their love. To a greater extent than in his other theatrical works, Telemann's music reflects the varying social positions of the characters, assigning an opera seria style to those who are high-born and a folklike or opera buffa style to those belonging to the servant class. But some characters, such as Emma and Eginhard, are treated almost as 'parti di mezzo carattere' (middle characters) who receive music in a *galant* 'middle' style – as befits their mixed

Die Last-tragende Liebe,

Oder

EMMA und EGINHARD,

in einem

Sing-Spiele

auf dem

Hamburgischen

Schau-Platze

ANNO 1728.

aufgeführet.

Gedruckt mit Stromerischen Schrifften.

6. Title page to the printed libretto of *Die Last-tragende Liebe oder Emma und Eginhard*, TVWV 21:25 (Hamburg, 1728; Staatsbibliothek zu Berlin – Preußischer Kulturbesitz, Music Department and Mendelssohn Archive, Mus. T 13-1/6). Image courtesy of Art Resources, NY. Reproduced by permission.

social status as a couple. One of the opera's musical high points is Hildegard's seria aria 'Meine Tränen werden Wellen' (No. 51), which mixes coloratura writing with a severe fugue featuring a descending chromatic subject. Instead of the usual French overture, the opera begins (like *Der neumodische Liebhaber Damon**) with a three-movement concerto* for violin and strings (TWV 51:a2). *Die Last-tragende Liebe oder Emma und Eginhard* has been published in volume 37 (2000) of the Telemann selective critical edition*. *HirPol, HobEmm.*

Late style Where to place Telemann's 'late' style is not a straightforward matter. There is the turning point of 1740, when, at nearly sixty, he ended his publishing* business by selling off the engraved plates to forty-four of his printed collections, moved away from composing in certain genres (instrumental ensemble music, opera and secular cantata), planned to write theoretical works (only some of which were realised), and took up the pastime of gardening* with evident zeal. This reorientation has sometimes been misunderstood as a semi-retirement or creative crisis. In fact, Telemann kept composing at a more than respectable pace and continued to explore new stylistic directions during the 1740s. For example, strong elements of musical *Empfindsamkeit* are evident in the 1745 St John Passion, *Ein Lämmlein geht und trägt die Schuld** (TVWV 5:30), and starting with the 1746 St Matthew Passion (TVWV 5:31) Telemann adapted several features of French recitative, including metrical shifts to improve declamation (as he noted in his correspondence with Carl Heinrich Graun*), active bass lines and more melodic vocal parts.

One could also point to 1750, at which time Telemann appears to have begun limiting his production of new church cantatas* (concentrating on works for feast days and ceasing composition of annual cycles), or to 1755, when he began producing a remarkable series of lyric oratorios, secular cantatas and odes for the concert hall (starting with *Der Tod Jesu**) to texts by young poets including Karl Wilhelm Ramler*, Friedrich Gottlieb Klopstock*, Friedrich Wilhelm Zachariae*, Daniel Schiebeler* and Christian Wilhelm Alers* (some of these poets also furnished the composer with librettos for sacred cantatas). Through all these professional watersheds, Telemann never stopped seeking new musical paths, and thus there are no definitive stylistic 'breaks' that may be considered a final compositional idiom. Still, one is reminded of the words of Charles Burney*, who in 1773 noted that 'this composer, like Raphael and some other great painters, had a first and second manner, which were extremely different from each other; in the first he was hard, stiff, dry, and inelegant; in the second, pleasing, graceful, and refined'. Burney may in fact have been referring to the concert works of 1755 and following years (he owned a copy of *Der Tod Jesu*). It is true that in his late oratorios, cantatas and odes Telemann blended a universality of expression with an increasingly individualistic musical language that is closely tailored to the text, a combination rarely found in his earlier works. *EicSpä, HirSpä, HobTom, LütDon, ReiBeo, ReiSpä, ReiRez.*

Le Clerc, Charles-Nicolas Le Clerc (1697–1774) owned a music publishing business in Paris from 1736 until his death. He received a privilege on 6 April 1736 to print 'five opuses of Telemann' and received another on 12 January 1751 (retroactive to 18 November 1750) to print instrumental works by Telemann and others. The five opuses appear to have been reprints of the *Quadri** (1736), *Sonates sans basse* (1736–37), *III Trietti methodichi e III scherzi* (1736–37), *Sei suonatine per violino e cembalo* (1737) and *Sonates corellisantes* (1737), all appearing shortly before Telemann's trip to Paris* in 1737–38. During the 1740s Le Clerc published a reprint of the *Six Quatuors ou Trios* and possibly also the *Sonate metodiche* and *Fantaisies pour le clavessin*. Between 1752 and 1760 a fourth 'book' of Telemann's quartets (the third being the *Nouveaux quatuors**, published in conjunction with the composer in 1738) appeared under Le Clerc's imprint as the *Quatrième livre de quatuors*. This is an arrangement, probably not by

Telemann, for flute, violin, viola and continuo of much older works for four-part strings. *RuhPar, ZohMix.*

Letters Judging from his ninety surviving letters, in addition to thirty-nine addressed to him, Telemann must have been a prolific correspondent throughout his life. Nearly three dozen of the composer's letters concern his official duties in Leipzig, Frankfurt, Hamburg, Bayreuth and Eisenach, and another twenty-one are addressed to his Frankfurt friend Johann Friedrich Armand von Uffenbach*. With few exceptions, Telemann's surviving correspondence with musicians consists of letters addressed to him. Among these musicians are Johann Friedrich Agricola*, Carl Philipp Emanuel Bach*, Franz Benda, Christoph Förster*, Carl Heinrich Graun*, George Frideric Handel*, Pantaleon Hebenstreit*, Johann Mattheson*, Lorenz Christoph Mizler*, Johann Georg Pisendel*, Johann Joachim Quantz*, Johann Adolph Scheibe* and Georg Andreas Sorge*. Conspicuous by his absence from this list is Johann Sebastian Bach*, though Telemann surely exchanged letters with him. Telemann must also have corresponded with Friedrich Wilhelm Marpurg*, Johan Helmich Roman* and Giuseppe Tartini*, since he acted as a publishing agent for all three. Particularly significant among the extant letters are three between Graun and Telemann concerning the merits of French recitative. The tone of Telemann's correspondence ranges from officious to intimate, affording us a clear glimpse of the composer's vivacious, witty personality, and in particular of his taste for irony and sarcasm. Telemann's complete letters were edited, with commentary, by Hans Grosse and Hans Rudolf Jung in 1972. The years since have seen the discovery of five additional letters addressed by Telemann to Hamburg's Collegium Scholarchale regarding his planned acceptance of the Thomaskantorat in Leipzig (1722), to Albrecht von Haller (1708–77) in Göttingen (1744), to Elias Caspar Reichard (1714–91) in Magdeburg (1755), to an anonymous correspondent (1757) and to Gottlob Immanuel Breitkopf* in Leipzig (1759). *BeiBri, FleBre, HobBri, HobRei, KreMem, NeuBot, RacSin, TelBri.*

Lied-Jahrgang This fragmentarily preserved annual cycle of sacred odes (also known as the *Lieder-Andachten-Jahrgang*) is based upon poetry by Erdmann Neumeister* that followed his Hamburg sermons during the 1742–43 church year. Neumeister's multi-stanza odes (which he called *Jesus-Lieder*) are to be sung to chorale melodies indicated by him. The sermons with odes were published in 1743, and Telemann's musical settings were first performed in Hamburg after sermons during the 1743–44 church year (later performances are documented for 1755–56 and 1760–61). At least thirty-nine of Neumeister's seventy-three odes were set by the composer, but just five settings are known to survive (three complete and two fragmentary). Instead of writing strophic forms, Telemann combines chorales in cantional style (sung by the congregation) with introductory sinfonias, contrapuntal chorale settings, solo arias and duets to create an updated, 'theatrical' version of a chorale-based genre with seventeenth-century roots. *HobNeu, NeuLie, NeuQue, PfaLie, PoeKir.*

Lingen-Jahrgang Telemann composed two annual cycles of church cantatas to librettos by the Eisenach court secretary Hermann Ulrich von Lingen (1695–1743). The first was performed simultaneously in Eisenach and Hamburg

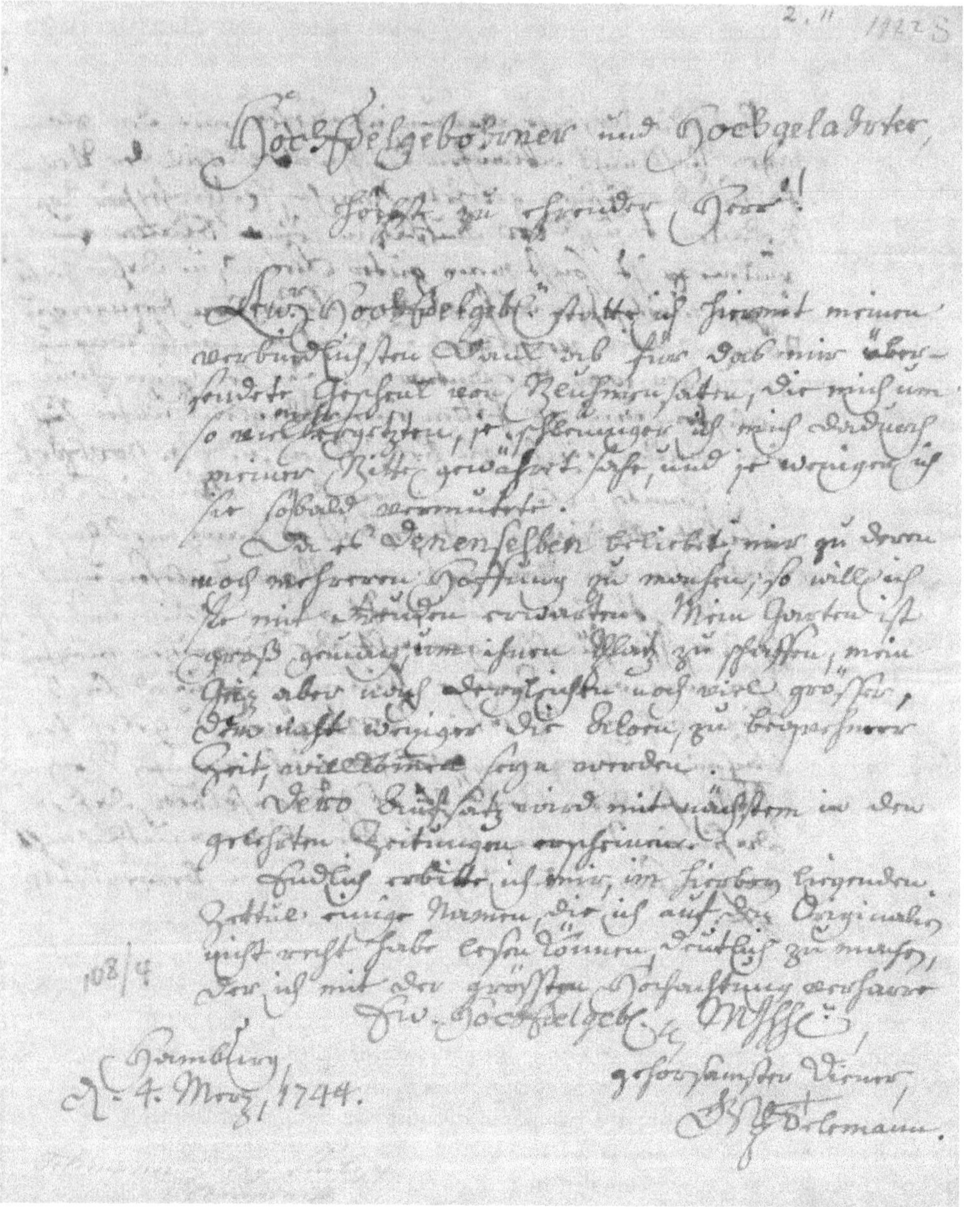
HochEdelgebohrner und Hochgelahrter,
Höchst zu ehrender Herr!

Ew. HochEdelgeb. statte ich hiermit meinen verbundlichsten Dank ab für das mir übersendete Geschenk von [illegible], die mich um so viel mehr ergetzen, je schleuniger ich mich dadurch meiner Bitte gewähret sehe, und je weniger ich sie sobald vermuthete.

Da es Denenselben beliebt, mir zu denen noch mehreren Hoffnung zu machen, so will ich sie mit Freuden erwarten. Mein Garten ist groß genug, um ihnen Platz zu schaffen; mein Geiz aber nach dergleichen noch viel größer, denn desto weniger [illegible], zu bequemer Zeit, [illegible] seyn werden.

Dero Aufsatz wird mit nächstem in den gelehrten Göttingen erscheinen.

Endlich erbitte ich mir, im hiebey liegenden Zettul einige Namen, die ich auf den Originalen nicht recht habe lesen können, deutlich zu machen, der ich mit der grössten Hochachtung verharre

Ew. HochEdelgeb. [illegible]
gehorsamster Diener,
G. P. Telemann.

Hamburg
d. 4. Merz, 1744.

7. Telemann's letter of 4 March 1744 to Albrecht von Haller (1708–77) in Göttingen (Bayerische Staatsbibliothek, Autogr. Cim. Telemann, Georg Philipp), fol. 1, first of two pages. Reproduced by permission.

(before the sermon) in 1722–23; a Frankfurt performance followed in 1723–24. The second cycle was heard in both Eisenach and Hamburg (before the sermon) in 1728–29. Upon publishing his librettos (*Poetische Aufmunterungen zur Andacht*; Eisenach, 1728), von Lingen noted that he had devised them according to Telemann's specifications. Only about half of Telemann's cantatas survive, and most of these open with an instrumental sonata that leads to an accompanied recitative, two da capo arias (in which, unusually, a second voice sings the B section) surrounding a chorale setting, and a concluding dictum (biblical verse) set for the full ensemble. *DraLin, FieWie, ReiJah, ReiLin.*

Magnificats Telemann composed the Magnificat in C major, TVWV 9:17, for the consecration of the rebuilt organ in Leipzig's Neukirche on 7 September 1704, during his brief tenure as the church's organist and music director. Municipal records relating to the occasion mention the performance of 'well composed pieces' including 'a beautiful Magnificat'. That TVWV 9:17 was the work in question seems confirmed by its preservation in a set of parts copied around 1705 by Telemann's successor at the Neukirche, Melchior Hoffmann. It is one of many Latin Magnificat settings that were performed in Leipzig on feast days, later examples including those by Johann Sebastian Bach* (BWV 243, 1723) and Carl Philipp Emanuel Bach* (Wq 215/H 772, 1755). Telemann's Magnificat in C major marks a high point in his early development as a composer of sacred vocal music, and is conceived in twelve compact movements, including an opening sinfonia. The six movements for one or two vocal soloists encompass a broad range of styles, affects and scorings (the most striking being 'Fecit potentiam', featuring two basses singing in canon to the accompaniment of fanfaring trumpets and drums), while the initial and concluding choral movements ('Magnificat anima mea' and 'Sicut erat in principio') alternate homophony with fugal writing.

The Magnificat in G major, TVWV 9:18, is a setting of Martin Luther's German translation of the Latin text, *Meine Seele erhebt den Herrn.* This work is more intimate and modestly scored than the Magnificat in C major (which probably predates it by some years), with pairs of recorders and oboes in place of trumpets and timpani; two horn parts were later added by Johann Gottlob Harrer (1703–55), Johann Sebastian Bach's successor in Leipzig. Another set of manuscript parts (lacking horns) may have been prepared for an earlier performance in Leipzig. The G major Magnificat's eight movements alternate solo and tutti scorings, the solos moving progressively from soprano down to bass (with contrasting accompaniments: two recorders, two oboes, violins in unison and continuo) and the motet-like tuttis featuring a variety of different choral textures. The last movement opens with a pastoral, 6/8 setting of the *Tonus peregrinus*, the Gregorian chant reciting tone associated in the Lutheran tradition with the Magnificat. *GlöNeu, GlöLei, HarMag.*

Marcello, Benedetto Telemann never met the dilettante composer Marcello (1686–1739), but sent him a 'fan' letter* praising the psalm settings of his eight-volume *Estro poetico-armonico* (Venice, 1724–26). Dated 6 October 1726, the letter was printed later that year by Marcello in the final volume of his series. In 1731 Telemann dedicated a collection of keyboard music*, the *XX Kleine Fugen*, to Marcello. *HobMar.*

Marpurg, Friedrich Wilhelm A Berlin composer and writer on music, Marpurg (1718–95) dedicated the first volume of his *Abhandlung von der Fuge* (1753–54) to Telemann (who acted as a publishing agent for the book), noting that 'the masterpieces from your pen have long since contradicted the erroneous notion that the so-called *galant* style cannot be combined with elements borrowed from counterpoint. The perfect model in this respect, fashioned by you to such universal approval, is known not only in Germany; your reputation has rendered admirable that of the Germans in France, in incomparable France, as well.' Marpurg goes on to hold up as exemplary models of fugal writing Telemann's flute duets* (from the *Sonates sans basse* and *XIIX Canons mélodieux*) and trios (from the *Sonates corellisantes*). Marpurg published Telemann's sonnet on the death of Johann Sebastian Bach* in a 1755 issue of his *Historisch-kritische Beyträge zur Aufnahme der Musik*. In his *Kritische Briefe über die Tonkunst* (1760), Marpurg praised fugal movements from Telemann cantatas written several decades earlier (TVWV 1:1106, 1238, 1451 and 1506), and his 1786 volume of musical anecdotes includes several about Telemann. *FleMar, ZohIma.*

Masses Telemann's masses constitute a relatively unfamiliar area of his output. In AB 1718 he recalled having written masses at Eisenach (1708–12), and it is possible that many of the extant works date from this period. Eleven of the masses (TVWV 9:1–11) are based upon chorale melodies and consist of Kyrie–Gloria pairs that are sometimes referred to as 'Lutheran masses' (since only these two parts of the mass ordinary were sung in Latin during Lutheran services). Their idiom is based on the *stile antico*, and the chorale melody provides a thematic basis for points of imitation instead of being quoted as a cantus firmus. Among the four Latin *missae breves* (9:12–15), that in B minor for alto, two violins and continuo (9:14) is exceptional for being organised into 'numbers', with both the Kyrie and Gloria divided into discrete movements. This work, together with a self-standing Sanctus setting (TVWV 9:*deest*), was apparently composed for the Leipzig Neukirche c. 1705. *CloMis.*

Mattheson, Johann If Telemann can be said to have had a 'frenemy', then it was surely the writer and composer Mattheson (1681–1764), a native of Hamburg who was active in the Opera as a singer and composer early in his career, served as Secretary to Sir John Wich, the English ambassador to Hamburg, from 1706, and was vicar then music director of Hamburg's cathedral (1715–28). Mattheson praised Telemann's trios in *Das neu-eröffnete Orchestre* (1713), and several years later the two established personal contact. In 1717 Telemann was one of the dedicatees of Mattheson's *Das beschützte Orchestre*, and months later he wrote to the author to thank him for this honour and compliment him on the book; Mattheson later published Telemann's letter, together with his response, both in the original French and in German translation. The following year Telemann wrote a poem of praise for Mattheson, which the latter soon published and reprinted, along with another Telemann poem, in his *Grosse General-Baß-Schule. Oder: Der exemplarischen Organisten-Probe* (1731). This book also included Telemann's first autobiography* (AB 1718), written for Mattheson's projected volume of musicians' lives. By the time this volume was published as the *Grundlage einer Ehren-Pforte* (1740), Telemann had supplied Mattheson with an updated autobiography (AB 1740).

Mattheson invited Telemann and Conrad Friedrich Hurlebusch* to his home several times in 1725 before the three made an 'honourable withdrawal' from each others' company, as Mattheson put it. During this period Mattheson criticised several works by Telemann, who nevertheless agreed to serve as a publishing agent for the second volume of Mattheson's journal *Critica musica* (1725). In asking Johann Friedrich Armand von Uffenbach* whether he would like to subscribe to the journal in 1724, Telemann playfully warned that a subscription would not 'provide assurance of being spared from [Mattheson's] prickly pen, from which neither friend nor foe has as a rule been spared until now'. Telemann may have been thinking of Mattheson's criticism of the word painting in his 1720 cantata *Das Wasser im Frühling* (TVWV 20:1, to a text by Barthold Heinrich Brockes*) and of his libretto for the opera *Sieg der Schönheit* (TVWV 21:10) in the first volume of the *Critica musica* (1722). Mattheson also had critical words for Telemann's opera *Die verkehrte Welt* (TVWV 21:23) in *Der Musicalische Patriot* (1728), but he praised the *Auszug derjenigen musicalischen und auf die gewöhnlichen Evangelien gerichteten Arien** and Telemann's French-style trios, noting in *Der volkommene Capellmeister* (1739) that 'whether Telemann used his Parisian journey to learn or to teach is in doubt. I believe it was more for the latter than the former purpose.' In 1729 the two collaborated on the opera *Aesopus bei Hofe* (TVWV 21:26), Mattheson adapting a libretto by Pietro Pariati and Telemann supplying the music. Evidence that the relationship between Mattheson and Telemann soured in later years comes from an epigram by the latter entitled 'To Legation Counsellor M[attheson]'. Apparently written after 1744 and first published by Friedrich Wilhelm Marpurg* in 1786, the poem reads: 'Once he called the genuine inferior, now he calls the inferior genuine in order to correct this mistake. But one considers that he was lying then and is lying now, and this increases the blame.' *CloHam, MarMat, SeiMat, TelBri, VosMiz, ZohJob.*

***Der May*, TVWV 20:40** Telemann's setting of Karl Wilhelm Ramler's* 1758 'musical idyll' celebrating the return of May and the feelings it evokes dates from c. 1760, his eightieth year. Although often classified as a cantata, the work does not conform to the genre's norms: in place of the usual succession of arias and recitatives is an alternating series of through-composed duets and strophic songs for two singers – representing, in the Arcadian tradition, the mythological-pastoral characters of Daphnis (bass) and Phyllis (soprano) – accompanied by a complement of winds that evokes the piping of shepherds (pairs of flutes, soprano recorders, oboes and bassoons along with chalumeau, trumpet and horn). The literary genre of the idyll had ancient models and became fashionable during the middle of the eighteenth century, when it seems to have offered readers a sort of pastoral escapism. Writing in 1777, the Berlin *Kapellmeister* Johann Friedrich Reichardt referred to Ramler's text as a 'shepherd's poem' (Schäfergedicht). Telemann's bucolic musical language emphasises tuneful and dance-based melodies, diatonic harmony, a richly *galant* rhythmic language and straightforward forms. Elements of his Polish style* animate the strophic drinking and dance song ('Seht, die Traube bricht hervor'; 'Seht der Wiese junges Grün'). *FleMay.*

Melante Telemann adopted his anagrammatic pseudonym by c. 1712, and used it occasionally until at least the 1730s. A number of scribal copies of Telemann's music, mostly dating from the 1710s, are attributed to 'Melante', suggesting that the pseudonym was most widely used during the composer's Eisenach and Frankfurt years (1708–21). In donning this transparent mask, Telemann was participating in a fashion, apparently derived from seventeenth-century French and Roman (Arcadian) literary traditions, of concealing the identities of real people behind pastoral pseudonyms. Among Telemann's German contemporaries, the poet August Bohse (1661–1740) was 'Talander', the writer and astronomer Johann Leonard Rost (1688–1727) styled himself 'Meletaon', the poet Christian Friedrich Hunold (1681–1721) published under the name 'Menantes', the opera librettist Georg Christian Lehms (1684–1717) went by 'Pallidor', the poet and amateur musician Johann Sigismund Scholze (1705–50) was known as 'Sperontes' and Telemann's Hamburg colleague Christoph Gottlieb Wend* (d. 1745) used the pseudonym 'Selimantes'. Already by the second half of the eighteenth century, some writers on music were unaware that Telemann and 'Melante' were one and the same. *ZohMix.*

Menke, Werner Menke (1907–93) completed his landmark doctoral dissertation on the dissemination and chronology of Telemann's vocal works under Max Seiffert* at the Staatliches Institut für deutsche Musikforschung in Berlin in 1940, publishing it two years later as *Das Vokalwerk Georg Philipp Telemanns: Überlieferung und Zeitfolge*. Building on early twentieth-century studies, he was able to assign many of the church cantatas to annual cycles (*Jahrgänge*). Menke was active as a solo trumpeter, singer in oratorios and pedagogue who founded and directed several music schools. He also wrote a well known book on the history of the trumpet in the time of Johann Sebastian Bach* and George Frideric Handel*. In the 1980s Menke published a two-volume thematic catalogue* of Telemann's vocal music, an abridged version of a thirty-two-volume manuscript catalogue he prepared in the 1930s in conjunction with his dissertation research, and which is currently in the Universitätsbibliothek Johann Christian Senckenberg Frankfurt am Main as part of his musical estate. He also published a pictorial biography of Telemann in 1987. *MenBil, MenFac, MenRic, MenVok, TVWV.*

***Der Messias*, TVWV 6:4** Although its title may bring to mind *Messiah* by George Frideric Handel*, Telemann's *Messias* is not an oratorio. Rather, it is a setting of two excerpts from the first and tenth parts (*Gesänge*) of the twenty-part epic poem *Messias* (1748–73) by Friedrich Wilhelm Klopstock (1724–1803). Telemann's two settings were first performed at a public concert on 29 March 1759 in Hamburg's Drillhaus, an exercise facility for the city's civic guard that doubled as a concert hall. The fact that they were separated on the programme by a performance of *Die Donner-Ode** suggests that the composer regarded them as independent works. A private performance of *Der Messias* in the Berlin home of Christian Gottfried Krause* took place the following 9 May. The first of the two Ramler texts, *Sing, unsterbliche Seele,* is in an epic poetic voice in which there is only one 'speaker' at a time, whereas the second, the *Wechselgesang der Mirjam und Debora,* is a dialogue in which these two women from the Hebrew Bible witness and lament the crucifixion of Jesus (though Telemann often ignores the text's dialogic structure and has Miriam and Deborah sing together). Telemann also set a third part of Klopstock's poem, the *Triumphgesang bey der*

Himmelfahrt, between 1764 and 1766, but this has not survived. *Der Messias* has been published in volume 41 (2010) of the Telemann selective critical edition*. *FleMes, GodMes, LütMon, ReiKlo, ReiMes, ReiOde, WacMes.*

Methodical sonatas This collective title encompasses three published sets of sonatas illustrating the art of free ornamentation: the *Sonate metodiche* (1728), containing six solos for flute or violin and continuo; the *III Trietti methodichi e III scherzi* (1731) for two flutes or violins and continuo; and a sequel collection of solos, the *Continuation des sonates méthodiques* (1732). Telemann advertised the first collection as being 'very useful' to those who 'wish to cultivate singing ornaments'. To this end, the opening slow movements of the solos and the middle slow movements of the first three trios all present the flute/violin parts in plain and ornamented versions, the ornaments being in a predominantly Italianate idiom. The idea may derive from the second, Amsterdam edition of the Op. 5 violin sonatas of Arcangelo Corelli*, in which slow movements in the first six sonatas are given in plain and embellished versions. Regardless of whether Telemann intended these examples as encyclopaedic illustrations of what is possible, or as models of what is desirable in performance, the ornaments are melodically and rhythmically inventive without obscuring the original melody – something that few similar examples of ornamentation from the eighteenth century manage to achieve to such good effect. Particularly valuable are the ornamented trio movements, which have few counterparts elsewhere in the eighteenth-century literature; in fact, Johann Joachim Quantz* is the only writer of the time to discuss the ornamentation of trio movements. But the methodical sonatas are more than their ornamented movements. The four-movement *Sonate methodiche* follow their serious opening slow movements with an attractive mixture of lively fast movements (often in da capo form) and *galant* airs. The *Continuation des sonates méthodiques* add a fifth movement and offer more stylistic variety among the opening slow movements. As their title indicates, the *III Trietti methodichi e III scherzi* include three 'small' (three-movement) trios in the Italian style and three in the Polish style* ('scherzo' referencing the jocularity Telemann associated with Polish music). *SwaSol, ZohMix.*

***Miriways*, TVWV 21:24** This 'Sing-Spiel', an opera seria in three acts to a libretto by Johann Samuel Müller (1701–73), who would become rector of Hamburg's Johanneum school, premiered at the Hamburg Opera on 26 May 1728. The opera's plot, which has few of the comic scenes that were favoured in Hamburg, is based on events in Persia (present-day Iran), as widely reported in Germany in 1722. These events were set in motion when the Persian governor of Kandahar (now in present-day Afghanistan) was murdered in 1709 by an Afghan uprising led by the tribal chief Mirwais Khan Hotek (1673–1715). Although Mirwais died in 1715, the power struggle he initiated led in 1722 to the Afghan invasion of Isfahan, then the Persian capital city. This resulted in the Persian Shah Husain being deposed and Mirwais' son Mahmud being installed as ruler. However, most German accounts in 1722 held that it was Mirwais, not Mahmud, who was the new Persian ruler. Müller's libretto is indebted to a 1723 German biography of Mirwais (entitled *The Persian Cromwell*) that celebrates him as a benevolent statesman whose atrocities resulted from the actions of others. The opera's plot

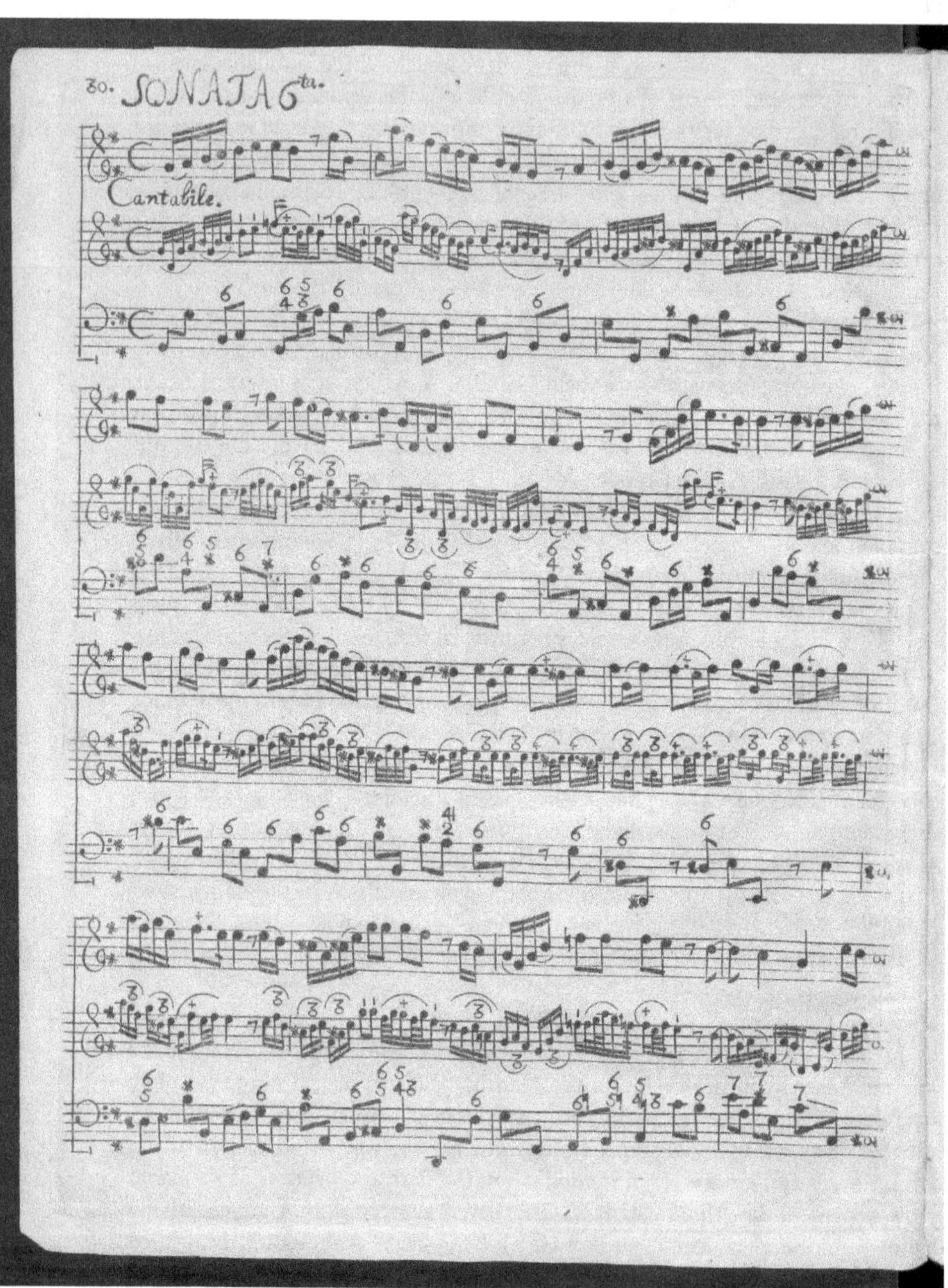

8. First movement of Sonata 6, TWV 41:G4, from the *Sonate metodiche* (Hamburg 1728; Staatsbibliothek zu Berlin – Preußischer Kulturbesitz, Music Department and Mendelssohn Archive, Am.B 350). Image courtesy of Art Resources, NY. Reproduced by permission.

begins after the conquering of Isfahan by Mirwais, who promises the Persian crown to the Shah's youngest son Sophi (sung by the soprano Maria Domenica Polon*) if he will marry the missing daughter of Mirwais. But Sophi, in love with Bemira, refuses this arrangement until it emerges, through various plot twists, that Bemira is in fact the daughter of Mirwais. The two lovers can now assume power without sacrificing their relationship. If Telemann's music is less colourfully scored than in some of his other Hamburg operas, its 'middle' style, featuring fresh, dance-based rhythms and tuneful melodies, helps humanise the high-born characters. Only a few numbers deploy local colour in the form of musically 'exotic' elements. The opera has been published in volume 38 (1999) of the Telemann selective critical edition*. *CloTon, ReiMir.*

Mixed taste Starting in the late seventeenth century, many German composers and writers on music described their national style as a superior mixture of idioms from other nations. In his 1728 thoroughbass treatise, Johann David Heinichen considered that 'a fortunate mixture [*glückliche Melange*] of the Italian and French tastes would most astonish the ear, and must win out over all other tastes of the world'. Johann Adolph Scheibe* advised in an unpublished treatise of c. 1728–36 that 'it is best if diligent German part writing, Italian *galanterie*, and French passion are combined' in trios and quartets. And Johann Joachim Quantz* noted in his 1752 *Versuch* that 'if one has the necessary discernment to choose the best from the styles of different countries, a mixed taste [*vermischter Geschmack*] results that, without overstepping the bounds of modesty, could well be called the German taste'; this taste 'displeases in neither Italy nor France, nor in other lands'. He later noted in his autobiography that the violinist Johann Georg Pisendel* had introduced the 'mixed taste' to the Dresden *Hofkapelle*. But no composer was as lavishly praised for his facility in blending national idioms as Telemann, who, according to the Leipzig literature professor Johann Christoph Gottsched, followed 'sometimes the Italian, sometimes the French, and often also a mixed manner [*einer vermischten Art*]'. For Telemann, the mixing of styles was not just a matter of alternating the French, Italian and Polish* idiolects within a work or movement, but also entailed investing styles and genres with new meaning through their amalgamation, as with his overture-suites* featuring a concerto-like soloist, solo concertos with a French or Polish sensibility, cantatas combining modern and historical idioms in the service of theological meaning, or German vocal declamation enhanced by applying the principles of French recitative. *ZohMix.*

Mizler, Lorenz Christoph A student of Johann Sebastian Bach*, Mizler (1711–78) founded the Correspondierende Societät der musikalischen Wissenschaften (Corresponding Society of Musical Science) in 1738. Telemann was elected a member the following year, and his theoretical contributions to the society included the *Beschreibung einer Augenorgel** (originally published in 1739 and reprinted by Mizler in a 1742 issue of his *Musikalische Bibliothek*) and the *Neues musikalisches System** (*Musikalische Bibliothek*, 1752). Mizler's plan to publish an annual cycle of church cantatas with librettos by himself and musical settings by society members was never realised, but Telemann contributed to the project with *Weint, weint, betrübte Augen*, TVWV 1:1542 (1754). According to Johann Adolph Scheibe*, Telemann was displeased with the songs of Mizler's *Sammlung auserlesener moralischer Oden* (Leipzig, 1740), and he objected in the preface of his second collection of songs*, *Vier und zwanzig, theils ernsthafte, theils scherzende, Oden*, to Mizler's rules of song composition. However, to judge from the five letters from Mizler to Telemann (four from February 1743 to March 1744, and a fifth from October 1753), this disagreement did not negatively impact their relationship. The letters mostly concern society business, but Mizler also responds at length to Telemann's critical remarks on one of his sonatinas. *JunMiz, ReiZus, TelBri, VosMiz.*

Moldenit, Joachim Erasmus von A colourful figure, the dilettante Moldenit (whose dates are unknown) attended Gymnasium in Hamburg and studied at the university in Kiel. He was resident in Hamburg by 1733, and remained there at least until 1756. In 1730 he was the dedicatee of Telemann's *Quadri**. In the dedication, which is found only in the copy of the collection belonging to the Sing-Akademie zu Berlin*, the composer praises Moldenit's flute playing (he had studied with Michel Blavet*, Pierre Gabriel Buffardin and Johann Joachim Quantz*) and his 'profound acuity in the beautiful science of harmony'. Moldenit did indeed compose: among his works is a self-published set of flute sonatas, the *Sei sonate da flauto traverso e basso continuo* (Hamburg, 1753). Yet his attainments as a flautist were called into question by Quantz in 1758, during a dispute between the two over the latter's *Versuch einer Anweisung die Flöte traversiere zu spielen*. Thus it would appear that Telemann was being exceedingly generous with his praise for Moldenit's playing. The two were apparently still in contact with each other during the 1750s, as is clear from letters* between Telemann and his Berlin colleagues Johann Friedrich Agricola*, Carl Heinrich Graun* and Christoph Nichelmann. Moldenit subscribed to both the *Musique de table** (1733) and *Nouveaux quatuors en six suites** (1738). *ReiMol, ReiQua, ZohMix.*

Moralische Cantaten Telemann published two sets of six 'moral' cantatas (Hamburg, 1735 and 1736), the first for voice and continuo (TVWV 20:23–28; to five librettos by Daniel Stoppe* and one unidentified poet), and the second for voice, flute or violin and continuo (20:29-35; to librettos by Joachim Johann Daniel Zimmermann*). Publication of both sets was planned as early as 1733, and the works' configuration as solo cantatas with two da capo arias surrounding a recitative makes them secular analogues to the cantatas of the *Harmonischer Gottes-Dienst** and *Fortsetzung des Harmonischen Gottesdienstes**. Telemann's vocal writing in these works is reminiscent of his songs, with memorable melodies and a narrow vocal range designed to render the cantatas singable by most voice types. The librettos align themselves with the didactic message promoted by many English and German moral periodicals of the time. Thus one should practice moderation in one's pleasures (*Die Zeit*, TVWV 20:23; *Das mäßige Glück*, 20:31), seek happiness and fortune in one's faith (*Hoffnung*, 20:24), be satisfied with one's lot in life (*Die Zufriedenheit*, 20:29) and reflect on what makes a true friend (*Die Freundschaft*, 20:34). Telemann adapted Stoppe's texts by abbreviating and reorganising them. Both collections of moral cantatas have been published in volume 44 (2011) of the Telemann selected critical edition*. *FleMor, LebDom, ZohMor.*

Motets Most of Telemann's motets were probably written during the first decade of the eighteenth century, and for a variety of pedagogical, liturgical and funereal purposes. Nine works have long been known (TVWV 3:92, 7:6 and 8:3, 4, 7–9, 11 and 13), and an additional seven (TVWV 8:17–23) were more recently identified in a late eighteenth-century manuscript. *Ein feste Burg ist unser Gott*, TVWV 8:7, was most likely written in Hamburg for the bicentenary of the Augsburg Confession in 1730, and both TVWV 8:11 and 13 may date from later in Telemann's Hamburg period, at least to judge from their more mature style. Five more 'motets' turn out to be movements taken from church cantatas (TVWV 8:2, 6, 10, 14 and 15), and this may also be true of some previously mentioned works. Several other works consisting only of vocal solos or duets (TVWV 8:1, 5, 12 and 16) are also unlikely to have been originally conceived as motets, which were understood during the eighteenth century as pieces for four or more voices, with or without instruments. All of these works stand apart from Telemann's *Deus judicium tuum regi da*, TVWV 7:7*, written for Paris* in the French grand motet tradition. *ReiAma, ReiMot.*

Musicalisches Lob Gottes in der Gemeine des Herrn For his fourth published annual cycle of church cantatas, Telemann commissioned librettos from Erdmann Neumeister*. It had been more than two decades since they last collaborated on such a cycle, and the composer now requested that each of the seventy-two cantatas follow the same seven-movement sequence of dictum (biblical verse)–chorale–recitative–aria–chorale–aria–dictum (repeat of the opening movement). The *Musicalisches Lob Gottes* did not appear under the composer's own imprint, as did the earlier *Harmonischer Gottes-Dienst, oder geistlichen Cantaten**, *Auszug derjenigen musicalischen und auf die gewöhnlichen Evangelien gerichteten Arien** and *Fortsetzung des Harmonischen Gottes-Dienstes**, but was engraved, printed, marketed and distributed by the organist and publisher Balthasar Schmid* in Nuremberg. It was the first of Telemann's published cycles to include dicta and chorales in addition to arias and recitatives – the type of project that he expressed a desire for already in the preface to the *Auszug*. A sample cantata was made available to prospective subscribers in October 1742, and the first half of the cycle was expected to be complete by St Michael's Day (29 September) 1743. But the publication schedule appears to have suffered some delays: Telemann's preface to the (nearly) completed cycle is dated 16 August 1744, and the final instalment of three cantatas with the cycle's title page and preface was not supplied to subscribers until 1 October. An engraved portrait* of Telemann, showing him holding the cantata for the first Sunday in Advent, was made available sometime later, and connected to the cycle as well is a printed biography* of the composer in German and French. When Telemann first performed the cycle in Hamburg is unknown, though this is most likely to have occurred in 1741–42 or 1742–43 (he repeated the cycle in 1757–58). Unlike his earlier published cycles, the *Musicalisches Lob Gottes* begins with the start of the liturgical calendar on the first Sunday of Advent (instead of New Year's Day), and like the *Harmonischer Gottes-Dienst*, it was published in score.

The musical forces called for by the cantatas, while fuller than in the first three published cycles, remain relatively modest: three voices (one each in high and middle ranges, plus optional bass that mostly doubles the continuo line) accompanied by two violins and continuo; cantatas for several major feast days add parts for three trumpets and timpani. No doubt as a concession to amateur performers, the upper voice parts are consistently doubled by instruments. In many dictum movements, which are often set as motets or fugues and are always scored for the full ensemble, indications of solo ('Einer') and tutti ('Alle') suggest how one might perform the music with extra (ripieno) singers and instrumentalists, as Telemann and others in fact did. (We are relatively well informed about Telemann's intentions in this respect: in addition to fifty-eight composing scores for the cycle, there are twenty-six sets of performance parts made by Hamburg copyists under the composer's supervision; all were inherited by his grandson, Georg Michael Telemann*.) Following Telemann's death, Carl Philipp Emanuel Bach* apparently performed the cycle in Hamburg, and Georg Michael Telemann continued to perform some of the cantatas in Riga as late as the 1820s. *HobNeu, PoeKir, TayCan.*

Musique de table This publication (Hamburg, 1733) is Telemann's magnum opus in the instrumental realm. Its title references a long tradition of banquet music (*Tafelmusik**), though no previous collection of music designed to be heard during meals comes close to it in terms of ambition and scope. Each of the three sets of music, called 'Production', contains an overture-suite*, concerto* with multiple soloists, quartet, trio, solo and one-movement 'Conclusion' (scored identically to the overture-suite). Although there is no evidence that the collection was actually used to accompany banquets, its three-part organisation may be seen as analogous to a festive three-course meal (which could last as long as several hours), with each set of six pieces representing the group of dishes served together during a course; alternatively, each 'Production' could provide music for a single, shorter meal, the six pieces accompanying the same number of courses. The music represents Telemann's mature instrumental style at its colourful and imaginative best. Some of the scorings are unique within Telemann's output (for example, oboe, trumpet and two violins as soloists in the second overture-suite, three solo violins in the second concerto, and recorder with two flutes in the second quartet), and the German mixed taste* is fully integrated with the *galant* style. In the printed parts, Telemann listed the names of 185 subscribers (ordering 206 copies), among whom were Michel Blavet*, Johann Michael Böhm*, four of the Burme(i)ster* brothers, George Frideric Handel*, Pantaleon Hebenstreit*, Johann Reinhold Hollander*, Johann Balthasar König*, Joachim Erasmus von Moldenit*, Johann Georg Pisendel*, Johann Joachim Quantz*, Johann Gottfried Riemschneider*, Johann Friedrich Armand von Uffenbach* and Christiane Mariane von Ziegler*. The *Musique de table* has been published in volumes 61–62 (1927) of the Denkmäler deutscher Tonkunst series, and in volumes 12–14 (1959–63; 2/2017) of the Telemann selective critical edition*. *FavNet, ZohMix, ZohTaf.*

Neues musikalisches System Telemann's 'New Musical System' of tuning intervals constitutes his most original contribution to music theory*, though it was intended in the first place for practical application. He sent it to Lorenz Christoph Mizler* in 1742 or 1743 as a contribution to the Correspondierende Societät der musikalischen Wissenschaften (Corresponding Society of Musical Science), of which he was a member. As the system circulated among the society's other members, the organist Georg Andreas Sorge* emerged as a proponent of the

Exemplaires.

1. Mr. Claussen . Ahrnsböck .
– S.A.S. Mgr. le Comte de Clermont . Paris .
– Mr. Cornabé . Cadix .
2. Mr. van der Cost . Delft .
1. Mr. James Crop . Hamb .
– S.A.S. Mgr. le Marggrave Brandenbourg-Coulmbac, Gouverneur general des Duchés de Schleswig-Holstein .

D.

– Mr. Demondorge, Maître de la Chambre aux deniers. Paris .
– Mr. de Dobbeler, Secretaire. Hamb.
– Mr. David Doormann, le jeune. Hamb.
– Mr. Jean Ulric Steiner zum Drachen. Winterthur.
– Mr. Dreÿer. Lünebourg .
– Madme. Droop . Hamb .
– Mr. Druckmüller. Hamb .

E.

– S. Excell: Mgr. le Comte d'Egmont. Paris.
S.A.S. Mgr. le Duc de Saxe-Eisenach . Eisenach .
– Mr. Erbach . Hildesheim .
– Madme la Marquise d'Erouville . Paris.
– S.A.S. Mgr. le Duc de Holstein-Eutin .

F.

– Mrs. I. M. F. Berlin .
– Mr. Fabritius, Ministre de l'Evangile . Loit .

Exemplaires.

1. Mr. de S. Fargeau . Paris .
– Mr. de Faussé . Paris .
– Mr. de Finck, Colonel . Celle .
– Mr. Foerster . Mersebourg .
– S. Exc: Mgr. le Comte de Franckenberg . Breslau .
– S.A.S. Mgr. le Prince regnant d'Ost-Frise . Aurich .
– Mr. Froede . Zerbst .

G.

2. Mr. Gleditsch . Leipzig .
1. Mr. Goll . Augsbourg .
– Mr. Gottfried . Hirschberg .
– S. A. Royale le Duc regnant de Holstein-Gottorf .
– Mr. le Chevalier de Guine . Paris .

H.

– Mrs. K. A. H. Berlin .
– Mr. Haas . Tundern .
– Mrs. les ordinaires de la Musique d'Hambourg .
– Mr. Bernard de Hamm. Marbourg
– Mr. le Baron de Hammerstein . Hamb .
– Mr. de Harling , Wittmund .
– Mr. Pantaleon Hebestreit . Dresde .
– Mr. Hendel, Docteur en Musique Londres .
– Mr. Herbst, Bleckede .
– Mr. von Höfften . Oldenbourg .
– Mr. Hollander . Riga .
– S. Exc: Mgr. le Comte de Holstein Copenhague .
– Mr. Detloff Hoppe . Hamb .

9. Second page of the list of subscribers to the *Musique de table* (Hamburg, 1733), engraved by Christian Fritzsch, including the musicians Christoph Förster, George Frideric Handel and Pantaleon Hebenstreit, as well as Telemann's friend Johann Reinhold Hollander (Paris, Bibliothèque nationale de France, Music Department, Vm^{7}-1536). Reproduced by permission.

system and Christoph Gottlieb Schröter (1699–1782) as a detractor; Mizler published only Schröter's commentary. Telemann refrained from entering the discussion, at least in print. Next, in a January 1750 letter to Telemann, Johann Adolph Scheibe* complained to his friend that the *Neues musikalisches System* was in fact derived from Scheibe's *Abhandlung von den musikalischen Intervallen* (1739), which had emerged in part from discussions with Telemann (Scheibe repeated this claim in 1773). Unfortunately, Telemann's response has not survived, though the two remained on friendly terms. Mizler finally published Telemann's system in a 1752 issue of the *Musikalische Bibliothek.*

Telemann explained that his system was not based on a keyboard temperament (though his division of the octave into fifty-five commas reflects an extended sixth-comma meantone system), but showed how 'unrestricted instruments, such as the violoncello, violin, etc. will be able to play purely, or nearly so', in keeping with 'everyday experience'. According to the system, each interval has four different sizes. Thus a fourth above the pitch C may be expressed as F-flat (smallest), F (small), F-sharp (large) and F-double sharp (largest), with the upper notes separated from each other by the distance of four commas (in other words, a chromatic semitone, as opposed to a diatonic semitone of five commas). The advantages of adjusting the size of intervals, Telemann explains, are seen in harmony, which 'gains not a little sonority' as a result. As Wolfgang Hirschmann* has shown, Telemann was apparently attempting to systematise the kind of enharmonic singing that he had heard in Paris*, when pitches sung too high or too low caused him aural discomfort while simultaneously creating a sweet effect. And it was apparently with this kind of singing in mind that Telemann composed several extreme modulations in his grand motet for Paris, *Deus judicium tuum regi da**, TVWV 7:7. In April 1767, just two months before Telemann's death, a revised version of his system was published in the Hamburg *Unterhaltungen* as the *Letzte Beschäfftigung Georg Philipp Telemanns, im 86sten Lebensjahre, bestehend in einer musikalische Klang- und Intervallen-Tafel* (Final pursuit of Georg Philipp Telemann, in his eighty-sixth year, consisting of a table of musical tones and intervals). Included with this new version is an example of chord progressions that includes one drawn from the motet, illustrating the 'largest' fourth. *HirInn, HirNeu, JunMiz, WacNeu.*

Neumeister, Erdmann In a 1714 letter to the Eisenach court, Telemann referred to Neumeister (1671–1756) as the 'most famous and best poet for sacred things', and for his part Neumeister regarded Telemann as an 'incomparable composer' in a 1726 publication of poetry. Collaborations between the two men helped shape the history of the sacred cantata over nearly half a century, and in fact most of Neumeister's annual cycles of sacred cantata librettos were written for Telemann, who set more of Neumeister's poetry than that of any other librettist. Telemann and Neumeister may have first met during the early years of the eighteenth century in Leipzig or Weißenfels, where Neumeister was court deacon. In any case, the two became colleagues in 1706, when Neumeister was appointed dean and court preacher at the Sorau court, following Telemann's appointment as *Kapellmeister* just months earlier. From 1715 Neumeister was head pastor at the Jacobikirche in Hamburg, in which capacity he provided essential support of Telemann's successful application in 1721 for the post of city music director and cantor of the Johanneum. By that time, Telemann had set at least five of

Neumeister's annual cantata cycles in whole or in part: the *Geistliche Cantaten** (at Leipzig or Sorau), the *Geistliches Singen und Spielen** (once at Eisenach and again at Frankfurt) and the so-called *Französischer Jahrgang** and first *Concerten-Jahrgang** (both at Frankfurt). Telemann also set at least twelve dicta from Neumeister's early cycle of strophic odes with a concluding dictum (*Poetische Früchte der Lippen, in Geistlichen Arien**, 1700); these vocal duets with an accompaniment of two violins and continuo (TVWV 1:100 and 10:21–31) may be the remainders of another complete annual cycle of church music (perhaps one of the two 'small annual cycles' mentioned in AB 1718), and most likely date from the first decade of the eighteenth century. Telemann again turned to Neumeister for church cantata cycles during the early 1740s with the *Musicalische Lob Gottes in der Gemeine des Herrn** and *Lied-Jahrgang**. In the cases of the *Geistliches Singen und Spielen, Französischer Jahrgang, Concerten-Jahrgang* and *Musicalische Lob Gottes,* Telemann made suggestions to Neumeister regarding the nature and order of cantata movements, resulting in a true collaboration. What Telemann may have made of Neumeister's well known and virulent anti-Semitism is unknown, and in fact we have no indication of whether the two were on especially friendly terms. *HobNeu, PfaTex, PoeKir, WacDic.*

***Der neu-modische Liebhaber Damon,* TVWV 21:8** Telemann's 'scherzhafte Singe-Spiele' (comic *Singspiel*), The Newfangled Lover Damon, premiered at the Hamburg Opera on 30 August 1724. It was a revised version of a work entitled *Die Satyren in Arcadien* (The Satyrs in Arcadia) that Telemann had written in Frankfurt for the Leipzig Opera, where it premiered in 1718 or 1719; only the libretto of this version of the opera is extant. The Hamburg revisions involved the composition of at least seven arias along with a duet and trio, but these notwithstanding, *Der neu-modische Liebhaber Damon* is the only work by Telemann for the Leipzig Opera to survive in more or less complete form, and it may have been his last work for the company before it permanently ceased operations in 1720. Telemann based his libretto on Pietro Pariati's *I Satiri in Arcadia* (Vienna, 1714), set to music by Francesco Bartolomeo Conti. The plot is a pastoral fantasy. The satyr Damon has returned to Arcadia with a band of satyrs following his banishment. Desiring all the nymphs he encounters, he also seeks revenge on the shepherd Tyrsis, who has laid a trap for the satyr by faking his own death and disguising himself as the nymph Caliste, with whom Damon now falls in love. Mirtilla, sister of Tyrsis, feigns insanity in order to fend off Damon's advances. During a feast of Bacchus, she slips a sleeping potion into the wine that renders Damon and his satyrs unconscious. Waking up bound in chains, Damon is forced to vow never to return to Arcadia. Much of Telemann's music is in the tuneful, dance-based 'middle style' reminiscent of his songs and secular cantatas, though there are also arias in buffa and seria style (an example of the latter is the heartbroken Mirtilla's chromatic arioso and aria toward the end of Act I). Perhaps unexpectedly, the pastoral-rustic style is mostly held in reserve. Among the instrumental dances are two burlesque chaconnes in Act III: the 'Chaconne comique' (entrance of the comic masks), and another providing entrance music for hunters, shepherds and a drunk satyr. Like *Die Last-tragende Liebe, oder Emma und Eginhard**, *Damon* opens with a three-movement violin concerto (TWV 51:C3) as a sinfonia. The opera has been published in volume 21 (1969) of the Telemann selective critical edition*. *MauLei, PegDam.*

Nouveaux quatuors en six suites Known popularly as the second set of Telemann's 'Paris' Quartets (following the *Quadri**), the *Nouveaux quatuors* were indeed premiered and published in Paris* in 1738, during the composer's visit to the city. In AB 1740 he mentions that the quartets 'found exceptionally attentive listeners at court and in the city, and quickly earned me a nearly universal honour, which was accompanied by great courteousness'. As French suites, they naturally appealed to a Parisian audience, but it is their Italianate stylistic elements – then all the rage in the French capital – that may have won them the most adherents. They represent the pinnacle of the quartet for three melody instruments and continuo, and as such take their place among the finest chamber music of the eighteenth century. Following the example of the last two works of the *Quadri**, the six quartets begin with substantial preludes, each different in form and character, and continue with suites of five or six movements, only some of which are explicitly dance-based. The printed parts include a list of the 287 subscribers (ordering 294 copies); these figures take into account a supplementary list printed after the first publication run. However, in AB 1738 Telemann claimed that the *Nouveaux quatuors* attracted over 400 subscribers in just a few weeks – an impressive number for the time (and which, according to Telemann, 'had never before happened with music'). Among the collection's named subscribers are Johann Sebastian Bach*, harpsichordist Anne Jeanne Boucon, Johann Friedrich Fasch*, viola da gambist Jean-Baptiste Antoine Forqueray, violinist Pierre Guignon, Johann Reinhold Hollander*, Johann Balthasar König*, Joachim Erasmus von Moldenit*, Johann Georg Pisendel* and Johan Helmich Roman*, in addition to numerous members of the nobility, royalty and merchant class. The *Nouveaux quatuors* have been published in volume 19 (1965) of the Telemann selective critical edition*. *FavNet, GiuGre, LanNou, ZohMix.*

Oboe Telemann appears to have had a special affection for the oboe, to judge from the high number of solo works he composed for the instrument, especially in the early decades of his career. During his Eisenach and Frankfurt periods (1708–21) he composed eight solo concertos for oboe (TWV 51:c1, c2, D5, d1, d2, e1, f1 and G2); three oboe d'amore concertos (TWV 51:e2, G3 and A2) may have been written slightly later. These works often exploit the instrument's 'vocal' eloquence through aria-, arioso- or recitative-inspired slow movements and close dialogues between the soloist and tutti in fast movements. The particularly fine E-minor oboe concerto (TWV 51:e1) was composed for the Dresden virtuoso oboist Johann Christian Richter. Two or three oboes are featured in many of Telemann's overture-suites*, often with a concertante role. Among his published works, *Die Kleine Cammer-Music** (1716) comes closest to being a collection of oboe music, as the six partitas are designated on the title page as being 'especially' for oboe (but also playable on violin, flute or keyboard), and the collection was dedicated to four prominent oboists (including Richter). The *Essercizii musici** (1726) includes two solos for oboe and continuo and four trios with the instrument, including one for oboe and obbligato harpsichord. Important solos, trios and quartets with oboe parts are found in *Der getreue Music-Meister** (1728–29) and the *Musique de table** (1733), which also contains two overture-suites with elaborate parts for one or two oboes. The lack of much other published oboe music by Telemann probably reflects the greater popularity of such instruments as the flute and violin among amateur musicians (though the oboe is sometimes listed as an alternative option). Among his vocal works, pairs of oboes became a nearly standard component of the instrumental ensemble by the Frankfurt period (1712–21). The virtuosic solo oboe part in the sinfonia to the *Brockes-Passion** (1716) was most likely written for the Darmstadt wind player (and Telemann's future brother-in-law) Johann Michael Böhm*. Prominent oboe parts appear in Telemann's first published cycle of church cantatas, the *Harmonischer Gottes-Dienst** (1725–27), and in the *Schubart-Jahrgang** (1731–32; excerpts published as the *Fortsetzung des Harmonischen Gottes-Dienstes*), as well as in many other church cantatas, oratorios, operas and occasional vocal works. *HayKle, ZohImi, ZohMix.*

Odes *See* **Songs**

Operas Telemann was active as an opera composer for over thirty years, spanning his directorship of the Leipzig Opera while a university student (1703–05) to his directorship of the Hamburg Opera from 1722 until its closing in 1738. He got his first taste of the genre as a boy in Magdeburg, writing an opera called *Sigismundus* at the age of twelve (he also sang the title role). In AB 1740 Telemann claimed to have written 'twenty-odd' operas for Leipzig and 'also the verses for many of them' while living in the city and, after 1705, while in Sorau, Eisenach and Frankfurt. He also reckoned that he had written 'about thirty-five' operas, intermezzi and prologues for Hamburg. These were in addition to several operas for courts in Bayreuth, Eisenach and Weissenfels. Of these dozens of works, only nine operas survive in complete form, along with most of the arias from a tenth. Additional operas are represented by one to a dozen or so arias, and many others have left behind only librettos. Even with so much music lost, Telemann may be considered the most important composer of German-language opera before 1750. He was particularly gifted when treating comic subjects; it is only a slight exaggeration to claim, as did Wilhelm Kleefeld at the turn of the twentieth century, that Telemann was the 'father of German comic opera'.

At present, only thirteen of Telemann's 'twenty-odd' Leipzig operas have been identified (seven more may be of his composition as well). Operas in Leipzig were performed during the thrice-yearly trade fairs (Michaelmas, New Year's and Easter), and Telemann's earliest works date from the 1703 New Year's and Easter fairs: *Ferdinand und Isabella* (TVWV 21:2) and *Lucius Verus* (21:*deest*). In 1704 Telemann composed three operas (performed during successive fairs) to librettos by Christine Dorothea Lachs (b. 1672): *Der lachende Democritus* (TVWV 21:1), *Cajus Caligula* (21:3) and *Germanicus** (21:*deest*), from which forty arias survive. He sang minor tenor roles in the first two operas, evidently splitting his time between the stage and the orchestra, which he would have directed from the keyboard or violin. From Sorau, Telemann supplied *Adonis* (1708; 21:4), and from Eisenach five more works: *Narcissus* (1709; 21:5), *Mario* (1709; 21:6), *Der Unglückliche Alcmeon, oder Jupiter und Semele* (1711; 21:7), *Die Syrische Unruh* (1711; 21:*deest*) and *Ariadne* (1712; 21:*deest*), in addition to a substantial reworking of *Germanicus*. *Mario* was a partnership between Telemann and his Eisenach colleague Pantaleon Hebenstreit*, and appears also to have included Italian arias by Giovanni Bononcini. Telemann wrote at least two operas for

Leipzig while at Frankfurt: *Die Königliche Schäferin Margenis* (1715; 21:*deest*) and *Die Satyren in Arcadien* (1718 or 1719; 21:8). The latter work is known only from its revised version, *Der neumodische Liebhaber Damon**, which premiered at Hamburg in 1724; it is therefore the most completely preserved of Telemann's Leipzig operas. Although he claimed to have written 'verses' to many of his works, this mostly involved translating and adapting pre-existing librettos; the same is true of several of his Hamburg operas.

Twenty operas and a dozen prologues are known to have been written for the Hamburg Opera, mostly between 1721 and 1733, in addition to music for operas by other composers (including George Frideric Handel*, Reinhard Keiser*, Giuseppe Maria Orlandini, Niccolò Porpora and Johann Gottfried Vogler). More than half of the operas and all of the prologues have been lost, though the surviving works offer a fair representation of Telemann's operatic style through the late 1720s. In keeping with Hamburg convention, many of the operas are comic or include comic scenes, and a number feature a bilingual libretto (with German recitatives and a mix of German and Italian arias). This is true of the comic and bilingual *Der geduldige Socrates** (1721; 21:9), which was written in Frankfurt and premiered in Hamburg some months before Telemann moved there. If the opposite pole is represented by the opera seria *Flavius Bertaridus, König der Langobarden** (1729; 21:27), other 'serious' operas such as *Der Sieg der Schönheit** (1722; 21:10), *Miriways** (1728; 21:24) and *Die Last-tragende Liebe oder Emma und Eginhard** (1728; 21:25) include some comic elements. All four of these works have historical subjects, though *Miriways* takes place in the recent past. An exceptional case is *Die wunderbare Beständigkeit der Liebe, oder Orpheus* (1726; 21:18), in which the myth of Orpheus and Eurydice is told in a trilingual libretto (French, German and Italian), with the musical style of individual numbers matching the language. Telemann wrote at least four comic intermezzos at Hamburg, but only *Pimpinone oder Die ungleiche Heyrath** (1725; 21:15) has survived; he printed the opera in 1728, the only one of his stage works to be published in full. This intermezzo, along with the late comic 'serenata' *Don Quichotte auf der Hochzeit des Comacho** (1761; 21:32), shows Telemann's comic gift to full effect.

Several more operas from the 1720s survive fragmentarily. The music of Telemann's opera for the Bayreuth court, *Adelheid oder die ungezwungene Liebe** (1724; 21:17), is known through his publication of fourteen comic numbers. Five more operas are even more fragmentarily preserved, being represented by one to four numbers in Telemann's music journal *Der getreue Music-Meister**: *Das Ende der babylonischen Gefangenschaft oder Belsazar* (1723; 21:11), *Calypso oder Sieg der Weisheit über die Liebe* (1727; 21:19), *Sancio oder Die siegende Großmuth* (1727; 21:20), *Die verkehrte Welt* (1728; 21:23) and *Aesopus bei Hofe* (1729; 21:26). In the case of *Omphale* (1724; 21:14), we have an aria and some ballet music, which is preserved in the overture-suite* 'L'Omphale', TWV 55:e8. *CloTon, DelGal, HirVer, HobLei, HutFra, HutTod, KiuFra, LauAri, LynOpe, MauAlm, MauLei, MauNar, PecOpe, RatOmp, RuhKom, RuhOpe, WolOpe.*

Oratorios When Telemann arrived in Hamburg in 1721, there was already a tradition of annual performances of liturgical Passion music. The Passion was heard thirteen times between the first Sunday in Lent and Good Friday, once in each of the five principal churches and eight secondary churches. Of the forty-six Passions Telemann wrote between 1722 and 1767, twenty-two are extant. This repertory is distributed unevenly across the period: only three works survive before 1737, eight more are extant from 1737–50 and another eleven date from 1755–67. As with the more familiar examples by Johann Sebastian Bach*, all of Telemann's works are based on a biblical narration of the Passion and death of Jesus Christ (the *narratio*) according to one of the four Evangelists – Matthew, Mark, Luke and John, in that order for each four-year cycle in Hamburg – and are subject to various poetic ('lyric') interpolations in the form of arias, chorales, choruses and recitatives. And as with Bach's Passions, the role of Evangelist is normally assigned to a tenor. After 1736 the *narratio* was curtailed to allow an expansion of the poetic interpolations. Atypical in this respect is the 1745 St John Passion, *Ein Lämmlein geht und trägt die Schuld** (TVWV 5:30; the only Passion setting that Telemann published), which has a full-length *narratio*. Narrative curtailment becomes intensified starting in 1755, revealing the influence of Telemann's late concert oratorios, and is balanced by sequences of chorales (sometimes involving chorale arias and fantasias), poetic depictions of events and substantial accompanied recitatives. The 1728 St Luke Passion and the 1745 St John Passion have been published in volumes 15 (1964) and 29 (1996) of the Telemann selective critical edition*.

Already during his Frankfurt years, Telemann established the oratorio as a concert genre with his *Brockes-Passion** (1716; TVWV 5:1), the five *Davidische Oratorien* (1718; 6:1), lost except for two arias, and *Das Muster wahrer Freundschaft oder David und Jonathan* (1720; 6:2), which is entirely lost. He continued this practice during his first Hamburg years with the *Seliges Erwägen** (1722; 5:2) and three passion oratorios performed in 1731: *Die Bekehrung des Römischen Hauptmans Cornelius* (5:3; lost), *Die gekreuzigte Liebe oder Tränen über das Leiden und Sterben unseres Heilandes** (5:4) and *Jesus, als die untergehende Sonne, wurde* (5:*deest*; lost). Telemann also gave public performances of his annual liturgical Passions following their presentation in the city's principal churches. With the *Oratorischer Jahrgang** (1730–31) and the *Stollbergischer Jahrgang** (1736–37), he blurred the line between sacred cantata and oratorio. During the 1750s and early 1760s Telemann composed a series of lyric oratorios (having little or no *narratio* and a cast of allegorical characters) specifically for the concert hall: the *Betrachtung der neunten Stunde an dem Todestag Jesu** (1755; 5:5), *Der Tod Jesu** (1755; 5:6), *Der Messias** (1759; 6:4), *Das befreite Israel** (1759; 6:5), *Die Auferstehung und Himmelfahrt Jesu** (1760; 6:6), *Die Auferstehung** (1761; 6:7) and *Der Tag des Gerichts** (1762; 6:8). *CarPas, GraCho, GraPas, HirJoh, HirPas, HirRez, HörPas, LanPas, LanTra, ReiPas, RuhPas, RuhSel, SchTex.*

Oratorischer Jahrgang For his 1730–31 cycle of church cantatas in Hamburg, Telemann turned to librettos by the Hamburg poet and musician Albrecht Jacob Zell (1701–54), hence the cycle's alternative name of *Zell-Jahrgang*. Zell's expansive librettos are oratorios populated with allegorical and biblical characters. Some are in two parts, to be performed before and after the sermon, and others further include movements to be heard at the end of the service (following Hamburg custom). This was Telemann's first cycle of oratorios, followed in 1731–32 by the more compact oratorios of the *Schubart-Jahrgang** and, in 1736–37, by the *Stollbergischer Jahrgang**, which includes several oratorio texts. The *Oratorischer Jahrgang* was performed complete in Gotha in 1742–43, and selected works were heard in Berlin as late as the 1760s.

Just over half of Telemann's cantatas are extant, and most of these were copied in score and parts by Jakob Ditmar, cantor of Berlin's Nikolaikirche from 1728 to 1780. Ditmar's manuscripts belong to the recently recovered music archive of the Sing-Akademie zu Berlin*, and thus were inaccessible for decades. The oratorios for Easter Sunday, the second Sunday after Easter, the Feast of St John, the Feast of St Michael and the twenty-fifth Sunday after Trinity have been published in volume 58 (2017) of the Telemann selective critical edition*. *HenSin, PoeFak, PoeGot, PoeOrd, PoeOra, ReiSin, VosDan.*

Orchestral suite *See* **Overture-suite**

Organ music *See* **Keyboard music**

Ornamentation *See* **Methodical sonatas**

Orpheus *See* ***Die wunderbare Beständigkeit der Liebe, oder Orpheus,*** **TVWV 21:18**

Ouverture Burlesque de Quixotte, **TWV 55:G10** This characteristic overture-suite* was inspired by Miguel de Cervantes Saavedra's famous novel *El ingenioso hidalgo Don Quijote de la Mancha* (The Ingenious Gentleman Sir Quixote of La Mancha; Madrid, 1605 and 1615). Along with the *Wasser-Ouverture**, it appears to have been among the most widely admired of Telemann's overture-suites during his lifetime, at least to judge by the number of surviving manuscript copies. Like Telemann's Gulliver Suite in *Der getreue Music-Meister**, the *Ouverture Burlesque de Quixotte* illustrates its subject through a series of character portraits or vignettes of famous scenes. The overture is in a mock-heroic, buffo style, and is followed by portraits of the knight-errant awakening ('Le Reveil de Quichotte'; a pastoral siciliana), his famous and ill-fated attack on windmills ('Son attacque des moulins à vent'; a parody of theatrical battle music), his amorous sighs for the imagined love-interest, Princess Dulcinea del Toboso ('Les Soupirs amoureux aprés la Princesse Dulcinée'; a theatrical *plainte*), his squire Sancho Panza tossed in a blanket ('Sanche Panse berné'), his horse Rocinante and Sancho Panza's ass Dapple ('Le Galope de Rosinante – Celui d'Ane de Sanche'; featuring limping and halting musical effects) and finally his dreams of his next misadventure ('Le couché de Quichotte'; in the rustic-Polish style). *FabWit, ZohMix.*

Ouverture des nations anciennes et modernes, **TWV 55:G4** This characteristic overture-suite* portrays ancient and modern peoples from Germany, Sweden and Denmark. As such, it is allied with two other Telemann overture-suites portraying peoples or characters: the *Ouverture burlesque* (TWV 55:B8) offering portraits of commedia dell'arte characters (Scaramouche, Harlequin, Columbine, Pierrot and Mezzetino) and the untitled TWV 55:B5, which portrays Turks, Swiss, Muscovites and Portuguese. All three suites belong to a balletic 'parade of nations' tradition going back to the seventeenth century, suggesting that they may in fact have been drawn from lost stage works. This impression is bolstered by the high number of movements in compound forms, something more characteristic of Telemann's theatrical dances than his stylised ones. In the *Ouverture des nations anciennes et modernes,* the 'ancient' dances are in slow or moderate tempos and feature dotted rhythms, whereas the 'modern' ones are faster and more rhythmically varied – probably a commentary on the superiority of the colourful modern style in comparison to the monochromatic ancient style. The suite's concluding movement, 'Les vieilles femmes' (The Old Women), is a grotesque, chromatic gavotte that references stock burlesque dance characters. *ZohMix.*

VI Ouverturen nebst zween Folgesätzen *See* **Keyboard music**

Overture-suite Telemann's approximately 125 surviving overture-suites (often called orchestral suites, though they were not always performed orchestrally) form the most important corpus of such works by a single composer, both for their quality and quantity. Although many of the extant works are not precisely datable, Telemann appears to have written overture-suites from his Leipzig years (1701–05) through the 1730s, returning to the genre briefly in the 1760s. In AB 1718 Telemann claimed that 'I have been able to produce up to two hundred *Ouverturen* from my pen' during the preceding thirteen years (in AB 1740 he recalled having written that number in only two years at Sorau between 1705 and 1708). This is a remarkable rate of production, even allowing for some exaggeration, though it is possible that by 'Ouverturen' he meant only French overtures or suites in all scorings. The figure of six hundred overture-suites, with which Telemann is sometimes credited, derives from a misreading of a passage in AB 1740, where he mentions that in his first eighteen years in Hamburg he wrote 'about six hundred *Ouvertüren*, trios, concertos, keyboard pieces, elaborated chorales, fugues, cantatas, etc. for local and out-of-town music lovers'; the number is surely inclusive of all these genres. Telemann's earliest surviving overture-suites owe much to late seventeenth-century works by the German followers of Jean-Baptiste Lully (*lullistes*), while later examples reveal the influence of the Vivaldian concerto and early symphony; in short, his works reflect the entire history of this short-lived genre.

Among the more innovative features of Telemann's overture-suites is the mixture of traditional French stylistic elements with Italianate concertato writing. Johann Adolph Scheibe* referred to works with soloistic wind or string instruments as 'Concertouverturen', and a subset of such works features one or two instruments functioning virtually as concerto soloists throughout the overture and most of the following suite movements. Telemann's best known example of the latter type is the Overture-suite in A minor for recorder and strings, TWV 55:a2, but he also wrote examples for solo violin, solo viola da gamba and (in the *Musique de table**) two winds with two violins. Telemann additionally composed several examples of the less common concerto-suite*, in which a concerto allegro movement precedes suite movements that also feature one or more soloists.

Telemann's programmatic or characteristic suites and movements include some of his most imaginative, witty and humorous instrumental works. At least eighteen overture-suites circulated with overall characteristic titles during the eighteenth century, but for the most part these titles cannot be connected with the composer himself; only the late *Ouverture, jointes d'une suite tragi-comique* (TWV 55:D22; from the 1760s) was certainly titled by Telemann. Several works justify their titles (or make a case for being given one) by maintaining a thematic or narrative thread through some or all movements. Thus the *Ouverture, jointes d'une suite tragi-comique* portrays medical conditions or character flaws and their 'remedies', the *Wasser-Ouverture** and *Alster-Ouverture** portray Hamburg as a centre of maritime commerce, *the Ouverture Burlesque de Quixotte** portrays characters or scenes from Cervantes' famous novel, the *Ouverture des nations anciennes et modernes** and the overture-suite TWV 55:B5 portray people of various nationalities, the *Ouverture burlesque* (TWV 55:B8) offers portraits of commedia dell'arte characters, the E-flat major suite TWV 50:21 portrays a courtly day whose focal point is a hunt, and the overture-suite TWV 55:B11 follows a series of oxymoronic movement titles ('Le repos interrompu' or Interrupted Rest; 'La guerre en la paix' or War in Peacetime; 'Les Vainquers vaincus' or Victors Vanquished; and 'La Solitude associée' or Communal Solitude) with one that references the growth and eventual bursting of the Mississippi Company stock bubble in 1719–20 ('L'Espérance de Mississippi' or Hope for the Mississippi).

Some overture-suites, or at least individual movements, may have been compiled from dance numbers belonging to lost stage works. This is demonstrably the case with *L'Omphale* (TWV 55:e8), at least several movements of which were drawn from the lost opera* *Omphale* (TVWV 21:14; Hamburg, 1724). The opening movements of a few overture-suites were used to introduce other Hamburg operas by Telemann, and the three suites portraying nationalities or commedia dell'arte characters mentioned above make explicit reference to a 'parade of nations' balletic tradition. Whether or not these works indicate a stage origin, individual movements in other suites with characteristic titles such as 'Harlequinade', 'Plainte', 'Entrée', 'Sommeille', 'La Tempête', 'Combattans' and 'Furies' all refer to stock characters or scenic types.

Telemann published a total of ten overture-suites, including one in the lost *Ouvertüre und Suite* (Hamburg, 1730), six in the *Six Ouvertures à 4 ou 6** (Hamburg, 1736; evidently the last-ever publication of such works) and three in the *Musique de table.* Six overture-suites have been published in volume 10 (1955) of the Telemann selective critical edition*, and seventy-one more have appeared in the Severinus Urtext Telemann Edition*. *BütKon, FabWit, HobBem, HofKon, PayFre, PayOve, PhiPro, ZohAes, ZohMix.*

Paris Telemann's eight-month visit to Paris commenced in October 1737 (he departed Hamburg on the Feast of St Michael, 29 September) and ran at least through May 1738. Our principal source of information about the visit is AB 1740, from which we learn that Telemann was invited to make the trip – his only known one outside German-speaking lands – by several unnamed Parisian virtuosos; these may have been the same instrumentalists who premiered the *Nouveaux quatuors en six suites** at the French court and in the city: flautist Michel Blavet*, violinist Jean-Pierre Guignon (1702–74), gambist Jean-Baptiste Antoine Forqueray (1699–1782) and cellist Eduoard (first name unknown). Telemann and Blavet appear to have been in contact for some years previously, as the flautist was most likely the composer's Parisian publishing agent for the *Musique de table** (1733). No doubt Telemann's visit was intended in part to put an end to unauthorised publications of his instrumental works, of which at least six had already appeared under the imprints of Charles-Nicholas Le Clerc* and François Boivin, whose *Six sonates en trio dans le goust italien* (1731–33) is probably the '6 trios for two transverse flutes

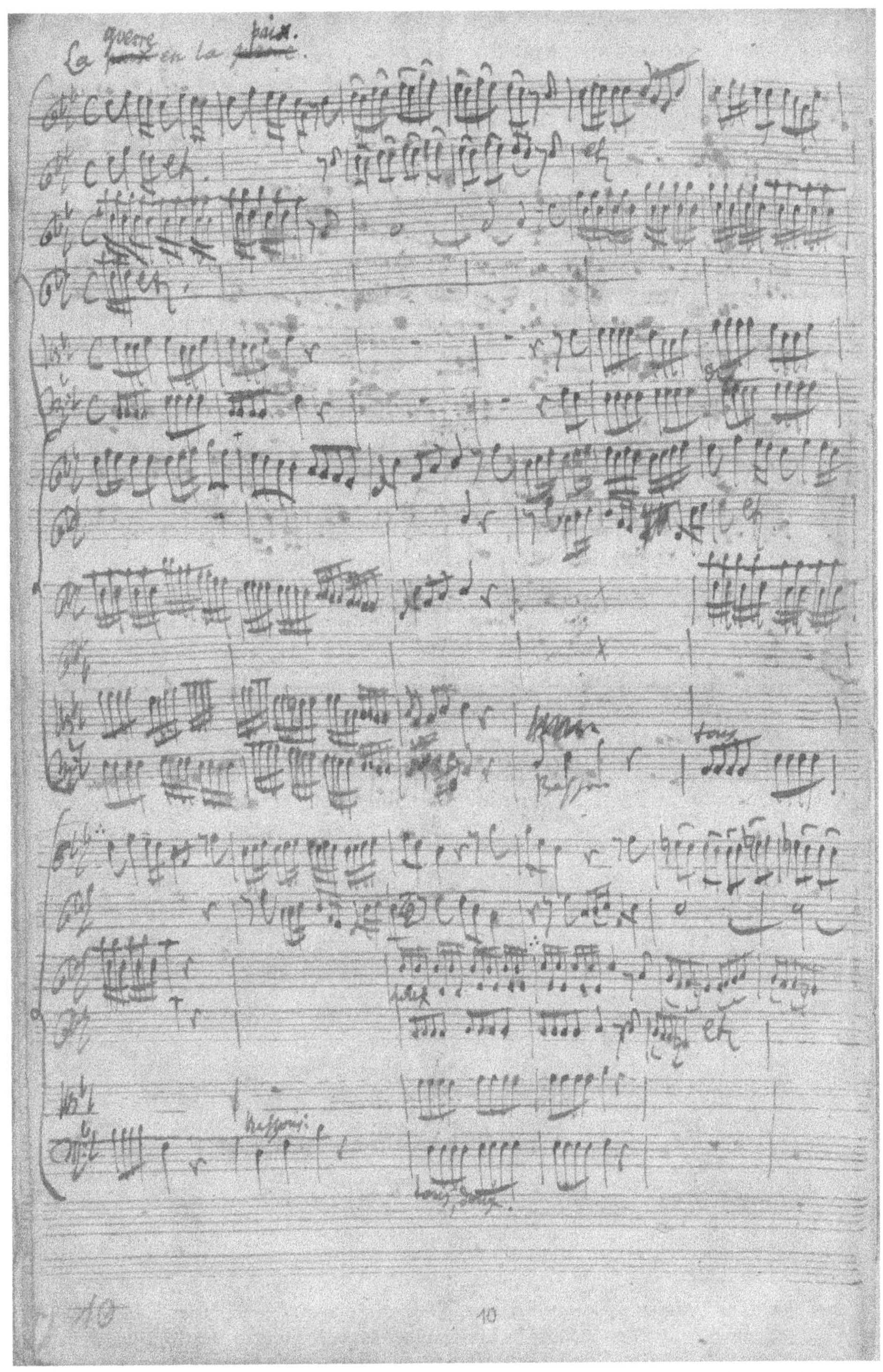

10. Telemann's c. 1719–20 composing score to the Overture-suite in B-flat major for two oboes, bassoon and strings, TWV 55:B11, showing the beginning of movement 3, 'La guerre en la paix' (War in Peacetime) (Dresden, Sächsische Landesbibliothek – Staats- und Universitätsbibliothek, Mus. 2392-O-34, p. 10). Reproduced by permission.

and continuo, engraved in Paris from a stolen manuscript' (AB 1740). While in Paris, Telemann was granted a royal publishing privilege on 3 February 1738 to protect 'several opuses of instrumental music without words' for twenty years beginning on the previous 31 January. In addition to the *Nouveaux quatuors*, Telemann published six canonic duets* (the *XIIX Canons mélodieux*) during his visit; a third set of instrumental works, the incompletely preserved *Sonates en trio* (three trios with continuo and three without), was published in the city after Telemann's return to Hamburg by the ex-patriot German harpsichord maker Antoine Vater, at whose Parisian home the composer had lodged. Telemann proudly recounted that his grand motet, *Deus judicium tuum regi da**, was performed twice at the Paris Concert Spirituel (25 and 27 March 1738) by nearly one hundred 'select' people. Telemann also wrote the following works during his stay in the city, all of which have been lost: two Latin, two-voice Psalms of David with instruments, a number of concertos, a French cantata titled *Polyphème* and a comic symphony on a popular tune. In the preface to his *Beschreibung der Augen-Orgel**, Telemann assures his readers that he will respond to the request of 'not a few' friends to publish his impressions of Parisian musical life, adding that he had already set down many of his ideas onto paper. Unfortunately, these impressions were never published. *LesCon, FavNet, LalPar, MahPar, ReiFra, RuhPar.*

'Paris' Quartets *See* ***Quadri*** and ***Nouveaux quatuors en six suites***

Passions *See* **Oratorios**

Pastorelle en Musique oder Musikalisches Hirtenspiel*, TVWV 11:*deest In AB 1718 Telemann noted that in Frankfurt 'I composed twenty-odd fully scored [*starcke*] *Dramata* for the most illustrious weddings both here and abroad, and for the

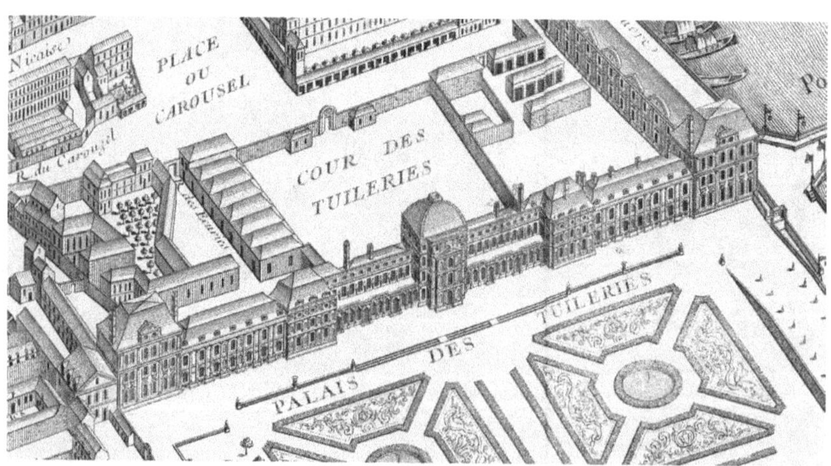

11. The Tuileries palace in Paris, detail from the city map commissioned by Michel-Étienne Turgot, and realised by cartographer Louis Bretez and engraver Claude Lucas in 1734–36; the map was published in twenty-one sections in 1739 (Main Library, Kyoto University, GG/355/122, as posted on Wikimedia Commons). On 25 and 27 March 1738 Telemann's grand motet, *Deus judicium tuum regi da*, TVWV 7:7, was performed in the Concert Spirituel series in the large 'Salle des cent Suisses' of the palace's central pavilion. Reproduced by permission.

attendance of great lords, also writing the poetry for all of them.' He refers to these works in AB 1740 as 'Hochzeitserenaten' or wedding serenatas, reiterates that he wrote all the librettos, and claims that 'in view of their freedom and none too palatable saltiness, [I] would have qualms about writing them today'. None of Telemann's wedding 'dramata' or serenatas was thought to be extant until a score of this one (a 'musical pastorale or musical shepherd's play') surfaced in the musical archive of the Sing-Akademie zu Berlin* in 2001. It is the earliest dramatic work by Telemann to survive intact, datable to c. 1713–16 based on its use of French airs first published in 1713 and its stylistic similarities with other works by Telemann from his Eisenach and early Frankfurt years. No doubt it was commissioned by one of Frankfurt's leading aristocratic, patrician or mercantile families, many of which had associations with the composer. Telemann's libretto is based in part on Molière's text for either Jean-Baptiste Lully's *Divertissement royal*, known as *Les Amans magnifiques*, LWV 42, or Lully's *Les Festes de l'Amour et de Bacchus*, LWV 47. Telemann included some of the original French texts, translated (and sometimes also adapted) others into German and added new German texts. He used none of Lully's music, but did adapt the music of several French composers for five airs. In addition to airs, arias, recitatives (all in German) and choruses, the serenata opens with a substantial, multi-movement concerto for pairs of oboes and trumpets with strings. The work has been published in volume 64 (2014) of the Telemann selective critical edition*. *PegPas, SchFra.*

Patronage *See* **Dedications**

Performance practice Telemann contemplated, but never completed, two books addressing performance. The *Traité du récitatif* was advertised by the composer in 1733 as among his forthcoming publications, and the *Musikalischer Practicus* was to address musical 'order and coherence' and continuo figuring, among other topics. Telemann discussed the latter with Carl Heinrich Graun* in 1743, and the 1744 Nuremberg biography* notes that the composer was 'preparing to publish serially a most important work under the title *Musikalischer Practicus*, in which he proposes faithfully to communicate all that he has observed through long experience'. Yet several of Telemann's publications include remarks on continuo playing and the proper performance of recitative, and three more provide invaluable examples of free ornamentation. The preface to the *Harmonischer Gottes-Dienst** discusses the so-called 'prosodic' appoggiatura in recitative and how to transpose *Kammerton* organ continuo parts in order to accommodate *Chorton*. At the conclusion of the *Fast allgemeines evangelisch-musicalisches Lieder-Buch**, Telemann gives advice on figured bass realisation (including the use of the cadential *tierce de Picardie*) and provides tonal plans for improvised organ preludes to precede the singing of chorales in unusual keys (Telemann later provided written-out examples of such preludes in the the *XX Kleine Fugen*, published in 1731). His first collection of songs*, the *Singe-, Spiel- und Generalbass-Übungen*, is virtually a continuo treatise, thanks to the commentaries accompanying each of the composer's realisations; further remarks on continuo realisation are found in the *Musikalisches Lob Gottes** preface. A new bass figure of a half circle for the diminished triad (the 'Telemannischer Bogen', as Carl Philipp Emanuel Bach* called it) is introduced in the *Avertissement* to the *Nouveaux quatuors en six suites**. Finally, some of the best examples of free ornamentation from the eighteenth century are found in slow movements of the methodical sonatas*. *See also* **Choir** *and* **Theory**. *HobBog, NeuKir, PoeTon, SwaPer, SynGen, ZohMix.*

***Pimpinone oder Die ungleiche Heyrath*, TVWV 21:15** This comic intermezzo (really three intermezzi) was first heard at the Hamburg Opera on 27 September 1725 between the acts of *Tamerlano* by George Frideric Handel*. Its great success led to numerous repeat performances, already in the following November (with Handel's *Giulio Cesare*) and again in 1727, 1729 (with *Mistevojus* by Reinhard Keiser*), 1730 and 1735. Telemann's publication of the intermezzo in 1728 is a further indication of its popularity (the only surviving copy of the print disappeared during World War II). In adapting a libretto by Pietro Pariati for Tomaso Albinoni* (Venice, 1708), Johann Philipp Praetorius* translated the Italian recitatives into German and retained the Italian aria texts, also adding two new Italian aria texts and a German duet. Inserted as well were aria texts by the English ambassador and music lover Cyril Wyche. Telemann and Praetorius had two of Hamburg's top singers for the intermezzo: the prima donna soprano Margaretha Susanna Kayser* and the bass Johann Gottfried Riemschneider*.

The plot is a variation on a common theme: the young Vespetta ('little wasp') is angling to marry a rich man, and has the older Pimpinone in her sights. Presenting herself as virtuous while leading him on, she is hired by him as a well-paid maid. When Vespetta complains that she doesn't have full run of the house, Pimpinone gives her the key to the safe and an expensive piece of jewellery. And when she claims that the whole city is gossiping about them, Pimpinone doesn't hesitate to marry her. Now Vespetta's demeanour changes, for she claims to have married to gain herself greater freedom, which she plans on exercising by doing exactly what she promised she wouldn't do: go out alone, attend meetings and the opera, dance, play cards and make visits. She and Pimpinone threaten each other, but in the end he resigns himself to letting her do as she pleases. Although long overshadowed by Giovanni Battista Pergolesi's *La serva padrona* (1733), *Pimpinone* includes music that is no less masterful. Telemann's comedic flair is on full display in Pimpinone's aria 'Sò quel che si dice' (really a trio for one singer), in which the character portrays two wives complaining about their husbands by singing the women's parts in falsetto while narrating in his natural bass register. A 1727 sequel to *Pimpinone, Die Amours der Vespetta oder Der Galan in der Kiste* (The Loves of Vespetta or The Galant in a Box, TVWV 21:22) has not survived. *Pimpinone* has been edited in volume 6 of the series Das Erbe deutscher Musik (1936). *KocPim, WolPim.*

Pisendel, Johann Georg The leading German violinist of his time, Pisendel (1687–1755) studied with both Giuseppe Torelli and Antonio Vivaldi*. He joined the Dresden* electoral *Hofkapelle* in 1712, ascending to the position of concertmaster in 1728. His close and long-standing friendship with Telemann dates from the autumn of 1709, when the two met in Leipzig; Pisendel was newly enrolled in the university and Telemann was visiting from Sorau*. At this time they appear to have had a mutual friend in Johann Sebastian Bach*, who presented Pisendel with a set of manuscript parts to Telemann's double violin concerto TWV 52:G2 during the violinist's visit to Weimar. Pisendel renewed his friendship with Telemann during a visit to Eisenach in 1711, and again in Dresden in September 1719, when Telemann spent weeks in the city during wedding festivities for the Habsburg archduchess Maria Josepha and the electoral prince Friedrich August II. On this last occasion, Telemann composed the violin concerto TWV 51:B1 for his friend, inscribing his composing score 'Concerto grosso, per il Sig.[r] Pisendel, da me GF Telemann, 14. Sept. 1719'. Additional works by Telemann, including the early violin concertos TWV 51:E3 and 53:D5, as well as the later violin concerto-suite* TWV 51:F4 (c. 1745–55), were probably written for Pisendel. In 1729 Telemann published the concluding movement of Pisendel's sonata for unaccompanied violin in *Der getreue Music-Meister**, and in 1732–33 Pisendel appears to have acted as Telemann's Dresden publishing agent for the *Musique de table**. In four letters* Pisendel wrote to Telemann in 1749–52 – clearly the remnants of an extensive correspondence – he addresses his friend as 'brother' and shares news (and occasionally gossip) from the Dresden court and their mutual acquaintances. He sent eleven plants to Hamburg in support of Telemann's gardening* hobby in 1749, and also supplied the composer with Bohemian music paper. Pisendel assembled a large manuscript collection of instrumental music that was purchased by the Dresden court a decade after his death, and this now constitutes one of the main sources* for Telemann's instrumental music. Upon Pisendel's death, Telemann wrote a memorial poem, the first stanza of which begins 'Friend! I shall kiss you no more, for death has wrested you from me. What a jewel I must do without! How much excellence dies with you!' *FecPis, FecStu, RacSin, SchTel, TelBri, ZohMix.*

Poetische Früchte der Lippen This is the title of an annual cycle of sacred texts published by Erdmann Neumeister* in Weißenfels in 1700. Each text consists of a strophic aria followed by a dictum (biblical quotation), and the dicta for the first Sunday in Advent through the first Sunday after Epiphany were set by Telemann as vocal duets with an accompaniment of two violins and continuo, TVWV 10:21–31. These works were apparently composed soon after the publication of Neumeister's texts, and it is possible that they represent a fragment of what would have been Telemann's earliest annual cycle of church music. *PfaTex, WacDic.*

Poetry Telemann not only wrote, adapted or translated librettos for a number of his operas, oratorios and church cantatas (for example, *Sieg der Schönheit** and *Seliges Erwägen**), but also authored non-musical poems that found their way into print. It was reported in 1716 that Telemann's 'abiding opinion was that nothing possible for a poet must be impossible for the composer', and he remained concerned with the music–text connection all his life. In 1711 the death of his first wife, Amalie Louise Juliane*, inspired substantial 'Poetic Thoughts' that appeared in a 1743 anthology of poetry by husbands on the deaths of their wives. Several of Telemann's poems appear in AB 1718, and two in praise of Johann Mattheson* (one dated 1718) were published by the dedicatee in 1731. Starting in 1723, a number of Telemann's cantata librettos and poems appeared in volumes of the *Poesie der Niedersachsen* anthology, edited by Christian Friedrich Weichmann*. Among these are a sarcastic epigram about Conrad Friedrich Hurlebusch* (1723) and a laudatory poem entitled 'On

Several German Composers' (1725) in which Telemann sings the praises of George Frideric Handel*, Pantaleon Hebenstreit*, Reinhard Keiser*, Johann Kuhnau*, Johann Christoph Pepusch and Johann Christoph Pez. In 1725 Telemann published a congratulatory poem for Johann Henrich von Seelen, rector at Lübeck's Katharineum, and in the following year he contributed three memorial epigrams for the prodigy Christian Henrich Heineken (1721–25), whom he had visited in Lübeck; one of these accompanied an engraving of the child by Christian Fritzsch*. Telemann was also apt to compose epigrams

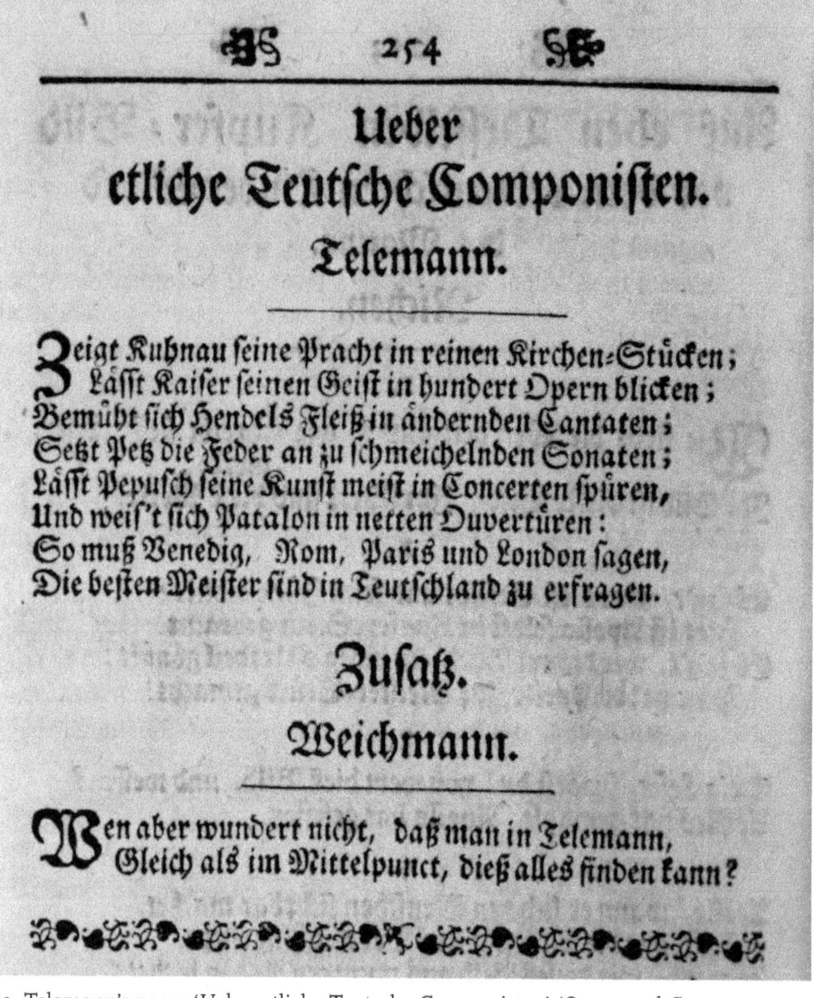

254

Ueber
etliche Teutsche Componisten.

Telemann.

Zeigt Kuhnau seine Pracht in reinen Kirchen-Stücken;
Lässt Kaiser seinen Geist in hundert Opern blicken;
Bemüht sich Hendels Fleiß in ändernden Cantaten;
Setzt Petz die Feder an zu schmeichelnden Sonaten;
Lässt Pepusch seine Kunst meist in Concerten spüren,
Und weis't sich Patalon in netten Ouvertüren:
So muß Venedig, Rom, Paris und London sagen,
Die besten Meister sind in Teutschland zu erfragen.

Zusatz.

Weichmann.

Wen aber wundert nicht, daß man in Telemann,
Gleich als im Mittelpunct, dieß alles finden kann?

12. Telemann's poem 'Ueber etliche Teutsche Componisten' (On several German composers), published in the second volume of Christian Friedrich Weichmann's poetry anthology *Poesie der Nieder-Sachsen* (Hamburg, 1723), p. 254 (digitised by Google Books). The poem reads in English translation: 'Kuhnau shows his splendour in pure church pieces; / Keiser reveals his spirit in a hundred operas; / Handel's diligence is stirred in varying cantatas; / Pez applies his pen to flattering sonatas; / Pepusch makes his art felt especially in concertos, / and Pantaleon [Hebenstreit] represents himself with enjoyable *Ouvertüren*: / Thus Venice, Rome, Paris and London must say / That the best masters are to be sought in Germany'. Weichmann's addendum reads: 'Who does not marvel that in Telemann, / Just as in a central point, one may find all of this?'

or brief poems in prefaces, guest albums and letters*. Writing to Johann Reinhold Hollander* in 1733, he offered a poem on the occasion of the death of Hollander's father. Telemann also wrote memorial poems for Reinhard Keiser* (1739), Johann Sebastian Bach* (1751) and Johann Georg Pisendel* (1755). *RacSin, RatSon, ReiGed, ReiLob, RuhSel, TelBri.*

Poetzsch, Ute After studies at the Martin-Luther-Universität Halle-Wittenberg, Poetzsch joined the research staff at the Zentrum für Telemann-Pflege und -Forschung* in Magdeburg in 1984. She earned her PhD at the Martin-Luther-Universität in 2003 with a dissertation on Telemann's church music to texts by Erdmann Neumeister* (published in 2006). Since 1992 she has served as Managing Editor of the Telemann selective critical edition*, also contributing six volumes of vocal and instrumental works. Although her research on Telemann has been wide-ranging, recent work has centred on the composer's church music and his relationship to librettists. *PoeBeh, PoeBro, PoeEdi, PoeFak, PoeGot, PoeKir, PoeOra, PoeOrd, PoeSel, PoeSie, PoeTon, PoeZer.*

Praetorius, Johann Philipp Following law studies at the university in Kiel and working in Rantzau, Praetorius (1696–c. 1775) arrived in Hamburg by 1724, and may have remained in the city until moving to Colmar bei Glückstadt in 1734 and to Trier (to teach at the university) in 1744. At Hamburg he supplied librettos to Telemann and Reinhard Keiser*, especially during the period 1725–28. His texts for Telemann include the 1724 *Kapitänsmusik** (TVWV 15:2), the Bayreuth opera *Adelheid oder die ungezwungene Liebe* (TVWV 21:17; repeated in Hamburg in 1727), the intermezzo *Pimpinone oder Die ungleiche Heyrath** (TVWV 21:15; 1725) and one of the *Sechs Cantaten** (1731). In 1724 Praetorius responded to a satire of the Hamburg Opera entitled 'Die Baßgeige' (The Double Bass), published in an issue of the journal *Der Patriot*, with his own counter-satire entitled 'Il Pregio del l'Ignoranza oder Die Baßgeige' (The Merit of Ignorance or The Double Bass). This was performed as a marionette play and skewered Telemann, among others. Yet it appears not to have affected Praetorius' working relationship with the composer. *CloHam, HobAdh, MaeKap, ThoPra.*

Polish style Unlike most of his contemporaries, Telemann eschewed the polite, courtly Polish style for a more rustic idiom evocative of the folk songs and dances he heard during his years at the Sorau court (1705–08). His recollection of experiencing the 'true barbaric beauty' of Polish and Moravian music in Pless (upper Silesia) and Kraków is among the most colourful passages in AB 1740: 'In the common taverns it consisted of a fiddle strapped to the body and tuned a third higher than usual so that it could drown out a half dozen others, a Polish Bock [bagpipe], a bass trombone, and a regal. At more respectable places there was no regal; instead, the fiddles and bagpipes were increased in number: I once saw thirty-six bagpipes and eight fiddles together. One can hardly believe what wonderful ideas such Bock players or fiddlers have when they improvise while the dancers rest. In eight days an observant person could snap up enough ideas from them to last a lifetime. Suffice it to say that there is very much in this music that is good, if it is handled properly. Since this time I have written various large concertos and trios in this style, clothing them in an Italian dress with alternating adagios and allegros.' One might accuse Telemann of cultural arrogance here – the music must be 'handled properly' and requires being 'clothed' in order to make its 'barbarity' more palatable – but his stance toward such 'folk' music is far more enlightened than was typical of the time. To be sure, for Telemann the Polish style was nearly as foundational to the German mixed taste* as the French and Italian styles were, and 'Polish' rhythms, melodic gestures and ornaments may be found in virtually every musical genre to which he contributed. His coinage of the phrase 'comic Polish seriousness' ('die lustige polnische Ernsthaftigkeit') in the commentary to his song* 'Sanfter Schlaf' (TVWV 25:63; *Singe-, Spiel- und General-Bass-Übungen*, No. 25) explains why his use of the Polish style often generates humorous, ironic or disruptive effects. Between 1737 and 1750 Johann Adolph Scheibe*, Friedrich Wilhelm Marpurg* and Telemann's former student* Jacob Wilhelm Lustig all credited Telemann with introducing or creating a vogue for the Polish style. *KocPol, SenHan, StePol, ZohMix.*

Polon (Pollone), Maria Domenica The Venetian soprano Polon (c. 1700–after 1750) trained at the Ospedale della Pietà and sang at the Arolsen court of the Prince of Waldeck from about 1719 to 1739. While on leave from the court between 1724 and 1730 she sang twenty-six roles at the Hamburg Opera and also performed in public concerts. Among the Telemann operas she sang in were *Das Ende der babylonischen Gefangenschaft oder Belsazar* (TVWV 21:11; 1723), *Calypso oder Sieg der Weisheit über die Liebe* (21:19; 1728), *Die verkehrte Welt* (21:23; 1728), *Miriways** (21:24; 1728), *Die Last-tragende Liebe oder Emma und Eginhard** (21:25; 1728) and *Flavius Bertaridus** (21:27; 1729). In 1730 she sang in Telemann's *Kapitänsmusik** and his cantata marking the bicentenary of the Augsburg Confession. One aria from *Emma und Eginhard* ('Ergrimmet nicht ihr holden Augen') published by Telemann in *Der getreue Music-Meister** notes that it was sung by Polon ('gesungen von Ma^{me} Polone'). Polon's employment at Arolsen may have helped Telemann establish a connection to the court, which he supplied with music from 1726 (including, in that year, the *Essercizii musici**). He also made several visits to Bad Pyrmont*, the court's summer residence, for the mineral water springs and baths. *JanPol, MaeMar.*

Portraits Although no paintings of Telemann have survived, there are five engraved portraits dating from his lifetime, and at least one of these was based on a painting. Perhaps the most frequently reproduced image of the composer in modern times is a 1750 mezzotint by Valentin Daniel Preißler (1717–65) after a lost painting by Ludwig Michael Schneider, part of a series of engravings of 'currently living' *Kapellmeister*. Here the seated Telemann wears an elegant, fur-trimmed cape and supports a book (possibly meant to represent the *Musikalischer Practicus*, a treatise he planned to write but never completed). The book rests upon ruled but otherwise blank music paper, and is next to an inkwell containing a quill pen – all of which portrays Telemann more as a man of letters than a composer. Below the portrait is a brief Latin biography of Telemann. An engraved portrait by Georg Lichtensteger (1700–81) had already been published in 1744 by Balthasar Schmid* in Nuremberg in conjunction with the *Musicalisches Lob Gottes** annual cantata cycle and a bilingual biography* of the composer. This engraving exists in two versions: in the first, Telemann's head

13. Engraved portraits of Telemann by Georg Lichtensteger (version 1 on left, version 2 on right), published c. 1744 by Balthasar Schmid in Nuremberg in connection with the *Musicalisches Lob Gottes* annual cantata cycle and a bilingual biography of the composer (version 1: Österreichische Nationalbibliothek, PORT_00015452_01; version 2: Stiftung Händel-Haus Halle (Saale)). Reproduced by permission.

faces the viewer and his eyes look sharply to the right, making for a slightly odd effect; in the second, the composer sports a different wig and his head points slightly to the right, with eyes directed toward the viewer. In both versions, the seated Telemann points to the first page of the opening cantata in the cycle. A rather crude copy of the second version of Lichtensteger's image was made by an anonymous engraver for the Correspondierende Societät der musikalischen Wissenschaften, founded by Lorenz Christoph Mizler*. Finally, an anonymous engraved portrait of the elderly Telemann was published in the eleventh volume of the *Bibliothek der schönen Wissenschaften und der freyen Künste* (Leipzig, 1764). *HobDru, MenBil, ZohMix.*

Printz, Wolfgang Caspar Telemann's senior colleague at the court of Count Balthasar Erdmann von Promnitz at Sorau (now Żary), Printz (1641–1717) became the count's *Capell-Director* in 1682. Between 1705 and 1708 the two musicians engaged in apparently heated discussions about melody, the same topic that Telemann had earlier explored with his friend George Frideric Handel*. In AB 1740 Telemann recalled that in these exchanges he took on the role of Democritus (the 'laughing philosopher') and Printz that of Heraclitus (the 'weeping philosopher'), as the older composer 'wailed bitterly about the melodic excesses of contemporary composers, while I laughed at the unmelodic artificiality of the old composers'. Telemann also noted that Printz hoped his younger colleague 'would be the first to depart Babel', that is, Sorau. *ZohRef.*

Programme music *See* **Overture-suite**

Publishing Telemann's pioneering activities as a publisher of his own music have scarcely any historical counterparts. In Frankfurt between 1715 and 1718 he published four collections of his sonatas and suites (the *Six sonates à violon seul**, *Die Kleine Cammer-Music**, *Six trio* and *Sei suonatine per violino e cembalo*) plus the *Six concerts à violon concertant* by Johann Ernst, Prince of Sachsen-Weimar*. Telemann hired others to typeset or engrave these publications. In Hamburg (including his Paris* trip) Telemann brought out forty-two entirely new publications containing his own music during the period 1725–39, in addition to three second editions; ten more publications were issued by other publishers between 1727 and 1765. These ranged from sets of fantasias* a mere dozen pages long, to a hundred-page music journal (*Der getreue Music-Meister**), to four complete annual cycles of seventy-two church cantatas apiece. Such a level of productivity and diversity of offerings was unmatched by the publications of any other German composer from the time. For his first Hamburg publications, including the *Harmonischer Gottes-Dienst** and *Sonates sans basse*, Telemann hired printers to typeset the music. But starting in late 1726, with the *Essercizii musici**, he engraved the music himself, using hammer-driven punches on copper and then pewter plates, in emulation of London music publishers. In a letter to Johann Friedrich Armand von Uffenbach* from November 1731, Telemann reported on the production of his cantata cycle *Fortsetzung des Harmonischen Gottes-Dienstes** that 'I am prepared to work on the music with extraordinary diligence; with regard to the beauty of the notation, one will scarcely believe that my hammered cripple-work could turn out so well.' The composer's engraving skills, while not quite expert, produced serviceable results and improved noticeably over the years. Telemann also undertook to market and distribute his publications through printed catalogues, single-sheet notices, press advertisements, personal correspondence and, most impressively, an extensive network of booksellers and musicians who collected subscriptions and sold copies on commission. At least fifteen of Telemann's publications were financed by subscribers (*Pränumeranten*) who paid a discounted advance rate. In two cases, the *Musique de table** (Hamburg, 1733) and the *Nouveaux quatuors** (Paris, 1738), he published the subscribers' names – something unheard of in Germany at the time.

In addition to music by fourteen composers in *Der getreue Music-Meister*, Telemann also published music and writings by others starting in the late 1730s: Christoph Förster's* Op. 1 violin duets (1737), Johann Graf's* Op. 3 violin sonatas (1737), Carl Johann Friedrich Haltmeier's* treatise on transposition (1737), the *Beschreibung einer Augen-Orgel** (1739), the *Musikalische Probe eines Concerts vors Clavier* (1741) by his student* Johann Hövet and two theoretical writings by Georg Andreas Sorge* (1744 and 1754). He also edited and wrote a preface to the second edition of David Kellner's popular continuo treatise *Treulicher Unterricht im General-Bass* (1737).

One sore point involving Telemann's Hamburg publishing activities concerned the printing of librettos for his annual liturgical Passions. The city printer Conrad Neumann had established his right to do so when, in 1722, Telemann's hiring of another printer set in motion an extended dispute between the two (with the city council initially ruling in the composer's favour). Neumann's successor, Conrad König, arranged to pay Telemann for the right to publish the 1724 Passion libretto, but when the composer promised the 1725 libretto to another printer, König successfully reclaimed the right to print Passion librettos by paying Telemann a fee. This arrangement periodically led to further disagreements in succeeding years, and in 1757 Telemann informed the city council that thirty-five years of conflict had left a bad taste in his mouth.

On 14 October 1740 Telemann announced that he was selling the engraved plates to his publications, which were to be purchased as a unit or divided into no more than two groups. Who claimed the plates is unknown, though they may have come into the possession of the Leipzig firm of Johann Gottlob Immanuel Breitkopf*, which sold a number of Telemann's publications in later years. The composer did not give up publishing his music, however, and instead turned to Balthasar Schmid* in Nuremberg to issue several collections of instrumental and vocal music during the 1740s. He also worked with several other publishers on single projects. As late as 1759, Telemann was in touch with Breitkopf about the possibility of issuing further publications, though these never appeared. *BönPub, BruAro, CloRat, FavNet, HobHer, HobVer, PohUrh, ReiVer, RuhPar, RuhVer, SatEss, SatNot, TayCan, ZohMar, ZohMix.*

Pupils *See* **Students**

Quadri Telemann's first publication of quartets (Hamburg, 1730) was dedicated to Joachim Erasmus von Moldenit* and is popularly regarded as the first half of the 'Paris' quartets because of its unauthorised reprinting in Paris* by Charles-Nicolas Le Clerc* (1736). The six quartets are scored for flute, violin, viola da gamba or cello (two separate parts, with the latter instrument apparently preferred by the composer) and continuo, a configuration that Telemann returned to for his *Nouveaux quatuors en six suites** (Paris, 1738; the other half of the 'Paris' quartets). In an embodiment of the German mixed taste*, these works juxtapose two three-movement 'concertos' (*Sonaten auf Concertenart**), two four-movement 'sonatas' (with fugues) and two 'balletti' (suites with preludes). The music displays Telemann's virtuosity in manipulating musical texture and instrumental colour. His mixed taste here encompasses not only the sonata, Italian concerto and French suite, but also elements as diverse as the capriccio*, operatic aria and polonaise. The *Quadri* have been published in volume 18 (1965) of the Telemann selective critical edition*. *GiuGre, ZohMix.*

Quantz, Johann Joachim Following studies with Jan Dismas Zelenka*, Quantz (1697–1773) joined the *Polnische Kapelle* of Friedrich August II, King of Poland, as an oboist in 1718. Later, as a member of the Dresden* electoral *Hofkapelle,* he studied composition with Johann Georg Pisendel* and flute with Pierre Gabriel Buffardin, switching permanently to that instrument in 1725 and leaving Dresden in 1741 to join the Potsdam *Hofkapelle* of Friedrich II, King of Prussia (Frederick the Great)*. To judge from his correspondence with Carl Heinrich Graun*, Telemann was in touch with Quantz ('whom I highly esteem') before 1751. In 1752 Telemann served as a publishing agent for Quantz's *Versuch einer Anweisung die Flöte traversiere zu spielen,* in which the author praises Telemann's trios in the French style, six unpublished quartets and overture-suites. In a lost letter* from the same year, Telemann asked Quantz why he had singled out these particular works, and Quantz provided explanations in his response of January 1753. Quantz had long been acquainted with Telemann's music, playing the composer's violin solos as a student in Merseburg (1708–13), copying out further instrumental works while at Dresden and subscribing to the *Musique de table**. He also appears to have used many of Telemann's flute duets* and trios in his teaching; the former works clearly inspired Quantz's own *Sei duetti a due flauti traversi* (1759). During a 1758 dispute with Joachim Erasmus von Moldenit*, Quantz challenged the dilettante flautist to play Telemann's fantasias for unaccompanied flute in a competition with one of Quantz's students. Whether Telemann ever composed music specifically for Quantz is unknown, but there are reasons to suppose that his *Sei duetti* for two flutes (TWV 40:130–35) were written for Quantz and Frederick the Great during the 1740s or 1750s. *AllQua, ReiQua, RuhQua, TelBri, ZohQua, ZohMix.*

Quatrième livre de quatuors This collection of six quartets for flute, violin, viola and continuo is the second of two unauthorised first editions of Telemann's music to appear in Paris* (the first was the *Six sonates en trio dans le goust italien* of 1731–33). Published by Charles-Nicholas Le Clerc* between 1752 and 1760, the quartets are sometimes clumsy arrangements (presumably not by the composer) of works originally written for two violins, viola and continuo and dating from much earlier in Telemann's career, probably before 1715. The quartets are in a purely Italianate idiom, with fast movements either fugal or in ritornello form, and slow movements often in a 'vocal' mode that encompasses accompanied recitative, arioso and the *stile antico. ZohMix.*

Rameau, Jean-Philippe Although there is no evidence that Telemann and Rameau ever met, it is probable that the two came into contact during Telemann's 1737–38 visit to Paris*. Telemann may well have attended the premiere of Rameau's third opera, the *tragédie en musique Castor et Pollux*, at the Académie Royale de Musique on 24 October 1737, and he discussed excerpts from the opera in his correspondence with Carl Heinrich Graun* about the merits of French recitative. The theme-and-variations movement concluding Telemann's Quartet in A minor, TWV 43:a2 (from the *Nouveaux quatuors en six suites**, published in Paris in 1738), is based upon the theme of the A-minor 'Gavotte et doubles' from Rameau's *Nouvelles suites de pièces de clavecin* (1729 or 1730), and may therefore be considered an homage to the French composer. *KliCas, RosRec, ZohMix.*

Ramler, Karl Wilhelm Following university studies in Halle with Christian Wolff, Ramler (1725–98) relocated to Berlin in 1745, settling into the city's rich literary and artistic life and teaching at the Kadettenschule. He provided librettos to several of Telemann's late passion oratorios and cantatas, including *Der Tod Jesu** (TVWV 5:6, 1755), *Die Hirten bei der Krippe zu Bethlehem** (TVWV 1:797, 1759), *Die Auferstehung und Himmelfahrt Jesu** (TVWV 6:6, 1760), *Der May** (TVWV 20:40, 1760?) and *Ino** (TVWV 20:41, c. 1765). With Christian Gottfried Krause* he edited the first volume of the *Oden mit Melodien* (Berlin, 1753), which included three of Telemann's songs* (TVWV 25:110–12). In the same year, he wrote to Johann Wilhelm Ludwig Gleim that he expected the third volume of the *Oden mit Melodien* would include songs from Telemann's *Vier und zwanzig Oden. CzoGra, FleMay, HobRam.*

Reception of Telemann's music If Telemann's music was almost universally admired during his lifetime in German-speaking lands, and indeed across much of central, western and northern Europe, his posthumous reception was rather more complicated. Between the 1760s and 1790s a number of vocal and instrumental works could be purchased in such cities as Paris, Leipzig (from the firm of Johann Gottlob Immanuel Breitkopf*) and Hamburg (from Johann Christoph Westphal*). In Berlin, where older music was especially appreciated, Telemann's flute duets and quartets were heard at least until the turn of the nineteenth century. Many of the church cantatas were still being performed in Frankfurt as late as the 1770s, and the *Seliges Erwägen**, along with some of the late concert works from the 1750s and 1760s, were presented in Hamburg by Telemann's successors Carl Philipp Emanuel Bach* and Christian Friedrich Gottlob Schwenke through the end of the century. The composer's grandson, Georg Michael Telemann*, performed various sacred vocal pieces in Riga into the 1820s. Many critical assessments of Telemann's music published between the 1760s and the 1780s are laudatory, and in 1799 the *Allgemeine Musikalische Zeitung* published an engraving of a sun in which the most important German composers of the past century are represented as rays, with Telemann featured as one of the leading lights (as it were). Several anecdotes published between 1776 and 1830 portray him as a witty, magically productive and masterful composer, and this was probably how much of the musical public thought of him during this period and beyond. Telemann was hardly forgotten in the decades following his death, and he was generally remembered fondly.

Yet the seeds for a more negative view, one that came to dominate Telemann's posthumous reception during the later nineteenth and twentieth centuries, had already been planted in 1770. In that year the Hamburg teacher and writer Christoph Daniel Ebeling* discussed the composer's vocal works in his 'Versuch einer auserlesenen musikalischen Bibliothek' (Essay on a choice musical library), criticising some of the older, unfashionable texts and what he saw as an excessive use of musical word-painting – common complaints directed at this time toward older composers, including Johann Sebastian Bach*. Ebeling's estimation of Telemann's music was generally positive, but he also remarked of the composer's legendary productivity that 'polygraphs seldom produce masterpieces'. This last criticism, echoed by Johann Friedrich Reichardt in 1782, reflects a shifting view of composers as artisans who effectively and efficiently fulfil their professional obligations, to composers as original geniuses who produce universally admired masterpieces. Telemann may have performed his duties as well as anyone of his generation, but he was now being judged according to different, proto-romantic criteria. Ebeling's criticisms were repeated by Ernst Ludwig Gerber in a dictionary article (*Historisch-Biographisches Lexicon der Tonkünstler*, 1792) that was to prove highly influential on nineteenth-century lexicographic accounts of Telemann. In a parallel example of how the composer's virtue became a liability, Sir John Hawkins quoted Handel as having once said that Telemann 'could write a church piece of eight parts with the same expedition as another would write a letter' (*A General History of the Science and Practice of Music*, 1776). This observation was no doubt meant by Hawkins to demonstrate Telemann's 'uncommon skill and readiness', but it eventually came to be seen as a mark of shallowness.

As admiration for the music of Johann Sebastian Bach grew during the nineteenth century, some scholars addressed the Telemann 'problem' – of his having been more successful than Bach – by branding him as insufficiently serious, rigorous and profound (qualities typically ascribed to Bach), and having earned his success the easy way, by 'selling out' or appealing to the lowest common denominator. Such pronouncements were as a rule made without much first-hand knowledge of Telemann's music. Philipp Spitta's ill-informed and error-filled comparison of cantatas by Bach and Telemann (*Johann Sebastian Bach*, 1873–80) had a particularly damaging and long-lasting effect on Telemann's reputation, as did Alfred Maczewski's dismissive dictionary article on the composer (Sir George Grove, *A Dictionary of Music and Musicians*, 1890), which was superseded only in 1980. Typical of late nineteenth-century estimations of Telemann is the following passage from Hugo Riemann's *Musik-Lexicon* of 1882 (as translated by John South Shedlock in 1893): '[Telemann] was the prototype of a German composer making a business of his profession, i.e. he wrote down his works with astonishing rapidity, just as he wanted them, just as they were wanted. His style was flowing and correct, and he was a master of counterpoint; but he lacked the purity, the depth, and the thoroughness of Bach.' Underpinning such writings is the master narrative of Bach as the isolated genius, misunderstood and undervalued during his lifetime in comparison to Telemann, who achieved greater, yet largely undeserved, fame. Modern scholarship had finally put things right.

Except that this narrative gradually changed once Telemann's music became better known in the course of the twentieth century. This was facilitated at first through the appearance of practical and critical editions, none more significant than Max Schneider's* 1907 volume containing *Der Tag des Gerichts** and *Ino**. Schneider included an extended biographical preface that almost single-handedly initiated the field of modern Telemann studies, and the composer's image was similarly transformed for a more general readership by Romain Rolland's 1919 essay on him as a 'forgotten master' (the French original was soon translated into German and English). By World War II, performances and recordings had established Telemann's instrumental music – particularly the sonatas – as a pillar of the baroque music revival. Interest in Telemann had grown so much by the 1940s, in fact, that a selective critical edition* of his works was launched, with the first volume appearing in 1950. Yet in that same year, Theodor Adorno could quip, with reference to the nascent Early Music movement's efforts to place Bach within the context of his contemporaries, 'They say Bach, mean Telemann.' The Telemann revival had not yet met with universal approbation, though by this time the question was not whether the composer merited rediscovery, but whether he should be considered a 'great' master. Even if this question no longer seems urgent, Telemann remains to some extent a polarising figure. The issue has largely been one of accessibility, for as the composer's music has steadily become better known, opinions of him have risen in equal measure. *FavNet, FinAng, FleUrt, HirHör, KleDok, KleSch, KocRez, KreRol, PisFra, ReiEbe, ReiMag, ReiTag, RuhBil, RuhFin, ZohIma, ZohRec.*

Recorder Telemann composed some of the most significant recorder music of the eighteenth century. The treble (alto) size of the instrument appears frequently in his vocal and instrumental works through the early 1730s, starting with some of the sacred concertos he wrote in Hildesheim and Leipzig (c. 1697–1705). Among Telemann's early publications, the *Six Trio* (1718) includes one trio with recorder, and the *Essercizii musici** (1726) includes two solos and four trios with the instrument, including one trio for recorder and obbligato harpsichord. Two more solos (TWV 41:C2 and F2) are included in *Der getreue Music-Meister** (1728–29), and a third (41:f1) may be played on recorder or bassoon. Some fine obbligato recorder parts appear in Telemann's first published cycle of church cantatas, the *Harmonischer Gottes-Dienst** (1725–27). Although he gradually stopped publishing recorder music in the 1730s, the *Musique de table** (1733) includes a quartet with recorder and two flutes. Significant works for the instrument are also found among the music Telemann left unpublished, including nine trios (TWV 42:c7, F5–9, F15, g9 and a6), three quartets (TWV 43:G6, a3 and g4) and a quintet (TWV 44:15). Particularly inspired are a series of concertos. In addition to two solo concertos (TWV 52:a2 and B1) and a solo concerto-suite (TWV 43:g3), there are double concertos for two recorders (TWV 52:a2 and B1) and for a recorder paired with flute (52:e1), bassoon (52:F1) and viola da gamba (52:a1). There are also two 'group' concertos involving one or two recorders (TWV 54:F1 and B2). But Telemann's best known work for the instrument is probably the brilliant overture-suite* in A minor for recorder and strings (TWV 55:a2), which is often played on the modern flute. This suite, like some of his other recorder music, may have been intended for the Darmstadt virtuoso Johann Michael Böhm*. *ZohMix.*

Reipsch, Brit Following musicological studies at the Martin-Luther-Universität Halle-Wittenberg, Reipsch joined the research staff of the Zentrum für Telemann-Pflege und -Forschung* in Magdeburg in 1989. She subsequently earned her PhD at Martin-Luther-Universität with a dissertation on Telemann's *Sicilianischer Jahrgang**. In 2011 she became a member of the Editorial Advisory Board of the Telemann selective critical edition*, to which she has contributed three volumes. She has also edited a critical edition of *Die Tageszeiten** for Carus, in addition to multiple volumes of the Magdeburger Telemann-Studien series and conference proceedings deriving from the Telemann-Festtage. Much of her research on Telemann has centred on the vocal works, especially the operas, sacred cantatas and motets, and on reception history. *ReiAma, ReiAnn, ReiCan, ReiDan, ReiDie, ReiEbe, ReiHel, ReiJah, ReiLin, ReiLob, ReiMir, ReiMot, ReiSic, ReiTag, ReiVer.*

Reipsch, Ralph-Jürgen Reipsch studied musicology at the Martin-Luther-Universität Halle-Wittenberg before taking a position at the Kultur- und Forschungsstätte Kloster Michaelstein bei Blankenburg/Harz in 1984. He joined the staff of Magdeburg's Zentrum für Telemann-Pflege und -Forschung* in 1986, and since 1992 has directed its library and archive. He is also editor of the centre's online Telemann bibliography*. In 1998 he curated the Magdeburg exhibition 'Telemann und Frankreich – Frankreich und Telemann' (also editing a published exhibition catalogue), and from 2014 he has conceived and directed the biennial Telemann-Festtage*. His research on Telemann has focused on sacred vocal works, musical source and documentary studies (including some significant discoveries), the composer's pastime of gardening* and reception history. He has also edited unpublished vocal works by Telemann, conference proceedings of the Telemann-Festtage and four volumes of vocal works for the Telemann selective critical edition*. *ReiAuf, ReiBea, ReiBeo, ReiBio, ReiBlu, ReiDok, ReiGed, ReiKlo, ReiMol, ReiOde, ReiPar, ReiPas, ReiRec, ReiMes, ReiRez, ReiSer, ReiSin, ReiSpä, ReiUff, ReiUnb, ReiZus.*

Richey, Michael As a professor of history and Greek at Hamburg's Johanneum school, Richey (1678–1761) was a professional colleague of Telemann. He was also a founder of the city's 'Teutsch-übende Gesellschaft' and 'Patriotische Gesellschaft', editing the latter society's moral weekly *Der Patriot*. One of Telemann's most important librettists, Richey provided the composer with texts for a number of occasional works, including wedding music (TVWV 11:3, 5–10, 12–14 and 17–18), the *Admiralitätsmusik** serenata *Unschätzbarer Vorwurf erkenntlicher Sinnen* (TVWV 24:1, 1724) and funeral music* for Hamburg mayors (TVWV 4:8 and 11; 11:15). Telemann also set five of his texts in his first collection of songs*, the *Singe-, Spiel- und Generalbass-Übungen. MenRic, RatRic.*

Riemschneider, Johann Gottfried Riemschneider (1691–1752 or later) studied law at the University of Halle from 1712, and according to AB 1718 performed as a baritone in Leipzig with the Collegium musicum founded by Telemann. He performed in Hamburg's cathedral under Johann Mattheson* in 1717, and then regularly in the city's churches and Opera from 1719 to 1739; he appears in rosters of Telemann's performances between 1725 and 1739. Riemschneider sang as a guest at the Cöthen court under Johann Sebastian Bach* in 1718, and sang operas for George Frideric Handel* in London in 1729–30. He became cantor of the cathedral in Bremen in 1739, but returned to Hamburg later that year to succeed Reinhard Keiser* as cantor of the cathedral. He left Hamburg for good in 1741 to become a court singer in Copenhagen, before holding similar positions in Braunschweig and Strelitz. In 1731 Telemann stood godfather to Riemschneider's son Georg Matthias, and in 1733 the singer subscribed to the *Musique de table**. *NeuKir.*

Roman, Johan Helmich Roman (1694–1758) was *Kapellmeister* to the Swedish royal court in Stockholm from 1727, after holding various other court positions. In 1726–27 Telemann was the Hamburg publishing agent for Roman's *12 Sonate a flauto traverso, violone e cembalo* (Stockholm, 1727), the only set of works Roman ever published. In 1728 and 1734 Roman purchased Telemann's published cantata cycles *Harmonischer Gottes-Dienst** and *Fortsetzung des Harmonischen Gottes-Dienstes** for the Swedish court, and in 1738 he subscribed to the *Nouveaux quatuors en six suites**. *HelRom, HobMis, RatRom.*

Romanus, Franz Conrad As mayor of Leipzig from 1701 to 1705, Romanus (1671–1746) commissioned Telemann, then a newly enrolled law student at the university, to provide music for the city's two main churches (the Thomaskirche and Nikolaikirche) every two weeks, even though Johann Kuhnau* had recently been installed as Thomaskantor. Romanus noted in 1704 that Telemann was 'one of the best composers' and 'capable of directing the choirs' in the two main churches. The work by Telemann that inspired this commission was a setting of Psalm 6 discovered by the composer's roommate (according to AB 1718 and AB 1740), perhaps *Ach Herr, strafe mich nicht in deinem Zorn*, TVWV 7:3 (another setting of the psalm with the same title, TVWV 7:1, may have been composed later during the Leipzig years). Romanus' daughter, Christiane Mariane von Ziegler*, would later become German poet laureate and provide Telemann with the libretto to a secular cantata. *GlöKuh.*

Ruhnke, Martin Following doctoral studies at the Christian-Albrechts-Universität in Kiel and a position at the Freie Universität Berlin, Ruhnke (1921–2004) taught at the Friedrich-Alexander-Universität Erlangen-Nürnberg from 1964 until his retirement in 1986. From 1960 to 2003 he served as General Editor of the Telemann selective critical edition* (from 1992 with Wolf Hobohm*), also contributing a volume of instrumental works and, as a supplement to the edition, a three-volume thematic catalogue* of Telemann's instrumental music. He also served as president of the Internationale Telemann-Gesellschaft (1991–97). A tireless and eloquent promoter of Telemann's music, Ruhnke's wide-ranging research on the composer addressed the composer's operas, passions, instrumental works and publishing practices. His articles on Telemann in *Die Musik in Geschichte und Gegenwart* (1966) and *The New Grove Dictionary of Music and Musicians* (1980) superseded outdated and misleading lexicographical articles while introducing the fruits of modern Telemann research to a broad audience. *RuhDon, RuhFug, RuhKom, RuhOpe, RuhPar, RuhPas, RuhQua, RuhSel, RuhUmt, RuhVer, TWV.*

Die Satyren in Arcadien *See* ***Der neu-modische Liebhaber Damon***

Scheibe, Johann Adolph A composer, keyboardist and writer, Scheibe (1708–76) studied law at Leipzig University before breaking off his studies to pursue a career in music. He unsuccessfully applied for organ positions in Leipzig, Prague and several other cities in 1729–36. While resident in Hamburg between 1736 and 1740, Scheibe composed large quantities of music (mostly lost) and wrote the important, serially published treatise *Der critische Musikus* (1737–40; revised in 1745 as *Critischer Musikus*), in which he regarded Telemann's music in a variety of instrumental and vocal genres as paradigmatic. He later noted that Telemann had seen the first fifteen issues of *Der critische Musikus* before leaving for Paris* in September 1737, and that the older composer had encouraged him to undertake, develop and publish the periodical. During Telemann's trip, Scheibe assumed some of his colleague's official duties, including the composition of church cantatas (at least one of these survives: *So ofte Jesus großer Name*, TVWV 1:1377, for the nineteenth Sunday after Trinity). Scheibe subsequently served as *Kapellmeister* to the Danish court in Copenhagen during two periods (1740–47 and after 1766) separated by various musical and literary activities in Sønderborg. In 1741 Telemann addressed a satirical letter of dedication to Scheibe in his second published collection of songs*, the *Vier und zwanzig, theils ernsthafte, theils scherzende, Oden*. Two extant letters* from Scheibe to Telemann in 1750 and 1757 are newsy and friendly in tone. *ReiZus, ZohMix.*

Scherzi melodichi *See* **Bad Pyrmont**

Schiebeler, Daniel Schiebeler (1741–71) was a student at Hamburg's Johanneum under Telemann. Following studies at the University of Göttingen he spent time in Leipzig and Dresden before returning to Hamburg and assuming a canonry at the cathedral. In 1759 Schiebeler provided Telemann with a libretto to the sacred ode *Er kam, lobsingt ihm, meine Lieder*, TVWV 1:462. He may also have provided the libretto for Telemann's *Kapitänsmusik** oratorio of that year, *Herr, unser Gott, von deiner Huld durchdrungen*, TVWV 15:22a. In 1761 Telemann arranged Schiebeler's libretto *Basilio und Quiteria* as the serenata *Don Quichotte auf der Hochzeit des Comacho**. The poet and former Telemann student Johann Joachim Eschenburg recalled in 1773 that Schiebeler had been on friendly terms with the composer, 'whose lively wit and jovial spirit, along with his art, remained faithful to him into extreme old age'. *BasDon, JahDon, ReiOde.*

Schieferlein, Otto Ernst Gregorius Schieferlein (1704–87) was active in Hamburg as a falsettist in church and at the Opera from 1732, if not earlier. By 1741 and until about 1780 he also served as a music copyist for Telemann and his successor, Carl Philipp Emanuel Bach*. Schieferlein is known in the Telemann literature as Hamburg Copyist A, and his hand appears in nearly 150 manuscript sources* for the composer's music now preserved at the Music Department and Mendelssohn Archive of the Staatsbibliothek zu Berlin – Preußischer Kulturbesitz. *JaeAut, NeuKir.*

Schmid, Balthasar Based in Nuremberg, Schmid (1705–49) was Telemann's publisher of choice after the composer ended his own publishing* business in 1740. Between 1742 and 1744 Schmid issued the *Musicalisches Lob Gottes** annual cycle of church cantatas along with an engraved portrait* and a biography* of the composer in French and German. These were followed by the *VI Ouverturen nebst zween Folgesätzen* (1745) and the 1745 St John Passion, *Ein Lämmlein geht und trägt die Schuld*, TVWV 5:30* (1747). *HobDru, ZohMix.*

Schneider, Max Schneider (1875–1967) studied musicology at Leipzig University prior to becoming choir director and *Kapellmeister* at the Stadttheater in Halle. He earned his doctorate from Berlin University (1917) while working in the Royal Library, and held teaching positions at the universities in Breslau (1915–28) and Halle (1928–60). His edition of Telemann's *Der Tag des Gerichts** and *Ino** in volume 28 (1907) of the Denkmäler deutscher Tonkunst series includes a lengthy biography* that set a new standard for Telemann scholarship – so much so, in fact, that the modern Telemann 'renaissance' is often said to have begun with this edition. *SchDen.*

Schubart-Jahrgang Telemann turned to Tobias Heinrich Schubart (1699–1747), preacher at Hamburg's Michaeliskirche from 1728, for the texts to his 1731–32 cycle of church cantatas. The cycle may have been performed the following year in Frankfurt, where it was in any case heard in 1741–42 under Johann Balthasar König*; extant musical sources for the cycle all stem from these later Frankfurt performances. Schubart's librettos are in fact oratorios in eighteenth-century parlance: allegorical characters sing arias and recitatives, and biblical characters sing Bible verses. The cycle was therefore Telemann's second 'oratorio' cycle in as many years, following the *Oratorischer Jahrgang** of 1730–31. The oratorios contain eight to ten movements mixing biblical verses (dicta), arias and recitatives with a concluding chorale. Arias frequently take the form of duets, and less often trios and quartets. Concurrently with the Hamburg performances, Telemann published excerpts of each oratorio – two arias surrounding a recitative arranged for voice, two obbligato instruments and continuo – as the *Fortsetzung des Harmonischen Gottes-Dienstes*, a sequel to the earlier *Harmonischer Gottes-Dienst** cycle. In suppressing the names of allegorical and biblical characters, along with the dicta and chorales, Telemann thereby turned his oratorios into cantatas. Like the *Harmonischer Gottes-Dienst* and *Auszug derjenigen musicalischen und auf die gewöhnlichen Evangelien gerichteten Arien* (drawn from the *Harmonisches Lob Gottes**), the *Fortsetzung* begins with the cantata for New Year's Day. But unlike these two earlier published cycles, the *Fortsetzung* was engraved rather than typeset and issued in parts (one for voice with continuo and two for the obbligato instruments). By including instrumental cues, the vocal-continuo part allows the cantatas to be performed by just one or two musicians. Most of the cantatas are for high or medium voice, but Telemann also included seven works specifically for bass voice. In addition to pairs of violins, flutes, oboes or recorders, some scorings call for dissimilar instruments and involve several instruments not called for in the *Harmonischer Gottes-Dienst*, such as violetta, cello, bassoon, trumpet and horn. Telemann's orchestrations for the cantatas' *Schubart-Jahrgang* versions, as performed in Frankfurt, are adapted in the *Fortsetzung* through 'solo' and 'tutti' indications in ritornellos. The *Schubart-Jahrgang* cantatas for the eighth through nineteenth Sundays after Trinity have been published in volume 59 (2014) of the Telemann selective critical edition*, and the entire *Fortsetzung* has been published by PRB Productions (1996–2006). *PoeFor, PoeOrd, SwaJud, TayCan.*

14. First page of the vocal-continuo part to *Der mit Sünden beleidigte Heiland*, TVWV 1:306, for New Year's Day 1732 (part of the *Schubart-Jahrgang*), published in the *Fortsetzung des Harmonischen Gottes-Dienstes* (Hamburg, 1731–32; Copenhagen, Royal Danish Library, mu 6510.0535, U260). Reproduced by permission.

Sechs Cantaten Scored for solo voice and strings with occasional obbligato wind instrument, this published set of secular cantatas* (Hamburg, 1731; TVWV 20:17–22) set librettos by several named poets (Johann Ulrich von König*, Achilles Augustus von Lersner, Johann Philipp Praetorius* and Johann Georg Hamann*) along with an unnamed one (possibly Telemann). The composer advertised these works as 'cantates galantes', noting that each of them and 'nearly every aria expresses a particular affect'. The heterogeneous nature of the librettos is reflected in the diverse origins of the music, for several arias in the collection borrow from or parody works composed by Telemann between 1724 and 1730. Although the cantatas are concerned with love (of a decidedly pastoral nature), they are also moralistic to varying degrees, thus anticipating the two sets of published *Moralische Cantaten**. The dance-like character of many arias reinforces the pastoral nature of the texts, as does the presence in three arias of obbligato parts for recorder, flute and oboe – the instruments most frequently used to evoke a shepherd's piping. It may have been this collection that deeply impressed the young Johann Friedrich Agricola* as a model for vocal writing; an extant manuscript copy of the cantatas is in his early hand. *ZohMor.*

Sei Duetti *See* **Duets**

Seiffert, Max After earning his doctorate in musicology at Berlin University in 1891, Seiffert (1868–1948) launched the series Denkmäler deutscher Tonkunst (DDT) in 1892. He taught in Berlin at the Hochschule für Musik, the Akademie für Kirchen and the Akademie der Künste, and founded and directed a musicology research institute based first in Bückeburg and then in Berlin. His work on Telemann includes the first modern editions of the *Singe-, Spiel- und Generalbass-Übungen** (1914), keyboard fantasias* (1923) and *Musique de table** (1927, DDT, vols. 61–62). During the 1940s he was one of the impulses behind establishing the Telemann selective critical edition*, and he edited its first volume (1950), containing the twelve methodical sonatas*.

***Seliges Erwägen des bittern Leidens und Sterbens Jesu Christi*, TVWV 5:2** Telemann's 'Blessed Contemplation of the Bitter Passion and Dying of Jesus Christ', with both text and music by the composer, was first performed in a Hamburg orangery on 9 March 1722. It was heard again ten days later during a benefit concert at which the printed libretto served as a ticket and proceeds were donated to the poor. It was the composer's second passion oratorio intended for the concert hall, following the *Brockes-Passion** of 1716, and would become his best known work during the eighteenth century; for decades it was performed not only in Hamburg's concert halls but also in the city's secondary churches (the principal churches were the site of liturgical passions). Telemann's successors Carl Philipp Emanuel Bach* and Christian Friedrich Gottlob Schwenke continued to perform the *Seliges Erwägen* until at least 1806, and the oratorio was also known in other parts of Germany: musical and textual sources document performances in Augsburg, Berlin, Brunswick, Frankfurt am Main, Göttingen, Leipzig and elsewhere. The oratorio's textual structure anticipates the 'lyric' oratorios of Telemann's last decade, in which there is little or no narrative. Thus there is no evangelist and the main 'roles' are given to Jesus (bass) and the allegorical character of Devotion (tenor), with a handful of numbers distributed among Peter (tenor), the high priest Caiphas (bass), Zion (soprano) and Faith (soprano). Divided into three parts (preparation, conviction and execution), the main events of Jesus' suffering and death are related through nine 'meditations' on the Last Supper, Peter's presumption, Jesus praying and sweating blood, Jesus accused and spat upon, Peter's penitence, the bloody Jesus, the crucifixion, Jesus dying and the burial. Each meditation is structured as a dramatic tableau containing two or three recitatives (some orchestrally accompanied) and as many arias, with a chorale usually placed at the end. Yet no two meditations offer the same sequence of movements, an attractive variety that is mirrored in the stylistic and affective diversity of the arias. The operatic quality of the arias and accompanied recitatives relates the oratorio to Telemann's opera *Sieg der Schönheit**, which premiered in Hamburg just a few months later. The two works, both set to the composer's librettos and very much of a piece musically, were among the most popular he wrote for Hamburg. The *Seliges Erwägen* has been published in volume 33 (2001) of the Telemann selected critical edition*. *RuhSel, RuhUmt, SieSel, SteSel.*

Sept fois sept et un menuet *See* **Keyboard music**

Serenata *See* ***Admiralitätsmusik*, Darmstadt, *Don Quichotte auf der Hochzeit des Comacho*, Funeral music, *Kapitänsmusik*, *Pastorelle en Musique oder Musikalisches Hirtenspiel*** and ***Tafelmusik***

Sicilianischer Jahrgang This annual cycle of church cantatas to librettos by Johann Friedrich Helbig* (and thus sometimes referred to as the first *Helbig-Jahrgang*) was first performed in Eisenach* by 1719–20. Telemann set at least sixty-nine of the seventy-two librettos, and nearly all of these are extant. Forty-five of the cantatas were performed by him in Hamburg, mainly following the sermon, in 1722–23 (selected pieces had already been performed there in 1721–22). The cycle was heard at the Roßla court by 1723–24 and in Frankfurt in 1727–28, and Johann Friedrich Fasch* performed it no fewer than seven times at the Zerbst court between 1723–24 and 1749–50. Its eighteenth-century nickname apparently derives from the consistently 'pastoral' use of two obbligato oboes (sometimes recorders), often playing in parallel thirds, and from the frequency of elements associated with the siciliana dance (compound duple meter, tuneful melodies and dotted rhythms). The cantatas are all in the five-movement sequence of dictum (biblical verse set as a chorus)–aria–recitative–aria–chorale. Twelve works for the seventh Sunday after Trinity through the Feast of St Michael have been published in volume 52 (2018) of the Telemann selective critical edition*. *JunKan, ReiAnn, ReiJah, ReiSic.*

***Sieg der Schönheit*, TVWV 21:10** 'The Triumph of Beauty' was the first opera Telemann wrote for the Hamburg Opera after moving to the city in 1721. At the time of its premiere, on 13 July 1722, he may already have assumed the directorship of the opera company. Further Hamburg performances of *Sieg der Schönheit* are documented for 1722–25, 1727–28 and 1734–35. Telemann's libretto is based on *Der Grosse König der Africanischen Wenden Gensericus, als Rom- und Carthagens Ueberwinder* by Christian Heinrich Postel (1658–1705), set to music for Hamburg in 1693 by Johann Georg Conradi (and apparently set anew at a later date by Johann Sigismund Kusser). The story is based on Roman history: in 455 CE Gaiseric (also Genseric), king of the Vandals, captured and plundered Rome before taking the empress Licinia Eudoxia and her daughters Eudocia and Placidia to Carthage, where Eudocia married Gaiseric's son Huneric. In keeping with Hamburg tradition, the comic character of Turpino is inserted into a plot involving four pairs of characters. Telemann made significant changes to Postel's libretto, expanding or contracting recitatives, modifying or replacing strophic arias in order to create modern da capo forms, consolidating scenes and adding new ones featuring choruses and ballets. A slightly abridged version of the opera (with newly composed recitatives, most likely by Georg Caspar Schürmann) was performed in Brunswick at the Hagemarkt Theatre in 1725, 1728 and 1732. It is this version, which used Postel's original title, that has survived in a score reflecting the 1728 performance; the Hamburg version of the opera is represented only by printed librettos and a manuscript copy of twenty-one arias. The close connection between the Hamburg and Brunswick companies is reflected in the 1722 cast, which featured several singers from Brunswick alongside those resident in Hamburg; among the latter were the bass Johann Gottfried Riemschneider*. Together, the numerous performances in Hamburg and Brunswick indicate that *Sieg der Schönheit* was, along with the intermezzo *Pimpinone**, Telemann's greatest operatic success – notwithstanding the criticism of Telemann's adaptation of Postel's libretto by Johann Mattheson*. The opera has been published in volume 42 (2009) of the Telemann selective critical edition*. *PoeSie, PoeStr.*

Simonis, Paul Gottfried The 'Gottfried Simonis' who provided Telemann with texts for an annual cycle of church cantatas known as the *Concerten-Jahrgang** was presumably Paul Gottfried Simonis (b. 1692), son of Paul Simonis (1656–1712), deacon and later senior pastor at St Johannis church in Groß-Salze. Paul Gottfried Simonis would have been a theology student at Martin-Luther-Universität Halle-Wittenberg when, in 1717, he provided librettos for the second half of Telemann's first *Concerten-Jahrgang* (Simonis' librettos were published, together with those provided by Erdmann Neumeister* for the first half of the cycle, as *Das Harmonische Zion*). Several years later (1720–21), Simonis provided new librettos for the first half of the cycle, which, when combined with his earlier librettos, became the second *Concerten-Jahrgang* (Simonis' complete librettos were now published as *Herrn Gottfried Simonis . . . neues Lied*). Cantata librettos (*Texte zur Music*) published in Hamburg in 1726 suggest that Telemann may have set another (lost) cantata cycle to texts by Simonis. *JunKan, PoeKir, SawSim.*

Sing-Akademie zu Berlin Founded by Carl Friedrich Christian Fasch in 1791, the Sing-Akademie zu Berlin is an amateur choral society. It was largely under Fasch's successor, Carl Friedrich Zelter, that the society assembled its archive of some five thousand musical sources from the eighteenth century. Following the allied victory in World War II, the archive – evacuated from Berlin for safekeeping – was discovered and claimed by the Russian Red Army. It ended up secreted in the Ukrainian State Library in Kiev, where it was rediscovered to great fanfare in 1999. Since 2001 it has been on deposit in the Music Department and Mendelssohn Archive of the Staatsbibliothek zu

Berlin – Preußischer Kulturbesitz. Among the archive's extensive Telemann holdings (including 242 vocal and ninety-four instrumental works, among which sixty-two works are preserved nowhere else) are thirty-seven works belonging to the *Oratorischer Jahrgang**, the funeral cantata *Du aber, Daniel, gehe hin**, the *Pastorelle en Musique oder Musikalisches Hirtenspiel** and a set of flute duets*. *HenSin, ReiDan, ReiQua, ReiSin, ReiUnb.*

Singe-, Spiel- und Generalbass-Übungen *See* **Songs**

Singende Geographie *See* **Songs**

Six concerts et six suites This collection of twelve trios (Hamburg, 1734) is a model of flexible scoring. As noted on the title page, the music can be performed in no fewer than five configurations: harpsichord and flute; harpsichord, flute and cello; violin, flute and cello; violin, flute and continuo; and harpsichord, violin, flute and cello. Thus the trios are some of the first with obbligato keyboard parts to appear in print, eight years after those in the *Essercizii musici**. The suites begin with a prelude and are comparable in style to the last two works of the *Quadri** (another mixed-genre collection representing the French and Italian idioms), whereas the 'concertos' contain some notable examples of the *Sonate auf Concertenart**. The *Six concerts et six suites* have been published in volumes 9 (1955) and 11 (1957) of the Telemann selective critical edition*. *ZohMix.*

Six Ouvertures à 4 ou 6 Telemann published this collection of six overture-suites* for strings (with optional horns in three of the works) by subscription in 1736. It was apparently the last published collection of overture-suites to appear anywhere in Europe. The only known copy of the print disappeared between the end of World War II and 2008, but two of the works had been published at the turn of the twentieth century and a third was known from an eighteenth-century manuscript copy; the other three works became available only with the print's recovery. The music suggests that one of Telemann's goals for the *Six Ouvertures* was to historicise the genre at a time when it was rapidly becoming unfashionable. Thus there is a stark contrast between movements referring, on the one hand, to the overture-suite's Lullian origins through theatrical titles or evocations of seventeenth-century style and, on the other, to the *galant* style of the 1730s. Telemann also sets up a tension between serious (urban-courtly) and humorous (pastoral-rustic) expression that is resolved in the concluding suite, which contains elements of both. Like many of his publications, the *Six Ouvertures* may also be seen as an encyclopaedic survey of movement types, in this case nearly all the stylised dances common to the genre. The collection was published by Ortus-Verlag soon after its recovery. *ZohAes.*

Six quatuors ou trios Unlike the other two quartet collections published by Telemann, the *Quadri** (1730) and *Nouveaux quatuors en six suites** (1738), the *Six quatuors ou trios* (1733) appear to have been calculated to appeal primarily to an amateur audience. Despite presenting two stylistic faces (learned/fugal in Nos. 1–3, and simple/diverting in Nos. 4–6, where concluding movements are entitled 'Divertimento'), the quartets as a whole are marked by uncomplicated textures, modest dimensions and an avoidance of the more expressive and challenging features of the *galant* style. Unusually, all six works may be played either as quartets or trios (the collection's full title reads: 'Six Quartets or Trios, for 2 transverse flutes or 2 violins, and for 2 cellos or 2 bassoons, the second of which can be left out entirely or played on the harpsichord'). This flexibility is facilitated by a first cello/bassoon part that both interacts with the treble instruments and provides a satisfying bass accompaniment; the optional, figured second cello/bassoon part is derived from the first part. Thus a trio performance will lack a chordal continuo accompaniment, and a quartet performance will feature both bass lines, with or without chordal accompaniment. The collection was reprinted by Charles-Nicholas Le Clerc* in Paris in 1746–48 and has been published in volume 25 (1981) of the Telemann selective critical edition*. *ZohMix.*

Six sonates à violon seul Telemann dedicated this set of solos for violin and continuo, his first-ever publication (Frankfurt, 1715), to the teenage Prince Johann Ernst of Sachsen-Weimar*, an ardent admirer of Italian music. The influence of the Op. 5 violin sonatas of Arcangelo Corelli*, and the sonatas of his Italian imitators, is reflected in Telemann's sonatas by the inclusion of both sonatas da chiesa and da camera (the latter following the traditional movement ordering of allemanda–corrente–sarabanda–giga), as well as the presence of florid Italianate ornaments (*passaggi*) in the collection's opening movement. The music mixes conservative and progressive elements, avoiding fugal movements (perhaps in deference to a target audience of amateurs) and including evocations of the aria and concerto (an early example of the *Sonate auf Concertenart**). Telemann's collection appears to have been popular, for it was not only reprinted by the composer (Hamburg, 1727–28), but also pirated by John Walsh as *Solos for a Violin . . . compos'd by Georgio Melande* (London, 1722). *SwaErn, SwaSol, SwaSon, SwaWal, ZohMix.*

Sonate auf Concertenart This term, coined by Johann Adolph Scheibe*, refers to a sonata composed 'in concerto style'. Although in practice the line between sonata and concerto may be difficult to discern (and Scheibe's definition is not as precise as one might wish), defining features in many works include the presence of ritornello form (generally not associated with the sonata) and 'display' figuration that marks one or more instruments as a soloist and the others as the 'orchestral' tutti. Once considered the exclusive domain of Johann Sebastian Bach* (as in the flute sonatas BWV 1030, 1032 and 1034; the violin sonata BWV 1016; and the viola da gamba sonata BWV 1029), the *Sonate auf Concertenart* was in fact cultivated by a number of German composers (as well as some French ones) during the first half of the eighteenth century. Echoes may also be found in later eighteenth-century repertories (for example, Mozart's K 452). Telemann was not only the most prolific composer of concerto-style sonatas, which appear with some frequency among his solos, trios and quartets, but he may well have invented the concept around 1710. Such generic amalgamations, also seen in the concerto-suite* and overture-suite* with soloistic writing, are characteristic of his mixed taste*. Telemann's sonatas *auf Concertenart*, like those of Bach, may involve sophisticated sleights of hand whereby the listener is not always sure who is 'soloing' and who is 'accompanying'; in many cases the instruments continuously switch roles, as is particularly common in Telemann's quartets. Closely related to the *Sonate auf Concertenart* is the *einstimmiges Concert* (also Scheibe's term), a concerto-like piece for a single instrument. If the most famous example is Bach's so-called Italian Concerto (BWV 971; singled out for praise by Scheibe), there are similar solo 'concerto' movements among Telemann's keyboard works and the fantasias* for unaccompanied violin and viola da gamba. *SchSon, SwaSon, TalViv, ZohSon, ZohMix.*

Sonate metodiche *See* **Methodical sonatas**

Sonates corellisantes *See* **Corelli, Arcangelo**

Sonates sans basse *See* **Duets**

Songs Among Telemann's most original and influential works are his published songs, which had a decisive effect on Berlin* composers of the younger generation, members of the so-called First Berlin Lieder School. What some have considered his earliest songs belong to a collection of thirty-six works for voice and continuo on geographical subjects known as the *Singende Geographie* (TVWV 25:1–36). This is the title of a geography textbook, including the song texts, that was published in 1708 by Johann Christoph Losius (1659–1733), rector of the Andreanum Gymnasium in Hildesheim while Telemann attended the school in 1697–1701. One extant copy of the book has manuscript copies of the anonymous song settings bound with the text, and because Telemann recalled in AB 1740 that at Hildesheim he made musical settings of the arias that were sung during Losius' annual school plays, it has been assumed – without any supporting evidence – that these arias included the songs of the *Singende Geographie.* In the book's introduction, Losius notes that the songs were sung by the Gymnasium students during a 'public play' on 30 October 1708, hence seven years after Telemann graduated from the school.

Telemann's other songs were all published between the 1730s and 1750s. Among their characteristics are idiomatic vocal writing (often with a restricted range to allow their performance by most voice types), avoidance of coloratura, close attention to text expression and declamation, and considerable rhythmic and harmonic interest. Telemann's first published collection, the 1733–34 *Singe-, Spiel- und Generalbass-Übungen* (Singing, playing and thoroughbass exercises; TVWV 25:39–85), is a landmark in the history of the eighteenth-century lied. It appears to have initiated interest in the genre among other composers after 1735, including Johann Friedrich Gräfe, Johann Valentin Görner, Conrad Friedrich Hurlebusch*, Lorenz Christoph Mizler* and Johann Sigismund Scholze (who published volumes of the *Singende Muse an der Pleiße* under the pseudonym Sperontes). Telemann's collection includes forty-eight songs of one or two stanzas that he excerpted from strophic poems by writers representing several generations, including Barthold Heinrich Brockes*, Friedrich von Hagdedorn*, Michael Richey*, Daniel Stoppe* and Joachim Johann Daniel Zimmermann*. About half of the song texts address moral topics, promoting a virtuous and sensible life. Each of the serially published songs (one issued per week) takes up a single sheet, and most are in binary form, though there are also through-composed, strophic and ternary (da capo) settings in addition to examples of arioso and recitative. The collection doubles as a continuo treatise, for Telemann provides realisations of the bass figures along with commentaries on them. The novelty of the enterprise is reflected in the title of the first song: 'Neues' (New).

Telemann's second set of songs, the 1741 *Vier und zwanzig, theils ernsthafte, theils scherzende, Oden, mit leichten und fast für alle Hälse bequehmen Melodien versehen* (Twenty-four serious and comic odes set to easy melodies suitable for nearly all throats; TVWV 25:86–109), was published in Hamburg by Christian Herold. It includes a satirical dedicatory letter to Johann Adolph Scheibe* in which Telemann attacks the pretence of those, like Mizler, who compose dismal odes by supposedly following ancient models (which they cannot live up to), while simultaneously offering his own works as a means toward improving musical taste. The letter may also be read as a defence of opera against the views of the Leipzig literature professor Johann Christoph Gottsched and his circle, who advocated replacing the genre with classical spoken tragedy and the simple strophic ode. For Telemann, the humble ode and the more elevated opera both justified their own existence. The poems Telemann selected by Johann Matthias Dreyer (1717–69), Johann Arnold Ebert (1723–95), Hagedorn and Stoppe emphasise the new anacreontic style, and the composer was the first to publish and set to music such poetry. This orientation toward the pastoral, amatory and convivial is signalled by the engraving, on the collection's title page, of a pastoral scene in the French tradition of the *fête galante* by the son of Christian Fritzsch* (though, as with the *Singe-, Spiel- und Generalbass-Übungen*, about half the texts are concerned with moral themes). Almost all of Telemann's strophic songs have binary forms, with the number of verses ranging from three to sixteen.

Finally, three of Telemann's songs (TVWV 25:110–12) were included in the the first volume of the *Oden mit Melodien* (Berlin, 1753), an anthology of thirty-one lieder edited by Christian Gottfried Krause* and Carl Wilhelm Ramler*. His inclusion in this collection is remarkable, since all the other songs are by Berlin composers of a younger generation, musicians with whom Telemann was in touch during the 1740s and 1750s: Johann Friedrich Agricola*, Carl Philipp Emanuel Bach*, Franz Benda, Carl Heinrich Graun*, Christoph Nichelmann (Telemann's former student*) and Johann Joachim Quantz*. Telemann's influence on these composers' songs, and on the theoretical discussion of lied composition in Krause's *Von der musicalischen Poesie* (Berlin, 1752), would be hard to overestimate. *CzoGra, HofSin, HotEin, HotKon, HotLie, LebDom, KroLie, ReiZus, RicHag, WerOde, ZohMor.*

Sorge, Georg Andreas An organist, composer and theorist, Sorge (1703–78) spent nearly his entire career as court and civic organist in Lobenstein. As a member of Lorenz Christoph Mizler's* Correspondierende Societät der musikalischen Wissenschaften (Corresponding Society of Musical Science), Sorge promoted Telemann's *Neues musikalisches System** in his *Gespräch zwischen einem Musico theoretico und einem Studioso musices* (Lobenstein, 1748), *Ausführliche und deutliche Anweisung zur Rational-Rechnung . . . des Monochords* (Lobenstein, 1749) and *Anleitung zur Fantasie* (Lobenstein, 1767). Telemann collected subscriptions for the last of these publications, and he published

15. 'Die Einsamkeit', TVWV 25:62, to a text by Joachim Johann Daniel Zimmermann (= 'Z'). No. 24 in the *Singe-, Spiel- und Generalbass-Übungen* (Hamburg, 1733–34; Staatsbibliothek zu Berlin – Preußischer Kulturbesitz, Music Department and Mendelssohn Archive, Mus. O. 12035). Image courtesy of Art Resources, NY. Reproduced by permission.

two of Sorge's writings: the *Anweisung zur Stimmung und Temperatur . . . der Orgelwerke* (Hamburg, 1744) and the *Gründliche Untersuchung, ob die . . . Schröterische Clavier-Temperaturen für gleichschwebend paßieren können, oder nicht* (Hamburg, 1754). Three letters from Sorge to Telemann (1750, 1766 and 1767) are friendly in tone and concern music-theoretical and family matters. *JunMiz, TelBri.*

Sources The principal sources for Telemann's music are 1) publications that he issued himself or authorised others to print, most of which survive; 2) his composing scores, of which a modest number survive for the vocal works and just eighteen for the instrumental works; 3) sets of manuscript performing parts copied under his supervision, also a limited corpus; and 4) many hundreds of scribal copies that vary widely in their reliability and relationship (if any) to the composer. Although the printed sources are scattered among libraries and archives throughout central and northern Europe, the manuscript sources are concentrated in several locations. The instrumental works that Telemann left unpublished are found principally in nearly three hundred copyists' manuscripts at the Universitäts- und Landesbibliothek Darmstadt, originally collected by members of the Darmstadt *Hofkapelle* (digitised copies at www.ulb.tu-darmstadt.de/spezialabteilungen/handschriften1.de.jsp), and in about 170 scribal copies at the Sächsische Landesbibliothek – Staats- und Universitätsbibliothek Dresden, largely assembled by Johann Georg Pisendel* while employed by the Dresden electoral *Hofkapelle* (digitised copies in the 'Instrumentalmusik der Dresdner Hofkapelle' database: digital.slub-dresden.de/kollektionen). Smaller but significant manuscript collections of instrumental works are in the Universitätsbibliothek Rostock (originating at the Württemberg-Stuttgart court) and the Landesbibliothek Mecklenburg-Vorpommen Günther Uecker in Schwerin. By far the largest and most significant collection of Telemann's church cantatas*, including some eight hundred works (in well over a thousand manuscript scores and sets of parts) that were performed in Frankfurt over much of the eighteenth century, is found in the Universitätsbibliothek Johann Christian Senckenberg Frankfurt am Main (digitised copies at sammlungen.ub.uni-frankfurt.de/telemann/nav/index/all). Another 150 sets of manuscript parts to sacred vocal works by Telemann originally belonging to the Fürstenschule in Grimma* are now at the Sächsische Landesbibliothek – Staats- und Universitätsbibliothek Dresden. Among these works are some of Telemann's earliest sacred concertos and cantatas, evidently composed in Hildesheim or Leipzig. One hundred and thirty-six of Telemann's composing scores of vocal works (mostly post-1740), along with several hundred scribal copies of vocal and instrumental works (particularly rich in secular cantatas, operas* and *Kapitänsmusik**), are preserved at the Staatsbibliothek zu Berlin – Preußischer Kulturbesitz. The composing scores, along with numerous sets of parts prepared on Telemann's behalf by Otto Ernst Gregorius Schieferlein* and others, were inherited by Georg Michael Telemann* from his grandfather's estate* (a selection has been digitised at digital.staatsbibliothek-berlin.de/). In 2001 the Staatsbibliothek's Telemann holdings were supplemented by the addition of 365 sources containing 336 vocal and instrumental works belonging to the music archive of the Sing-Akademie zu Berlin*.

In recent decades significant headway has been made toward identifying copying hands and paper types in the manuscript sources, and this has resulted in a refined sense of the music's chronology and dissemination. Additionally, a re-examination of Telemann's publishing* practices has resulted in the redating of some of his engraved collections of music and the identification of multiple states of others. *FalRis, FecStu, HenSin, JaeAut, KerQue, KrüRos, LanNot, LanQue, ReiSin, SatEss, SatNot, SchKat, WeiPap, ZohPap, ZohMix.*

Stolbergischer Jahrgang Also known as the *Behrndt-Jahrgang*, this annual cycle of church cantatas to librettos by the civil servant, historian and poet Gottfried Behrndt (1693–1743) was first performed in Hamburg and Roßla during the 1736–37 church year (the earliest Frankfurt performance, from which most surviving musical sources derive, took place sometime during the following four years). The revision of Behrndt's 1731 librettos and, presumably, Telemann's settings (sixty-one of which are extant) were commissioned by Count Jost Christian of Stolberg-Roßla. The cantatas are richly scored with wind instruments (particularly flute) and exhibit a wide formal variety, with textual and musical types (recitative, aria, chorale, biblical verses) often interconnected with one another; six works are fashioned as miniature oratorios by virtue of their named characters, not unlike the *Oratorischer Jahrgang**. The 1736–37 church year had not yet ended when Telemann left Hamburg on St Michael's Day (29 September) 1737 to embark on his eight-month trip to Paris*. Johann Adolph Scheibe recalled in 1773 that he was entrusted by Telemann to complete the cycle, and indeed Scheibe composed the cantata for the nineteenth Sunday after Trinity (27 October), *So ofte Jesus großer Name*, TVWV 1:1377. However, there is otherwise no evidence that the remainder of the cycle was composed by anyone other than Telemann. The twelve cantatas for Quinquagesima Sunday through the third Sunday after Easter have been published in volume 48 (2010) of the Telemann selective critical edition*. *EicKan, EicSpä, PfaSto, PoeBeh.*

Stoppe, Daniel Stoppe (1697–1747) studied at Leipzig University, then returned to his native Hirschberg to work as a private tutor and then as deputy rector at the Evangelical Church of Grace (Gnadenkirche). He provided five librettos for Telemann's second set of *Moralische Cantaten** and was the author of fourteen song* texts in the *Singe-, Spiel- und Generalbass-Übungen* and of six more in the *Vier und zwanzig, theils ernsthafte, theils scherzende, Oden.* Before his death he furnished Telemann with librettos through the sixth Sunday after Trinity for the *Engel-Jahrgang**. *HauSto, KocSto.*

Students Although none of Telemann's students became composers of the first rank, he trained a number of significant musicians. Jacob Wilhelm Lustig (1706–96) was organist at Hamburg's Pesthofkirche and then at the city's cathedral in 1727, studying composition with Telemann and Johann Mattheson* before accepting an organist post in Groningen in 1728 and another at the Nieuwe Kerk in The Hague in 1741; Lustig recalled that Mattheson stressed the theoretical and Telemann the practical. Around 1730 Johann Jeremias Du Grain (d. 1756) sang bass for Telemann and most likely studied with him before moving to the Polish town of Elbing (1732) and then to Danzig (1739), where he later became organist at the reformed church of St Elisabeth. Between

1733 and 1739 Christoph Nichelmann (1717–62), later harpsichordist at the Berlin court of Friedrich II, King of Prussia (Frederick the Great)*, studied the theatrical style with Telemann, Reinhard Keiser* and Mattheson. In February 1756, following the granting of his request for dismissal from the Berlin court, Nichelmann wrote to Telemann asking for his assistance in securing a new position. Johann Hövet (c. 1715–99) studied with Telemann from about 1736, and in 1741 Telemann published his *Musikalische Probe eines Concerts vors Clavier* (unfortunately lost). In 1754 Telemann claimed that Johann Christoph Schmügel (1727–98), who served as organist at the Johanniskirche in Lüneburg from 1758, was one of the best composition students he had ever had. In later years Telemann trained his grandson, Georg Michael Telemann*, who came to live with him in 1755. Georg Michael wrote at least six cantatas during the period 1764–66 while assuming some performing duties for his grandfather. Writing to Georg Johann Daniel Poelchau in 1823, he recalled that his grandfather, in looking over his early compositional efforts, remarked in all seriousness 'truly, you will be greater than me'. Also during his last decade, Telemann gave three years of instruction to the trumpeter, organist and composer Caspar Daniel Krohn (1736–1801), who became organist at Hamburg's Petrikirche and performed at least one of Telemann's cantatas (at Easter 1763) while studying with him. *HobSch, NeuKir, ReiBeo, Telbri.*

Stuttgart The Stuttgart *Hofkapelle* of Eberhard Ludwig, Duke of Württemberg (1676–1733), resident in the city until its 1725 removal to nearby Ludwigsburg, owned a number of Telemann's instrumental works. These belonged to the flute-playing Crown Prince Friedrich Ludwig (1698–1731), who assembled a large collection of instrumental music starting in 1716, following his travels to Italy, Holland and France. Now at the Universitätsbibliothek Rostock, the collection remains largely intact and contains some three dozen manuscripts of Telemann's instrumental works. The composer appears to have travelled from Frankfurt to Stuttgart in August 1720, for the autograph score of his cantata for the thirteenth Sunday after Trinity, *In Christo Jesu gilt weder Beschneidung*, TVWV 1:929, bears the date 'Stuttgardt d. 19. Aug. 1720'. At that time, Reinhard Keiser* was resident at court. *FalStu, KrüRos, ZohMix.*

Swack, Jeanne R. After performance studies at the University of Southern California and earning a PhD in musicology from Yale University with a dissertation on Telemann's solo sonatas (1988), Swack joined the musicology faculty of the University of Wisconsin at Madison, where she also holds an appointment in the Center for Jewish Studies. Her work on Telemann and related topics has centred on the composer's sonatas and church cantatas, performance-practical issues and anti-Semitism in texts for vocal works. She has also published editions of the *Douze Solos à violon ou traversière** and *Fortsetzung des Harmonischen Gottesdienstes**, and prepared two annotated bibliographies* of writings on Telemann. *SwaBib, SwaCho, SwaErn, SwaJud, SwaOuv, SwaPer, SwaRes, SwaSol, SwaSon, SwaWal.*

Tafelmusik The *Musique de table** is only the most famous of Telemann's music associated with banquets, as many of the cantatas and serenatas he wrote for weddings, birthdays and political events are most likely to have accompanied meals. As *Konzertmeister* at the Sorau court in 1705, Telemann played violin 'bey der Tafel'. And upon being named secretary of the Eisenach court in 1709, he earned a place at the 'Marschallstafel' (an honour he had also enjoyed at Sorau), thus presumably dining to *Tafelmusik*. One of his duties as Eisenach *Kapellmeister* in absentia from 1717 was to provide works 'for ordinary Tafel-Music', which consisted of instrumental pieces. In addition, three of his vocal works for the court are identified as 'Taffel-Music' in their printed librettos. At Hamburg Telemann's annual *Kapitänsmusik** included a serenata heard during a banquet for the captains of the city's civil guard. During a celebratory meal marking the organisation's centennial in 1723, the so-called *Admiralitätsmusik** (the allegorical serenata, *Unschätzbarer Vorwurf erkenntlicher Sinnen*, TVWV 24:1) was introduced by the *Wasser-Ouverture**. Telemann performed further serenatas as *Tafelmusik* on various special occasions in Hamburg. The lost *Auf zur Freude, zum Scherzen, zum Klingen* (TVWV 13:6) was heard during a 1725 dinner for the visiting Duke August Wilhelm of Brandenburg-Wolfenbüttel, and in 1732 *O erhabnes Glück der Ehe* (TVWV 11:15c) served as *Tafelmusik* for the golden wedding anniversary of the Hamburg senator Matthias Mutzenbecher (1663–1735) and his wife Maria Catharina. One of the composer's last examples of *Tafelmusik* was a serenata for the centennial celebration of Hamburg's Handlungs-Deputation (Commerce Deputation), the lost *Hamburgs Flor* (TVWV 24:4) to a libretto by Christian Wilhelm Alers*. *ZohTaf.*

***Der Tag des Gerichts*, TVWV 6:8** Telemann's last oratorio was first performed on 17 March 1762 in Hamburg's new, heated concert hall 'auf dem Kamp' (in the field). The eighty-one-year-old Telemann probably did not conduct on this occasion. Christian Wilhelm Alers* provided the composer with a 'lyric' libretto in which there is little dramatic action and the mostly allegorical characters express their sentiments about the subject matter. Thus the story is divided into four 'contemplations', the first of which features the characters of Disbelief, the Mocker, Reason, Religion and a Chorus of Believers. Telemann provides the Mocker with a buffa-style aria, fills Reason's aria with mimetic effects and symphonic writing, and portrays the 'horrible howls of vice' in the Chorus of Believers through striking chromaticism. In the second contemplation, the elements rage and Jesus condemns tyrants while Faith soars to Him. Chaos is represented both in the thrilling opening chorus and Devotion's harmonically adventurous accompanied recitative. The third contemplation portrays The Last Judgement: the Archangel raises the dead, Devotion is blessed and rewarded, and Disbelief is filled with despair. Vivid dissonances are heard in the Chorus of Vices, the F-minor tonality of which is the farthest removed from the work's principal key of D major. Finally, the fourth contemplation, set in heaven, is marked by praise and thanksgiving. Here a touching aria for One of the Blessed Spirits includes an obbligato viola da gamba. In a fine expression of the 'mixed taste'*, Telemann ends the oratorio with two choruses separated by a brief recitative for Faith, the first concluding with a Handelian 'Amen' fugue and the second cast as a passepied *en rondeau*. *Der Tag des Gerichts* has become the best known among Telemann's late vocal masterpieces, due in large measure to the edition by Max Scheider* in volume 28 (1907) of the series Denkmäler deutscher Tonkunst, where the oratorio is paired with the late cantata *Ino**.

***Die Tageszeiten*, TVWV 20:39** This cycle of four secular cantatas illustrating the times of day for solo voices, chorus and orchestra is set to pastoral-sacred librettos by Justus Friedrich Wilhelm Zachariae*, who fashioned texts for Telemann from the much longer poems of his *Tageszeiten* cycle (1756). The librettos as published by Zachariae in his *Poetische Schriften* (1764) each include two arias surrounding a recitative (orchestrally accompanied in Telemann's cantatas), but do not include the concluding chorus found in the musical settings. Thus Telemann himself may have authored the choral texts. *Die Tageszeiten* was first performed on 20 October 1757, at a public concert of Telemann's music in Hamburg's Drillhaus, an exercise facility for the city's civic guard that doubled as a concert hall. Also on the programme was Telemann's *Deus judicium tuum regi da** and the first part of *Die Donnerode**. Further documented performances of *Die Tageszeiten* during the composer's lifetime occurred in 1759 and 1763. Following a three-movement instrumental sinfonia that begins with a musical sunrise, the solo vocal and instrumental timbres gradually darken throughout the day as the sun traverses the sky: soprano with trumpet for *Der Morgen* (morning), alto with viola da gamba for *Der Mittag* (noon), tenor with flutes for *Der Abend* (evening) and bass with bassoon for *Die Nacht* (night). Telemann's music is filled throughout with vivid expressions of the librettos' natural imagery and moral-theological messages through nuanced shadings of style, texture and scoring. *HobBri, ReiTag, WacNat.*

Tartini, Giuseppe One of the most celebrated violinist-composers of his time, Tartini (1692–1770) was also an important writer on music. He and Telemann must have corresponded with each other, for Telemann acted as a publishing agent for an unidentified set of the Italian's violin sonatas; in a February 1749 letter, Franz Benda reported to Telemann that some of his colleagues in the Berlin *Hofkapelle* were interested in purchasing copies. *TelBri.*

Telemann, Amalie Louise Juliane (née Eberlin) The daughter of the composer Daniel Eberlin, Amalie Louise Juliane (1681–1711) married Telemann in Eisenach on 13 September 1709 but died just over a year later, on 21 January 1711, during the birth of their daughter, Maria Wilhelmina Eleonora (1711–42), among whose godparents was Erdmann Neumeister*. The death of his wife inspired Telemann's lengthy and moving poem 'Poetische Gedanken, mit welchen die Asche seiner hertzgeliebten Louisen beehren wollte' (Poetic thoughts with which to honour the ashes of his dearest Louise), which was published in a 1743 anthology of poetry* by husbands on the deaths of their wives. *HobDok.*

Telemann, Andreas Andreas (1715–55) was the eldest child of Georg Philipp and Maria Catharina Telemann*. Following studies in Hamburg at the Johanneum school and academic Gymnasium, he attended the university in Jena. Starting in 1741, he served as adjunct pastor and then deacon in Plön before becoming pastor in Ahrensbök. Andreas had four children, the third of which, Georg Michael Telemann* (1748–1831), went to live with his grandfather in Hamburg following Andreas' death. *HobDok, RübAut.*

Telemann, Georg Michael The son of Andreas Telemann*, Georg Michael (1748–1831) left Ahrensbök when his father died in 1755 to live with his grandfather in Hamburg. From about 1762 he assisted Georg Philipp as a director, singer, keyboardist and copyist for church music while attending Hamburg's Johanneum school (1756 until at least 1765); he then attended the academic Gymnasium starting in 1768. Following his grandfather's death in June 1767, Georg Michael temporarily took over the interim direction of the city's five principal churches, corresponding about the position with Carl Philipp Emanuel Bach*, under whose direction he continued his activities as an accompanist between 1768 and 1770. He was a theology student at the university in Kiel (1770–72), but broke off his studies and briefly returned to Hamburg to teach at the Nikolaikirche school before taking the position of cantor in Riga (1773–1828), where he also served as teacher (1773–1801) and organist (1813–28) at the cathedral. Georg Michael's continuo treatise, the *Unterricht im Generalbass-Spielen* (Hamburg, 1773; indebted to books by Carl Philipp Emanuel Bach and Friedrich Wilhelm Marpurg*), was completed during his university studies. His *Beytrag zur Kirchenmusik* (Königsberg and Leipzig, 1785) includes vocal-instrumental anthems along with chorale preludes and fugues for organ. He also published a hymnal (Riga, 1800), a collection of chorale melodies (Mittau, 1811–12) and a brief treatise on selecting chorale melodies (Riga, 1821). His few surviving compositions are mostly sacred.

Having inherited many sacred vocal works from his grandfather's estate*, Georg Michael performed dozens of passions, funeral cantatas and other occasional compositions in Riga over the course of several decades. In line with the practices of his time, he altered both the texts and scores of these works to suit his tastes and needs, sometimes updating the music by adding instrumental interludes or modifying the original instrumentation. These alterations were generally entered directly onto composing scores and copyists' manuscripts, rendering the original musical texts difficult to decipher. Georg Michael's intentions are usually made clear through explanatory notes, and in an 1823 letter to his former student Georg Johann Daniel Poelchau (1773–1836) he reasoned that 'I stand on the shoulders of giants, and can naturally see farther than them.' He also wrote to Poelchau about preserving his grandfather's music legacy through the publication of selected works (including cantatas and motets) and the correspondence with Carl Heinrich Graun* and other composers; he admitted feeling too 'weak' in 1816 to write a 'worthy biography of this patriarch'. (Georg Michael had already mentioned the possibility of publishing some of his grandfather's feast-day cantatas in the preface to the *Beytrag zur Kirchenmusik*.) In the end, neither music nor letters made it into print. Poelchau received about two hundred works by Georg Philipp in performing parts from Georg Michael in 1829, and after the latter's death he came into possession of fifty composing scores (he would later acquire more) that he found in the tower of Riga's cathedral in the summer of 1834. In 1841 Poelchau's Telemann manuscripts were acquired by the Königliche Bibliothek in Berlin, now the Staatsbibliothek zu Berlin – Preußischer Kulturbesitz. *AriHör, ClaLet, HirSch, HobDok, HobErb, KleDok, ReiBea, SatRez, SucTel.*

Telemann, Heinrich Telemann's father Heinrich Telemann (1646–85) spent his first twelve years in Cochstedt before attending school in Scherleben, Halberstadt, Egeln, Quedlinburg and Schöningen. After theology studies at the university in Helmstedt (1664–68), he was first a school rector in Hadmersleben and then a pastor in Hakeborn, finally serving as deacon at the

Heligen-Geist-Kirche in Magdeburg from 1676 until his death at thirty-eight. He and his wife Johanna Maria* had seven children, of whom only Heinrich Matthias* and Georg Philipp lived full lives; the brothers were twelve and almost four when he died (the two-year-old Johann Gerhard would die less than two months after his father). Heinrich sketched a family tree on which he encouraged following generations to add to the family's genealogy. This passed to his eldest son, Heinrich Matthias Telemann*, who bequeathed it to his nephew Andreas Telemann* (the composer's eldest son). Upon Andreas' death in 1755, the family tree passed to his father and then, no later than 1767, to Andreas' son Georg Michael Telemann*. Georg Philipp, Andreas and Georg Michael, representing three generations, all fulfilled Heinrich Telemann's wish by writing autobiographies. *HobDok, ReiBio.*

Telemann, Heinrich Matthias The composer's older brother Heinrich Matthias (1672–1746) attended the cathedral school in Magdeburg then studied at the universities in Jena and Halle. In the Thuringian town of Wormstedt, about twenty-two kilometres from Weimar, he served as a substitute pastor (from 1704) and then pastor (from 1716). He married Dorothea Maria Petri in 1704, and the couple had five children; the third child, Johanna Maria, married in 1731, and Telemann stood godfather to her second child (a son) on 4 July 1737 (thus the composer appears to have travelled to Jena for the baptism). In 1717 Telemann named his son Heinrich Matthias after his brother, who was not present in Frankfurt for the baptism on 5 April. Yet a scribal copy of the score to Telemann's cantata for Exaudi Sunday from the first *Concerten-Jahrgang** (9 May 1717), *Wer will uns scheiden von der Liebe Gottes*, TVWV 1:1613, bears the inscription 'Wormstedt, 26. April 1717', which may indicate that the composer travelled the three hundred kilometres from Frankfurt to visit Heinrich Matthias. *HobDok, ReiWor.*

Telemann, Johanna Maria (née Haltmeier) Telemann's mother Johanna Maria (1642–1711) was not financially well off after the early death of her husband Heinrich Telemann* in 1685, and her son Georg Philipp helped support her through his singing while still a schoolboy in Magdeburg (as he noted in AB 1738). Although it was Johanna Maria who sent her son away to boarding school in Zellerfeld with the goal of preventing him from becoming a professional musician, Telemann deflects blame from her in AB 1718 and AB 1740 by pointing to unnamed persons who convinced his mother of the perils of music as a career. Telemann also notes that his mother supported him financially during his university studies in Leipzig, and that once he resolved to become a musician, she was also supportive of his new path. Johanna Maria spent her later years living with her eldest son, Heinrich Matthias Telemann*, in Wormstedt, where she died on 15 December 1711. Although Telemann claimed to have inherited his musical talent from Johanna Maria, only her nephew Joachim Friedrich Haltmeier (1668–1720; cantor in Verden from 1696) and his son Carl Johann Friedrich Haltmeier* (c. 1698–1735; organist in Hanover from 1720) were professional musicians. *HobDok.*

Telemann, Maria Catharina (née Textor) Telemann's second wife Maria Catharina (1697–1775) belonged to a middle-class Frankfurt family (her father was the city's 'Kornschreiber', in charge of managing the intake and disbursement of grain) and was sixteen years old – seventeen years younger than her husband – when she married in Frankfurt in August 1714. Over the next dozen years Maria Catharina and Telemann had nine children: Andreas* (1715–55), Johannes (Hans) (1716–?), Heinrich Matthias (1717–?), Anna Clara (1719–?), Friedrich Carl (1720–22), Augustus Bernhard (1721–38), Johann Barthold Joachim (1723–?), Benedictus Eberhard Wilhelm (1724–?) and Ernst Conrad Eibert (1726–27). But by 1726 the marriage appears to have begun unravelling: Maria Catharina had accumulated a large debt that eventually reached 5,000 Reichstalers (roughly five times the amount Telemann earned from his official Hamburg duties plus directing the Opera). Some 3,000 Reichstalers had been been paid back by the time Telemann wrote to his friend Johann Reinhold Hollander* on 1 September 1736 ('I have no idea where they came from'), and 600 Reichstalers had been contributed by Hamburg's citizenry. In the same letter, Telemann states that 'my wife is away from me and the wastefulness is finished'. Until recently it was assumed that Maria Catharina and her husband permanently separated in 1735, but a paylist for the 1738 annual performance of the oratorio *Seliges Erwägen**, which occurred while Telemann was still in Paris*, is in Maria Catharina's handwriting. Moreover, further documentary evidence reveals that she adopted a girl in Hamburg in 1741. Thus either the couple separated on a temporary basis, or Telemann could occasionally count on his estranged wife to help with professional matters. In any event, Maria Catharina died in her native Frankfurt in 1775 and was buried in the courtyard of the city's Dominican cloister. The oft-repeated claim that the source of marital discord between Maria Catharina and Telemann was her affair and abscondence with a Swedish military officer is based on an 1804 misinterpretation of 'Die Baßgeige' (The Double Bass), a satire on the Hamburg Opera published in a 1724 issue of the journal *Der Patriot. CloHam, HobDok, NeuKir, SieLeb.*

Telemann-Festtage This biennial celebration of the life and music of Telemann consists of an extensive series of concerts (usually including an opera) and an international scholarly conference. Held since 1962 in Magdeburg, the composer's birthplace, the celebration is organised by the Zentrum für Telemann-Pflege und -Forschung*. From the 1960s through the 1980s the celebration was held every three or four years, but since 1990 it has been offered every two years with an increasingly international roster of performers. The scholarly conference has accompanied all but a few of the celebrations, with papers later published in volumes of conference proceedings.

Telemann societies Three active Telemann societies are devoted to promoting the composer's life and music through lectures, conferences, exhibitions, concerts and publications. The Internationale Telemann-Gesellschaft, based in Magdeburg, partners with the Zentrum für Telemann-Pflege und -Forschung* to sponsor the concert festival and scholarly conference that make up the Telemann-Festtage*, co-sponsors similar events in other locations, runs a biennial music competition and publishes an annual newsletter containing brief scholarly articles, listings of new Telemann publications and recordings, and news items relating to the composer from around the world. Both the Hamburger Telemann-Gesellschaft (founded 1958) and the Frankfurter

Telemann-Gesellschaft (founded 1992) focus on the composer's activities in their respective cities. The Hamburg society opened a small Telemann museum in 2015, which remains the only one of its kind.

Thematic catalogues Somewhat confusingly, Telemann's vocal and instrumental works have been catalogued separately. Werner Menke* produced a thematic catalogue of the vocal works (TVWV) in conjunction with his doctoral studies in the 1930s, and a condensed version of this catalogue was published in two volumes (1982 and 1988) covering, respectively, the church cantatas (listed alphabetically according to text incipit) and other vocal works. Each genre is assigned a number, with individual works receiving their own numbers following a colon. Menke was able to consult works prior to their disappearance during World War II, many of which were recovered after the publication of his catalogue (especially manuscripts belonging to the Sing-Akademie zu Berlin*). The three-volume catalogue of Telemann's instrumental works (TWV), edited by Martin Ruhnke*, appeared as a supplement to the Telemann selective critical edition* over a period of fifteen years (1984, 1992 and 1999). It continues the numbering system of the TVWV, but for sonatas, concertos, overture-suites and other ensemble music, individual works are identified with a letter (standing for the key) and a number. The appendix to volume 1 includes transcriptions of Telemann's publishing* catalogues, a list of publications by the composer and others, and a list of the contents of *Der getreue Music-Meister**. Volume 3 includes an appendix that lists Telemann's instrumental works according to scoring and provides transcriptions of title pages to his publications. *TVWV, TWV.*

Theory It may have been Telemann's contact with Johann Mattheson* and Johann Adolph Scheibe* in Hamburg that inspired him to make his own music-theoretical contributions, many of which never saw the light of day. Already in his 1717 letter* to Mattheson, Telemann (then in Frankfurt) mused that 'perhaps I will soon bring to light a treatise in which I address composing for the most commonly used instruments, and their natural qualities'. In 1728 he advertised a forthcoming translation of the *Gradus ad parnassum* by Johann Joseph Fux, and several years later mentioned treatises on musical invention and another on recitative (*Traité du récitatif*). In 1735 Telemann announced he would publish a *Theoretisch-practischer Tractat vom Componiren* (*Theoretical-Practical Treatise on Composition*) 'wherein the most important [aspects] of Fux's and Heinichen's great works will be brought together and supplemented by the author's own ideas and discoveries, the whole, however, summarised with the utmost brevity and clarity'. This treatise was again mentioned as forthcoming in the preface to Telemann's 1744 published cantata cycle *Musikalisches Lob Gottes**, where he had hoped to address the incorporation of the theatrical style into church music, the setting of German recitative texts to Italianate melodies and the handling of both 'usual and unusual' dissonance. Finally, in 1759 Telemann proposed to Johann Gottlob Immanuel Breitkopf* that he might write a short discourse on the 'descriptive manner of writing' and another on the 'correct use of the German language' in composing vocal music. Despite all these unrealised plans, Telemann did in fact complete some theoretical-practical projects. His *Fast allgemeines Evangelisch-Musicalisches Lieder-Buch** concludes with a practical 'lesson' (*Unterricht*) 'on four-part composition and on the continuo accompaniment associated with it'. He claimed to have tried out his method 'on a thirteen-year-old boy who knew little about music and found that this is a direct path to attaining four-part composition'. His *Neues musikalisches System** offers a method of tuning by recognising, and applying in performance, four sizes of each musical interval. *See also* **Performance practice**.

***Der Tod Jesu*, TVWV 5:6** Along with the *Betrachtung der neunten Stunde an dem Todestag Jesu**, this passion oratorio helped initiate a series of oratorios, odes and cantatas composed over Telemann's last decade. The libretto, by Karl Wilhelm Ramler*, was commissioned in 1754 by Princess Anna Amalia of Prussia (sister of Friedrich II, King of Prussia, known as Frederick the Great*), apparently so that it could be set by Carl Heinrich Graun*, who received the text in August and finished composing by the following February. By this time Telemann had also come into possession of the libretto, undoubtedly through one of his many contacts in Berlin*. This may have been Graun himself, perhaps with the intent of setting Ramler's text in friendly competition with his older colleague. In any case, Telemann's *Der Tod Jesu* premiered on 19 March 1755 in Hamburg's Drillhaus (a double-bill with the *Betrachtung der neunten Stunde an dem Todestag Jesu*), and Graun's received its first public performance just a week later, on 26 March, in Berlin's cathedral. The next year, each work was performed in the other city: Graun's in the Drillhaus on 29 March 1756, and Telemann's in Berlin's Petrikirche on 11 and 16 April 1756. Graun, who attended one of the Berlin performances, praised Telemann's *Der Tod Jesu* and *Betrachtung der neunten Stunde an dem Todestag Jesu* (he owned scores of both) in a letter* of 15 May 1756. For a Hamburg performance of Telemann's setting on 18 March 1756 the composer lightly revised his score to better reflect Ramler's libretto (the copy he originally worked from was faulty). He also added an introduction to the oratorio: an orchestral chorale prelude on a melody associated with the texts 'Wenn meine Sünd mich kränken' and 'Hilf Gott, daß mir's gelinge'. In 1760 Ramler published a revised version of his libretto, and although neither Graun nor Telemann followed suit in revising their settings, Telemann did make a setting of the new trio 'Rette mich, ich flehe dir'.

Ramler's libretto is unconventional for a passion oratorio in being more contemplative than dramatic, and this appears to have inspired Telemann, whose setting diverges from Graun's in providing orchestral accompaniment for all recitatives and including a high number of movements in minor mode. Among the most striking numbers is the chorus 'Unsere Seele ist gebeugt zur Erden', with its 'updating' of the venerable *stile antico* through forward-looking chromaticism. Yet Graun's approach to matching 'stirring' songs to Ramler's lyrical monologues fit better with the Zeitgeist, and it was consequently his setting that was performed to great acclaim into the nineteenth century while Telemann's gradually fell into obscurity. The oratorio has been published in volume 31 (2006) of the Telemann selected critical edition*. *CzoGra, CzoTod, HobTod, LölTod, LütMon, SchAuf.*

***Trauer-Musik eines Kunsterfahrenen Canarienvogels*, TVWV 20:37** The full title of this funeral music*, 'Trauermusik eines Kunsterfahrenen Canarienvogels, als derselbe zum grössten Leidwesen seines Herrn Possessoris in diesem Jahre verstorben. Alle Liebhabern der edlen Musik in einer Cantate publicieret'

(Cantata or funeral music for an artistically skilled canary whose death this year brought the greatest sorrow to his owner. Made public in a cantata for all lovers of noble music) suggests that it was commissioned by a bereaved pet owner, though the circumstances of the work's origin remain obscure (including the librettist's identity). One manuscript source bears the date of 16 October 1737 and preserves what is probably Telemann's original scoring of soprano, violin or flute and continuo. Another manuscript reflects Justus Wilhelm Lorber's arrangement for soprano, two violins, viola and continuo; this was the basis for a 1942 edition of the cantata by Werner Menke*, with the result that the work's original version has remained obscure. Although the cantata has often been considered tragi-comic, there is nothing humorous about its text or music (the canary is devoured by death, not a cat, as some translations have it). The four arias, alternating with secco recitatives, encompass two laments, an operatic rage aria and a lullaby in the form of a sarabande. In a surprising twist, the concluding recitative acquires an instrumental accompaniment and switches to low German at the 'reading' of the canary's tombstone.

Uffenbach At Frankfurt Telemann was in contact with two members of the patrician von Uffenbach family: Zacharias Conrad (1683–1734) and his brother Johann Friedrich Armand (1687–1769), both of whom were amateur musicians. Zacharias Conrad may have been the unnamed person who 'recommended' Telemann for the Frankfurt post in December 1711 or January 1712, and as a member of the Frauenstein Society he may have helped Telemann acquire his position as the organisation's secretary and director of the Collegium musicum*. But Johann Friedrich Armand appears to have been the greater music enthusiast, in addition to being an alderman, juror, writer, poet, artist and art collector. During Telemann's early years in Frankfurt (1712–16) he was studying in Strasbourg and then on a grand tour through southwest Germany, France, Italy and England; his travel diaries are full of musical experiences. Johann Friedrich Armand was already familiar with Telemann's music before he left Frankfurt, and upon his return he became a supporter of the Frauenstein Collegium musicum. After he left Frankfurt for Hamburg in 1721, Telemann engaged in an extensive correspondence with Johann Friedrich Armand, who subscribed to the *Musique de table** and purchased a number of the composer's other publications. Twenty-one of the composer's letters* survive from the period 1723–42. Some concern Uffenbach's sacred cantata librettos that Telemann set in 1727–28 (the *Emblematischer Jahrgang**), and the latest concern gardening*, a pastime the two shared in common.

Between 1728 and 1733 Johann Friedrich Armand created a parody annual cycle of sacred cantatas for domestic worship (*Der genesenen Vernunft*) by supplying new texts to eighty arias and duets from Telemann's *Harmonischer Gottes-Dienst**, *Auszug derjenigen musicalischen und auf die gewöhnlichen Evangelien gerichteten Arien* and other works, in addition to newly composed recitatives by Christoph Graupner* and Gottfried Grünewald and arias by several more German and Italian composers. This parody cycle contains two arias from the otherwise lost five-oratorio cycle *Der Königliche Prophet David, als ein Fürbild unseres Heylandes Jesu*, TVWV 6:1 (1718), to texts by Uffenbach. In 1730 Johann Friedrich Armand provided Telemann with an engraving for the frontispiece of the *Fast allgemeines Evangelisch-Musikalisches Lieder-Buch**. The composer had praised his friend's engravings in an October 1724 letter: 'I couldn't be more astonished at how far you have come in this pleasant science in such a short time. From what I have seen so far, the invention of [your engravings] cannot be improved; the inner harmony is exemplary, and the niceties of using a burin are observed with the greatest care.' *PegUff, ReiPar, ReiUff, TelBri.*

Uffenbach-Jahrgang *See* **Emblematischer Jahrgang**

***Unsterblicher Nachruhm Friedrich Augusts,* TVWV 4:7** *See* **Funeral Music**

Vier und zwanzig, theils ernsthafte, theils scherzende, Oden *See* **Songs**

Viola There is scarcely a violist worldwide who has not studied Telemann's viola concerto (TWV 51:G9), which therefore may lay claim to being one of the composer's best known works. Less well known today is the concerto for two violas ('violette'; TWV 52:G3), though Telemann was recognised as early as 1738 for his concertos in which the viola is given a concertante role (Johann Philipp Eisel, *Musicus Autodidaktos, oder Der sich selbst informirende Musicus*). There are also a number of sonatas featuring the instrument, including a canonic solo (TWV 41:B3) in *Der getreue Music-Meister** (1728–29) and seven trios with violin and viola in the *Scherzi melodichi* (1734). Among the works Telemann left unpublished, there is a further trio for violin and viola (TWV 42:D11) and six string quintets for two violins, two violas and continuo (TWV 44:5, 11 and 32–35); these last works were most likely composed in Leipzig (1701–05). *ZohMix.*

Viola da gamba Telemann contributed significantly to the solo viola da gamba repertory during his Hamburg years. His *Essercizii musici** (1726) includes the instrument in two solos and four trios, one with obbligato harpsichord, and among the viola da gamba music in *Der getreue Music-Meister** (1728–29) is a particularly fine unaccompanied sonata in D major (TWV 40:1), a canonic solo (with various alternative scorings; TWV 41:B3) and a solo for treble viol (TWV 41:G6). Both sets of 'Paris' quartets, the *Quadri** (1730) and *Nouveaux quatuors en six suites** (1738), include elaborate parts for viola da gamba or cello, though the former instrument appears to have been favoured by the composer. The recovery in 2015 of Telemann's set of twelve fantasias* for unaccompanied viola da gamba, the *Fantaisies pour la basse de violle* (1735), represents a major addition to the instrument's repertory. Telemann featured the viola da gamba as a soloist in three works: a solo concerto (TWV 51:A5), a popular overture-suite with a concertante part for the instrument (TWV 55:D6), and an equally fine double concerto for recorder and viola da gamba (TWV 52:a1). The viola da gamba is also well represented among the sonatas the composer left unpublished. Nine trios for recorder or oboe with treble viol appear to date from the late Frankfurt or early Hamburg years (TWV 42:C2, c3, d7, e5, F6, G8, g6, g9 and A10). The more usual bass instrument appears in six later trios in combination with violin (TWV 42:E6, E7, F10, G10, g10 and g11), and a seventh work replaces violin with flute (42:a7). There are also two excellent quartets with flute and two violas da gamba (TWV 43:G10 and G12), as well as two with flute, viola da gamba and bassoon (TWV 43:C2 and h3) and one for oboe, violin and viola da gamba (43:g2).

The viola da gamba makes occasional appearances as an obbligato instrument in Telemann's vocal works, especially as part of the 'soft' instrumental ensemble in funeral music, as in *Du aber, Daniel, gehe hin** and the early *Ach, wie nichtig, ach, wie flüchtig* (TVWV 1:38). A remarkably late instance of the instrument's use in Telemann's music is the obbligato part in the tenor aria from the fourth 'contemplation' of *Der Tag des Gerichts** (1762). *ZohFan, ZohMix.*

Vivaldi, Antonio Although evidence of Telemann's direct contact with Vivaldi's music is sparse, there can be little doubt that the Italian's concertos exerted a strong influence on him from the 1710s onward. This is clear from Telemann's use of formal and harmonic innovations pioneered by Vivaldi, especially modular ritornellos, temporary shifts to the parallel minor key (a prominent example of which occurs in the first movement of the concerto for three violins, TWV 53:F1, from the *Musique de table**) and a type of slow movement in which a central solo episode is framed by brief ritornellos (found in both sonatas and concertos by Telemann). At Hamburg, Telemann appears to have performed Vivaldi's violin concerto Op. 7, No. 2 between acts of his comic intermezzo *Pimpinone oder Die ungleiche Heirat**. A further point of contact between Telemann and Vivaldi has recently come to light. The latter's father, Giovanni Battista Vivaldi (c. 1655–1736), copied three Telemann trios in Venice in 1716 or 1717 for performances by visiting Dresden* court musicians in the retinue of Crown Prince Friedrich August I. These musicians included the violinist Johann Georg Pisendel*, the oboist Johann Christian Richter (a recent dedicatee of *Die Kleine Cammer-Music**) and the keyboard player Christian Pezold (who would later publish a suite in *Der getreue Music-Meister**). The Telemann trios, formerly believed to be in the hand of Giovanni Alberto Ristori, were probably sent by Telemann to Venice at the request of Pisendel, who eventually brought the manuscripts back to Dresden with him. It may have been Giovanni Battista or Antonio Vivaldi who substituted for Pisendel (away visiting other Italian cities for much of 1717) in Venetian performances of the trios. *AnsViv, TalViv, ZohViv.*

Walther, Johann Gottfried Walther (1684–1748) was organist at Weimar's Stadtkirche from 1707, also serving as the music and composition teacher to Prince Johann Ernst of Sachsen-Weimar* and eventually becoming a member of the ducal *Hofkapelle*. It may have been at the prince's request that he made organ arrangements of Telemann's concerto for oboe and violin, TWV 52:c1 (= Anh. 33:2), violin concerto TWV 51:B2 (= Anh. 43:B1 and Anh. 33:6) and overture-suite TWV 55:E2 (fourth movement). Walther requested that Telemann provide him with an autobiography* for inclusion in the *Musicalisches Lexicon* (1732), which the composer did in 1729, noting that 'what I have accomplished in the area of musical style is well known. First came the Polish style, followed by the French, church, chamber and operatic styles, and [finally] what is called the Italian style, which currently occupies me more than the others do.' Walther is known to have owned copies of Telemann's *Harmonischer Gottes-Dienst**, *Der getreue Music-Meister** and *Singe-, Spiel- und General-Bass-Übungen*.

***Wasser-Ouverture*, TWV 55:C3** Perhaps Telemann's best known overture-suite*, this work was known variously during his lifetime as the 'Wasser-Ouverture',

'Hamburger Ebb und Fluht' (Hamburg tides or Hamburg ebb and flow), 'Musica maritima' and 'Ouverture à 7, qui réprésente L'eau avec ses divinités et le commerce de la mer' (Overture in seven parts, which represents the water with its divinities and maritime commerce). The work's first documented performance occurred on 6 April 1723 in Hamburg's Niederbaumhaus, where it served as *Tafelmusik** during a dinner celebrating the centennial of the city's Admiralty and preceded a performance of Telemann's allegorical serenata *Unschätzbarer Vorwurf erkenntlicher Sinnen*, TVWV 24:1, known today as the *Admiralitätsmusik**. Along with the *Ouverture Burlesque de Quixotte**, the *Wasser-Ouverture* appears to have been the best known of Telemann's overture-suites during his lifetime, at least to judge by the number of surviving scribal copies. Unusually for a characteristic suite, the movements include both dance and descriptive titles. This, along with the evidence of two recently recovered manuscripts belonging to the Sing-Akademie zu Berlin*, suggests that an early version of the suite may have lacked at least some of the descriptive titles. Following the overture (without a descriptive title but representing, according to a contemporary account, the calm, surge and agitation of the sea) are 'sleeping Thetis' (a sarabande with elements recalling the *sommeil*, or French theatrical sleep scene), 'waking Thetis' (a pair of bourrées), 'amorous Neptune' (a loure), 'playful Naiads' (a gavotte *en rondeau*), 'joking Tritons' (a *harlequinade en rondeau*), 'storming Aeolus' (a French theatrical *tempête*), 'pleasant Zephyr' (a pair of minuets), 'tides' (a gigue) and 'merry mariners' (a canarie). *ZohMix.*

Wedding music *See* ***Pastorelle en Musique oder Musikalisches Hirtenspiel*** and ***Tafelmusik***

Weichmann, Christian Friedrich Resident in Hamburg as privy councillor to the Duke of Braunschweig-Lüneburg and closely associated with the city's 'Patriotische Gesellschaft' (Patriotic Society), Weichmann (1698–1770) was a poet and editor of the multi-volume *Poesie der Niedersachsen*, in which Telemann's poetry* appeared during the 1720s and 1730s. He provided Telemann with a number of librettos, including those to a serenata for the Petri-Mahl (the Feast of the Chair of St Peter, on 22 February), *Hamburgs Glückseligkeit* (TVWV 24:2; 1724), and another for the Duke of Braunschweig-Lüneburg, *Hamburgs Freude* (TVWV 13:6; 1725). *CloHam.*

Weiss, Sylvius Leopold As lutenist at the Dresden* electoral court from 1717, Weiss (1686–1750) would have met Telemann no later than the latter's visit to the city in 1719. In 1729 Telemann published a movement from one of Weiss' lute suites in *Der getreue Music-Meister**, the only work by Weiss to be printed during his lifetime.

Wend, Christoph Gottlieb Wend (d. 1745) was active in Hamburg from 1725 as a private teacher, journalist and writer. For Telemann he provided librettos to the comic intermezzo *Buffonet und Alga* (TVWV 21:21; 1727), the operas *Die Last-tragende Liebe oder Emma und Eginhard** (TVWV 21:25; 1728) and *Flavius Bertaridus** (TVWV 21:27; 1729), three operatic prologues (TVWV 23:3, 6 and 7; 1727–29) and a German translation of the libretto to *Riccardo Primo* by George Frideric Handel* (TVWV 22:8; 1729). Wend was also active as a translator of

English and French literature. In 1727–28 he published the first German translation of Jonathan Swift's novel *Gulliver's Travels.*

Westphal, Johann Christoph Owner of a Hamburg publishing and bookselling firm, Westphal (1727–99) played an important role in disseminating Telemann's music during the late eighteenth century. Like the Leipzig firm of Johann Gottlob Immanuel Breitkopf*, Westphal dealt mostly in manuscript copies, offering both scores and performing parts for many works; in fact, some of his stock consisted of 'written musical things from the Breitkopf firm'. Manuscripts and prints of music by Telemann – mainly oratorios, odes, cantatas and occasional vocal works from the 1750s and 1760s – appear in Westphal's non-thematic catalogues from 1772 until the firm ceased operations in 1799. Mostly single works were advertised, but a 1772 notice following a church cantata advised that 'the entire annual cycle can be produced on request'. Some of the Telemann manuscript sources* now at the Staatsbibliothek zu Berlin – Preußischer Kulturbesitz were handled by the Westphal firm. *HobGru.*

Wilkens, Matthäus Arnold Wilkens (1704–59) attended Hamburg's Johanneum and Gymnasium before studying law in Leipzig. Returning to Hamburg, where he became a councilman, he provided librettos for a number of Telemann's vocal works, including most cantatas of the *Harmonischer Gottesdienst**, the 1726 St Matthew Passion (TVWV 5:11) and the 1728 St Luke Passion (5:13). In a letter of 26 July 1728 to Wilkens, Telemann requested that the poet provide him with librettos for eight feast-day cantatas he wished to publish. After telling Wilkens that 'no one in the world makes better verses for music than you', the composer suggested how the cantatas might be organised into six movements. *TelBri.*

***Die wunderbare Beständigkeit der Liebe, oder Orpheus*, TVWV 21:18** Telemann's 'The Marvellous Constancy of Love or Orpheus' was first heard in a concert performance arranged by Margaretha Susanna Kayser* at the Hamburg Opera on 9 March 1726 (during Lent, when staged opera performances were forbidden). This followed an aborted stage performance in 1725 or 1726, which appears to be documented in the two surviving manuscript copies of the opera's score (discovered in the 1970s). The opera was finally staged on 15 October 1736, now in modified form and under the title *Die Rachbegierige Liebe, oder Orasia, verwittwete Königin in Thracien* (The Revengeful Love, or Orasia, Widowed Queen in Thrace). Although neither the manuscript scores nor the anonymous printed librettos name Telemann as composer, his authorship of the music is almost certain and his authorship of the text is a strong possibility. The principal source for the libretto is Michel Du Boulay's *Orphée* (Paris, 1690; music by Jean-Louis Lully), though some texts are drawn from various other French and Italian operas, including Jean-Baptiste Lully's *Amadis* and *Armide* and George Frideric Handel's* *Rinaldo.* The result of this textual heterogeneity is a trilingual libretto with recitatives in German and arias in Italian, French and German – exceptional for the Hamburg Opera, where bilingual librettos were common. The plot offers a fresh take on the familiar myth. Orasia, Queen of Thrace, is in love with Orpheus, who has fled her court, and plots with her friend Ismene to be rid of her rival Eurydice. When Eurydice is bitten by a snake and dies, Orasia believes she will succeed in winning the affection of Orpheus, who is encouraged by his friend Eurimedes to bring Eurydice back from Hades. Orpheus' song persuades Pluto to free Eurydice, but Pluto's minister Ascalax attaches the condition that Orpheus must not look at Eurydice as they leave the underworld. He also reveals that Orasia was responsible for Eurydice's death. As Orpheus and Eurydice depart, he fails to observe the condition by looking at her, and she is pulled back into the underworld. When the returning Orpheus rejects Orasia (and Eurimedes), she becomes enraged and orders the Baccantes to tear him to pieces. Now repentant, she resolves to end her suffering through death.

The trilingual aspect of the libretto is reflected in Telemann's music, which alternates between the idioms of opera seria, opera buffa and tragédie lyrique; the latter is reflected not only in a number of French airs (especially those of Orasia), but by *divertissements* in the first and second acts and the prominent use of the chorus throughout. As in some of his other Hamburg operas, Telemann reflects and deepens characterisation through his manipulation of musical style. Thus the emotionally volatile Orasia toggles between opera seria arias (themselves spanning a wide affective range) and French-pastoral airs, whereas Orpheus and Eurydice are marked as pastoral-comic characters through their rustic or buffa arias. Yet Orpheus' 'Ach Tod, ach süßer Tod' represents an entirely different (and non-operatic) idiom: its chorale-like melodic writing, scoring with pizzicato strings and through-composed form strongly invoke the Lutheran funeral music* tradition. Although it is not known which singers were involved in the opera's 1726 premiere, the principal roles of Orasia and Orpheus may well have been sung by Kayser and Johann Gottfried Riemschneider*. *Die wunderbare Beständigkeit der Liebe, oder Orpheus* has been published in volume 50 (2011) of the Telemann selective critical edition*. *CloTon, HutFra, PegOrp, RuhOpe, SchFra.*

Zachariae, Justus Friedrich Wilhelm Zachariae (1726–77) studied law at Leipzig University (1743–47) and was still a student when he published his epic poem *Der Renommist* (1744). Following further study in Göttingen, he moved to Brunswick, where he became a professor of literature in 1761 and was active as a translator, editor and author. During the 1750s and early 1760s he provided librettos for Telemann's *Die Tageszeiten** (TVWV 20:39; 1757), *Das befreite Israel** (TVWV 6:5; 1759) and *Die Auferstehung** (TVWV 6:7; 1761). In reaction to Telemann's concert works of 1755–56, including *Der Tod Jesu** and *Die Donner-Ode**, Zachariae ended his poem *Der Abend* (part of his *Tageszeiten* cycle of poems) with the lines '*Telemann*, niemand als du, du Vater der heiligen Tonkunst, / dessen erhabnen Gesang der Gallier selber bewundert, / Kann mit irdischen Tönen die Chöre der Engel entzücken' (Telemann, no one but you, you father of holy composition, whose sublime song is admired by the French themselves, can enrapture choirs of angels with earthly tones).

Zelenka, Jan Dismas Zelenka (1679–1745), first a violone player and eventually church composer in the Dresden* electoral *Hofkapelle*, would have met Telemann no later than September 1719, when the latter visited Dresden on the occasion of the wedding between the Habsburg archduchess Maria Josepha and the electoral prince Friedrich August II. In 1728 Telemann published Zelenka's retrograde canon *Cantilena circularis 'Vide Domine'*, ZWV 179, in *Der getreue Music-Meister**; this was the only work by Zelenka to be printed during his lifetime. But some years later Telemann attempted to publish another one. In a letter* to Telemann of 16 April 1749, Johann Georg Pisendel* sent his friend a manuscript of Zelenka's twenty-seven *stile antico* motets, the *Responsoria pro hebdomada sancta*, ZWV 55, that he had copied surreptitiously in fulfilment of a long-standing promise. Pisendel asked that his involvement in the matter be kept confidential and urged Telemann to abbreviate Zelenka's title and omit the concluding 'Gratias' so as to avoid suspicion that he possessed the complete score, which was the exclusive property of the Dresden court. In three subsequent letters from Pisendel over as many years, it emerges that Telemann intended to publish the *Responsoria*. Pisendel suggested that the works be issued together, rather than piecemeal, and that they might be printed in Paris, England or Holland. In the end, though, Zelenka's music remained unpublished. In 1756, the year after Pisendel's death, Telemann remarked on his manuscript of the *Responsoria* that 'owing to the exceptional effort it contains, this work deserves an admirer [*Liebhaber*] who can afford at least one hundred Reichstalers to possess it'. *MaeZel, TelBri.*

Zell-Jahrgang *See* ***Oratorischer Jahrgang***

Zentrum für Telemann-Pflege und -Forschung The Centre for Telemann Promotion and Research in Magdeburg was founded in conjunction with the study group 'Georg Philipp Telemann', established in 1961 under the aegis of the German Democratic Republic's cultural alliance. Under the direction of Carsten Lange*, who in 2003 succeeded Wolf Hobohm*, the centre employs three additional full-time researchers (Brit Reipsch*, Ralph-Jürgen Reipsch* and Ute Poetzsch*), is the editorial home of the Telemann selective critical edition*, organises the biennial Telemann-Festtage*, runs an annual concert series, houses an extensive library of materials relating to the life and works of Telemann, and produces in-house editions with performing parts available for hire. Its extensive list of publications include conference reports deriving from the Telemann-Festtage (since 1963), the series Magdeburger Telemann-Studien (since 1966), editions of librettos and facsimiles of documentary and musical sources.

Ziegler, Christiane Mariane von A celebrated poet and *salonnière*, Ziegler (1695–1760) was the daughter of Franz Conrad Romanus*, mayor of Leipzig during Telemann's university years in the city. Thus Telemann most likely knew her when she was still a child. Ziegler later studied in Leipzig with the literature professor Johann Christoph Gottsched and published three volumes of poetry and one of letters (1728–39), winning the Deutsche Gesellschaft's prize for poetry in 1732 and 1734. She was crowned imperial poet laureate in 1733 by the philosophical faculty of the University of Wittenberg. Telemann is the first composer known to have set her secular poetry, in the cantata *Ich kann lachen, weinen, schertzen*, TVWV 20:15 (published in *Der getreue Music-Meister**). Ziegler's *Moralische und vermischte Send-Schreiben, an einige Ihrer vertrauten und guten Freunde gestellet* (Moral and miscellaneous epistles to several of her acquaintances and good friends), includes one letter, possibly fictitious, to an unidentified *Kapellmeister* who may well be Telemann. In 1733 she subscribed to the *Musique de table**. *ZohFai.*

Zimmermann, Joachim Johann Daniel Zimmermann (1710–67) attended Hamburg's Johanneum school before undertaking theology studies in Rostock and Helmstedt. Returning to Hamburg, he was catechist at the Werk- und Zuchthaus from 1738 and in 1741 became deacon (later archdeacon) at the Katharinenkirche. As one of Telemann's most important librettists, he provided the composer with texts to numerous sacred, secular and occasional vocal works over three decades, among which are the 1733 funeral music* for Friedrich August I (Augustus the Strong), *In dunkler Nacht* (TVWV 4:7); four songs* in the *Singe-, Spiel- und Generalbass-Übungen* (he is probably the author identified only as 'Z.'); the *Kapitänsmusik** for 1734, 1736 and 1737 (TVWV 15:7, 9 and 10); the second set of six *Moralische Cantaten**; *Ein Lämmlein geht und trägt die Schuld** (the 1745 St John Passion; TVWV 5:30); the *Betrachtung der neunten Stunde an dem Todestag Jesu** (TVWV 5:5); and the 1762 inauguration music* for Hamburg's Great St Michaeliskirche (TVWV 2:12). *HirJoh.*

Zweytes sieben mal sieben und ein Menuet *See* **Friedrich Carl, imperial count of Erbach and Limburg** and **Keyboard music**

Works

Introductory notes

1 TVWV numbers are taken from Werner Menke, *Thematisches Verzeichnis der Vokalwerke von Georg Philipp Telemann*, 2nd edn, 2 vols (Frankfurt: Klostermann, 1988 and 1995).
2 TWV numbers are taken from Martin Ruhnke, *Georg Philipp Telemann: Thematisch-Systematisches Verzeichnis seiner Werke (TWV): Instrumentalwerke*, 3 vols (Kassel: Bärenreiter, 1984–99).
3 Works not listed in either of the above catalogues are indicated by '*deest*'.
4 When published sources are given, only the earliest such source is named.
5 Some lost works and pieces likely to have been written by Telemann are included, but misattributed ones are not.
6 A basso continuo part is assumed to be present unless otherwise stated.
7 Major keys are indicated by capitals, minor keys by lower case.
8 An 'equals' sign stands for 'equivalent to' or 'textually identical with'.
9 A forward slash is used to separate alternatives.

Abbreviations

A	alto voice (choral)
a	alto voice (solo)
ad lib.	ad libitum
anon.	anonymous
arr.	arrangement
attrib.	attributed to
B	bass voice (choral)
b	bass voice (solo)
bc	basso continuo
bn	bassoon
cal	calcedono
chal	chalumeau
cor	*corno* (horn in F)
corn	cornetto
edn	edition
fl	flute
frag.	fragmentary
hpd	harpsichord
kbd	keyboard (as obbligato part)
incompl	incompletely preserved
lib.	libretto
movt	movement
ob	oboe
obbl	obbligato
ob d'am	oboe d'amore
org	organ

perf.	performance
picc.	piccolo
poss	possibly
pub	published
rec	recorder (treble)
rev	revised by
S	soprano voice (choral)
s	soprano voice (solo)
str	strings – assumed, unless otherwise stated, to comprise parts for two violins, viola and cello (plus violone as appropriate)
T	tenor voice (choral)
t	tenor voice (solo)
tim	timpani
tr	trumpet in C or D
trb	trombone
vers	version
v	voice (solo)
va	viola
va d'am	viola d'amore
vadg	viola da gamba
vc	cello
vn	violin (solo)
vne	violone

Contents

The list of works is divided into the following sections:

1 Church cantatas

Listed alphabetically are extant works with secure attributions to Telemann. Scoring is SATB, str, bc unless otherwise stated; wind, brass and timpani parts supplement this basic ensemble.

Abbreviations for Sundays and feast days:

Ad	Advent
Ann	Annunciation of Mary
Asc	Ascension Day
Chr	Christmas Day
Eas	Easter Sunday
EasMon	Easter Monday
EasTue	Easter Tuesday
Ep	Epiphany Sunday
John	Feast of St John the Baptist
LSun	Low Sunday
Mich	Feast of St Michael
MThu	Maundy Thursday
NYD	New Year's Day
Palm	Palm Sunday
Pen	Pentecost (Whit Sunday)
Pur	Purification of Mary
Quin	Quinquagesima Sunday
Sept	Septuagesima Sunday
Sexa	Sexagesima Sunday
SuAsc	Sunday in Ascension Week
SuChr	Sunday after Christmas
SuNY	Sunday after New Year
Tr	Trinity Sunday
Vis	Visitation of Mary

Note that Ad1 = first Sunday in Advent; Chr2 = second day of Christmas; Eas2 = second Sunday after Easter; Ep1 = first Sunday after Epiphany; Lent1 = first Sunday in Lent; Pen2 = second day of Pentecost; Tr2 = second Sunday after Trinity.

Abbreviations for annual cycles (*Jahrgänge*):

PoetFr	*Poetische Früchte der Lippen*, librettos by E. Neumeister, 1700
GeistC	*Geistliche Cantaten*, librettos by E. Neumeister c. 1702–06
GSuS-I	*Geistliches Singen und Spielen*, librettos by E. Neumeister, 1710–11
GSuS-II	*Geistliches Singen und Spielen* (second setting), librettos by E. Neumeister, 1717–18
FranzJ	*Französischer Jahrgang*, librettos by E. Neumeister, 1714–15
ConcJ	*Concerten-Jahrgang*, librettos by E. Neumeister, 1716–17 and 1719–20
NeuL	*Neues Lied*, librettos by P.G. Simonis, 1717 and 1720–21
SicJ	*Sicilianischer Jahrgang*, librettos by J.F. Helbig, 1719–20
RambGP	*Geistliche Poesien*, librettos by J.J. Rambach, 1720
Ling1	First *Lingen-Jahrgang*, librettos by U. von Lingen, 1723–24?
BranJ	*Brandenburg-Jahrgang*, librettos by M.C. Brandenburg, 1723–24
JoR	*Jahrgang ohne Rezitativ*, librettos by J.F. Helbig and B. Neukirch, 1724–25
HarmGD	*Harmonischer Gottesdienst*, librettos by M.A. Wilkens and others, 1725–26; publ. Hamburg, 1725–27
HarmLG	*Harmonisches Lob Gottes*, librettos by J.F. Helbig, 1726–27
AdA	*Auszug derjenigen musicalischen und auf die gewöhnlichen Evangelien gerichteten Arien*, (Hamburg, 1727; 2nd edn, 1733)
EmbJ	*Emblematischer Jahrgang*, librettos by J.F.A. von Uffenbach, 1727–28
Ling2	Second *Lingen-Jahrgang*, librettos by U. von Lingen, 1728–29
OratJ	*Oratorischer Jahrgang*, librettos by J. Zell, 1730–31
SchuJ	*Schubart-Jahrgang*, librettos by T.H. Schubart, 1731–32
FoHarmGD	*Fortsetzung des Harmonischen Gottesdienstes* (Hamburg, 1731–32)
StolbJ	*Stolbergischer Jahrgang*, librettos by G. Behrndt, 1736–37
MusLG	*Musicalisches Lob Gottes*, librettos by E. Neumeister, 1742–43; publ. Nuremberg, 1742–44
LiedJ	*Lied-Jahrgang*, librettos by E. Neumeister, 1743–44
EngelJ	*Engel-Jahrgang*, librettos by D. Stoppe and anon. (from Tr7), 1747–49, publ. Hermsdorf, 1748–49
HornJ	*Horn-Jahrgang*, librettos by anon. poets, 1739–40
49/50J	Cycle with librettos by anon. poets, 1749–50

TVWV	*Title*	*Occasion*	*Scoring*	*Cycle/Comments*
1:1	*Abscheuliche Tiefe des großen Verderbens*	SuChr	2 fl	SchuJ, FoHarmGD
1:358a	*Absteigende Gottheit in menschliche Tiefe!*	Ann	v, bc	AdA
1:3	*Ach bleib mit deinem Worte*	EasMon	2 vn	EngelJ
1:4	*Ach, daß der Herr aus Zion käme*	Ad1	2 ob	49/50J
1:5	*Ach, daß der Herr aus Zion käme*	Chr2	cor	HornJ
1:7	*Ach, daß du den Himmel zerrissest*	Chr	3 tr, tim	1725
1:9	*Ach ewiges Wort, in Herz und Mund*	Chr3	s, vn, va, bc	FoHarmGD
1:10	*Ach Gott, dein Zion klagt und weint*	Tr17		EngelJ
1:11	*Ach Gott, du bist gerecht*	Tr22	2 ob	GSuS-I
1:12	*Ach Gott, es geht gar übel zu*	Tr8		EngelJ
1:14	*Ach Gott vom Himmel sieh darein*	Tr10		EngelJ
1:16	*Ach Gott, wie drückt die Last der Sünden*	Tr19	2 ob	SchuJ, FoHarmGD
1:18	*Ach Gott, wie manches Herzeleid*	Ad3	2 ob	FranzJ
1:19	*Ach Gott, wie manches Herzeleid*	EasTue	2 ob	FranzJ
1:20	*Ach Gott, wie manches Herzeleid*	Chr2	2 ob	JoR
1:21	*Ach Gott, wie manches Herzeleid*	SuAsc		EngelJ
1:24	*Ach Herr, lehr uns bedenken wohl*	Tr16	2 ob	
1:26	*Ach Herr, wie ist meiner Feinde so viel*	SuNY	2 ob ad lib.	ConcJ
1:27	*Ach Herr, wie sind meiner Feinde so viel*	SuNY	2 ob	Ling1
1:29	*Ach mein Herze schwimmt im Blute*	Tr11	2 ob	GSuS-I

1:30	*Ach Not, wenn Gottes Hand*	Tr25	s, v, va, bc	FoHarmGD
1:31	*Ach sagt mir nichts von Gold und Schätzen*	Tr15		EngelJ
1:294	*Ach Seele, hungre, dürste*	Tr2	s, 2 rec, bc	FoHarmGD
1:32	*Ach, sollte doch die ganze Welt*	Tr18	2 ob	FranzJ
1:33	*Ach süße Ruh, die stets mein Geist*	Tr22	2 ob	SchuJ, FoHarmGD
1:34	*Ach, welche Bitterkeit der Schmerzen*	Tr16		SchuJ, FoHarmGD
1:*deest*	*Ach, wer flößet*			frag.
1:35	*Ach, wer verkündigt mir, was mir ins zukünftige*	Eas4		OratJ
1:36	*Ach, wie beißt mich mein Gewissen*	Tr11	2 ob	FranzJ
1:37	*Ach, wie nichtig, ach wie flüchtig*	Tr25	2 fl, 2 ob	StolbJ
1:38	*Ach, wie nichtig, ach wie flüchtig*	Tr 24	3 rec, bn, 4 vadg	Hildesheim or Leipzig?
1:39	*Ach, wie so gut ist hier zu sein*	Ep6	with 2 T, 3 B	OratJ
1:40	*Ach, wie so lang, ach, Herr*	Ep2	2 ob	BranJ
1:41	*Ach, wo bin ich hingeraten*	Tr3	t, ob	
1:42	*Ach, wo bin ich hingeraten*		2 fl	lib. by E. Neumeister
1:43	*Ach, wo flieh ich Armer hin*	Tr3	2 ob	GSuS-I
1:45	*Ach, wo kömmt doch das böse Ding her*	Tr23	SAB	MusLG
1:47	*Ach wundergroßer Siegesheld*	Asc	ob, 2 tr, tim	49/50J
1:48	*Ach, zu den tiefsten Jammer-Höhlen*		2 ob	SchuJ, FoHarmGD
1:50	*Alle, die gottselig leben wollen*	SuChr	2 ob	NeuL
1:51	*Alle, die gottselig leben wollen*	SuAsc	2 ob, 2 cor	FranzJ

1:52	*Alle, die gottselig leben wollen*	Eas3	2 ob, 3 tr	Ling1
1:54	*Alle, die gottselig leben wollen*	SuNY		GSuS-I
1:71	*Alle eure Sorge werfet auf den Herrn*	Tr15	2 ob	GSuS-I
1:55	*Alle gute Gaben und alle vollkommene Gabe*	Eas4	2 ob	Ling1
1:57	*Allein die Anfechtung lehret*	Lent2	2 ob	JoR
1:58	*Allein Gott in der Höh sei Her*	Chr	tr	
1:59	*Allein Gott in der Höh sei Ehr*		SBB	for Christmas; frag.
1:60	*Allein zu dir, Herr Jesu Christ*	Ann	2 ob, 2 bn, 2 tr, tim	49/50J
1:62	*Allein zu dir, Herr Jesu Christ*	Lent2	SATBB, ob, ob d'am	OratJ
1:64	*Allenthalben ist dies Leben*	Tr14		
1:65	*Aller Augen warten auf dich*	Lent4	2 ob	GSuS-I
1:66	*Aller Augen warten auf dich*	Tr7	3 ob	ConcJ
1:67	*Aller Augen warten auf dich*	Tr15	2 ob	JoR
1:68	*Alles Fleisch ist Heu*	Tr16	2 ob	HarmLG, AdA
1:69	*Alles, was ihr tut*	NYD	fl, 2 tr, tim	1756
1:70	*Alles, was von Gott geboren ist*	Tr	2 ob, 2 tr, tim	Ling1
1:72	*Allmächtiger, heiliger, starker Gott*	Lent1	SSAABBB, 2 fl, 2 ob	OratJ
1:73	*All's Glück und Ungelücke*	Tr12	ob	
1:74	*Also hat Gott die Welt geliebet*	Pen2	2 ob	GSuS-II
1:75	*Also hat Gott die Welt geliebet*	Pen2	2 ob, bn	NeuL
1:76	*Also hat Gott die Welt geliebet*	Pen2	2 fl, 2 ob	GSuS-I

1:77	*Also hat Gott die Welt geliebet*	Pen2	2 ob, 3 tr, tim	Ling1
1:80	*Also hat Gott die Welt geliebet*	Pen2	2 tr, tim	lib. by Simonis, 1726
1:82	*Also hat Gott die Welt geliebet*	Pen2	SAB	MusLG
1:86	*Also hat Gott die Welt geliebet*	Pen2	3 tr, tim	frag.
1:87	*Also hoch und also sehr*	Pen2		EngelJ
1:89	*Also schweig, mein Mund*	Pen2	2 ob ad lib., 2 cor	FranzJ
1:93	*Am göttlichen Segen ist alles gelegen*	Tr7	2 fl, 2 ob	StolbJ
1:94	*Am guten Tag sei guter Dinge*	Lent2	2 ob	SchuJ, FoHarmGD
1:91	*Amen, Lob und Ehre*	Chr	SAB	MusLG; first movt = TVWV 8:2
1:92	*Amen, Lob und Ehre*	SuChr	2 ob	lib. partly E. Neumeister
1:96	*Auf ehernen Mauern*	LSun	v, rec, bc	HarmGD
1:97	*Auf ein gleich erhörtes Flehen*	Tr14	2 ob	BranJ
1:98	*Auf, erwachet meine Sinnen*	Chr3		EngelJ
1:99	*Auf, fröhliches Zion, auf*	NYD	b	
1:100	*Auf Gott will ich mich stets verlassen*		s, b, vn, vc	
1:101	*Auf grüner Auen wollest du*	Pen or Pen3	2 ob, 2 tr, tim	lib. by Telemann
1:103	*Auf ihr Priester, auf zum Schlachten*	Palm	with 2 T, 3 B, fl	OratJ
1:104	*Auf, lasset in Zions geheiligten Hallen*	Eas	2 fl, 2 ob, 2 tr, tim	1756
1:106	*Auf, mein Herz, rüste dich*	Ad2	ob	for Communion, lib. by Schmolck
1:108	*Auf, und lasset uns besingen*	Eas	t, 2 vn	
1:109	*Auf Zion, und laß in geheiligten Hallen*	Chr	fl, 2 ob, 3 tr, tim	1760

1:110	*Augenweide, Fleischeslust*		2 b	
1:112	*Aus Gnaden seid ihr selig worden*	Sept	2 ob, 3 tr, tim	Ling1
1:113	*Aus Gnaden seid ihr selig worden*	Sept	SAB	MusLG
1:*deest*	*Aussatz hat mich ganz gefressen*	Ep3		1740
1:114	*Aus Zion bricht an der schöne Glanz*	Ad2	ob	HarmLG, AdA
1:116	*Barmherzig und gnädig ist der Herr*	Tr22	2 ob	HarmLG, AdA
1:261a	*Beglückte Mutter*	Ep	v, bc	AdA
1:118	*Beglückte Zeit, die uns*	Tr24	v, vn, bc	HarmGD
1:119	*Begnadigte Seelen, gesegneter*	Tr5	v, ob, bc	HarmGD
1:120	*Bei dem Herrn findet man Hilfe*	Tr12	2 ob	JoR
1:121	*Bekehret euch zu mir*	Tr3	ob	SchuJ, FoHarmGD
1:122	*Belebende Lüfte*	Eas	2 ob, 2 tr, tim	1763
1:123	*Bequemliches Leben, gemächlicher Stand*	Eas2	SATBB	OratJ
1:124	*Bestelle dein Haus*	Tr16	s, b, 2 rec	
1:127	*Bittet, so wird euch gegeben*	Eas5	2 ob	GSuS-I
1:128	*Bittet, so wird euch gegeben*	Lent2	fl, 2 ob	NeuL
1:130	*Bleib, o Jesu, bleib bei mir*		s, 2 vn	
1:131	*Brannte nicht unser Herz in uns*	EasMon	2 ob	JoR
1:132	*Brausende Stürme, wallende Wellen*	Ep4	2 ob	BranJ
1:133	*Brich an und werde Licht*	Chr	ob, 2 tr, tim	49/50J
1:134	*Brich dem Hungrigen dein Brot*	Tr13	2 ob	FranzJ

1:135	*Christen heißen und nicht sein*	Ad4	2 ob	FranzJ
1:136	*Christ ist erstanden*	Eas1	2 ob	FranzJ
1:137	*Christum lieb haben ist besser*	Tr18	fl, 2 ob	GSuS-I
1:149	*Christus aber ist gekommen*	SuAsc	2 ob	HarmLG, AdA
1:138	*Christus der ist mein Leben*	Eas	2 ob	lib. by M. Vulpius; Danzig, 1754?
1:139	*Christus hat ausgezogen die Fürstentümer*	Eas1 and 2	2 fl, 3 tr, tim	1757
1:140	*Christus hat einmal für die Sünde gelitten*	Quin	2 ob	FranzJ
1:141	*Christus hat gelitten für uns*	Palm	2 ob ad lib.	ConcJ
1:142	*Christus hat sich selbst für uns gegeben*	Tr17	2 ob	JoR
1:144	*Christus hat unsre Sünde selbst geopfert*	Ann/Palm	2 ob	
1:145	*Christus ist aufgefahren*	Asc	2 ob	SicJ
1:148	*Christus ist der Glanz*	Pur		JoR
1:150	*Christus ist nicht eingegangen*	Eas4	2 ob	ConcJ
1:151	*Christus ist um unserer Missetat willen*	Quin	2 ob, 2 tr	NeuL
1:152	*Christus ist wahrlich der Prophet*	Lent4	2 ob	JoR
1:154	*Da die Zeit erfüllet war*	Chr2	2 tr, tim	lib. by Behrmann, 1726
1:*deest*	*Da ich mich hier eingefunden*	Pur	2 fl, 2 ob	lib. by E. Neumeister, before 1721
1:156	*Da Jesus nun merkte*	Lent4	2 ob	ConcJ
1:175	*Da sie aber davon redeten*	EasTue		ConcJ
1:155	*Dafür halte uns jedermann*	Tr9	2 ob	SchuJ, FoHarmGD
1:157	*Danket dem Herrn, denn er ist freundlich*	SuChr	2 ob, 2 cor	ConcJ

1:158	*Danket dem Herrn, denn er ist freundlich*	John		Ling1
1:159	*Danket dem Herrn, denn er ist freundlich*	NYD	fl, 2 ob, 2 cor	FranzJ
1:163	*Danket dem Herrn Zebaoth*	SuChr	2 chal, 2 ob	GSuS-I
1:165	*Daran ist erschienen die Liebe Gottes*	Pen2	fl, 2 ob	ConcJ
1:167	*Daran ist erschienen die Liebe Gottes*	Chr2		Ling1
1:168	*Daran ist erschienen die Liebe Gottes*	Pen2	2 ob, 2 cor	SchuJ, FoHarmGD
1:169	*Darum, wenn sie zu euch sagen*	Tr25	fl, ob	
1:166	*Darzu ist erschienen die Liebe Gottes*	Chr3	2 ob	NeuL
1:170	*Das Blöken der Schafe, das Brüllen der Rinder (Der für Saul erwählte und gesalbte David)*	Ann	SSATTBB, 2 tr	OratJ
1:171	*Das Blut Christi wird unser Gewissen reinigen*	Tr14	2 ob	SicJ
1:172	*Das Blut Jesu Christi, des Sohns Gottes*	LSun	with 2 S, 2 ob, cor	NeuL
1:173	*Das ew'ge Licht geht da herein*	Chr3		
1:174	*Das heulende Winseln aus Belias Rachen*	Eas	2 fl, 2 ob, 2 tr	1755
1:176	*Das ist das ewige Leben*	Pen3	2 ob	SicJ
1:177	*Das ist das ewige Leben*	Tr18	2 ob	ConcJ; lib. by Telemann
1:178	*Das ist die Freudigkeit*	Eas5	SAB	MusLG
1:180	*Das ist ein köstlich Ding*	Tr14	2 ob, tr	GSuS-I
1:181	*Das ist je gewißlich wahr*	Tr3	2 ob	NeuL; falsely attrib. to J.S. Bach (BWV 141)
1:182	*Das ist je gewißlich wahr*	Tr3	2 ob	ConcJ
1:183	*Das ist je gewißlich wahr*	Ad3	2 ob	SicJ

1:184	*Das ist je gewißlich wahr*	Ad3	2 fl, 2 ob	SchuJ, FoHarmGD
1:186	*Das ist meine Freude und Zuversicht*		SAB	before 1758
1:187	*Das ist meine Freude*		b, 2 ob	lib. by Helbig
1:188	*Das ist meine Freude*	Vis	2 ob	SicJ
1:189	*Das ist sein Gebot, da wir gläuben*	Tr13	SAB	MusLG
1:190	*Das Kreuz ist eine Liebesprobe*	Tr21	2 ob	GSuS-I
1:191	*Das macht Gottes Vaterherz*	John		EngelJ
1:192	*Das Manna deiner Speise*		b, 2 fl	lib. by Lehms; for Communion
1:193	*Das Reich Gottes ist nicht Essen und Trinken*	Tr2	2 ob	SicJ
1:195	*Das sollst du wissen, daß in den letzten Tagen*	Tr25	SAB	MusLG
1:196	*Das weiß ich fürwahr*	EasTue	2 ob	ConcJ
1:197	*Das weiß ich fürwahr*	John	2 ob	NeuL
1:198	*Das weiß ich fürwahr*	Tr24	SAB	MusLG
1:199	*Das Wetter rührt mit Strahl und Blitzen*	Tr9	v, ob, bc	HarmGD
1:200	*Das Wort Jesus Christus*	Chr3	2 ob	GSuS-I
10:22	*Das Wort unsers Gottes bleibt ewiglich*		a, t, 2 vn, bc	PoetFr
1:202	*Das Wort ward Fleisch*	Ad3		Ling1
1:203	*Das Wort ward Fleisch*	Chr	2 ob	HarmLG, AdA
1:194	*Daß Herz und Sinn, o schwacher*	Tr27	v, vn, bc	HarmGD
1:204	*Davids Sohn, laß mich Hülfe schauen*	Lent2	2 ob	StolbJ
1:205	*Dazu ist erschienen der Sohn Gottes*	Lent3	2 ob	NeuL

1:206	*Dazu ist erschienen der Sohn Gottes*	Chr3	2 ob, 2 tr, tim	Ling1
1:207	*Dazu ist erschienen der Sohn Gottes*	Lent3	2 ob	SicJ
1:208	*Dazu ist erschienen der Sohn Gottes*	Lent3	with 2 S	
1:209	*Deine Liebe, liebster Jesu*	EasMon		
1:211	*Deiner Sanftmut Schild*	Tr6		EngelJ
1:212	*Deines neuen Bundes Gnade*	Tr13	v, fl, bc	HarmGD
1:214	*Dein gnädig Ohr*	Eas5		EngelJ
1:215	*Dein Schade ist verzweifelt böse*	Tr14	ob	ConcJ
1:1133	*Dein Schade ist verzweifelt böse*		s, ob, vn	before 1721
1:*deest*	*Dein Schade ist verzweifelt böse*		fl, ob	lib. by E. Neumeister, 1750
1:216	*Dein Wort ist meinem Munde süßer denn Honig*	Sexa	fl, 2 ob	NeuL
1:213	*Deine Toten werden leben*	Eas5	v, rec, bc	HarmGD
1:218	*Dem Herren mußt du trauen*	Tr15	2 ob	StolbJ
1:219	*Dem höchsten Gott zu loben*		b, cor, 2 vn	for harvest festival (*Erntedank*)
1:221	*Den Frommen geht das Licht auf*	Quin		Ling1
1:227	*Den Reichen von dieser Welt gebeut*	Tr9	2 ob	JoR
1:228	*Den Reichen von dieser Welt gebeut*	Tr9		JoR
1:220	*Denen, die Gott lieben*	Tr21	2 ob	ConcJ; lib. by Telemann
1:222	*Dennoch bleib ich immer stille*	Tr17	fl, 2 ob, 3 tr, tim	lib. by Telemann
1:226	*Denn so jemand das ganze Gesetz hält*	Tr13	2 ob	JoR
1:223	*Dennoch bleib ich stets an dir*	Tr12	2 ob	ConcJ

1:224	*Dennoch bleib ich stets an dir*	Lent2	2 ob	SicJ
1:225	*Dennoch bleib ich stets an dir*	Lent2		EngelJ
1:229	*Der allergrößeste, von Weisheit*	Tr17	2 ob	SchuJ, FoHarmGD
1:231	*Der arme Mensch muß durch der Sünden Schuld*	Eas4	2 ob	StolbJ
1:*deest*	*Der Demut will ich mich befleißen*			frag.
1:232	*Der Engel des Herrn lagert sich*	Mich	2 cor	GSuS-I
1:235	*Der Engel des Herrn lagert sich*	Mich	2 ob	SicJ
1:237	*Der Feind ist viel*	Tr9	2 fl, ob, cor	1758
1:238	*Der feste Grund Gottes bestehet*	EasMon	2 ob, 2 chal, bn	NeuL
1:239	*Der Friede Gottes, welcher höher ist*	LSun	2 ob, 2 cor, trb	Ling1
1:241	*Der Fromme muß allhier gar vieles*	SuAsc		Ling2
1:242	*Der Geist des Herrn*	Pen3		JoR
1:243	*Der Geist gibt Zeugnis*	Pen	2 tr, tim	EngelJ
1:245	*Der Gerechte kommt um*	Pur	2 fl, 2 ob	ConcJ
1:246	*Der Gerechte muß viel leiden*	Tr1	2 ob	ConcJ
1:247	*Der Gerechte muß viel leiden*	Tr1	2 ob, 3 tr, tim	Ling1
1:249	*Der Gott des Friedens zertrete*	EasTue	2 ob	NeuL
1:250	*Der Gott des Friedens*	EasMon	2 ob	SicJ
1:254	*Der Gott unsers Herrn Jesu Christi*	Eas4	2 ob	SicJ
1:251	*Der Gottlose ist wie ein Wetter*	Tr23	2 ob	NeuL
1:252	*Der Gottlose lasse von seinem Wege*	Tr10	2 ob	Ling1

1:253	*Der Gottlose lauret*	Tr22	2 ob	StolbJ
1:257	*Der Herr bewahret die Seelen*	SuNY	2 fl, 2 ob	NeuL
1:260	*Der Herr hat gesagt zu meinem Herrn*	Tr18	2 ob	JoR
1:262	*Der Herr hat offenbaret*	Chr	2 ob, 2 tr, tim	1762
1:*deest*	*Der Herr hats gemacht*	Pen2		1756; falsely listed as 1:1528
1:*deest*	*Der Herr ist König*			for the Leipzig council, 1722? = TVWV 8:6
1:263	*Der Herr ist mein getreuer Hirt*	EasMon	2 ob, tr	FranzJ
10:24	*Der Herr ist mein Gut und mein Theil*		a, b, 2 vn, bc	PoetFr
1:264	*Der Herr ist mein Hirte*	Pen3		FranzJ
1:265	*Der Herr ist mein Hirte*	Eas2	2 ob, 3 tr, tim	Ling1
1:266	*Der Herr ist mein Hirte*	Eas2	2 ob	JoR
1:268	*Der Herr ist mein Hirte*	Pen3	SAB	MusLG
1:273	*Der Herr ist nahe allen*	Lent2		HarmLG, AdA
1:274	*Der Herr ist nahe allen*	Ep3	2 ob	SicJ
1:275	*Der Herr ist nahe bei denen*	EasMon	2 ob	SicJ
1:276	*Der Herr ist nahe bei denen*	EasMon	2 ob	HarmLG, AdA
1:277	*Der Herr ist Sonn und Schild*	John	3 tr, tim	1725
1:278	*Der Herr ist unser Gott*	Sept	2 ob	
1:279	*Der Herr Jesus wird offenbaret werden*	Tr1	2 ob	JoR
1:280	*Der Herr kennet die Tage der Frommen*	Lent4	2 fl, 2 ob	NeuL
1:281	*Der Herr kennet die Tage der Frommen*	Lent4	2 ob	SchuJ, FoHarmGD

1:282	*Der Herr kennet die Tage der Frommen*	Tr5	2 ob	Ling1
1:283	*Der Herr kennet die Tage der Frommen*	Ep2		MusLG
1:284	*Der Herr lebet*	Eas	2 tr, tim	EngelJ
1:285	*Herr Herr regieret*	Ad4		EngelJ
1:286	*Der Herr schauet vom Himmel*	Tr20		frag.
1:287	*Der Herr sprach zu meinem Herrn*	Asc		1724 or earlier
1:288	*Der Herr verstößet nicht ewiglich*	Tr21	2 ob	FranzJ
1:289	*Der Herr weiß die Gottseligen*	Lent1	2 ob	Ling1
1:290	*Der Herr weiß die Gottseligen*	Lent3	2 ob	1724
1:291	*Der Herr wird den Elenden*	SuAsc	2 ob	SicJ
1:292	*Der Herr wird dich schlagen*	Tr10	2 ob	StolbJ
1:293	*Der Herr wird ein neues im Lande schaffen*	Tr20	2 ob	GSuS-I
1:295	*Der Himmel ist offen*	Asc	2 ob	FranzJ
1:297	*Der Himmel wird heiter*	Asc	ob, 2 tr, tim	1757
1:300	*Der höchste Gott ist rein*	Ep5	2 ob	FranzJ
1:301	*Der jüngste Tag wird bald*	Ad2		GSuS-II
1:302	*Der jüngste Tag wird bald*	Ad2		GSuS-I
1:303	*Der Kern verdammter Sünder*	Lent5	2 ob	SchuJ, FoHarmGD
1:306	*Der mit Sünden beleidigte Heiland*	NYD	2 ob, 3 tr, tim	SchuJ, FoHarmGD
1:308	*Der natürliche Mensch verstehet nicht*	Tr	2 ob ad lib.	HarmLG, AdA
1:312	*Der Regen Gottes fällt auf gute Sprossen*	Ep5	v, 2 vn, bc	FoHarmGD

1:313	*Der Reichtum macht allein beglückt*	Lent2	v, ob, bc	HarmGD
1:309	*Der Segen des Herrn machet reich ohne Mühe*	Tr9	2 ob	StolbJ
1:310	*Der Segen des Herrn macht reich ohne Mühe*	Tr5	2 ob	GSuS-I
1:311	*Der Segen des Herrn macht reich ohne Mühe*	Tr5	2 ob	GSuS-II
1:316	*Der Segen des Herrn macht reich*	Tr5	SAB	MusLG
1:317	*Der Sohn Gottes hat mich geliebet*	EasMon	2 ob	ConcJ
1:319	*Der Stein, den die Bauleute*	SuChr	ob	HarmLG, AdA
1:320	*Der Tod ist verschlungen in den Sieg*	Eas	2 ob, 2 tr, tim	NeuL
1:322	*Der Tod ist verschlungen in den Sieg*	EasTue	2 ob	SicJ
1:323	*Der Tod ist verschlungen in den Sieg*	Eas	with 4 T, 2 B, fl, 2 tr, tim	OratJ
1:324	*Der treue Freund, der unser Elend schaut*	Tr20	2 fl, 2 ob	StolbJ
1:327	*Des Königs Tochter ist ganz herrlich*	Ep2	ob	HarmLG, AdA
1:328	*Dich, den meine Seele*	Ep6	v, 2 vn, bc	FoHarmGD
1:329	*Dich rühmen die Welten*	Mich	2 ob, 3 tr, tim	lib. by J.J. Eschenburg, 1762
1: 330	*Die auf den Herrn hoffen, die werden*	Ad3		first movt as TVWV 7:8
1:331	*Die Bosheit siehet oft die größesten*	Tr6	2 ob	SchuJ, FoHarmGD
1:*deest*	*Die dicken Wolken schneiden sich*		fl, 2 tr, tim	1760
1:332	*Die Ehe soll ehrlich gehalten werden*	Ep2	2 ob	ConcJ
1:333	*Die Ehe soll ehrlich gehalten werden*	Ep2	2 ob	JoR
1:334	*Die Ehre des herrlichen Schöpfers*	Tr20	v, vn, bc	HarmGD
1:335	*Die Engel sind allzumal dienstbare Geister*	Mich		HarmLG, AdA

1:336	*Die Furcht des Herrn ist der rechte*	Ep1	2 ob	JoR
1:337	*Die Furcht des Herrn ist Ehre und Ruhm*	Eas	SSB, bc	1737
1:338	*Die G'bot uns all gegeben sind*	Pen, Pen2	2 fl, 2 ob	1755
1:339	*Die Gnadentüre stehet offen*	Tr1		EngelJ
1:344	*Die Gott vertrauen, die erfahren*	Tr25	2 ob	SicJ
1:341	*Die Gottes Gnad alleine*	Ep1	ob, 3 tr, tim	49/50J
1:343	*Die Gottlosen ziehen das Schwert aus*	SuNY	ob	HarmLG, AdA
1:345	*Die Grube ist von gestern her zugerichtet*	Tr1	2 ob ad lib.	HarmLG, AdA
1: 346	*Die Güte des Herrn ist, daß wir nicht*		s, b	for harvest festival (*Erntedank*)
1:347	*Die Hauptsumme der Gebote ist: Liebe*	Tr18	SAB	MusLG
1:348	*Die ihm vertrauen, die erfahren*	Ad3	SAB	MusLG
1:349	*Die Kinder des Höchsten*	John	v, vn, bc	HarmGD
1:350	*Die Liebe gegen meinen Gott*	Tr13	fl	
1:352	*Die mit Tränen säen*	Tr21	s, b, 2 vn, bc	
1:353	*Die Opfer, die Gott gefallen*	Ep	2 ob, 3 tr, tim	Ling1
1:*deest*	*Die so das Land des Lichts bewohnen*			
1:362	*Die, so ihr den Herren fürchtet*	Ep4	2 ob	ConcJ
1:363	*Die stärkende Wirkung des Geistes der Gnade*	Tr16	v, vn, bc	HarmGD
1:364	*Die stille Nacht umschloß den Kreis (Der am Öhlberg zagende Jesus)*	MThu	b	lib. by Telemann, by 1741
1:365	*Die Sünd hat uns verderbet sehr*	Lent5	2 fl, 2 ob	StolbJ
1:366	*Die Sünd macht Leid, Christus beut Freud*	Chr	fl, ob, 2 tr, tim	HornJ

1:367	*Die Wahrheit fällt auf der Gasse*	Lent5	2 ob, tr ad lib.	ConcJ
1:368	*Die Warheit ist ein edles Kind*	Pen2	2 ob	StolbJ
1:370	*Die Weisheit ruft, und keiner hört*	Tr2	2 fl, 2 ob	StolbJ
1:371	*Die Welt bekümmert sich*	SuAsc	2 ob	StolbJ
1:372	*Die Welt kann ihre Lust*	Tr21	ob	StolbJ
1:373	*Die Welt vergehet mit ihrer Lust*	Tr16	2 fl, ob	1758
1:356	*Dies ist der Gotteskinder Last*	Eas3	v, ob, bc	HarmGD
1:*deest*	*Dies ist der Tag, den der Herr*		t, vn, bn, bc	1741
1:359	*Dies ist der Tag, den der Herr*	Ann	SAB	MusLG
1:355	*Dieser Jesus, welcher von euch ist*	Asc	2 ob	
1:374	*Drei sind, die da zeugen im Himmel*	Tr	3 tr, tim	GSuS-II
1:375	*Drei sind, die da zeugen im Himmel*	Tr	2 ob, 2 cor, 2 tr, tim	lib. by E. Neumeister, 1725
1:376	*Drei sind, die da zeugen im Himmel*	Tr		JoR
1:377	*Drei sind, die da zeugen im Himmel*	Tr	2 ob, 2 x 3 tr, tim	GSuS-I; frag.
1:379	*Du aber, was richtest du deinen Bruder*	Tr4	2 ob	Ling1
1:382	*Du bist erschrecklich*	Tr22	2 ob	ConcJ; lib. by Telemann
1:384	*Du bist mein Vater, ich dein Kind*	SuChr		EngelJ
1:385	*Du bist verflucht, o Schreckensstimme*	Lent4	v, rec, bc	HarmGD
1:386	*Dünke dich nicht weise sein*	Tr4	2 ob	ConcJ
1:387	*Du fährest mit Jauchzen und heller Posaune*	Asc	v, vn, bc	HarmGD
1:389	*Du Gott, dem nichts ist verborgen*	LSun	2 fl, 2 ob	StolbJ

I:391	*Du Hirte Israel, höre*	Eas2		HarmLG, AdA
I:392	*Du machst mir, strenger Tod*	Tr24	v, 2 ob, bc	FoHarmGD
I:394	*Du, o schönes Weltgebäude*		2 fl, 2 ob	Danzig, 1754?
I:395	*Durch Adams Fall ist ganz verderbt*	Tr12	ob	1726
I:396	*Durch Adams Fall ist ganz verderbt*	Tr19		
I:402	*Du riefest einst aus tiefen Schlünden*	Pen	2 fl, ob, tr, tim	1761
I:403	*Du sollst lieben Gott deinen Herrn*	Tr13	2 ob	NeuL
I:404	*Du teure Liebe*	Tr18	2 ob	SchuJ, FoHarmGD
I:405	*Du Tochter Zion, freue dich*	Ad1	2 ob, 2 cor	JoR
I:406	*Du Tochter Zion, freue dich*	Ad1	2 ob, 2 cor	SchuJ, FoHarmGD
I:407	*Du Tochter Zion, freue dich*	Ad1	3 tr	EngelJ
I:408 = 405?	*Du Tochter Zion, freue dich*	Ad1	2 cor	JoR
I:409	*Du unbegreiflich höchstes Gut*	Pen	2 ob, 3 tr, tim	1747
I:397	*Durch Christi Auferstehungskraft*	EasTue		EngelJ
I:398	*Durch Christum habt ihr gehöret*	Pen3		ConcJ
I:400	*Durch tausend gekünstelte Ränke*	Lent1	2 ob	SchuJ, FoHarmGD
I:401	*Durch Trauren und durch Plagen*	NYD	2 fl, 2 tr, tim	49/50J
I:399	*Durchsuche dich, o stolzer Geist*	Tr11	v, rec, bc	HarmGD
I:410	*Edler Geist ins Himmels Throne*			lib. by J.G. Herrmann; for Pentecost
I:413	*Ehr und Dank sei dir gesungen*	Mich	2 tr, tim	EngelJ

1:411	*Ehre sei Gott in der Höhe*	Chr, Chr2	2 fl, 2 ob, 2 tr, tim	1756
1:412	*Ehre sei Gott in der Höhe*		3 tr, tim	for Christmas
1:432	*Ei nun, mein lieber Jesu*	Ep6		EngelJ
1:437	*Ei, warum sollt ich dich lassen*	Ep1		EngelJ
1:414	*Eilt hinweg, verfolgte Sinnen*	SuNY	2 ob	BranJ
1:415	*Eilt zu, ruft laut, ihr längst verlangten Boten*	Ad1	2 fl, 2 ob	OratJ
1:416	*Ein Arzt ist uns gegeben*	Ep3		EngelJ
1:417	*Ein Aussatz ist die Sünde*	Tr14	ob	FranzJ
1:419	*Ein feste Burg ist unser Gott*	Mich	b, bc	based on chorale by Martin Luther
1:420	*Ein feste Burg ist unser Gott*	Tri18	3 tr, tim	based on chorale by Martin Luther
1:421	*Ein gläubigs Flehn, in Jesu Namen*	Eas5	2 ob	StolbJ
1:*deest*	*Ein großer König überall*	Asc	2 ob, 3 tr, tim	frag.
1:422	*Ein gütiges Herz ist des Leibes Leben*	Tr4		
1:424	*Ein Jammerton, ein schluchzend Ach*	Ep2	2 ob	SchuJ, FoHarmGD
1:425	*Ein jeder läuft, der in den Schranken*	Sept	v, ob, bc	HarmGD
1:426	*Ein Kindelein so löbelich*	Chr2	2 ob	FranzJ
1:427	*Ein lispelnd murmelndes Gedränge*	Ep1	2 ob	SchuJ, FoHarmGD
1:429	*Ein Richter muß im Urteil sprechen*	Quin	2 ob	StolbJ
1:430	*Ein sanftes Erfreuen, ein ruhiges Ergetzen*	Sept	2 ob d'am	OratJ
1:434	*Ein ungefärbt Gemüte*	Tr4	2 ob, 2 cor, 2 tr	FranzJ
1:435	*Ein Weiser rühme sich nicht*	Ad4	2 ob ad lib.	NeuL

1:436	*Ein zartes Kind hat nirgends*	Tr25	v, vn, bc	HarmGD
1:418	*Einen solchen Hohen-Priester*	Lent5	2 ob	SicJ
1:431	*Eins bitte ich vom Herren*	Ep1	2 ob	ConcJ
1:433	*Eins ist not, ach Herr, dies eine*	Tr2		
1:440	*Endlich wird die Stunde schlagen*	Ad2	v, ob, bc	HarmGD
1:442	*Entzückende Lust, unendliche Freuden*			for Communion; frag.
1:444	*Er, der Herr des Friedens*	EasTue	2 ob	GSuS-I
1:445	*Er, der Messias, ist ein Stein des Anstoßens*	SuChr	2 ob	SicJ
1:452	*Er hat alles wohlgemacht*	Tr12	SAB	MusLG
1:453	*Er hat ein Gedächtnis gestiftet*	Lent3	ob	1758
1:455	*Erhebet den Herrn*		3 tr, tim	frag.
1:460	*Er ist auferstanden*	Eas	2 tr	
1:461	*Er ist mein, und ich bin sein*	Pen3		EngelJ
1:462	*Er kam, lobsinget ihm*	Asc	ob, fl, 3 tr, tim	1759
1:464	*Er kennt die rechten Freudenstunden*	Ep2		EngelJ
1:443	*Erbarm dich mein*	Tr22		1721
1:447	*Ergeuß dich zur Salbung*	Pen3	v, vn, bc	HarmGD
1:448	*Ergötzt euch nur, ihr eitlen Seelen*	Eas2	ob, vn, bc	lib. by E. Neumeister
1:467	*Er neigte den Himmel*	Asc	ob, 3 tr, tim	1276
1:484	*Er wird trinken vom Bach auf dem Wege*	EasMon	SSAATTBBB, 2 fl, 2 ob, 3 tr, tim	OratJ

1:449	*Erhalt mich, o Herr, in deinem*	Tr22	v, fl, bc	HarmGD
1:450	*Erhalt mein Herz im Glauben*	LSun		EngelJ
1:451	*Erhalt uns, Herr, bei deinem Wort*	Tr8	2 ob	FranzJ
1:457	*Erhebt euch, weil Christus gen Himmel gefahren*	Asc	2 ob	BranJ
1:458	*Erhöhet die Täler*	Ad4	v, vn, bc	HarmGD
1:459	*Erhöre mich, wenn ich rufe*	Eas5	2 ob, corn, 2 trb	ConcJ
1:465	*Erkenntliche Christen, frohlocket und lachet*	Pen3	2 ob	BranJ
1:129a	*Erleuchtet uns, wesentliche Klarheit*	Eas5	v, bc	AdA
1:466	*Ermuntert euch, bestürzte Sinnen*	EasMon		BranJ
1:*deest*	*Ermuntre dich, mein schwacher Geist*	Ep		HarmLG, AdA; falsely listed as 1:261
1:468	*Eröffne dich, du Reich der Seligkeiten*	Asc	ob, 3 tr, tim	
1:469	*Erquickendes Wunder*	Chr	v, vn, bc	HarmGD
1:470	*Erquicktes Herz, sei voller Freuden*	Chr2	b, vn, bc	
1:471	*Erscheine, Gott, in deinem Tempel*	Pur	v, fl, bc	HarmGD
1:472	*Erschrick, im Geiz versenkter Sünder*	Tr9	2 ob	Ling1
1:473	*Erschrick, mein Herz, vor dir*	Tr14		
1:474	*Erstanden ist der heilge Christ*		ob, bn, 2 tr, tim	1737
1:475	*Erster Anfang, letztes Ende*	Ad4	2 v	BranJ
1:476	*Ertönet bald herrlich, ihr letzten Posaunen*	Ad2	ob, cor, tr	SchuJ, FoHarmGD
1:479	*Ertrage nur das Joch der Mängel*	Tr1	2 ob	SchuJ, FoHarmGD

1:480	*Erwachet, entreißt euch den sündigen Träumen*	SuAsc	v, vn, bc	HarmGD
1:481	*Erwachet zum Kriegen*	Ad1	v, vn, bc	HarmGD
1:482	*Erwecke dich, Herr, warum schläfest du*	Ep4	2 ob	NeuL
1:485	*Erzittre, Welt, vor dem Gericht*	Ad2		BranJ
1:486	*Es danken dir, Gott, die Völker*	Sexa	ob	HarmLG, AdA
1:487	*Es erhub sich ein Streit im Himmel*	Mich	2 tr	
1:488	*Es erhub sich ein Streit im Himmel*	Mich	ob, cor	
1:489	*Es fähret Jesus auf, mit Jauchzen*	Asc	2 ob, 3 tr, tim	SchuJ, FoHarmGD
1:491	*Es gleitet mein Fuß auf schlüpfrigen Wegen*	Ep1	SATBB	OratJ
1:492	*Es hat mich umgeben Leiden ohne Zahl*	Tr12	2 ob	Ling1
1:494	*Es ist das Heil uns kommen her*	Sept	2 ob	GSuS-I
1:495	*Es ist das Herz ein trotzig und verzagt Ding*	Tr19	2 ob	NeuL
1:496	*Es ist dir gesagt, Mensch, was gut ist*	Tr4	2 ob	JoR
1:497	*Es ist dir gesagt, Mensch, was gut ist*	Tr17	SAB	MusLG
1:498	*Es ist ein elend jämmerlich Ding*	Tr16	2 ob	JoR
1:500	*Es ist ein Gott und ein Mittler*	Pen2	2 ob	JoR
1:501	*Es ist ein großer Gewinn*	Sept	2 ob	ConcJ
1:502	*Es ist ein großer Gewinn*	Tr15	2 ob	ConcJ
1:503	*Es ist ein großer Gewinn*	Tr7	2 ob	SicJ
1:504	*Es ist ein köstlich Ding*	Eas3	2 ob	SicJ
1:506	*Es ist ein schlechter Ruhm*	Tr19	v, rec, bc	HarmGD

1:499	*Es ist eine Stimme eines Predigers*	John	2 fl, ob	1758
1:507	*Es ist erschienen die heilsame Gnade*	Chr	2 ob	SicJ
1:508	*Es ist erschienen die heilsame Gnade*	Ann	ob	1754
1:509	*Es ist gewißlich an der Zeit*	Tr25		EngelJ
1:510	*Es ist gewißlich an der Zeit*	Ad2	2 tr	OratJ
1:511	*Es ist gewißlich an der Zeit*	Tr25 and Tr26	s, a	
1:512	*Es ist gut, auf den Herrn vertrauen*	Tr21	2 ob	JoR
1:513	*Es ist keine Obrigkeit ohne von Gott*	Tr23	2 ob	HarmLG, AdA
1:514	*Es ist um aller Menschen Leben*	Tr14	2 ob	SchuJ, FoHarmGD
1:515	*Es ist umsonst, daß ihr früh aufsteht*	Tr5	2 ob	NeuL
1:516	*Es ist umsonst, daß ihr früh aufsteht*	Tr5	2 fl, 2 ob, bn	HarmLG, AdA
1:*deest*	*Es ist umsonst, daß ihr früh aufstehet*	Tr5	2 fl, 2 ob, bn	1720
1:517	*Es jauchzen die Engel entzückende Lieder*	Chr	fl, 2 ob, 2 tr, tim	1758
1:*deest*	*Es kann nicht anders sein*	Eas3		Ling2; replaces falsely attributed 1:518
1:519	*Es komm mein End heut oder morgen*	Pur	rec, 2 fl, ob	1758
1:520	*Es kömmet die Stunde*	Tr26	2 ob	SicJ
1:521	*Es kommt die Zeit heran*	Asc	2 T, 7 B, fl, 3 tr, tim	OratJ
1:523	*Es lebt so mancher Mensch in Sünde*	Ad2		1728
1:524	*Es sei denn, daß jemand*	Ad4		JoR
1:526	*Es sei fern von mir rühmen*	Palm	fl, 2 ob	NeuL

1:527	*Es sind mancherlei Gaben*	Pen	2 ob	JoR
1:528	*Es sind schon die letzten Zeiten*	Ad2		EngelJ
1:529	*Es sind schon die letzten Zeiten*	Tr25	b, ob	OratJ
1:530	*Es soll auf diesen Tag niemand sterben*	Ann		JoR
1:531	*Es spielen die Strahlen der göttlichen Stärke*	Tr12	2 fl, 2 ob	SchuJ, FoHarmGD
1:532	*Es spricht, der solches zeuget*	Ad2	SAB	MusLG
1:*deest*	*Es spricht der Unweisen Mund*	Tr8		GSuS-I
1:533	*Es spricht der Unweisen Mund*	Tr8		GSuS-II
1:535	*Es werden nicht alle, die zu mir sagen: Abba*	Tr8	2 ob	JoR
1:*deest*	*Es werden nicht alle, die zu mir sagen: Herr*	Tr8	2 ob	by 1725
1:536	*Es werden sich viele falsche Propheten*	Tr25	2 ob	Ling1
1:537	*Es wird des Herrn Tag kommen*	Tr23	2 ob	NeuL
1:538	*Es wird des Herrn Tag kommen*	Tr27	rec, 2 ob	1759
1:539	*Es wird ein Durchbrecher vor ihnen herauffahren*	Eas	2 ob, 3 tr, tim	StolbJ
1:541	*Es wird ein Tag sein*	Tr25	fl, ob	
1:542	*Es wird ein unbarmherzig Gericht*	Tr1	2 ob ad lib.	NeuL
1:543	*Es wird geschehen, daß des Menschen Sohn*	Tr26	2 ob	JoR
1:544	*Es wollt uns Gott genädig sein*	Tr14	2 ob	LiedJ
1:545	*Euch zuvörderst hat Gott auferwecket*	Tr10		JoR
1:546	*Ewge Quell, milder Strom*	Eas4	v, fl, bc	HarmGD
1:547	*Feiert, Kinder des Höchsten*	Pen	2 fl, 2 ob, 2 tr, tim	1760

1:548	*Findet nun im Grabe Ruh*			extant only in modern edn
1:549	*Findet nun im Grabe Ruh*	Lent1	v, vn, bc	HarmGD
1:550	*Fleuch der Lüste deiner Jugend*	SuNY	SSATTB	OratJ
1:552	*Flügel her, nur Flügel her*	Pur	fl, ob, cor	HornJ
1:553	*Fraget nicht, was mich betrübet*	Ep1	2 ob	FranzJ
1:554	*Fragst du, Jesu, was ich liebe*		b	for Communion, c. 1721
1:555	*Freu dich sehr, o meine Seele*	Tr16	fl, 2 ob	1721
1:557	*Freuet euch, die ihr mit Christo*	Chr2	SAB	MusLG
1:558	*Freuet euch, ihr Himmel*	Mich	SSATB, 2 tr, tim	1758
1:559	*Freuet euch mit Jerusalem*	Eas	2 fl, 2 ob, 2 tr, tim	1762
1:561	*Friede! Jesus lebt*	LSun	2 ob	BranJ
1:564	*Frolocket, ihr Engel, und jauchzet*	Asc	2 fl, 2 ob, 2 tr, tim	StolbJ
1:565	*Frohlocket, ihr Völker*	Asc	2 ob, 2 cor, 2 tr, tim	1750
1:568	*Frohlocket vor Freuden*	Chr	2 ob, 2 tr, tim	BranJ
1:574	*Für Schmeicheln, List und Heuchelei*	Tr8	2 ob	
1:577	*Furcht und Zittern kommt mich an*		fl, 2 ob	for Communion, before 1721
1:570	*Fürchtet den Herrn, ihr seine Heiligen*	Tr15	2 ob	SicJ
1:571	*Fürchtet den Herrn, ihr seine Heiligen*	Lent4	fl, 2 ob	Ling1
1:572	*Fürchtet euch nicht für denen*	SuAsc	2 ob	JoR
1:573	*Fürchtet Gott, ehret den König*	Tr23	2 ob	Ling1
1:575	*Fürwahr, er (der Messias) trug unsre Krankheit*	Palm	2 ob	SicJ

1:576	*Fürwahr, er trug unsre Krankheit*	Sexa	2 fl	1724
1:578	*Gebet dem Kaiser, was des Kaisers ist*	Tr23		GSuS-I
1:579	*Gebet dem Kaiser, was des Kaisers ist*	Tr23	2 ob	JoR
1:581	*Gedenke des Sabbat-Tages*	Tr17	2 ob	Ling1
1:582	*Gedenke doch, wie herrlich hoch*	Ann	fl, cor	HornJ
1:583	*Gedenke doch, wie ich so elend*	Lent2	SAB	MusLG
1:584	*Gedenket an den, der ein solches Widersprechen*	Lent5	2 ob	JoR
1:585	*Gedenke an den, der ein solches Widersprechen*	Lent3 or Lent5		HarmLG, AdA
1:586	*Gedenket an Jesum*	Lent3	2 ob	ConcJ
1:587	*Geduldig sein und hoffen*	Tr24	2 ob	StolbJ
1:589	*Geduld, wenn Menschen sich zu Teufeln machen*	Lent3	2 ob	GSuS-I
1:590	*Gefährten zum Ewgen*	NYD	ob, 3 tr	1758
1:591	*Gehe hin, mein Volk, in deine Kammer*	Pur	2 B, 2 fl, 2 ob	OratJ
1:592	*Gehet ein durch die enge Pforte*	Tr1	2 ob	SicJ
1:593	*Gehet hin, gehet hin durch die Tore*	Ad1	2 fl, 2 ob	1757
1:594	*Geht heraus, ihr Zions Töchter*	Lent5		c. 1726
1:596	*Gelobet sei der Herr*	John	2 tr, tim	GSuS-I
1:597	*Gelobet sei der Herr*	Chr	3 tr, tim	Ling1
1:*deest*	*Gelobet sei der Herr*		tr	frag.
1:598	*Gelobet sei der Herr, der Gott*	John	2 ob	SicJ
1:599	*Gelobet sei der Herr, der Gott*	John		JoR

1:600	*Gelobet sei der Herr täglich*	Tr24	2 ob	Ling1
1:602	*Gelobet sei der Herr*	John	3 fl, 2 ob, 4 cor, tim	1733
1:603	*Gelobet sei des Herrn Nam'*	Tr16	ob, cor	HornJ
1:604	*Gelobet sei Gott, der Herr*	John	2 fl, 2 ob, 2 ob d'am, 3 tr	1725
1:605	*Gelobet sei Gott, der Herr*	NYD	2 ob	HarmLG, AdA
1:606	*Gelobet sei Gott, der mein Gebet*	Tr24	2 ob	JoR
1:607	*Gelobet sei Gott und der Vater*	Tr	2 ob	NeuL
1:610	*Gelobet sei Gott und der Vater*	Tri	SAB	MusLG
1:608	*Gelobet sei Gott und Vater*	Eas	2 ob	SicJ
1:611	*Gelobet seist du, Jesu Christ*	Chr2	2 ob	GSuS-II
1:612	*Gelobet seist du, Jesu Christ*	Chr2		GSuS-I
1:613	*Gen Himmel zu dem Vater mein*	SuAsc	2 ob	GSuS-I
1:614	*Gerechter Gott, ach strafe nicht*			
1:616	*Gesegnet ist die Zuversicht*	Tr7	2 ob	GSuS-I
1:617	*Gesegnet sei die Zuversicht*	Tr7	2 ob	GSuS-II
1:620	*Gib auch den Göttern dieser Erden*	Tr23	v, vn, va, bc	FoHarmGD
1:621	*Gib, daß ich mich nicht*	Tr23		EngelJ
1:622	*Gib mildiglich dein' Segen*	Tr5		EngelJ
1:623	*Gib mir ein fröhliches Herz*		SSATB	for Communion; lib. by E. Neumeister
1:624	*Gib uns Segen an die Hand*	Sept		EngelJ

1:625	*Gläubst du? Willig. Gläubst du? Nein!*	LSun	SATBB	OratJ
1:626	*Glaubet, hoffet, leidet, duldet*	Tr26	v, vn, bc	HarmGD
1:627	*Glaubet nicht einem jeglichen Geist*	Tr25	2 ob	JoR
1:628	*Gleich, wie der Blitz aufgehet*	Ad2		Ling1
1:630	*Gleichwie der Regen und Schnee*	Sexa	2 ob	GSuS-I
1:633	*Gott, bei dir ist die lebendige Quelle*	Ad4	2 fl, 2 ob	StolbJ
1:79a	*Gott, dem nichts verborgen*	Chr3	v, bc	AdA
1:634	*Gott der Hoffnung, erfülle euch*	Pen	2 ob, 2 hn	ConcJ; falsely attrib. J.S. Bach (BWV 218)
1:635	*Gott, der liebt nicht nur die Frommen*	Tr10		
1:636	*Gott der Vater wohnt uns bei*	Lent1	ob, cor	HornJ
1:637	*Gott, du erhörest Gebet*	Eas5	2 ob	JoR
1:638	*Gott, du lässest mich erfahren*	Eas3	2 ob	StolbJ
1:642	*Gott fähret auf mit Jauchzen*	Asc	tr	ConcJ
1:644	*Gott fähret auf mit Jauchzen*	Asc		HarmLG, AdA
1:645	*Gott fähret auf mit Jauchzen*	Asc	SAB, 3 tr, tim	MusLG
1:646	*Gott fähret auf mit Jauchzen*	Asc	2 fl, 2 ob, 2 tr, tim	1756
1:647	*Gott fähret auf mit Jauchzen*	Asc	3 tr, tim	c. 1730
1:648	*Gott fähret auf mit Jauchzen*	Asc		frag.
1:650	*Gott hält gewiß, was er versprochen*	John	2 fl, 2 ob	1754
1:653	*Gott hat Geduld mit uns*	Tr22	2 ob	SicJ

1:654	*Gott hat Jesum erhöhet*	NYD	2 ob	1727
1:656	*Gott hat uns berufen*	Sept	2 ob	SicJ
1:657	*Gott hat uns das ewige Leben*	Pen2	2 ob	SicJ
1:659	*Gott, ich weihe dir mein Herze*	Quin	v, ob	
1:660	*Gott ist die Liebe*	Tr18	2 ob	Ling1
1:663	*Gott ist ein rechter Richter*	Tr10	2 ob	SicJ
1:665	*Gott ist unsre Zuversicht*	Ep4		JoR
1:668	*Gott ist unsre Zuversicht*	Ep4	2 fl, cor, tr	
1:673	*Gott Lob und Dank, heut grüßet uns*	NYD	t, vn, bc	GeistC
1:674	*Gott Lob und Dank*	Eas	2 tr, tim	
1:676	*Gott mein Ruhm, schweige nicht*	Tr8		
1:678	*Gott, schweige doch nicht also*	Lent5	3 bn	FranzJ
1:679	*Gott segnet den Frommen ihre Güter*	Tr5	2 ob	SchuJ, FoHarmGD
1:681	*Gott sei mir gnädig*	Tr11	2 ob	ConcJ
1:683	*Gott, strafe nicht nach meiner Schuld*	Tr22		
1:684	*Gott straft den Kranken*	Tr19	2 ob	ConcJ; lib. by Telemann
1:686	*Gott, unser Heiland, will*	Tr20	SAB	MusLG
1:689	*Gott verläßt die Seinen nicht*	SuNY	2 fl, 2 ob, 3 cor	FranzJ
1:691	*Gott widerstehet den Hoffärtigen*	Tr17	2 ob ad lib.	HarmLG, AdA
1:692	*Gott, wie dein Name ist auch dein Ruhm*			for Epiphany
1:693	*Gott will, daß allen Menschen geholfen werde*	Chr2	2 ob	SicJ

1:694	*Gott will Mensch und sterblich werden*	Ann	v, vn, bc	HarmGD
1:695	*Gott will uns alle selig haben*	Tr2		Ling2
1:696	*Gott wird geben einem jeglichen*	Tr1	SAB	MusLG
1:698	*Gott Zebaoth, in deinem Namen*	Tr16	2 ob	StolbJ
1:699	*Gott Zebaoth, wende dich*	Sept		HarmLG, AdA
1:640	*Gottes Liebe gehet weit*	Ann		EngelJ
1:641	*Gottes Wort, was ist das vor ein Schatz*	Sexa	2 ob	FranzJ
1:639	*Gottesfurcht, der Weisheit Quelle*	Ep1	fl, 2 ob	StolbJ
1:670	*Gottlob, die Frucht hat sich gezeiget*	Vis	v, vn, bc	HarmGD
1:671	*Gottlob! nun geht das Jahr zu Ende*	SuChr	2 ob	FranzJ
1:*deest*	*Gottloses, schändliches Gebot* (*Der aus der Löwengrube errettete Daniel*)	Mich		OratJ
1:700	*Greulich sind die letzten Zeiten*	Tr25	2 ob	FranzJ
1:703	*Groß sind die Werke des Herrn*	Vis	fl, ob, 2 bn	1757
1:701	*Große Gottheit, deine Stärke*			frag.
1:702	*Große Städte, große Sünden*	Tr10	2 ob	SchuJ, FoHarmGD
1:704	*Gute Nacht, vergangnes Jahr*	NYD	2 ob, 2 tr, tim	StolbJ
1:705	*Habe deine Lust an dem Herrn*	Tr5	2 ob	SicJ
1:708	*Habt ihr nicht gesehen den meine Seele liebet*	Ep		JoR
1:709	*Habt nicht lieb die Welt*	Tr1	2 ob	GSuS-I
1:710	*Habt nicht lieb die Welt*	Chr3	2 ob	SicJ

1:711	*Habt nicht lieb die Welt*	Tr20	2 ob	JoR
1:712	*Halleluja, er lebt!*	EasMon		StolbJ
1:713	*Halleluja! Lobet den Namen des Herrn*	NYD	SAB, 2 tr, tim	MusLG
1:714	*Halleluja. Singet dem Herrn*	Vis	3 tr, tim	Ling1
1:715	*Halt ein mit deinem Wetterstrahl*	NYD	v, vn, bc	HarmGD
1:717	*Halt im Gedächtnis Jesum Christ*	EasMon	SAB	MusLG
1:716	*Haltet fest an der Demut*	Tr17	2 ob	NeuL
1:718	*Hast du dann, Jesu, dein Angesicht*	Ad1	2 fl, 2 ob	StolbJ
1:1688a	*Hat Gott nicht zu seiner Wohnung*	Tr25	v, bc	AdA
1:724 = 726	*Heilig ist der Herr Zebaoth*	Tr	2 ob, 2 tr, tim	lib. by E. Neumeister
1:727	*Heilig ist der Herr Zebaoth*		3 tr, tim	ConcJ; frag.
1:719	*Heilige Flamme der ewigen Liebe*	Pen	2 fl, 2 ob, 2 cor, tim	StolbJ
1:722	*Heilige sie, Vater, in deiner Wahrheit*	Sexa	2 ob	JoR
1:720	*Heiliger Samengöttlicher Kraft*	Sexa	2 ob	StolbJ
1:721	*O Heiliges Fest, dein liebreicher West*	Tr	2 ob, 2 tr, tim	StolbJ
1:730	*Hemmet den Eifer, verbannet*	Ep4	v, rec, bc	HarmGD
1:731	*Herr Christ, den rechten*	Ep5		EngelJ
1:732	*Herr Christ, der einge Gottessohn*	Ann		FranzJ; falsely attrib. to J.S. Bach (BWV Anh. 156)
1:733	*Herr Christ, der einge Gottessohn*	Ann	2 rec, 2 ob	1758
1:734	*Herr, deine Augen sehen nach dem Glauben*	Ep3	2 ob	StolbJ

1:735	*Herr, dein Wort erhält*	Lent1	2 ob	StolbJ
1:736	*Herr, die Demut fällt zur Erden*	Ep3	2 ob	BranJ
1:737	*Herr, die Wasserströhme erheben sich*	Ep4	2 ob	HarmLG, AdA
1:738	*Herr, erhöre meine Stimme*	Eas5	b	before 1758
1:740	*Herr, gehe nicht ins Gericht*	Tr22		
1:741	*Herr Gott, barmherzig und gnädig*	Tr19	2 ob	JoR
1:742	*Herr Gott, der du uns hast von*	Tr14		Ling2
1:745	*Herr Gott, dich loben wir*	NYD	fl, bn	OratJ
1:746	*Herr Gott, du König aller Himmel*	Chr	3 tr, tim	Ling2
1:749	*Herr Gott, wer wird es dir genug verdanken*	Vis		Ling2
1:750	*Herr Gott Zebaoth, wer ist wie du*	Ep4	2 ob	SicJ
1:751	*Herr Gott Zebaoth, wie lange*	Tr15	2 ob	SchuJ, FoHarmGD
1:752	*Herr hilf uns, wir verderben*	Ep4	SATBBB, 2 ob	OratJ
1:753	*Herr, ich bin beide*	EasMon	fl, 2 ob	NeuL
1:755	*Herr Jesu Christ, dich zu uns wend*	Pen3		GSuS-I
1:757	*Herr Jesu Christ, groß ist die Not*	Ep4	2 ob	FranzJ
1:758	*Herr Jesu Christ, ich schrei zu dir*	Lent2	2 ob	GSuS-I
1:763	*Herr, lehre uns bedenken*	Tr16	fl/va d'am/vadg	ConcJ
1:764	*Herr, meiner Sehnsucht Seltenheit*	Tr11	2 fl, 2 ob	SchuJ, FoHarmGD
1:*deest*	*Herr, nimmst du mir was Liebes ab*	Tr24	2 fl	frag.
1:766	*Herr, nun laß in Frieden*	Pur		EngelJ

1:767	*Herr, schau doch meine matte Seele*	LSun	2 ob	SchuJ, FoHarmGD
1:768	*Herr, segne meinen Tritt*	SuNY		EngelJ
1:769	*Herr, sei mir gnädig, denn mir ist angst*	Tr11	2 ob ad lib.	NeuL
1:770	*Herr, sei mir gnädig, heile meine Seele*	Ep3	2 ob	Ling1
1:771	*Herr, strafe mich nicht in deinem Zorn*	Tr19	2 ob, 3 tr, tim	Ling1
1:774	*Herr, warum trittest du so ferne*	EasMon	2 fl, 2 ob	SchuJ, FoHarmGD
1:775	*Herr, was muß ich tun, daß ich das ewige*	Tr	2 tr, tim	
1:777	*Herr, wie lange willst du*	Lent2	2 ob	FranzJ
1:778	*Herr, wie lange willst du*	Lent2		lib. partly by E. Neumeister
1:779	*Herr, wie sind deine Werke so groß*	Tr15	fl, 2 ob	Ling1
1:780	*Herr, wie sind deine Werke so groß*	Tr7	2 ob ad lib.	HarmLG, AdA
1:781	*Herr, wir liegen vor dir mit unserm Gebet*	Tr6	2 fl	ConcJ
1:782	*Herr, wir liegen vor dir mit unserm Gebet*	Eas5	2 ob	SicJ
1:783	*Herzlich lieb hab ich dich, Herr*	Tr18	2 fl, 2 ob	StolbJ
1:784	*Herzlich tut mich verlangen*	Pur		GSuS-I; movt 4 = 1:1303
1:785	*Herzliebster Jesu, was hast du verbrochen*	Palm	2 ob	JoR
1:786	*Herzog meiner Seligkeit*	Tr16	2 fl	LiedJ
1:789	*Heut ist die werte Christenheit*	Ad1	2 tr	1728 or earlier
1:*deest*	*Heut ist unsers Königs Fest*		s, vn, bc	
1:790	*Heut lebst du, heut bekehre dich*	John	ob	49/50J
1:791	*Heut schleußt er wieder auf die Tür*	Asc	ob, 2 tr, tim	1758

1:793	*Heut triumphieret Gottes Sohn*	EasMon	2 fl, 3 tr, tim	
1:787	*Heute geht aus seiner Kammer Gottes Held*	Chr	2 ob	StolbJ
1:794	*Hier hab ich meine Plage*	Tr13		EngelJ
1:795	*Hier ist mein Herz, geliebter Jesu*		s, t	for Epiphany, c. 1715
1:798	*Hilf, daß ich sei von Herzen froh*	Tr11	ob	
1:799	*Hilf Herr! die Heiligen haben abgenommen*	Tr25	2 ob	NeuL
1:800	*Hilf Herr, die Heiligen haben abgenommen*	Tr8	2 ob	SicJ
1:802	*Hilf Jesu, hilf, ich bin in Sünden krank*		s	for Communion
1:803	*Hilf Herr, o hilf, du großer König*	Palm	2 ob	StolbJ
1:805	*Hirt' und Bischof unsrer Seelen*	Eas2	v, vn, bc	HarmGD
1:806	*Horche nur, dort regt sich was*	EasTue	2 fl, 2 ob	OratJ
1:808	*Hosianna dem Sohne David*	Ad1	SSATB, fl, 2 ob	NeuL
1:809	*Hosianna dem Sohne David*	Ad1	SAB	MusLG
1:810	*Hosianna, dieses soll die Losung sein*	Chr2	2 fl, 2 ob, 3 tr, tim	StolbJ
1:811	*Hütet euch, daß eure Herzen*	Ad2	2 ob	ConcJ
10:30	*Ich aber, Herr! Hoffe auf dich*		s, b, 2 vn, bc	PoetFr
1:812	*Ich armer Mensch, ich armer Sünder*		fl, 2 ob	before 1722
1:814	*Ich bin arm und elend, der Herr*	SuNY	SAB	MusLG
1:815	*Ich bin das A und das O*	Eas	2 fl, 2 ob, 2 tr, tim	with C.D. Krohn, 1762
1:816	*Ich bin der erste und der letzte*	Eas	2 ob, tr	ConcJ
1:817	*Ich bin der Herr, dein Arzt*	Tr12	2 ob	NeuL

1:818	*Ich bin der Weg, die Wahrheit und das Leben*	Chr3		JoR
1:819	*Ich bin dir, Herr, mehr als zehntausend*	Tr22		Ling2
1:820	*Ich bin getauft in Christi Tode*	Tr6	v, fl, bc	HarmGD
1:821	*Ich bin getrost im Leben*	Mich	2 ob, 2 tr	FranzJ
1:822	*Ich bin ja, Herr, in deiner*		2 ob, ob d'am, bn, tr	for Danzig, 1754
1:823	*Ich bin vergnügt an diesen Gütern*	Tr9		GSuS-I
1:824	*Ich danke dir und preise*	Tr12		EngelJ
1:825	*Ich fahre auf zu meinem Vater*	Asc	fl, 2 ob ad lib., 2 cor	NeuL
1:826	*Ich freue mich im Herren*	Tr20	t, b, ob d'am	
1:827	*Ich fürchte keinen Tod auf Erden*	Tr24	fl, 2 ob	GSuS-I
1:829	*Ich gehe voll Freuden zum Hause des Herrn*		SSATB, ob, 2 tr	lib. by E. Neumeister
1:831	*Ich glaube aber, daß ich sehen werde*		2 ob, 2 cor	
1:833	*Ich habe Lust abzuscheiden*	Tr16		GSuS-I
1:834	*Ich habe Lust abzuscheiden*	Tr16	2 ob	FranzJ
1:836	*Ich habe Lust abzuscheiden*	Pur	SAB	MusLG
1:838	*Ich habe oft des Himmels Mann verachtet*	Tr		Ling2
1:839	*Ich habe Wächter über euch gesetzt*	Chr2	2 ob	SchuJ, FoHarmGD
1:840	*Ich halte aber dafür*	SuAsc	fl, 2 ob	NeuL
1:841	*Ich halte es dafür, daß dieser*	SuAsc	SAB	MusLG
1:842	*Ich hatte mich verirret*	Tr3		EngelJ
1:843	*Ich hatte viel Bekümmernüsse*	Lent2	2 ob	ConcJ

1:845	*Ich hebe meine Augen auf*	Ep3	2 ob	JoR
1:*deest*	*Ich hebe meine Augen auf zu den Bergen*		a, 2 vn, bc	
1:846	*Ich hebe mich ein wenig kaum empor*	Lent5	SATBBBB	OratJ
1:847	*Ich hoffe darauf, daß du so gnädig bist*	Eas3	2 fl, 2 ob, tim	NeuL
1:848	*Ich hoffe darauf, daß du so gnädig bist*	Tr21	SAB	MusLG
1:*deest*	*Ich hoffe darauf, daß du so gnädig bist*		s, 2 vn, bc	
1:830	*Ich irre, seufze, klage*	Tr3	2 ob	Ling1
1:849	*Ich komme, o höchster Gott, zu dir*	Tr2		1724
10:21	*Ich lebe, aber doch nun nicht ich*		s, b, 2 vn, bc	PoetFr
1:850	*Ich lebe, und ihr sollt auch leben*	Eas	2 fl, 2 ob, 2 tr, tim	1754
1:851	*Ich muß auf dem Berge weinen*	Tr10	fl	1722; performed in Leipzig on 9 August
1:852	*Ich muß im Leben immer wandeln*	Eas3		OratJ
1:854	*Ich recke meine Hand aus*	Tr2	2 ob	FranzJ
1:857	*Ich ruf zu dir, Herr Jesu Christ*	Tr6		
1:855	*Ich rufe dich demütig flehend an*	Pen		Ling2
1:858	*Ich sage euch, dieser ging hinab*	Tr11	2 ob	JoR
1:859	*Ich schaue bloß auf Gottes*	Tr18	v, fl, bc	HarmGD
1:860	*Ich schicke mich zu meinem Ende*	Tr16	s, 2 vn, bc	GeistC
1:861	*Ich schlafe, aber mein Herz wachet*		s, b, 2 vn, bc	
1:863	*Ich sehe mich mit Finsternissen*	John		Ling2

1:*deest*	*Ich sonst beglücktes Land*			
1:866	*Ich suchte des Nachts in meinem Bette*	Ep1	2 tr	Ling1
1:867	*Ich taumle vor Freuden*	Tr27	v, bc	AdA
1:868	*Ich traue auf Gott*	Palm		EngelJ
1:871	*Ich wandle mit furchtsamen Schritten*	Ep5		OratJ
1:872	*Ich war tot. Und siehe*	Eas	2 ob	JoR
1:873	*Ich weiß, daß mein Erlöser lebt*	EasMon	2 ob	ConcJ
1:874	*Ich weiß, daß mein Erlöser lebt*	Tr24		FranzJ
1:876	*Ich weiß, daß mein Erlöser lebt*	Tr24		FranzJ
1:877	*Ich weiß, daß mein Erlöser lebt*	Eas	s/t, vn, bc	GeistC; falsely attrib. J.S. Bach (BWV 160)
1:878	*Ich weiß, daß mein Erlöser lebt*	Eas	3 tr, tim	
1:879	*Ich weiß, daß mein Erlöser lebt*	EasMon	2 fl, 2 ob	
1:880	*Ich weiß wohl, was ich für Gedanken*	EasTue		JoR
1:881	*Ich werde fast entzückt*	Ann	v, 2 ob, bc	FoHarmGD
1:882	*Ich werfe mich zu deinen Füßen*	Tr19	2 ob	FranzJ
1:884	*Ich will den Kreuzweg gerne gehen*	Tr21	b, v, bc	GeistC
1:885	*Ich will dich erhöhen*	Tr14	2 ob, 2 tr	NeuL
1:*deest*	*Ich will dulden*			frag.
1:888	*Ich will mich mit dir verloben*	Tr20	2 fl, 2 ob	ConcJ
1:889	*Ich will mich mit dir verloben*	Ep2	2 ob	SicJ

1:890	*Ich will mit Danken kommen*	Tr10		1759, = 1:1220 with different movt order and scoring
1:891	*Ich will rein Wasser über euch sprengen*	Tr14	ob	StolbJ
1:893	*Ich will singen von der Gnade des Herrn*	Lent3	ob, bn	OratJ; = 1:1655
1:894	*Ich winselte wie ein Kranich*	Ep3	2 fl, 2 ob	SchuJ, FoHarmGD
1:896	*Ihr Christen, wollt ihr selig sein*	Tr14		
1:897	*Ihr, deren Leben mit banger Finsternis*	Tr12	v, vn, bc	HarmGD
1:898	*Ihr, die ihr Christi*	Lent5		EngelJ
1:899	*Ihr, die ihr euren Nächsten sucht zu fällen*	Tr4		Ling2
1:900 = 1416	*Ihr fromme Christen, auf*	Quin	2 ob	
1:901	*Ihr Gerechten, freuet euch*	Palm	SAB	MusLG
1:904	*Ihr habt nicht einen knechtischen Geist*	Pen	2 ob, 3 tr, tim	SchuJ, FoHarmGD
1:905	*Ihr habt nicht einen knechtischen Geist*	Pen	rec, 2 fl, 2 ob, 2 tr, tim	1757
1:906	*Ihr Heuchler, die ihr euch*	Tr11	2 cor	Ling2
1:1353a	*Ihr in Sünden toten Glieder*	EasTue	v, bc	AdA
1:908	*Ihr Lieben, gläubet nicht einem jeglichen Geist*	Tr8		MusLG
1:909	*Ihr Lieben, lasset uns untereinandern liebhaben*	Tr13	2 ob	SicJ
1:912	*Ihr schüchternen Blicke*	Tr26	v, vn, va, bc	FoHarmGD
1:913	*Ihr Seelen, die ihr denkt an jenen*	Tr6		Ling2
1:914	*Ihr seid alle Gottes Kinder*	Ad4	2 ob	ConcJ
1:915	*Ihr seid alle Gottes Kinder*	Ad4	2 ob	GSuS-II

1:916	*Ihr seid alle Gottes Kinder*	Ad4		GSuS-I
1:917	*Ihr seligen Stunden erquickender Freuden*	Tr4	v, vn, bc	HarmGD
1:918	*Ihr sollet geschickt sein*	Tr26	SSATB, 2 ob	ConcJ
1:919	*Ihr Völker, bringet her*	Ep		GSuS-I
1:920	*Ihr Völker, bringet her*	Ep	2 ob	NeuL
1:921	*Ihr Völker hört, wie Gott aufs neue*	Ep	v, fl, bc	HarmGD
1:922	*Ihr werdet, aus Gottes Macht*	Tr21	2 ob	Ling1
1:923	*Ihr werdet weinen und heulen*	Eas3	2 ob	
1:924	*Ihr Wölfe droht mit euren Klauen*	Pen3	v, vn, va, bc	FoHarmGD
1:926	*Im hellen Glanz der Glaubenssonne*	Chr3	SATTB	OratJ
1:927	*Im sechsten Monat war der Engel Gabriel*	Ann	2 ob, tr	
1:928	*In allen meinen Taten*	Tr5	2 ob	
1:929	*In Christo Jesu gilt weder Beschneidung*	Tr13	2 ob	ConcJ; composed at Stuttgart, 19 August 1720
1:930	*In Christo Jesu gilt weder Beschneidung*	NYD	2 ob	SicJ
1:931	*In deinem Wort und Sakrament*	Ad1		LiedJ
1:934	*In den Seilen deiner Liebe, Jesu*	Eas	t, b, 2 vn, bc	
1:936	*In der Welt habt ihr Angst*	Eas3		GSuS-I
1:938	*In dich wollst du mich*	Tr20		EngelJ
1:939	*In dulci jubilo*	Chr	2 ob, 2 cor	FranzJ
1:940	*In Ephraim sind allenthalben Lügen*	Tr17	ob	StolbJ

1:941	*In gering und rauhen Schalen*	Ep	v, rec, bc	HarmGD
1:942	*In Gott vergnügt zu leben*	Tri	b, fl, ob, cor, 2 vn, bc	
1:944	*Ist auch das Kreuz bitter und schwer*	Tr13	2 ob	StolbJ
10:25	*Ist Gott für uns, wer mag wider uns sein?*		s, a, 2 vn, bc	PoetFr
1:946	*Ist Gott versöhnt*	NYD		EngelJ
1:948	*Ist Widerwärtigkeit den Frommen eigen*	Ep2	v, vn, bc	HarmGD
1:949	*Ja! Selig sind, die Gottes Wort hören*	Sexa	SAB	MusLG
1:950	*Jauchze, du Tochter Zion*	NYD	SSATB, 2 fl, 2 ob, 2 tr, tim	1762
1:951	*Jauchzet dem Herrn, alle Welt*	Ep	ob, 6 tr, tim	1733
1:952	*Jauchzet dem Herrn, alle Welt*	NYD	b, 2 tr, bc	= 7:21
1:959	*Jauchzet dem Höchsten, alle Welt*		2 ob, 2 tr, tim	for Easter
1:953	*Jauchzet, frohlocket*	Chr2	v, vn, bc	HarmGD
1:955	*Jauchzet, ihr Christen*	EasTue	v, vn, bc	HarmGD
1:956	*Jauchzet, ihr getreuen Herze*		s, t, vn, bc	
1:957	*Jauchzet, ihr Himmel, freue dich, Erde*	Lent4	SAB	MusLG
1:958	*Jauchzet, ihr Himmel, freue dich, Erde*	Ann	fl, ob, bn	1756
1:960	*Jederman sei untertan der Obrigkeit*	Tr23	2 ob	SicJ
1:962	*Jedermann sei Untertan der Obrigkeit*	Tr23	v, vn, va, bc	FoHarmGD
1:964	*Jesu, in deinem Namen bin ich heute*	NYD		
1:965	*Jesu, meine Freude*	Tr13	2 ob	GSuS-I

1:966	*Jesu, meine Freude*	Tr20	2 ob	FranzJ
1:967	*Jesu, meine Freude*	Ep6		FranzJ
1:970	*Jesu, meine Freude*		2 ob, 2 bn	Danzig, 1754?
1:973	*Jesu, meine Freude*		2 ob ad lib.	for Communion; lib. by E. Neumeister
1:974	*Jesu, meiner Seelen Weide*		s, 2 fl, 2 ob, bc	1725
1:*deest*	*Jesu, meines Lebens Sonne*	Ad3		excerpted from 1:1657
1:988	*Jesu, wirst du bald erscheinen*	Tr26	ob, 2 corn, 3 trb	GSuS-I
1:975	*Jesus Christus ist kommen*	EasTue	SAB	MusLG
1:976	*Jesus Christus, unser Heiland*	EasTue	2 ob	FranzJ
1:980	*Jesus ist der Heilandsname*	Name Day of Jesus	fl, ob	
1:981	*Jesus ist der Heilandsname*	Name Day of Jesus	2 fl, 2 ob	
1:982	*Jesus Liebe mich vergnüget*		s, vn, b	
1:983	*Jesus liegt in letzten Zügen (Der sterbende Jesus)*		b, 2 ob	1758
1:984	*Jesus, meine Zuversicht*		rec, fl, ob, ob d'am, cor	Danzig, 1754?
1:985	*Jesus nimmt die Sünder an*		SSATB, fl, 2 ob	for Communion, lib. by L.H. Schlosser
1:986	*Jesus sei mein erstes Wort*	Tr5	2 ob	FranzJ
1:989	*Jetzt geht der Lebensfürst zum Tode*	Palm		SchuJ, FoHarmGD
1:1671a	*Kann euch dieser Donnerschlag*	Tr26	v, bc	AdA

1:990	*Kann man auch Trauben lesen*	Tr8	2 ob ad lib.	HarmLG, AdA
1:991	*Kaum ist Heiland auf der Erden*	NYD	b	
1:992	*Kaum wag ich es, dir, Richter, mich zu nahn*	Tr19		1762
1:993	*Kein Hirt kann so fleißig gehen*	Tr3	2 vn, bc	
1:994	*Kein Vogel kann in Weiten fliegen*	Tr10	v, fl, bc	HarmGD
1:997	*Kinder, es ist die letzte Stunde*	Tr8	2 ob	Ling1
1:999	*Komm, Geist des Herrn*	Pen	2 ob, 3 tr	1759
1:1000	*Komm, Gnadentau, befeuchte mich*	Pen	SAATTBBB, 2 fl, 3 tr, tim	OratJ
1:1001	*Komm, heiliger Geist, Herr Gott*	Pen	fl, 2 ob, 4 tr, tim	49/50J
1:998	*Kommet herzu, lasset uns dem Herrn*	Tr14	2 ob ad lib.	HarmLG, AdA
1:1003	*Kommt alle, die ihr traurig seid*	Ep3	2 ob	FranzJ
1:1004	*Kommt alle, die von so manchem Sündenfalle*	Tr3	2 ob	FranzJ
1:1005	*Kommt, Christen, laßt uns Christum fragen*	Ad3		BranJ
1:1006	*Kommt, die Tafel ist gedeckt*	Tr2		c. 1723
1:1007	*Kommt her zu mir alle*	Tr2	2 ob	ConcJ
1:1008	*Kommt her zu mir alle*	Tr3		ConcJ
1:1009	*Kommt herzu, lasset uns*	Tr14		HarmLG, AdA
1:1010	*Kommt, ihr Schäflein, laßt euch weiden*	Eas2	2 fl, 2 ob	StolbJ
1:1012	*Kommt, laßt uns anbeten und knien*	Pen3		Ling1
1:1013	*Kommt und laßt uns Jesum lehren*	Tr18		

1:1014	*Kommt, verruchte Sodoms-Knechte*	Tr10	s, b, 2 ob, 4 bn	
1:1017	*Kindlich groß ist das gottselige Geheimnis*	Ch3	2 ob ad lib.	ConcJ
1:1019	*Kindlich groß ist das gottselige Geheimnis*	Chr	2 ob	JoR
1:1020	*Kindlich groß ist das gottselige Geheimnis*	Chr	2 ob, 3 tr, tim	SchuJ, FoHarmGD
1:*deest*	*Lad o Herre Ordets sœd, riigelig*		ob, fl	
1:1033	*Laß mich an andern üben*	Tr24	b, 2 ob	
1:1034	*Laß mich beizeit mein Haus bestellen*	Tr		EngelJ
1:1037	*Laß mich, o mein Gott*	Tr7		EngelJ
1:1038	*Laß vom Bösen und tue Gutes*	Ep4	2 ob	1724
1:1023	*Lasset uns aufsehen auf Jesum*	Quin	2 ob	SicJ
1:1024	*Lasset uns beweisen, als die Diener Gottes*	SuAsc	2 ob	HarmLG, AdA
1:1025	*Lasset uns den Herrn preisen*	Eas	3 trb, tim	49/50J
1:1036	*Laßt uns eins ums ander singen*			frag.
1:1026	*Lasset uns Gott lieben*	Tr18	2 ob	SicJ
1:1027	*Lasset uns Gott lieben*	Pen3	2 ob	1724
1:1028	*Lasset uns nicht eitler Ehre geizig sein*	Tr17	2 ob, 2 bn	ConcJ
1:1029	*Lasset uns rechtschaffen sein*	Ep1	2 ob, 2 bn	SicJ
1:1031	*Lasset uns von Gnade singen*		s, b, vn, bc	for Communion, before 1721
1:1040	*Lauter Wonne, lauter Freude*	Ad4	v, rec, bc	HarmGD
1:1041	*Leben wir, so leben wir dem Herrn*	Pur	2 fl, ob, bn	1756
1:1085	*Lebensfürst, auf dein Erblassen*	Eas	v, bc	AdA

10:31	*Lehre mich tun nach deinem Wohlgefallen*		a, b, 2 vn, bc	PoetFr
1:*deest*	*Lehre mich tun*		ob, 3 tr, tim	frag.
1:1042	*Lehre uns bedenken, daß wir sterben müssen*	Tr9	SAB	MusLG
1:1043	*Lehre uns bedenken, daß wir sterben müssen*	Tr27	SAB	MusLG
1:1044	*Liebe, die vom Himmel flammet*	Ep5	v, vn, bc	HarmGD
1:1045	*Liebe muß der Christen Merkmal sein*	Tr13	2 ob	BranJ
1:1046	*Liebet eure Feinde*	Tr6	2 ob	NeuL
1:1047	*Liebet eure Feinde*	Tr4	2 ob	SicJ
1:1048	*Lieblicher Saiten ergetzendes Schallen*	Ad4	2 fl/ob	SchuJ, FoHarmGD
1:1051	*Liebster Jesu, kehre wieder*	Ep1	s, 2 fl	only one aria extant
1:1052	*Liebster Jesu, meine Lust*	Tr18	2 ob	
1:1056	*Lob den Herrn, meine Seele*	Tr7	s, b	
1:1057	*Lob, Ehr und Preis sei Gott*	Mich	fl, ob, 3 tr, tim	1760
1:1053	*Lobe den Herrn, meine Seele, Halleluja*	Vis	2 tr	FranzJ
1:1054	*Lobe den Herrn, meine Seele*	Tr12	2 ob	SicJ
1:1058	*Lobet den Herrn, alle Heiden*	Ep	2 ob	ConcJ
1:1059	*Lobet den Herrn, alle Heiden*	Ep	SAB	MusLG
1:1060	*Lobet den Herrn, alle Heiden*	John	SAB	MusLG
1:1061	*Lobet den Herrn, alle seine Heerscharen*	NYD	2 ob, 3 tr, tim	NeuL
1:1063	*Lobet den Herrn, ihr seine Engel*	Mich	2 fl, 2 ob, 2 tr, tim	1756
1:1064	*Lobsinget dem Herrn*	NYD	2 ob	BranJ

1:1066	*Lobt Gott, ihr Christen allzugleich*	Chr3	SATB, SATB, 2 ob, 4 tr, tim	FranzJ, concluding chorus = TVWV 8:10
1:1067	*Lobt ihn mit Herz und Munde*	Vis		EngelJ
1:1069	*Locke nur, Erde*	Tr23	v, rec, bc	HarmGD
1:1079	*Mach mich an meiner Seele reich*	Tr15		Ling2
1:1080	*Mach mir stets zuckersüß*	Tr2		EngelJ
1:1070	*Mache dich auf, werde Licht*	Chr	3 tr	lib. by von Holten
1:1072	*Mache dich auf, werde Licht*	Ep	ob, bn	OratJ
1:1073	*Machet Bahn dem, der da sanft herfähret*	Pen	2 fl, 2 ob, 2 tr	
1:1074	*Machet die Tore weit*	Ad1	2 ob	SicJ
1:1075	*Machet die Tore weit*	Ad1	2 fl, 2 ob, tr, cor	
1:1076	*Machet euch Freude mit dem ungerechten Mammon*	Tr9	2 ob	FranzJ
1:1077	*Machet euch Freude mit dem ungerechten Mammon*	Tr9	2 ob	
1:1078	*Machet keusch eure Seelen*	Sexa	2 ob	SicJ
1:1082	*Man muß nicht zu sehr trauren*	Tr24	2 fl, 2 ob	ConcJ; lib. by Telemann
1:1084	*Man singet mit Freuden von Sieg*	Lent1	2 ob, 2 tr	GSuS-I
1:1086	*Man singet mit Freuden von Sieg*	Eas	SSATB, 3 tr, tim	1734
1:1087	*Man singet mit Freuden von Sieg*	Eas	SAB	MusLG
1:1088	*Man singet mit Freuden von Sieg*		2 ob, 3 tr, tim	for Easter, 1711 or 1718
1:1089	*Maria stund auf in den Tagen*	Vis	2 ob	GSuS-I

1:1090	*Mein Alter kömmt*	Pur		
1:1093	*Mein Augen sehen stets zu dem*	Lent3	SAB	MusLG
1:1112	*Mein Gott, ich bin gesinnt*	Tr7	s, b, ob d'am, 2 vn, bc	lib. by Telemann, 1725
1:1114	*Mein Gott, ich schäme mich*	Tr22	2 ob, bn	NeuL
1:1115	*Mein Herz ängstet sich*	LSun	2 ob	FranzJ
1:1065a	*Mein Herze muß, an Freuden*	Vis	v, bc	AdA
1:1116	*Mein Herze, heg Barmherzigkeit*	Tr4	ob	
1:1117	*Mein Herz, warum betrübst du dich*	Ep2	cor	RambGP
1:1119	*Mein Jesu, ist dirs denn verborgen*	Ep2	2 ob	GSuS-I
1:1120	*Mein Jesu, meines Herzens Freude*	Pen3	t, vn, bc	GeistC
1:1122	*Mein Jesus ist mein Leben*		s/t, vn, bc	
1:1124	*Mein Jesus nimmt die Kranken an*	Ad3		
1:1127	*Mein Jesus wirft mit voller Hand*	Sexa	SATBB	OratJ
1:1128	*Mein Kind, verwirf die Zucht des Herrn nicht*	Tr21	2 ob	NeuL
1:1129	*Mein Kind, willst du Gottes Diener sein*	Ad3	2 ob, bn	ConcJ
1:1130	*Mein Kind, willst du Gottes Diener sein*	Ad3	2 ob	GSuS-I
1:1132	*Mein Schutz und Hülfe kömmt*	Tr19		EngelJ
1:1134	*Mein Sünd mich werden kränken*	Tr19		GSuS-I
1:*deest*	*Mein Sünd mich werden kränken*			GSuS-II
1:1094	*Meine Brüder, seid stark in dem Herrn*	Lent3	2 ob	Ling1
1:1095	*Meine Liebe lebt in Gott*	Pen2	baritone, ob, vn, bc	lib. by G.C. Lehms, 1725

1:1099	*Meine Rede bleibt betrübt (Der geliebte und verlorne Jesus)*		s, ob, 2 vn, bc	c. 1715
1:1102	*Meine Schafe hören meine Stimme*	Eas2	ob	GSuS-I
1:1103	*Meine Schafe hören meine Stimme*	Eas2	SAB	MusLG
1:1104	*Meine Seele erhebt den Herrn*	Vis	2 ob	NeuL
1:1105	*Meine Seele erhebt den Herrn*	Ann	2 ob	1722
1:1106	*Meine Seele erhebt den Herrn*	Ann		Ling1
1:1107	*Meine Seele erhebt den Herrn*	Vis	v, vn, va, bc	FoHarmGD
1:1108	*Meine Seele erhebt den Herrn*	Vis	SAB	MusLG
1:*deest*	*Meine Seele erhebt den Herrn*	Vis	2 ob	1754
1:1109	*Meine Seele harret nur auf Gott*	Lent2	2 fl, 2 ob, 2 bn	c. 1730
1:1110	*Meine Seele trägt Verlangen*	SuAsc	2 vn, bc	for Communion; lib. by E. Neumeister
10:27	*Meine Seele verlanget nach deinem Heÿl*		s, b, 2 vn, bc	PoetFr
1:1096	*Meinem Jesu will ich singen*	Eas3	SAB, fl	frag.
1:1097	*Meinen Jesum laß ich nicht*	Pur	2 ob	for Communion; lib. by E. Neumeister
1:1098	*Meinen Jesum will ich lieben*	Pur	2 ob, cor	StolbJ
1:1101	*Meines Bleibens ist nicht hier*	EasMon	a, 2 vn, bc	GeistC
1:1135	*Me miserum, miseriarum conflictu*		a, 2 vn, bc	lib. by E. Neumeister
1:1136	*Michael, wer ist wie Gott*	Mich	2 ob, 2 tr, tim	1764
1:1137	*Mir hat die Welt trüglich gericht*	Tr17		GSuS-I

1:1138	*Mir hat die Welt trüglich gericht*	Lent3		EngelJ
1:1140	*Mit Fried und Freud ich fahr dahin*	Pur		before 1729
1:1141	*Mit Gott im Gnadenbunde stehen*	Ep3	SSB, 2 ob, 2 chal, 2 cor	1722
1:*deest*	*Mit Fried und Freud ich fahr dahin*			
1:1144	*Möchte ich, Jesu, mein Amt verwalten*	Pen	fl, ob, 2 tr, tim	1763
1:1145	*Muntre Gedanken fliehet*	Ep	v, 2 fl, bc	FoHarmGD
1:1146	*Muß nicht der Mensch immer im Streit sein*	Lent1	2 ob	FranzJ
1:1147	*Nach ausgelöschtem Feindschafts-Feuer*	EasTue	v, vn, va, bc	FoHarmGD
10:29	*Nach dem Ungewitter läßest du die Sonne wieder scheinen*		s, t, 2 vn, bc	PoetFr
1:1148	*Nach dem Weinen, nach dem Leiden*	Eas3	2 ob	BranJ
1:1149	*Nach dir will ich mich sehnen*	Eas4		EngelJ
1:1150	*Nach Finsternis und Todesschatten*	John	v, tr/ob, vn	FoHarmGD
10:28	*Nach seiner Barmherzigkeit macht Gott uns selig*		a, t, 2 vn, bc	PoetFr
1:1156	*Nicht viel Weise nach dem Fleisch*	Sept	2 ob	JoR
1:1153	*Nichts kann mich*	Lent1		EngelJ
1:1157	*Niedrigkeit ist ein Spott*	SuChr	2 fl, 2 ob	StolbJ
1:1159	*Nimm von uns, Herr, du treuer Gott*	Tr10	2 ob	FranzJ
1:1160	*Nimm nicht zu Herzen, was die Rotten*	Tr8	2 fl, 2 ob	StolbJ
1:1161	*Nun aber, die ihr in Christo Jesu seid*	LSun	2 ob	HarmLG, AdA
1:1162	*Nun aber gehe ich hin*	Eas4	2 ob	GSuS-I
1:1163	*Nun aber gehe ich hin*	Eas4	fl, 2 ob	NeuL

1:1166	*Nun danket alle Gott*		fl, 2 tr, tim	chorale verses by M. Rinckart
1:1167	*Nun freut euch, Gottes Kinder*	Asc		EngelJ
1:1170	*Nun ist das Heil und die Kraft*	Mich	2 fl, ob, 2 tr, tim	1754
1:1172	*Nun ist das Heil und die Kraft*	Mich	2 fl, 2 ob, 2 cor, 2 tr, tim	1761
1:1173	*Nun ist das Reich des göttlichen Sohnes*	Pen	fl, ob, 2 tr, tim	1762
1:1174	*Nun komm der Heiden Heiland*	Ad1	2 ob, 2 tr, tim	GSuS-II
1:1175	*Nun komm der Heiden Heiland*	Ad1	2 ob, bn, 2 tr	FranzJ
1:1177 = 1755	*Nun komm der Heiden Heiland*	Ad1		GSuS-I
1:1179	*Nun kömmt die große Marterwoche*	Palm	2 ob	GSuS-I
1:1181	*Nun lernet dich mein Herze kennen*	SuNY	2 fl, 2 ob	StolbJ
1:1184	*Nun wir denn sind gerecht worden*	LSun	2 ob	SicJ
1:1182	*Nunmehr hab ich ausgeruft*	Tr12	2 ob	StolbJ
1:1185	*Nur getrost und unverzagt*	Eas5	ss/tt, ob	before 1719
1:1188	*O ein gütiges Befehlen*	Tr15	2 ob	BranJ
1:1190	*O fröhliche Stunden, der Lebensfürst lebt*	Eas	t, 2 ob, 2 cor	frag.
1:1191	*O Gotteslamm, o Liebesflamm*	Tr18		EngelJ
1:1192	*O Gottes Sohn, Herr Jesu Christ*	Tr21		
1:1193	*O Gott, gedenke mein am besten*		t, b	
1:1194	*O Gott, wie groß ist deine Güte*	Sept	2 ob	BranJ
1:1195	*O große Lieb*	Quin		EngelJ

1:1196	*O großer Gott von Macht*	Tr10	2 ob	GSuS-I
1:*deest*	*O großer Gott von Macht*	Tr10		GSuS-II
1:*deest*	*O! hörer I Oeer I folk som langt borte*		s, 2 vn, bc	
1:1200	*O Jesu Christ, dein Kripplein*	Chr2		EngelJ
1:1201	*O Jesu, meine Wonne*	Tr20		
1:1202	*O Jesu, treuer Hirte*	Eas2		EngelJ
1:1203	*O Land, höre des Herren Wort*	Tr10	2 ob	ConcJ
1:1204	*O liebster Gott, was mangelt mir*	Pen		lib. by E. Neumeister; frag.
1:1205	*O mein Gott, vor den ich trete*	LSun		GSuS-I
1:1206	*O mein Gott, vor den ich trete*	LSun	2 ob	GSuS-II
1:1207	*O Mensch, bedenke stets dein Ende*	Tr1		
1:1209	*O Mensch, wer du auch immer bist*	Tr9		
1:1212	*O selig Vergnügen, o heilige Lust*		a, b, 2 fl, 2 vn ad lib., bc	for Communion; lib. by E. Neumeister
1:1214	*O setze alles Leid hintan*	Pen	2 fl, ob	1756
1:1215	*O tausendmal gewünschter Tag*	Ann		GSuS-I
1:1216	*O weh, schaut der Ägypter Heer*	John	ob, 3 cor	1732
1:1217	*O, wie herrlich wirds im Himmel*	Pur		FranzJ
1:1219	*O, wie ist die Barmherzigkeit des Herrn*	Tr12	2 ob ad lib.	HarmLG, AdA
1:1220	*O, wie selig ist die Stunde*	Tr6	2 fl, ob	1759, = 1:890 with different movt order and scoring
1:1221	*O, wie wird der Mensch geliebt*		2 cor	

1:1186	*Ob bei uns ist der Sünden viel*	Tr3	2 ob	StolbJ
1:1199	*Ohne Glaube ist's unmöglich*	LSun	SAB	MusLG
1:1210	*Opfre Gott Dank*	Tr23		StolbJ
1:1222	*Packe dich, gelähmter Drache*	Mich	v, vn, bc	HarmGD
1:1223	*Posaunen wird man hören gehen*	Tr26	2 ob, tr	
1:1225	*Redet untereinander mit Psalmen*	NYD	2 ob, 3 tr, tim	GSuS-I
1:1226	*Redet untereinander mit Psalmen*	Vis		JoR
1:1228	*Reiner Geist, laß doch mein Herze*	Pen	b, fl, vn, bc	lib. by G.C. Lehms, 1725
1:1229	*Reiß los, reiß von dem Leibe*	Ep6	v, bc	AdA
1:1230	*Ruft es aus in alle Welt*	Chr	3 tr, tim	
1:1232	*Sag nicht, ich bin ein Christ*	Tr4	2 ob	StolbJ
1:1231	*Sage mir an, du, den meine Seele liebet*	Ep1	2 fl, 2 ob	NeuL
1:1233	*Saget dem verzagten Herzen*	Ad1	2 ob	HarmLG, AdA
1:1235	*Saget der Tochter Zion: Siehe dein Heil*	Ad1	2 ob, 3 tr, tim	Ling1
1:1236	*Sanftmut und Geduld sind die Schilder*	Lent3	2 ob	EmbJ
1:1238	*Schaffe in mir, Gott, ein rein Herz*	Pen	2 ob, 3 tr, tim	Ling1
1:1240	*Schaffe in mir, Gott, ein rein Herz*			for Communion
1:1241	*Schaffe in mir, Gott, ein rein Herz*	Pen2		
1:1243	*Schau nach Sodom nicht zurücke*	Tr14	v, ob, bc	HarmGD
1:1244	*Schau, Seele, Jesus geht zum Vater*	Eas4	2 ob	SchuJ, FoHarmGD
1:1242	*Schaue Zion, die Stadt unsers Stifts*	NYD	2 fl, ob, 2 tr, tim	1761

1:1245	*Schaut die Demut Palmen tragen*	Palm	v, ob, bc	HarmGD
1:1247	*Schicket euch in die Zeit*	Tr25	2 chal, 2 ob d'am	NeuL
1:1248	*Schlage bald, erwünschte Stunde*	Ep2	ob	OratJ
1:1250	*Schmecket und sehet, wie freundlich*	Tr7	SAB	MusLG
1:1251	*Schmecket und sehet, wie freundlich*	Chr	SATTBBBB, 2 fl picc., 2 ob, 3 tr, tim	OratJ
1:1252	*Schmecket und sehet unsres Gottes*	SuNY	v, ob, bc	HarmGD
1:1253	*Schmücke dich, o liebe Seele*	Tr20		for Communion; lib. by E. Neumeister
1:1254	*Schmücke dich, o liebe Seele*		ob	before 1721
1:1255	*Schmücket das Fest mit Maien*	Pen	fl, 2 ob, 3 tr, tim	
1:1256	*Schmückt das frohe Fest mit Maien*	Pen2	v, vn, bc	HarmGD
1:1257	*Schwing dich auf zu deinem Gott*	Eas4	2 ob	FranzJ
1:*deest*	*Schnöder Hochmut, weg mit dir*			frag.
1:801a	*Seel und Leib sind fest*	Tr13	v, bc	AdA
1:1258	*Seele, lerne dich erkennen*	Quin	v, rec, bc	HarmGD
1:1662a	*Segensreicher Gang*	Eas4	v, bc	AdA
1:1259	*Sehet an die Exempel der Alten*	Ep2	2 ob ad lib., corn, 3 trb	NeuL
1:1260	*Sehet auf, und hebet eure Häupter*	Ad2	2 ob	FranzJ
1:1262	*Sehet nun zu, wie ihr fürsichtiglich wandelt*	Tr8		NeuL
1:1263	*Sehet, wir gehn hinauf gen Jerusalem*	Quin	2 ob	GSuS-I
1:1264	*Seht, wir gehen hinauf gen Jerusalem*	Quin	2 ob	SchuJ, FoHarmGD

1:1282	*Sei du mein Anfang*	Ad1	ob	1755
1:1283	*Sei getreu bis in den Tod*	Ad3	2 ob, 2 bn	NeuL
1:1284	*Sei getreu bis in den Tod*	SuAsc		
1:1290	*Sei zufrieden, meine Seele*	EasMon	b, vn, bc	
1:1266	*Seid allesamt gleich gesinnet*	Tr6	2 ob ad lib.	HarmLG, AdA
1:1267	*Seid allezeit bereit*	Ad4	2 ob	HarmLG, AdA
1:1268	*Seid barmherzig, wie auch euer Vater*	Tr4	v, ob, bc	GSuS-I
1:1269	*Seid dankbar in allen Dingen*	Tr14	SAB	MusLG
1:1270	*Seid getrost, fürchtet euch nicht*	Lent3	2 ob	1757
1:1271	*Seid getrost und hoch erfreut*	Tr26		EngelJ
1:1272	*Seid ihr mit Christo auferstanden*	Asc	2 ob, 3 tr, tim	Ling1
1:1273	*Seid nüchtern und wachet*	Ep5	2 ob ad lib.	ConcJ
1:1274	*Seid nüchtern und wachet*	Lent1	2 ob, 2 cor	NeuL
1:1275	*Seid nüchtern und wachet*	Ep5	2 ob	GSuS-I
1:1276	*Seid nüchtern und wachet*	Lent1	2 ob	SicJ
1:1278	*Seid nüchtern und wachet*	Lent1	SAB	MusLG
1:1279	*Seid stark in dem Herrn*	Lent1	2 ob	ConcJ
1:1280	*Seid stark in dem Herrn*	Quin	2 ob	HarmLG, AdA
1:1281	*Seid wacker allezeit, und betet*	Ad2	2 ob	NeuL
1:1288	*Sein starker Arm hat mit dem Tod gerungen*	EasMon	2 ob, 3 tr, tim	
1:1291	*Selig ist der Mann, der die Anfechtung*	SuAsc	2 ob	1723

1:1292	*Selig ist der Mann, der die Anfechtung*	Chr2		
1:1293	*Selig ist der, und heilig*	Tr24	2 ob	SicJ
1:1294	*Selig sind die Augen*	Tr13	2 ob	SchuJ, FoHarmGD
1:1295	*Selig sind, die das Wort Gottes hören*	Sexa	2 ob	ConcJ
1:1296	*Selig sind, die Gottes Wort hören*	Sexa	2 ob	Ling1
1:1298	*Selig sind die Toten*	Tr24	2 ob	NeuL
1:1299	*Selig sind die Toten*	Tr24	2 ob, 2 bn	NeuL
1:1300	*Selig sind die Toten*	Tr16	2 ob	Ling1
1:1302	*Selig sind die Toten*			= TVWV 4:1
1:1304	*Selig sind, die zum Abendmahle*	Tr2	ATB, 2 vn/fl, bc	GSuS-I
1:1305	*Selig sind, die zum Abendmahl*	Tr20	2 ob, 3 tr, tim	Ling1
1:1306	*Selig sind, die zum Abendmahl*	Tr2	2 fl, 2 ob, bc	lib. by E. Neumeister, 1725
1:1307	*Selig sind, die zum Abendmahl*	Tr2	2 tr, tim	1726
1:1308	*Selig sind, die zum Abendmahl*	Tr2	SAB	MusLG
1:1309	*Selig sind, die zum Abendmahl*	Tr2	2 ob	
1:1310	*Selig sind, die zum Abendmahl*		s, t	1743
1:1311	*Sie gehen dahin unter den Sorgen*	Chr2	SATTB, ob	OratJ
1:1312	*Sie gehen in die Welt*	Tr24	ob, cor	HornJ
1:1313	*Siehe an meinen Jammer und Elend*	Tr14	2 ob	JoR
1:1314	*Siehe da, eine Hütte Gottes*	Pen	2 ob	HarmLG, AdA
1:1315	*Siehe da, ich lege in Zion einen Stein*	SuChr	2 ob	JoR

1:1316	*Siehe, das ist Gottes Lamm*	Quin	2 ob	ConcJ
1:1317 = 1319	*Siehe, das ist Gottes Lamm*	Quin	2 ob	JoR
1:1318	*Siehe, das ist Gottes Lamm*	Quin	SAB	MusLG
1:1320	*Siehe, das ist Gottes Lamm*	Pal	2 ob	
1:1322	*Siehe, der Herr kommt*	Ad2	2 ob	JoR
1:1324	*Siehe, des Herren Auge siehet auf die*	Tr7	2 ob	Ling1
1:1325	*Siehe, dieser wird gesetzt zu einem Fall*	SuChr		OratJ
1:1326	*Siehe, eine Jungfrau ist schwanger*	Ann	2 ob	ConcJ
1:1327	*Siehe, eine Jungfrau ist schwanger*	NYD	2 ob	JoR
1:1328	*Siehe, es hat überwunden der Löwe*	Mich	2 ob, 3 tr, tim	Ling1; falsely attrib. to J.S. Bach (BWV 219)
1:1329	*Siehe, es hat überwunden der Löwe*	Eas	2 ob, 3 tr, tim	
1:1330	*Siehe, es kommt ein Tag*	Tr26		Ling1
10:23	*Siehe, hieer bin ich*		s, t, 2 vn, bc	PoetFr
1:1331	*Siehe, ich komme*	Quin		
1:1332	*Siehe, ich komme*	Quin		
1:1333	*Siehe, ich verkündige euch große Freude*	Chr	ob, 2 tr, tim	1755
1:1334	*Siehe, ich verkündige euch große Freude*	Chr	2 fl, 2 ob, 2 tr, tim	1761
1:1336	*Sie ist gefallen, Babylon*	Lent3	2 ob	JoR
1:1337	*Sie ist gefallen, Babylon*	Lent3		HarmLG, AdA
1:1339	*Sie verachten das Gesetz*	Tr10	SAB	MusLG

1:1340	*Sind sie nicht allzumal dienstbare Geister*	Mich		JoR
1:1341	*Sing Dank und Ehr*	Mich	2 fl, ob, 2 tr, tim	1759
1:1343	*Singet dem Herrn ein neues Lied*	Asc	2 ob, 2 tr, tim	JoR
1:1344	*Singet dem Herrn ein neues Lied*	Eas	2 fl, 2 ob, 2 tr, tim	lib. by Peticius, 1761
1:1345	*Singet dem Herrn ein neues Lied*	John	2 cor, tr, harp	
1:1346	*Singet Gott, lobsinget*	Pen	2 ob, 3 tr, tim	EmbJ
1:1347	*Singt umeinander dem Herrn*	NYD	SATBB, 2 fl, 2 ob, 2 tr, tim	1764
1:1348	*So der Geist des, der Jesum von den Toten*	Tr24	2 ob ad lib.	HarmLG, AdA
1:1349	*So du freiest, sündigest du nicht*	Ep2		Ling1
1:1350	*So du mit deinem Munde bekennest*	Eas	2 ob, 3 tr, tim, glockenspiel	Ling1
1:1351	*So du mit deinem Munde bekennest*	LSun		JoR
1:1352	*So du mit deinem Munde bekennest*	LSun		
1:1354	*So fahre hin, du tolle Schar*	Tr14		EngelJ
1:1356	*So Feuer als Flamme*	Tr6	2 ob	StolbJ
1:1357	*So folgt der Fesseln schütternd Klingen*	Ad3	SATTBBB	OratJ
1:*deest*	*So gehest du, mein Jesu, hin*		SATTB, 2 ob	1744
1:1358	*So hoch hat Gott geliebet*	Pen2		Ling2
1:1359	*So ihr den Menschen ihre Fehler vergebet*	Tr22		Ling1
1:1361	*So ist der Mensch gesinnt*	Ep4	2 ob	StolbJ
1:1362	*So jemand Christi Wort wird halten*	Lent5	2 ob	Ling1

1:1363	*So lasset uns nun hinzutreten mit Freudigkeit*	Eas5	SATTBB	OratJ
1:1364	*So lasset uns nun nicht schlafen*	Ep5	SAB	MusLG
1:1366	*So leget ab alle Unsauberkeit*	Sexa	fl, 2 ob	SchuJ, FoHarmGD
1:1367	*So leget nun ab von euch*	Tr20	2 ob	NeuL
1:1368	*So leget nun ab von euch*	NYD	2 ob, 3 tr, tim	Ling1
1:1369	*So leget nun ab von euch*	Tr	2 ob	SchuJ, FoHarmGD
1:1370	*So leget nun von euch ab*	Tr	2 ob	SicJ
1:1376	*So nun das alles soll zergehen*	Ad2	2 ob	SicJ
1:1383	*So spricht der Herr: Man höret eine klägliche Stimme*	SuNY	2 ob	
1:1384	*So spricht der Herr Zebaoth: Richtet recht*	Tr4	2 ob ad lib.	NeuL
1:1385	*So töricht ist die Welt*	Eas3	2 fl, 2 ob	SchuJ, FoHarmGD
1:1386	*So wie das alte Jahr mit Tagen*	NYD	3 tr, tim	Ling2
1:1387	*So wir denn nun haben*	Eas4	SAB	MusLG
1:1388	*So wir sagen, daß wir Gemeinschaft mit Gott haben*	Tr11	2 ob	SicJ
1:1389	*So wir sagen, wir haben keine Sünde*	Tr11	2 ob	Ling1
1:1390	*So ziehet nun an, als die Auserwählten Gottes*	Tr6	2 ob	SicJ
1:1391	*So ziehet nun an, als die Auserwählten Gottes*	Tr4	2 ob	SchuJ, FoHarmGD
1:1371	*Soll ich nicht von Jammer sagen*	Tr19	b, fl ad lib.	BranJ
1:1373	*Sollt ein christliches Gemüte*	Mich	b, fl, ob	1721
1:1374	*Sollt uns Gott nun können lassen*	Pen2	2 ob	

1:1392	*Sprich nicht im Mangel*	Lent4		EngelJ
1:1393	*Sprich nur ein Wort*	Tr21		EngelJ
1:1394	*Spricht der Herr aber also*	Ep3	2 ob ad lib.	ConcJ
1:1397	*Stehe auf, Nordwind, und komm, Südwind*	Pen2	2 rec	
1:1398	*Stern aus Jakob, Licht der Heiden*	Ep	2 tr	FranzJ
1:1401	*Stille die Tränen der winselnden Armen*	Tr2	v, fl, bc	HarmGD
1:1403	*Suchet den Herrn, weil er zu finden ist*	Tr3	2 ob	JoR
1:1404	*Suchet den Herrn, weil er zu finden ist*	Tr3	ob	HarmLG, AdA
1:1405	*Suchet den Herrn, weil er zu finden ist*	Tr11	SAB	MusLG
1:1406	*Suchet den Herrn, rufet ihn an*	Tr11		= 1:1405 with altered text, 1758
1:1408	*Süße Ruh in herben Leiden*	Ep5	v, bc	AdA
1:1407	*Süßer Trost für meine kranke Seele*	Tr14	2 ob	Ling1
1:1410	*Tönet die Freude*	Chr	2 fl, 2 tr, tim	1757
1:1411	*Trachtet am ersten nach dem Reiche Gottes*	Lent4	2 ob	SicJ
1:1412	*Trachtet am ersten nach dem Reiche Gottes*	Tr15	SAB	MusLG
1:1413	*Trag mit Geduld die herben Schmerzen*		t, b, vn, bc	
1:1414	*Trauert ihr Himmel*		2 fl, 2 ob, 2 tr, tim	for Easter, 1760
1:1415	*Traurigs Herz, verzage nicht*	Mich	2 ob	
1:1417	*Trifft menschlich und voll Fehler sein*	Tr15	v, rec, bc	HarmGD
1:1418	*Tritt Arbeit und Beruf in Gottes Namen an*	Sept	2 ob, 2 cor	FranzJ
1:1420	*Tritt auf die Glaubensbahn*	SuChr		lib. by Franck

1:1421	*Triumph! Denn mein Erlöser lebet*	Eas	2 ob, 2 tr, tim	BranJ
1:1423	*Triumph, Triumph*	Eas	fl, ob, 2 tr, tim	1758
1:1424	*Triumph, Triumph*	Eas	3 tr, tim	Ling2
1:1422	*Triumphierender Versöhner*	EasMon	v, vn, bc	HarmGD
1:1425	*Tröstet mein Volk, spricht euer Gott*	John	2 tr, tim	
1:1426	*Umschlinget uns, ihr sanften*	Tr17	v, ob, bc	HarmGD
1:1745	*Unbegreiflich ist dein Wesen*	Tr	v, vn, bc	HarmGD
1:1427	*Und alle Engel stunden um den Stuhl*	Mich	SAB	MusLG
1:1428	*Und als der Tag der Pfingsten erfüllet war*	Pen	ob, 2 tr, tim	1758
1:1429	*Und als er nahe hinzu kam*	Tr10	2 ob ad lib.	NeuL
1:1430	*Und da die Engel von ihnen*	Chr2	2 ob ad lib.	ConcJ
1:1431	*Und das Wort ward Fleisch*	Chr3	SAB	MusLG; first movt = TVWV 8:14
1:1432	*Und der Herr Zebaoth*	Tr2	2 fl, 2 ob	
1:1433	*Und die Apostel sprachen zu dem Herrn*	LSun	2 ob	ConcJ
1:1434	*Und es erhub sich ein Streit*	Mich	3 tr, tim	NeuL
1:1436	*Und Gott ruhte am siebten Tage*	Tr17		
1:1437	*Und siehe, eine Stimme aus den Wolken*	Ep6	SAB	MusLG
1:1438	*Und sie redeten miteinander*	EasMon	SSATB, 2 ob	FranzJ
1:1440 = 1441	*Unschuld und ein gut Gewissen*	Lent3	2 ob	FranzJ
1:1442	*Unser keiner lebt ihm selber*	Tr16	2 ob	SicJ
1:1443	*Unser keiner lebt ihm selber*	Tr16	SAB	MusLG

1:1444	*Unser Leben währet siebenzig Jahr*	Pur	rec, 2 fl, 2 ob	1760
1:1445	*Unser Trost ist der*	Lent5	SAB	MusLG
1:1450	*Uns ist ein Kind geboren*	Chr	2 fl, 2 ob, 2 tr, tim	ConcJ
1:1451	*Uns ist ein Kind geboren*	Chr	3 tr, tim	GSuS-I
1:1452	*Uns ist ein Kind geboren*	Chr	SSATB, 2 ob, 2 cor	NeuL
1:1453	*Uns ist ein Kind geboren*	Chr	SAB	MusLG
1:1454	*Uns ist ein Kind geboren*	Chr	2 tr, tim	EngelJ
1:1455	*Uns ist ein Kind geboren*	Chr	2 ob	frag.
1:1456	*Unverzagt in allem Leide*	Chr3	v, vn, bc	HarmGD
1:1457	*Unverzagt und ohne Grauen*	Ad3		EngelJ
1:1458	*Valet will ich dir geben*	Tr17	SATTBB, 2 ob	FranzJ
1:1459	*Vater, Gott von Ewigkeit*	Vis	2 fl, ob	1758
1:1460	*Vater unser im Himmelreich*	Eas5	2 ob	FranzJ
1:1461	*Vater unser im Himmelreich*		2 ob	
1:1462	*Vater unser im Himmelreich*	Tr19		
1:1463	*Verdammet, fluchet, ihr Gesetze*	Pur	v, vn, va, bc	FoHarmGD
1:1466	*Verflucht sei jedermann*	Tr11	2 ob ad lib.	HarmLG, AdA
1:1467	*Verfolgter Geist, wohin*	Tr21	v, ob, bc	HarmGD
1:1468	*Verirrter Knecht der Welt*	Ad3		Ling2
1:1469	*Verirrte Sünder, kehret*	Chr2		Ling2
1:*deest*	*Verklärte Majestät*		s, vn, bc	

1:1470	*Verlaß doch einst, o Menschenkind*	EasTue		Ling2
1:248a	*Verliere nur gebrochen dich*	Pur	v, bc	AdA
1:1471	*Verlöschet, ihr Funken*	Tr1	v, ob, bc	HarmGD
1:1473	*Versuchet euch selbst*	Tr21	2 ob	SicJ
1:*deest*	*Verwirrter Geist, wie wird wir (Der ungerathne Sohn)*	Tr3		OratJ
1:1746	*Victoria, mein Jesu ist erstanden*		b, tr, vn, va, bc	for Easter
1:1475	*Victoria, Triumph, Victoria*		3 tr, tim	for Easter
1:1477	*Viel Menschen sind noch heut*	Tr20		Ling2
1:1478	*Viel(e) sind berufen*	Tr2	2 ob, 3 tr, tim	Ling1
1:1479	*Viel tausend sind*	Tr27	v, vn, va, bc	FoHarmGD
1:1481	*Vor allen Dingen ergreifet*	Lent1	2 ob	before 1730
1:1482	*Vor allen Dingen habt unter einander*	Tr9	2 ob ad lib.	HarmLG, AdA
1:1483	*Vor des lichten Tages Schein*	Ad3	v, fl, bc	HarmGD
1:1484	*Vor Gott gilt keine Heuchelei*	Tr8	s, b, 2 fl, vn, bc	before 1721
1:1485	*Vor Wölfen in der Schafe Kleider*	Tr8	2 ob	SchuJ, FoHarmGD
1:1487	*Wachet auf, ruft uns die Stimme*	Tr27		EngelJ
1:1488	*Wachet auf, ruft uns die Stimme*		s, b, b	Danzig, 1754?
1:1489	*Wachet und betet*	Lent1	2 ob	JoR
1:1490	*Wachet und betet*	Lent1	s, b, vn, bc	lib. by E. Neumeister
1:1491	*Wachset in der Gnade*	Ad4	SAB	MusLG

1:1492	*Wacht auf, ruft uns die Stimme*	Tr20	2 fl, 2 ob, 3 tr, tim	1721
1:1494	*Wahrlich ich sage euch: Ein Reicher wird*	Tr1	2 ob	FranzJ
1:1495	*Wahrlich ich sage euch: Ein Reicher wird*	Tr1		lib. by E. Neumeister
1:1493	*Wahrlich ich sage euch, so ihr den Vater*	Eas5	2 ob	NeuL
1:1497	*Wahrlich ich sage euch, so ihr den Vater*	Eas5	2 rec, 2 ob	
1:1498	*Wandelt in der Liebe*	Lent3	v, fl, bc	HarmGD
1:1499	*Warum betrübst du dich, mein Herz*	Ep2	2 ob	FranzJ
1:1500	*Warum betrübst du dich, mein Herz*	Ep2	ob	lib. by E. Neumeister
1:1502	*Warum verstellst du die Gebärde*	Ep3	v, ob, bc	HarmGD
1:1503	*Warum währet doch unser Schmerz so lange*	Ep3	2 ob	HarmLG, AdA
1:1504	*Warum währet doch unser Schmerz so lange*	Ep3		OratJ
1:1505	*Was betrübst du dich, meine Seele*	Tr7	2 ob	NeuL
1:1506	*Was betrübst du dich, meine Seele*	EasMon	2 ob, 3 tr, bc	Ling1
1:1507	*Was fehlt dir doch*	Tr12	2 ob	FranzJ
1:1508	*Was frag ich nach der Welt*	Chr	2 fl, ob, 3 tr, tim	1754
1:1509	*Was für ein jauchzendes Gedränge*	Ad1	2 ob	
1:1510	*Was gibst du denn, o meine Seele*	Tr23	fl, 2 ob	
1:1511	*Was gleicht dem Adel wahrer Christen*	SuChr	v, ob, bc	HarmGD
1:1512	*Was Gott im Himmel will*	Ep3	2 ob	MusLG
1:1747	*Was Gott tut, ist wohlgetan*	Eas4	s, b, vn, bc	
1:1513	*Was hast du, Mensch!*	Tr9	2 ob, bn	NeuL

1:1514	*Was hat das Licht*	Tr15	2 ob	NeuL
1:1516	*Was ist das Herz*	Ep6	v, vn, bc	HarmGD
1:1517	*Was ist dein Freund vor andern Freunden*	Ep6	2 ob	
1:*deest*	*Was ist denn auch der Mensch*			frag.
1:1520	*Was ist ein Mensch*	Tr4		HarmLG, AdA
1:1521	*Was ist mir doch das Rühmen nütze*	Sexa	v, fl, bc	HarmGD
1:1522	*Was ist schöner als Gott dienen*	Sexa		EngelJ
1:1523	*Was Jesus nur mit mir wird fügen*	Tr12	2 ob	GSuS-II
1:1525	*Was Jesus nur mit mir wird fügen*	Tr12	2 ob	GSuS-I
1:1526	*Was Jesus tut, ist wohlgetan*	Tr12	s, vn, bc	GeistC
1:1529	*Was mein Gott will*	Ep3	2 ob	GSuS-I
1:1530	*Was meinst du, was will aus dem Kindlein*	John		
1:*deest*	*Was sorgst du dich so ängstlich*			frag.
1:1531	*Was suchet ihr den Lebendigen bei den Toten*	EasTue		Ling1
1:1534	*Weg mit Sodoms giftgen Früchten*	Eas	v, vn, bc	HarmGD
1:1535	*Weg, nichtige Freude*			
1:1536	*Weiche, Lust und Fröhlichkeit*		v	for Passiontide
1:1537	*Weichet fort aus meiner Seele*	Tr15	2 ob, cor	FranzJ
1:1538	*Weicht ihr Sünden, bleibt dahinten*	Tr8	v, vn, bc	HarmGD
1:1539	*Weich, verborgner Pharisäer*	Sept	2 ob	StolbJ
1:1540	*Weil ich denn rufe*	Tr2	2 ob	NeuL

1:1541	*Weine nicht, siehe, es hat überwunden*	Eas	2 ob, 3 tr	SchuJ, FoHarmGD
1:1542	*Weint, weint, betrübte Augen*	Lent2	2 fl, ob	lib. by L.C. Mizler, 1754
1:1545	*Welcher unter euch*	Lent5	2 fl, 2 ob	NeuL
1:1546	*Welch Getümmel erschüttert den Himmel*	Mich	2 ob, 2 tr, tim	1757
1:1547	*Welt, hinaus aus meinem Herzen*		t, vn, bc	frag.
1:661a	*Welt, verlange nicht mein Herz*	Tr18	v, bc	AdA
1:1550	*Wende dich zu mir*	Tr3	SAB	MusLG
1:1551	*Wende meine Augen ab*	Tr8	2 ob	ConcJ
1:1552	*Wenn aber der Tröster*	Eas4	2 ob	JoR
1:1553	*Wenn aber des Menschen Sohn*	Tr26	fl, ob	after 1755
1:1555	*Wenn böse Zungen stechen*	TR4		EngelJ
1:1556	*Wenn der Herr Friede gibt*	Eas3	2 ob, bn	HarmLG, AdA
1:1557	*Wenn du deine Gabe*	Tr6	SAB	MusLG
1:1559	*Wenn Gott in diesem Leben*	Tr1		Ling2
1:1561	*Wenn ich ein gut Gewissen habe*	Lent5	2 ob	GSuS-I
1:1562	*Wenn Israel am Nilus-Strande*	Tr7	v, rec, bc	HarmGD
1:1563	*Wenn jemand das Gesetz Mosis bricht*	Tr2		HarmLG, AdA
1:1564	*Wenn langer Seuchen Heftigkeit*	Tr21	fl, 2 ob	SchuJ, FoHarmGD
1:1565	*Wenn meine Sünd mich kränken*			for Danzig, 1754?
1:1566	*Wenn mich die böse Rott anfällt*	Lent3	2 ob, hn	StolbJ
1:1567	*Wenn mir angst ist*	Ep4	SAB	MusLG

1:1568	*Wenn wir in höchsten Nöten sein*	Ep4	3 ob, 3 tr, tim	GSuS-I
1:1569	*Wenn wir in höchsten Nöten*	Ep4		EngelJ
1:1570	*Wenn wir nicht Kreuz und Trübsal hätten*	Eas3		EngelJ
1:1572	*Wer Arges tut*	Pen2	2 ob	HarmLG, AdA
1:1573	*Wer bei Gott in Gnaden ist*	John	2 ob	FranzJ
1:1574	*Wer bringt dir nicht Ehre*		fl, 2 ob, 2 cor, 2 tr	frag.
1:1575	*Wer da saget, ich kenne ihn*	Tr18	2 ob	NeuL
1:1578	*Wer der Barmherzigkeit*	Tr4	SAB	MusLG
1:1582	*Wer hofft in Gott*	Tr17		
1:1583	*Wer ist aber, der die Welt überwindet*	Ad4		Ling1
1:1584	*Wer ist, der dort von Edom*	Lent5	v, vn, bc	HarmGD
1:1585	*Wer ist der, so von Edom kömmt*	Palm	2 ob	FranzJ
1:1586	*Wer ist der, so von Edom kommt*	Quin		HarmLG, AdA
10:26	*Wer ist jemals zu Schanden worden*		a, t, 2 vn, bc	PoetFr
1:1587	*Wer ist wohl wie du, Jesu*	Ep		EngelJ
1:1588	*Wer Jesum kennt*	Tr7	2 ob	FranzJ
1:1589	*Wer mich liebet, der wird*	Pen	fl, 2 ob, hn, 2 tr	NeuL
1:1590	*Wer mich liebet, der wird*	Pen	2 ob	FranzJ
1:1591	*Wer mich liebet, der wird*	Pen	fl, 2 tr, tim	1754
1:1593	*Wer nur den lieben Gott läßt walten*	Lent4	2 ob	FranzJ
1:1594	*Wer sehnet sich nach Kerker*	Tr3	v, rec, bc	HarmGD

1:1595	*Wer seinen Bruder hasset*	Tr6	2 ob	Ling1
1:1596	*Wer seinen Bruder hasset*	Tr6	fl, 2 ob	
1:1597	*Wer sich auf seinen Reichtum*	Tr1		
1:1598	*Wer sich des Armen erbarmet*	Tr13	2 ob	Ling1
1:1599	*Wer sich des Armen erbarmet*	Tr1	2 fl, 2 ob, bn, 2 tr, tim	StolbJ
1:1600	*Wer sich rächet*	Tr6		GSuS-I
1:1601	*Wer sich rächet*	Tr22	SAB	MusLG
1:1602	*Wer sich rächet*	Tr6	2 ob	GSuS-II
1:1603	*Wer sich selbst erhöhet*	Tr17	2 ob	SicJ
1:1604	*Wer sich selbst erhöhet*	Ad4	2 ob	OratJ
1:1605	*Wer sich vor dir, o Gott*	Tr11	2 fl, 2 ob	StolbJ
1:1609	*Wer weiß, wie nahe mir mein Ende*	Chr2		49/50J; = 1:762
1:1610	*Wer weiß, wie nahe mir mein Ende*	Tr9		EngelJ
1:1611	*Wer weiß, wie nahe mir mein Ende*	Tr16		EngelJ
1:1613	*Wer will uns scheiden von der Liebe Gottes*	SuAsc	2 ob	ConcJ; composed in Wormstedt, 26 April 1717
1:1614	*Wer zu Gott kommen will*	Tr21	2 ob ad lib.	HarmLG, AdA
1:1615	*Wer zweifelt, daß man unser Herze*	Ep4	2 ob	SchuJ, FoHarmGD
1:1580	*Werfet Panier auf im Lande*	Chr2	2 ob, 2 tr, tim	HarmLG, AdA; first movt = TVWV 8:15
1:1579	*Werd ich denn zu deiner Rechten*	Tr26	2 ob	FranzJ

1:1576	*Werde munter, mein Gemüte*			for Communion; lib. by E. Neumeister
1:1606	*Wertes Zion, sei getrost*	Tr26	2 ob, 3 tr, tim	FranzJ
1:1607	*Wertes Zion, sei getrost*	Tr23	SS/TTB	lib. by E. Neumeister; doubtful
1:1616	*Wie der Hirsch schreiet*	Tr16	2 ob	NeuL
1:1617	*Wie der Hirsch schreiet*	Pur	3 tr, tim	Ling1
1:1618	*Wie der Hirsch schreiet*	Ann	2 ob	
1:*deest*	*Wie der Hirsch schreiet*		b, 2 vn, bc	before 1721
1:1619	*Wie ein Lämmlein sich dahin läßt*	Quin	SATBB, fl, ob	OratJ
1:1620	*Wie fehlet doch ein Herz*	Tr20	2 ob	SchuJ, FoHarmGD
1:1621	*Wie freudig seh ich dir entgegen*		2 fl, 2 cor, 3 trb, tim	
1:1625	*Wie, kehren sich, bei Jesu Krippen*	SuNY	v, vn, va, bc	FoHarmGD
1:1626	*Wie lange hinket ihr auf beiden Seiten*	Lent4	SAATT, 2 fl	OratJ
1:1627	*Wie lieblich sind deine Wohnungen*	Ep1	2 ob	GSuS-I
1:1628	*Wie lieblich sind deine Wohnungen*	Ep1	SAB	MusLG
1:*deest*	*Wie lieblich, wie schöne ist dieses zu hören*	Pen	s	
1:1629	*Wie liegt die Stadt so wüste*	Tr10	2 ob ad lib.	HarmLG, AdA
1:1630	*Wie mancher baut sich Schlösser*	EasMon		Ling2
1:1633	*Wie ofte hört man nicht*	Ep2	fl, 2 ob	StolbJ
1:1634	*Wie schmerzlich drückt*	Tr7	2 ob	SchuJ, FoHarmGD
1:1640	*Wie schön wirds nicht im Himmel sein*	Asc	fl, 2 ob, bn	GSuS-I

1:1641	*Wie sich ein Vater über Kinder erbarmet*	Lent2	2 ob	Ling1
1:1643	*Wie, sollte Jesus von mir gehen*	Eas4		Ling2
1:1644	*Wie Spinnen Gift aus Blumen saugen*	Lent3	2 ob	BranJ
1:1646	*Wie teuer ist deine Güte, Gott*	Chr2	fl, 2 ob ad lib., 2 tr	NeuL
1:*deest*	*Wie will ich, Höchster, dich besingen*		fl, 4 tr, tim	frag.
1:1649	*Wie würde es uns (mir) ergehen*	Mich		Ling2
1:1648	*Wiewohl er, Jesus Christus, Gottes Sohn war*	NYD	2 fl, 2 ob, 2 tr, tim	1757
1:1652 = 1653	*Willkommen, segensvolles Fest*	Eas	SSATB, 2 ob, 4 tr, tim	GSuS-I
1:1654	*Wir aber, die wir des Tages Kinder sind*	Ad2	2 ob	StolbJ
1:1657	*Wir danken dir, Gott*	Ad3		HarmLG, AdA
1:1659	*Wir gingen alle in der Irre*	Eas2	2 ob	SchuJ, FoHarmGD
1:1660	*Wir glauben an den heiligen Geist*	Pen	2 ob, vadg, bn	GSuS-I
1:1661	*Wir haben den funden*	Ad3		JoR
1:1663	*Wir haben ein festes prophetisches Wort*	Ep5		JoR
1:1665	*Wir haben hier keine bleibende Statt*	Vis	2 fl, bn	1732; = TVWV 4:9
1:1666	*Wir haben hier keine bleibende Stätte*		SSATB	for Feast of the Circumcision of Christ
1:1667	*Wir haben nicht mit Fleisch und Blut*	Lent3	2 ob	SchuJ, FoHarmGD
1:1668	*Wir liegen, großer Gott, vor dir*	Tr22	2 ob, 2 bn	FranzJ
1:1669	*Wir müssen alle offenbar werden*	Tr9	2 ob	ConcJ
1:1670	*Wir müssen alle offenbaret werden*	Tr9	2 ob	SicJ

1:1672	*Wir müssen alle offenbar werden*	Tr26	SAB	MusLG
1:1674	*Wir sind allesamt wie die Unreinen*	Tr6		JoR
1:1675	*Wir sind allesamt wie die Unreinen*	Tr20	2 ob ad lib.	HarmLG, AdA
1:1676	*Wir sind allzumal Sünder*	Sept	2 ob	NeuL
1:1677	*Wir sind Gottes Mitarbeiter*	Ep5	2 ob	1757
1:1678	*Wir sollen selig werden*	Tr	2 ob	FranzJ
1:1679	*Wirst du den Herrn suchen*	Ep1		frag.
1:1681	*Wir wissen, daß denen, die Gott lieben*	SuNY	2 ob	SicJ
1:1682	*Wir wissen, daß denen, die Gott lieben*	Eas3	SAB	MusLG
1:1683	*Wir wissen, daß Gott die Sünder nicht höret*	Eas5	2 ob	Ling1
1:1685	*Wisset ihr nicht, daß alle*	Ad4	2 ob	SicJ
1:1686	*Wisset ihr nicht, daß euer Lieb*	Pen	SAB, 3 tr, tim	MusLG
1:1687	*Wisset ihr nicht, daß ihr Gottes Tempel*	Pen	2 ob	SicJ
1:1689	*Wo bleibt die brüderliche Lieb*	Tr22		EngelJ
1:1690	*Wo find ich meinen Jesum wieder*	Ep1		BranJ
1:1716	*Wo ist dann dein Freund hingegangen*	Ep1	2 ob	HarmLG, AdA
1:1717	*Wo ist denn mein Jesus hin*		b, vn, bc	
1:1719	*Wo ist ein solcher Gott, wie du bist*	Tr22		RambGP
1:1720	*Wo ist solch ein Gott, wie du bist*	Tr3	2 ob	SicJ
1:1721	*Wo ist solch ein Gott, wie du bist*	Tr19	SAB	MusLG
1:1722	*Wo Jesus Hunger merkt*	Lent4	2 ob	StolbJ

1:1724	*Wo soll ich fliehen hin*	Tr22	fl, 2 ob, bn	
1:1725	*Wo soll ich fliehen hin*		s, 2 vn, bc	
1:1692	*Wohin ich nur die Augen wende*	Tr25		GSuS-II
1:1693	*Wohin ich nur die Augen wende*	Tr25		GSuS-I
1:1701	*Wohl dem, dem die Übertretung*	Tr19	SSATB, 3 trb	
1:1698	*Wohl dem, dem die Übertretung*	Tr19	2 ob	SicJ
1:1699	*Wohl dem, dem die Übertretungen*	Tr22	2 ob	JoR
1:1700	*Wohl dem, dem die Übertretungen*	Tr19	2 ob ad lib.	HarmLG, AdA
1:1703	*Wohl dem, der den Herrn fürchtet*	Tr15	2 ob ad lib.	HarmLG, AdA
1:1704	*Wohl dem, der den Herren fürchtet*	Eas4		
1:1708	*Wohl dem, des Hülfe der Gott Jacob ist*	Ep3	2 ob	NeuL
1:1709	*Wohl dem, des Hülfe der Gott Jacobs ist*	Lent4		HarmLG, AdA
1:1710	*Wohl dem Volke, das jauchzen kann*	Tr10	2 fl, 3 cor	1761
1:1713	*Wohl her nun und lasset uns wohlleben*	Eas3	2 ob, 3 tr, tim	RambGP
1:1694	*Wohlan alle, die ihr dürftig seid*	Tr2	2 ob	JoR
1:1696	*Wohlan, ich will meinem Lieben*	Sept	2 ob	SchuJ, FoHarmGD
1:1697	*Wohlauf Herze, sing und spring*	Tr24		EngelJ
1:1723	*Wollüstiger Sinnen bemühtes Beginnen*	Ad3	fl, 2 ob	StolbJ
1:1726	*Wünschet Jerusalem Glück*	NYD	2 ob, 2 cor	ConcJ
1:1727	*Wünschet Jerusalem Glück*	NYD	2 ob, 3 tr, tim	1734
1:1728	*Zeuch ohn Verzug in deinen Nöten*	Eas5	2 ob	SchuJ, FoHarmGD

1:1730	*Zions Hülf und Abrams Lohn*	NYD	ob, cor	HornJ
1:1731	*Zion spricht: Der Herr hat mich verlassen*	Eas3	2 ob	JoR
1:1732	*Zischet nur, stechet, ihr feurigen*	Pen	v, ob, bc	HarmGD
1:1733	*Zorn und Wüten sind Gräuel*	Tr6	2 ob	FranzJ
1:1735	*Zu dir flieh ich, verstoß mich nicht*	Tr11		EngelJ
1:1736	*Zu Mitternacht ward ein Geschrei*	Tr20	2 ob	SicJ
1:1738	*Zween Jünger gehn nach Emmaus*	EasMon	2 fl, 2 ob	GSuS-II
1:*deest*	*Zween Jünger gehn nach Emmaus*	EasMon		GSuS-I
1:1739	*Zwei Menschen, welche Saba hat geboren*	Ep		Ling2
1:1751	*Der Segen des Herrn macht reich ohne Mühe*	Tr5	2 ob	JoR
1:1752	*Gott ist die Liebe*	Tr17	2 ob, bn	frag.
1:1753	*Es ist umsonst, daß ihr früh aufsteht*	Tr5		ConcJ

2 Cantatas for church inaugurations

2:*deest*	*Erhebt euch zum Opfer*, for the Stadtkirche in Hersbruck near Nuremberg, 19 October 1738; music lost
2:3	*Siehe da! eine Hütte Gottes bei den Menschen* (lib. M. Richey), for the St Nicolaikirche in Billwerder, 1739, SATB, fl, ob, bn, 3 tr, tim, str
2:4	*Ich halte mich, Herr, zu deinem Altar* (lib. Telemann from texts by E. Neumeister) for the altar of the St Getrudkirche in Hamburg, 14 August 1742, SATB, 3 tr, tim, str
2:*deest*	*Bebt, Mauren und Pfosten* (lib. E.C. Reichard), for the principal Lutheran church in Altona, 8 September 1743; music lost
2:5	*Kommt, lasset uns anbeten* (lib. H.G. Schellhaffer), for the church in the St Hiob-Hospital in Hamburg, not performed on 15 February 1745 due to the mourning period for Emperor Charles VII, SATB, fl, ob, 2 vn
2:6	*Heilig, heilig, heilig ist Gott* (lib. H.G. Schellhaffer), for the Heilige Dreieinigkeitskirche in St Georg near Hamburg, 26 October 1747, SATB, ob, ob d'am, chal., 2 cor, 3 tr, tim, str
2:7	*Zerschmettert die Götzen*, for the church in Neuenstädten (Nienstedten), 16 May 1751, s, b, fl, ob, 2 tr, tim, 2 vn
2:9	*Singet Gott! Lobsinget seinem Namen* (lib. L.W. Ballhorn), for the church in Rellingen, 18 July 1756, SAB, fl, ob, cor, 2 tr, tim, 2 vn; incompl
2:10	*Ich will die zerfallene Hütte Davids wieder aufrichten* (lib. C.F. Schaub), for the small Michaeliskirche in Hamburg, 14 June 1757; music lost
2:12	*Komm wieder, Herr, zu der Menge der Tausenden in Israel* (lib. J.J.D. Zimmermann), for the Great St Michaeliskirche in Hamburg, 19 October 1762, SATBB, 2 fl, 2 ob, 2 cor, 6 tr, 2 tim, str

3 Music for the institution of preachers

For SATB and str, unless otherwise stated

3:56	*So sind wir nun Botschafter an Christi statt*, for Samuel Seeland as deacon in St Nicolai, Hamburg, 16 July 1749, with ob; incompl
3:57	*Alles was Odem hat, lobe den Herrn* (chorus), for Anton Kühl in St Jacobi, Hamburg, 18 June 1749
3:61	*Wie lieblich sind auf den Bergen die Füße der Boten*, for Joachim Lütkens in Steinbeck near Hamburg, 8 October 1754, with 2 ob, 3 tr, tim, str; incompl
3:67	*Nimm Dank und Weisheit*, for Christoph Gottlob Baumgarten in Moorburg near Hamburg, 15 June 1758, with SAB
3:82	*Veni sancte spiritus*, 1739, with ob
3:83	*Veni sancte spiritus*, 1756, with 3 tr, tim
3:84	*Veni sancte spiritus*, 1760?, with 3 tr, tim

3:85 *Veni sancte spiritus*, 1760?, for SB, bc
3:86 *Veni sancte spiritus*, with 3 tr, tim; incompl
3:87 *Veni sancte spiritus*, for SATB, bc
3:88 *Veni sancte spiritus*, for SSB, bc
3:89 *Veni sancte spiritus*, for SSS, bc
3:90 *Veni sancte spiritus*, with 2 ob, tr, tim
3:91 *Veni sancte spiritus*, for SATB, SATB
3:92 *Komm heiliger Geist, erfülle die Herzen* (motet), 1742?, for SSB, bc
3:93 *Komm heiliger Geist* (chorus), 1727, with 3 tr, tim
3:94 *Komm heiliger Geist, erfülle die Herzen* (motet), c. 1725, with 2 ob
3:95 *Wahrheit und das Licht*, with ob; incompl

Music and/or text lost: seventy-seven works for Hamburg and the neighbouring towns of Allermöhe, Billwerder, Curslac, Doos, Eppendorf, Hamm und Horn, Hornbostel, Mohrflet, Moorburg and Ochsenwerder, 1723–66

4 Funeral music

For SATB and str, unless otherwise stated; all composed for Hamburg ceremonies

4:1 *Selig sind die Toten*, for Bürgermeister Ludwig Becceler, 7 July 1722
4:2 *Ach wie nichtig, ach wie flüchtig* (lib. C.F. Weichmann), for Bürgermeister Gerhard Schröder, 1723, with 2 fl, 2 ob, 3 tr, timp, str, bc; incompl
4:3 *Das Leben ist ein Rauch, ein Schaum* (lib. M. Richey), for Bürgermeister Heinrich Dietrich Wiese, 10 February 1728, with fl, ob, 3 tr, tim
4:4 *Selig sind die Toten*, *Ich fürchte keinen Tod auf Erden* and *Alles Fleisch ist Heu* (3 cantatas) for Anna Maria Elers (wife of a pastor) in Hamm and Horn near Hamburg, 4 January 1729; music lost
4:5 *Ich hab, gottlob, das mein vollbracht* (lib. M. Richey), for Bürgermeister Hans Jacob Faber, 22 November 1729, with 3 tr, tim
4:6 *Ach wie nichtig, ach wie flüchtig*, for Bürgermeister Hartlieb Sillem, 5 January 1733, with fl, ob, 3 tr, tim
4:7 *In dunkler Nacht, bestürzt und bang* (*Unsterblicher Nachruhm Friedrich Augusts*; lib. J.J.D. Zimmermann), for Elector Friedrich August I, 1733, with 2 rec, 2 fl, 2 ob, ob d'am, chal, 2 bn, 2 cor, 6 tr, tim
4:8 *Dränge dich an diese Bahre* (lib. M. Richey), for Bürgermeister Daniel Stockfleth, 6 February 1739, with fl, 2 ob, 3 tr, tim
4:9 *Wir haben hier keine bleibende Statt*, for pastor Andreas Elers in Hamm and Horn near Hamburg, 28 May 1739, with 2 fl, bn
4:10 *Gönne jammervollen Klagen* (lib. J.J.D. Zimmermann), for the Holy Roman Emperor Charles VI, 1740; music lost
4:11 *Gott, du hast deinem Volke ein hartes erzeiget* (lib. M. Richey), for

	Bürgermeister Johann Hermann Luis, 25 September 1741; music lost
4:12	*Wer Gott vertraut, hat wohl gebaut* (lib. M.A. Wilkens), for Bürgermeister Rütger Ruland, 30 November 1742; music and text lost
4:13	*Ich hoffete aufs Licht* (lib. J.J.D. Zimmermann), for the Holy Roman Emperor Charles VII, 14 March 1745, with 2 tr, tim
4:14	*Der Mensch ist in seinem Leben wie Gras* (lib. H.G. Schellhaffer), for Bürgermeister Nicolai Stampeel, 2 June 1749; music lost
4:15	*Lieber König, du bist tot*, for King George II of England, 19 November 1760, B, 2 tr
4:16	*Wie ist der Held gefallen*, for the Holy Roman Emperor Franz I, 1765; music lost
4:17	*Du aber Daniel, gehe hin*, for an unknown occasion, for SATB, rec, ob, vn, bn, 2 vadg, bc
4:18	*Ein Mensch ist in seinem Leben*, for an unknown occasion, by 1729
4:19	*Fliehet hin, ihr bösen Tage*, for an unknown occasion, for b, vn, bc; music and text lost
4:20	*Nun geh ich aus der Sorgen Banden*, for an unknown occasion, for b, bc
4:21	*Wie so kurz ist unser Leben*, for an unknown occasion, for s, fl, cor, 2 vn, bc
4:22	*Gottlob, es ist vollbracht*, for an unknown occasion, with 2 ob
4:23	*Herr, nimmst du mir was Liebes*, for an unknown occasion, for a, b, 2 fl, str, bc; incompl

5 Passion oratorios and passions

For SATB, str and composed for Hamburg, unless otherwise stated

5:1	*Der für die Sünden der Welt gemarterte und sterbende Jesus* (*Brockes-Passion*; lib. B.H. Brockes), Frankfurt, 2–3 April 1716, with SSSAATTBBB, 3 rec, 2 fl, 2 ob, bn, 2 cor, 2 tr, 3 violetta, va d'am
5:2	*Seliges Erwägen des bittern Leidens und Sterbens Jesu Christi* (lib. Telemann), 9 March 1722, with 2 ob, 2 chal, 2 vn, 2 cor
5:3	*Die Bekehrung des Römischen Hauptmans Cornelius* (lib. A.J. Zell), 9 March 1731; music lost
5:*deest*	*Jesus, als die untergehende Sonne, wurde*, 1731; music lost
5:4	*Die gekreuzigte Liebe oder Tränen über das Leiden und Sterben unseres Heilandes* (lib. J.U. von König), 22 March 1731, with rec, 2 fl, 2 ob, ob d'am, chal, 2 cor
5:5	*Betrachtung der neunten Stunde an dem Todestag Jesu* (lib. J.J.D. Zimmermann), 19 March 1755, with SATBB, 2 fl, ob d'am, 2 cor
5:6	*Der Tod Jesu* (lib. K.W. Ramler), 19 March 1755, SAATBB, 2 fl, 'grosse' fl, 2 ob, ob d'am, cor
5:8	St Mark Passion (lib. B.H. Brockes), 1723, with fl, 2 ob, ob d'am; only 1 aria extant, transcribed in P. Spitta, *Johann Sebastian Bach*, vol. 1 (Leipzig, 1873), musical appendix, 12–13.

5:13 St Luke Passion (lib. M.A. Wilkens), 1728, with rec, 2 fl, 2 ob, bn
5:15 St Matthew Passion (lib. T.H. Schubart), 1730, with 2 fl, ob
5:18 St John Passion, 1733, with fl, 2 ob
5:22 St John Passion, 1737, with fl, 2 ob
5:26 St John Passion, 1741, with 2 fl, 2 ob
5:29 St Luke Passion (lib. J. Gesenius), 1744, with fl, ob, ob d'am
5:30 St John Passion (lib. J.J.D. Zimmermann), 1745, with SATTTBBB, rec, 2 fl, ob, ob d'am, bn; pub. as *Music vom Leiden und Sterben des Welt Erlösers* (*Ein Lämmlein geht und trägt die Schuld*; Nuremberg, 1746)
5:31 St Matthew Passion, 1746, with rec, ob, ob d'am, 2 cor
5:33 St Luke Passion, 1748, with 2 fl, ob, ob d'am
5:34 St John Passion (parody of 5:26), 1749, with 2 fl, 2 ob
5:35 St Matthew Passion, 1750, with 2 fl, ob, ob d'am
5:40 St Mark Passion, 1755, with 2 fl, 2 ob
5:42 St John Passion, 1757, with fl, ob
5:43 St Matthew Passion, 1758, with fl, ob
5:44 St Mark Passion, 1759, with 2 fl, 2 'grosse' fl, 2 ob, ob d'am, 2 bn
5:45 St Luke Passion, 1760, with 2 ob
5:46 St John Passion, 1761, with 2 fl, 'grosse' fl, ob, ob d'am
5:47 St Matthew Passion, 1762, with 2 fl, 2 ob, ob d'am, 2 cor
5:49 St Luke Passion, 1764, with fl, 2 ob
5:50 St John Passion, 1765, with 2 ob, ob d'am, 2 bn
5:51 St Matthew Passion, 1766, with SSATTB, 2 fl, ob d'am
5:52 St Mark Passion, 1767, with 2 fl, ob, bn, 2 cor

Lost Passions: St Matthew, 1722, 5:7; St Luke, 1724, 5:9; St John, 1725, 5:10; St Matthew, 1726, 5:11; St Mark, 1727, 5:12; St John, 1729, 5:14; St Mark, 1731, 5:16; St Luke, 1732, 5:17; St Matthew, 1734, 5:19; St Mark, 1735, 5:20; St Luke, 1736, 5:21; St Matthew, 1738, 5:23; St Mark, 1739, 5:24; St Luke, 1740, 5:25; St Matthew, 1742, 5:27; St Mark, 1743, 5:28; St Mark, 1747, 5:32; St Mark, 1751, 5:36; St Luke, 1752, 5:37; St John, 1753, 5:38; St Matthew, 1754, 5:39; St Luke, 1756, 5:41; St Mark, 1763, 5:48

6 Sacred oratorios

For SATB, str and composed for Hamburg, unless otherwise stated

6:1 *Davidsche Gesänge* (*Der Königliche Prophet David, als ein Fürbild unseres Heylandes Jesu*, lib. J.U. von König), five oratorios, Frankfurt, 1718; 2 arias extant
6:2 *Das Muster wahrer Freundschaft oder: David und Jonathan* (lib. Telemann), Frankfurt, 1720; music lost
6:*deest* *Die höchst tröstliche Fastenzeit*, Eisenach, 1711, lost
6:3a *Wie ist dein Name so groß* (*Die Donner-Ode*, part 1; Psalms 8 and 29, translated J.A. Cramer), 15 November 1756, with ob, bn, cor, 3 tr, tim
6:3b *Mein Herz ist voll vom Geiste Gottes* (*Die Donner-Ode*, part 2;

Psalm 45, translated J.A. Cramer), 26 April 1762, with 2 fl, ob, cor, 3 tr, tim

6:4 *Der Messias* (lib. F.G. Klopstock), 29 March 1759, with SAT, 2 fl, 2 ob, ob d'am, 2 bn; additional setting of the *Triumphgesang bey der Himmelfahrt*, 1764–66, lost

6:5 *Das befreite Israel* (lib. F.W. Zachariae), 29 March 1759, with SATBB, 2 fl, 2 ob, ob d'am, 2 bn, 2 cor, 3 tr, tim

6:6 *Die Auferstehung und Himmelfahrt Jesu* (lib. K.W. Ramler), 28 April 1760, with 2 fl, 2 ob, 2 cor, 3 tr, tim

6:7 *Die Auferstehung* (lib. F.W. Zachariae), 13 April 1761, with SATBB, fl, ob, ob d'am, bn, 2 cor, 3 tr, tim

6:8 *Der Tag des Gerichts* (lib. C.W. Alers), 5 March 1762, with SATBB, 2 ob, ob d'am, 3 cor, 2 tr, tim

7 Psalm settings

For SATB and str, unless otherwise stated

7:1 *Ach Herr, strafe mich nicht* (Ps. 6, 2–11), c. 1705? (3rd Sunday after Trinity), for a, 2 vn, bc

7:2 *Ach Herr, strafe mich nicht* (Ps. 6, 2–11) for s, ob, bn, vn, bc

7:3 *Ach Herr, strafe mich nicht* (Ps. 6, 2 and 10), c. 1698–1701?

7:4 *Alleluja, singet dem Herrn ein neues Lied* (Ps. 149, 1; Ps. 147, 1 and 7–11), with 2 ob

7:5 *Danket dem Herrn, denn er ist freundlich* (Ps. 118, 1), with 2 ob, 2 cor, bn

7:6 *Das ist ein köstlich Ding* (Ps. 92, 2–3), for a Hamburg school examination

7:7 *Deus judicium tuum regi da* (Ps. 72, 1–18), grand motet, Paris, 15 March 1738, with 2 fl, 2 ob, 2 bn

7:8 *Die auf den Herren hoffen* (Ps. 125, 1–5), for s, a, 2 ob, 2 vn, bc

7:9 *Die auf den Herrn hoffen* (Ps. 125, 1 and 3–4), for t, b, 2 ob, 2 vn, bc

7:10 *Das ist der Tag, den der Herr gemacht hat* (Ps. 118, 24), with 2 ob, 2 cor

7:11 *Domine ad adjuvandum me* (Ps. 69, 2)

7:12 *Domine, Dominus noster* (Ps. 8, 2) with 2 fl

7:13 *Exaltabo te Deus* (Ps. 145, 1–3), for s, b, bc

7:14 *Ich danke dem Herrn von ganzem Herzen* (Ps. 111, 1–6 and 9–10), with 2 ob, tr

7:15 *Ich hebe meine Augen auf zu den Bergen* (Ps. 121, 1–8), for t, vn, bc

7:17 *Ich hebe meine Augen auf* (Ps. 121, 1–3, 5 and 7), for SBB, ob

7:18 *Ich will den Herrn loben* (Ps. 34, 2–4), for s, a, bc

7:19 *Ihr seid die Gesegneten des Herrn* (Ps. 115, 15), with ob

7:20 *Jauchzet dem Herrn alle Welt* (Ps. 100, 1–5), for b, ob, tr, str, bc

7:21 *Jauchzet dem Herrn alle Welt* (Ps. 100, 1 and 3–5), for Feast of the Circumcision, for b, 2 tr, bc; = 1:952

7:22 *Jauchzet dem Herrn alle Welt* (Ps. 100, 1–5), for STB, 2 fl, str, bc

7:23	*Jehova pascit me* (Ps. 23, 1–6), for s, b, 2 fl, 2 ob, str, bc
7:24	*Jubilate deo, omnis terra* (Ps. 100, 1–5)
7:25	*Laudate Jehovam omne gentes* (Ps. 117, 1–2), for Hamburg school examination, 1757
7:26	*Laudate pueri dominum* (Ps. 113, 1, 3–6 and 9), for s, str, bc
7:27	*Lobe den Herrn meine Seele* (Ps. 104, 1, 24–25, 31, 33 and 35), with 2 ob, 2 tr
7:28	*Lobet den Herrn alle Heiden, Halleluja!* (Ps. 117, 1–2)
7:29	*Lobet den Herrn alle Heiden* (Ps. 117), for Hamburg school examination, Easter 1767, for t, t, b, bc
7:30	*Singet dem Herrn ein neues Lied* (Ps. 96, 1–9)
7:31	*Der Herr ist König und festlich geschmückt* (Ps. 93, 1–5), for b, ob, bn, str, bc
7:32	*Schmecket und sehet, wie freundlich der Herr ist* (Ps. 34, 9–10), for s, vn, bc

8 Motets

For SATB and str, unless otherwise stated

Additional motets in sections 3 and 14

8:1	*Amans disciplinam* (Proverbs 12:1–3), for a, t, bc
8:3	*Danket dem Herrn, denn er ist freundlich* (Ps. 118, 1–2 and chorale *Lob Ehr und Preis*), for Christmas, for SATB, SATB
8:*deest*	*Das ist meine Freude*
8:4	*Der Gott unsers Herrn Jesu Christi* (Ephesians 1:17–18), for Pentecost
8:5	*Der Herr gibt Weisheit* (Proverbs 2:6–8), for SAB, bc
8:7	*Ein feste Burg ist unser Gott* (M. Luther, verses 1 and 3), Hamburg, 1730; = 14:3c
8:8	*Es segne uns* (Ps. 67, 8)
8:*deest*	*Fürwahr, er trug unsere Krankheit*
8:9	*Halt, was du hast, daß niemand deine Krone nehme* (Acts 3:11 and 15),
8:*deest*	*Ich habe Lust abzuscheiden*
8:*deest*	*Ich will schauen dein Antlitz in Gerechtigkeit*
8:*deest*	*Rufe mich an in der Zeit der Not*
8:*deest*	*Saget der Tochter Zion*
8:11	*Laudate dominum* (Ps. 116), for SATB, bc
8:12	*Non aemulare* (Proverbs 24: 1–3), for s, b, bc
8:13	*Selig sind die Toten* (Off. 14:13)
8:*deest*	*Selig sind die Toten*
8:16	*Wohl dem, der den Herrn fürchtet* (Ps. 112, 1–3), for s, a, bc

9 *Masses, mass movements and magnificats*

A. Masses on chorale melodies

For SATB and bc, unless otherwise stated

9:1	*Ach Gott vom Himmel sieh darein*, with 2 ob
9:2	*Allein Gott in der Höh sei Ehr*
9:3	*Christ lag in Todesbanden*
9:4	*Durch Adams Fall ist ganz verderbt*
9:5	*Ein Kindelein so löbelich*, for SATB, bc
9:6	*Erbarm dich mein, o Herre Gott*
9:7	*Es wird schier der letzte Tag herkommen*, SATTB
9:8	*Es woll uns Gott gnädig sein*
9:9	*Gott der Vater wohn uns bei*, for Trinity
9:10	*Komm heiliger Geist*, for Pentecost
9:11	*Komm heiliger Geist*

B. Latin masses, mass movements and magnificats

For SATB and str, unless otherwise stated

9:12	*Missa alla siciliana* in F major
9:13	Kyrie and Gloria in B minor
9:14	Kyrie and Gloria in B minor, for a, 2 vn, bc, c. 1705
9:15	Kyrie and Gloria in C major, for s, SATB, bc
9:16	Sanctus in D major, with 3 tr, tim
9:*deest*	Sanctus in F major, c. 1705
9:17	Magnificat in C major (Latin), 1704, SATBB, 3 tr, tim
9:18	Magnificat in G major (German), with 2 rec, 2 ob, 2 cor
9:19	Amen in D major, with 2 tr

10 *Canons, chorales and sacred arias*

10:1	*Fast allgemeines Evangelisch-Musicalisches Lieder-Buch* (Hamburg, 1730; 2nd edn 1751), hymnal with two thousand chorales and over five hundred melodies
10:2–13	*Telemanns Canones à 2, 3, 4* (Hamburg, 1735), 12 canons for 2–4vv on Psalm texts
10:14–20	7 sacred arias for s, str, bc
10:21–31	See Church cantatas

11 *Music for weddings*

11:1	*Ihr lieblichen Täler, annehmliche Felder*, serenata for Duke Johann

Wilhelm of Sachsen-Eisenach and Margravine Maria Felicitas of Baden-Durlach, Eisenach, 29 May 1727, SATB, 2 ob, str

11:15 *Herr Gott, dich loben wir* and *Nun hilf uns Gott, den Dienern dein*, two-part oratorio (lib. M. Richey), SATB, fl, ob, 3 tr, tim, str; and *O erhabnes Glück der Ehe*, serenata (lib. M. Richey), SATB, fl, chal, ob, str; for the Mutzenbecher-Ecken golden wedding anniversary, Hamburg 20 February 1732

11:22 *Drei schöne Dinge sind*, SATB, 2 ob, 3 cor, str

11:23 *Ein wohlgezogen Weib ist nicht zu bezahlen*, SATB, str

11:24 *Es woll uns Gott genädig sein*, s, s, b, str

11:25 *Herr, hebe an zu segnen das Haus*, s, b, str

11:26 *Liebe, was ist schöner als die Liebe*, s, t, 2 ob, str

11:27 *Lieblich und schön sein ist nicht*, a, t, b, 2 cor, str

11:*deest* *Mein Zepter gibt der Welt Gesetze*, 4 December 1754, s, a, b, fl, bn, str

11:*deest* *Pastorelle en Musique oder Musikalisches Hirtenspiel* (lib. Telemann), Frankfurt, c. 1713–16, SSATB, rec, 2 ob, 2 cor, 2 tr

11:29 *Seid fruchtbar, mehret euch*, SATB, 2 fl, 2 cor, str

11:30 *Sprich treuer Himmel: Ja*, b, ob, str

11:31 *Wem ein tugendsam Weib bescheret ist*, s, b, 2 cor, 2 tr, tim, str

Music or music and text lost: eighteen cantatas and serenatas, 1722–65

12 *Music for birthdays*

For SATB and str, unless otherwise stated

12:1 *Auf Christenheit, begeh ein Freudenfest* (lib. J.G. Pritius), cantata for Archduke Leopold of Austria, Frankfurt, with 2 fl, 2 ob, 3 tr, tim; together with *Deutschland grünt und blüht in Friede* (lib. J.G. Pritius), with 2 ob, 2 cor, 3 tr, tim; Frankfurt, 17 May 1716

12:2 Music for Count Palatine of the Rhine Joseph Carl Emanuel (lib. Telemann), Frankfurt, 17 March 1718, music lost

12:3 *Willkommen, schöner Freudentag*, serenata for Duke Johann Wilhelm of Sachsen-Eisenach, Eisenach, 17 October 1718, with 2 ob

12:4 *Unsre Freude wohnt in dir*, Eisenach, 3 September 1723, with 2 rec

12:5 *Erheitre dich mit güldnen Strahlen* and *Herr, Herr, lasse meinen Mund deines Ruhms* (lib. Telemann), for senior pastor Petrus Theodor Seelmann, Hamburg, 21 August 1724, music lost

12:6 *Erklingt durch gedoppelt annehmliche Töne*, serenata for Eisenach?, with 2 ob

12:7 *Kommt mit mir, ihr süßen Freuden* (*Die Plaisir*), serenade for Duchess Magdalena Sibylle of Sachsen-Eisenach and her daughter, Eisenach, 3 September 1725, with rec, 2 ob, 2 cor

12:8 *Ich will dem Herrn singen mein Lebelang*, for Duchess Anna Sophie of Sachsen-Eisenach, Eisenach, 1731 or 1732, with 2 ob

12:9 Cantata for King Christian of Denmark, Altona near Hamburg, 30 December 1741, music lost

12:10 *Lyksalig Tvillung-Rige!*, for King Friedrich V of Odense, Altona near Hamburg, 31 March 1757, with SB, fl, 3 tr, tim; pub. as *De danske, norske og tydske undersaatters glaede* (Hamburg, 1757)

12:11 *Großmächtiger Monarch der Britten*, for King George II of England, c. 1760, with SB, fl, 3 tr, tim

Music lost: thirty-four cantatas and serenatas for the Eisenach court, 1717–31

13 *Music for political celebrations*

For SATB and str, unless otherwise stated

13:*deest* *Ich sonst beglücktes Land*, for an unknown occasion, 1711?, with 2 ob, 2 cor, 3 tr, tim

13:5b *Zeuch, teures Haupt, zeuch mit den Deinen*, cantata for *Tafelmusik* at the Eisenach court, 22 August 1722, with 2 ob

13:9 *Sei tausendmal willkommen, o auserwählter Tag*, for s, str, and *Du bleibest dennoch unser Gott*, for s, b, str (both lib. J.G. Hamann), for bicentennial of the Augsburg Confession, Hamburg, 25 June 1730; as pub. in abbreviated form by Telemann (Hamburg, 1731)

13:13 *Gebeut, o Vater der Gnade*, for the inauguration of the Gymnasium in Altona near Hamburg, 1744, with 2 fl, 3 tr, tim

13:14 *Geschlagene Pauken, auf, auf!*, for the same occasion as 13:13, with 2 fl, 2 ob, 2 tr, tim

13:18 *Holder Friede, heilger Glaube* (lib. J.J.D. Zimmermann), oratorio for the bicentennial of the Peace of Augsburg, Hamburg, 5 October 1755, with 2 rec, 2 fl, 3 tr, tim

13:19 *Halleluja, amen, Lob und Ehr*, for the thanksgiving for the victory of Lowoschütz (1756), Hamburg, 1 August 1757, with 2 fl, 3 tr, tim

13:20 *Hannover siegt, der Franzmann liegt*, oratorio for a victory celebration in 1758, 1759 or 1761, for s, 2 fl, 2 ob, str

13:*deest* *Die dicken Wolken scheiden sich*, for the centennial of the hereditary sovereignty of the Danish royal family in Altona near Hamburg, 16 October 1760, with fl, 2 tr, tim

13:21 *Bleibe, lieber König, leben*, for an unknown occasion, for s, 2 tr, tim, str

13:22 *Herr, wir danken deiner Gnade*, aria for b, str

13:25 *Von Gnade und Recht will ich singen* (Ps. 101) for an unknown occasion, with 2 ob, 2 cor

13:*deest* *Nunc auspicato sidere*, ode for the Danish king

Music lost: eighteen cantatas and serenatas for Eisenach, Frankfurt and Hamburg, 1715–64

14 *Music for schools in Hamburg, Altona and Lübeck*

14:1 *Actu* for an examination at the Johanneum, Hamburg, 1722, music lost
14:2 *Sey gegrüsset, edle Feier* and *Das ist ein köstlich Ding*, cantatas for the bicentennial of the Augsburg Confession, Hamburg, academic Gymnasium, 26 June 1730, music lost
14:3 *Komm heiliger Geist, Halleluja, Ein feste Burg ist unser Gott* and *Heilig, heilig, heilig ist Gott* (= first movt of TVWV 2:6), all for the bicentennial of the Augsburg Confession, Hamburg, Johanneum, 1730; music to first three works lost
14:4 *Wo sich Ruh' und Friede küssen*, aria for a school *Actus*; incompl
14:5 Oratorio in the Johanneum, Hamburg, 21–22 October 1734, music and text lost
14:6 *Nunc auspicato sidera*, ode for the Christianeum in Altona near Hamburg, 29 October 1749, music and text lost
14:7 *O quam lata vis amoris dei*, SS, str
14:8 *Mit Danken und mit Loben* and *Der Herr, unser Gott, sey uns freundlich* (lib. M. Richey), cantatas for the inauguration of Hamburg's academic Gymnasium, 16 March 1751, music lost
14:9 *Sonder Ansehn der Person* and *In der ersten Unschuld*, arias for a school *Actus*, Hamburg, 1752, S, str
14:10 *Gott ist in Juda bekannt* and *Jauchzet dem Herrn* (lib. H.G. Schellhafer), cantatas for the bicentennial of the Peace of Augsburg, Hamburg, academic Gymnasium, 7 October 1755, music lost
14:11 *Laetare juvenis in juventute tua* (Proverbs 11:9–10), cantata for a Hamburg school examination, 1758, SATB, 2 vn
14:12 *Gott, man lobet dich in der Stille*, cantata for the celebration of the peace of Hubertusburg (end of the Seven-Year War), Hamburg, academic Gymnasium, 15 May 1763, SATB, 2 fl, 2 ob, bn, 2 cor, tr, tim
14:13 *Deus aperi coelorum* (text C.F. Hunold), duet for SS/AA, bc
14:14 *O terra felicissima* (text C.F. Hunold), duet for SA, bc
14:15 *Friede, dich grüssen die Hirten und Herden*, aria for s, str
14:16 *Friede, dich preisen die Hirten und Herden*, duet for an examination in the Hamburg academic Gymnasium, 1755, SS, 2 vn, bc
14:17 *Gehet hin zur Ameise, du Fauler* (Proverbs 6:6), motet for Hamburg school examination, 1756, 1760 and 1764, S/A, B, bc
14:18 *Fein säuberlich müsst ihr verfahren*, aria, incompl
14:19 *Holder Frühling muntrer Jugend*, aria, incompl
14:20 *In omni tempore dedit confessionem*, cantata for a school examination, SATB, fl, 2 ob, str
14:21 *Studiosa salve te corona*, cantata, incompl
14:*deest* Installation music for rector Johann Daniel Overbeck at the Katharineum in Lübeck (1763); parody of TVWV 3:63 (1755)

15 Kapitänsmusiken

232 All works with str and composed for Hamburg

15:2	*Freuet euch des Herrn, ihr Gerechten*, oratorio (lib. J.P. Praetorius), with STB, 2 rec, and *Geliebter Aufenthalt, beglückte Stille*, serenata (lib. Praetorius), with STBB, fl, ob, ob d'am, 2 bn, 31 August 1724
15:4	*Mit innigstem Ergetzen*, serenata (lib. C.G. Wend or J.P. Praetorius), with SSTBB, 3 fl, 2 ob, ob d'am, 2 chal, 3 tr, tim, 29 August 1728; oratorio lost
15:5	*Jauchze, jubilier und singe*, oratorio (lib. Telemann), with SATBB, and *Zu Walle, zu Walle, ruft alle*, serenata (lib. J.G. Hamann), with SATBBB, fl, ob, tim, 31 August 1730
15:9	*Preise, Jerusalem, den Herrn*, oratorio, with SSATBB, 2 fl, and *So kömmt die kühne Tapferkeit*, serenata (J.J.D. Zimmermann), with SSATBB, fl, 30 August 1736
15:11	*Wohl dem Volke, des der Herr sein Gott ist*, oratorio, with SSATTBB, 2 rec, 2 fl, 2 ob, bn, 2 cor, and *Es locket die Trommel mit wirbelnden Schlägen*, serenata (lib. J.F. Lamprecht), with SSATTBB, fife, fl, 2 ob, 2 cor, tim, 28 August 1738
15:13	*Der Herr ist meine Stärke und mein Schild*, oratorio, with SATBB, ob, 2 cor, *Schlagt die Trommel, blast Trompeten*, serenata (lib. F.W. Roloffs), with SATBBB, 2 fl, chal, ob, 2 tr, tim, 30 August 1742
15:15	*Vereint euch, ihr Bürger und singet mit Freuden*, oratorio, with SSATB, 2 ob, ob d'am, bn, 2 cor, and *Freiheit, Göttin, die Segen und Friede begleiten*, serenata (lib. N.D. Giseke), with SSATB, fife, rec, 2 ob, 2 cor, tim, 3 September 1744
15:20	*Danket dem Herrn*, oratorio (lib. H.G. Schellhaffer), with SAATBB, 2 rec, 2 fl, 'grosse' fl, 2 ob, ob d'am, 2 cor, tr, and *Ihr rüstigen Wächter Hamburgischer Zinnen*, serenata (lib. M. Richey), with SAATBB, fife, 2 rec, fl, ob, 2 cor, 2 tr, tim, 28 August 1755
15:21	*Wohl dem Volk, das jauchzen kann*, oratorio, incompl, and *Rast, lärmende Trommeln*, serenata (lib. W.A. Paulli), with 2 fl, 2 ob, 2 bn, 2 cor, 26 August 1756
15:23	*Herr, du bist gerecht*, oratorio, with SATBB, rec, 2 fl, 2 ob, 2 chal, 2 cor, tr, and *Wir nähren, wir zieren, wir schützen die Staaten*, serenata (W.A. Paulli), with SSATTBB, rec, 2 fl, 2 ob, tr, tim, 18 September 1760
15:*deest*	*Freuet euch des Herrn, ihr Gerechten*, oratorio (W.A. Paulli), with SSATB, 2 fl, 2 ob, 2 cor, tr, tim, 27 August 1761; serenata lost
15:25	*Der Herr Zebaoth ist mit uns*, oratorio, with SAATBB, 2 ob, 2 cor, 2 tr, tim, and *Trompeten und Hörner erschallet*, serenata (W.A. Paulli), with SAATTTBBB, fife, 2 fl, 2 ob, 2 cor, 2 tr, tim, 30 August 1764

Music or music and text lost: oratorios and serenatas for 1723, 1725, 1731, 1734, 1735, 1737, 1739, 1743, 1749, 1752, 1753, 1754, 1759 and 1765

16 Secular cantatas

20:1 *Das Wasser im Frühlinge* (lib. B.H. Brockes), Frankfurt, 1720, music lost

20:2 *Ertöne muntrer Musen-Chor*, Frankfurt, 18 October 1720, music lost

20:3 *Hans ohne Sorge* (J.U. von König), Frankfurt, 1720, music lost

20:4–9 Six cantatas for Count Friedrich Carl von Erbach, to the count's French librettos, c. 1720, music lost

20:10 *Alles redet itzt und singet* (lib. B.H. Brockes) for s, b, picc., 3 fl, 3 ob, bn, str, bc, Frankfurt, 1720

20:11 *Der Herbst* (lib. B.H. Brockes), Hamburg, 1721, music lost

20:12 *Der Winter* (lib. B.H. Brockes), Hamburg, 16 and 23 January 1722, music lost

20:13 *Wie? Schlafet ihr, verstummte Saiten?* (lib. Telemann), Hamburg, 15 November 1721, music lost

20:14 *Tönet, schallet, klingt ihr Saiten* (lib. Telemann), Hamburg, 12 January 1723

20:15 *Ich kann lachen, weinen, scherzen* (lib. C.M. von Ziegler), s, bc, pub. in *Der getreue Music-Meister* (Hamburg, 1729)

20:16 *Voll feuriger Regung* (lib. J.G. Hamann), Hamburg, 1730, music lost

20:17–22 *Sechs Cantaten* (Hamburg, 1731) to librettos by J.G. Hamann, J.U. von König, A.A. von Lersner, J.P. Praetorius and an anon. poet, for v, rec, fl, ob, str, bc: *Dich wird stets mein Herz erlesen, Mein Vergnügen wird sich fügen, Mein Schicksal zeigt mir nur von ferne, Dein Augue trängt, ach weine nicht, Lieben will ich, aber binden lässet* and *In einem Tal, umringt von hohen Eichen*

20:23–28 *VI moralische Cantaten* (Hamburg, 1735) to librettos by D. Stoppe and an anon. poet for v and bc: *Die Zeit, Die Hoffnung, Das Glück, Der Geiz, Die Falschheit* and *Die Großmut*

20:29–34 *VI moralische Cantaten* (Hamburg, 1736) to librettos by J.J.D. Zimmermann for v, fl/vn, bc: *Die Zufriedenheit, Die Tonkunst, Das mäßige Glück, Die Liebe, Die Landlust* and *Die Freundschaft*

20:35 Serenata for the Collegium musicum in Jena, 7 February 1737; text and music lost

20:36 *Polyphème*, Paris, 1737 or 1738; text and music lost

20:37 *Trauermusik eines Kunsterfahrenen Canarienvogels* (*O weh, mein Canarin ist tot*), for s, vn or fl, bc (arr. J.W. Lorber for s, str, bc), Hamburg, 16 October 1737

20:38 *Hinkende Dichter an Helikons Rande*, for the installation of Elias Caspar Reichard as Professor at the Akademischer Gymnasium in Altona near Hamburg on 27 January 1741; chorus and aria extant

20:39 *Die Tageszeiten* (lib. F.W. Zachariae), four cantatas for s, a, t, b, 2 fl, bn, tr, vadg, str, bc, Hamburg, 1757: *Der Morgen, Der Mittag, Der Abend* and *Die Nacht*

20:40 *Der Mai* (lib. K.W. Ramler) for s, b, 2 rec, 2 fl, 2 ob, chal., cor, tr, str, bc, Hamburg, c. 1760

20:41	*Ino* (lib. K.W. Ramler) for s, 2 fl, 2 cor, str, bc, Hamburg, c. 1765
20:42	*La Tempesta* (*No non turbarti;* lib. P. Metastasio) for s, 2 cor, str, bc
20:43	*Amor heißt mich freudig lachen*, for s, bc
20:44	*Bin ich denn so gar verlassen*, for s, vn, bc
20:45	*Bist du denn gar von Stahl und Eisen*, for b, ob/vn, bc
20:46	*Bleicher Sorgen Kummer-Nächte*, for b, 2 vn, bc
20:47	*Der Mond zog nach und nach*, for t, bc
20:48	*Die Hoffnung ist mein Leben*, for b, 2 vn, bc
20:49	*Du angenehmer Weiberorden*, for s, str, bc
20:50	*Geht, ihr unvergnügten Sorgen*, for s, b, ob, str, bc
20:51	*Gönne doch dem freien Munde*, for s, vn, bc
20:52	*Gute Nacht, du Ungetreuer*, for s, b, ob, vn, va, bc
20:53	*Ha, ha, wo will wi hüt noch danzen*, for s, vn, bc
20:54	*Haltet ein, ihr schönsten Blicke*, for s, bc
20:55	*Ich haß und fliehe zwar die Liebe*, for s, bc
20:56	*Ich liebe dich wie meine Seele*, for s, bc
20:57	*Der Schulmeister* (*Ihr Jungen, sperrt die Augen auf*), for s, a, t, b, 2 ob, 2 bn, 2 cor, str, bc
20:58	*Mein Herze lachet vor Vergnügen*, for b, vn, bc
20:59	*Mein Vergnügen heißt mich sterben*, for b, vn, bc
20:60	*Nichts vergnügters ist auf Erden*, for b, vn, bc
20:61	*Parti mi lasci*, for s, fl, vn, bc
20:62	*Pastorella venga bella*, s, vn, bc, doubtful
20:63	*Per che vezzoso*, for s, vn, bc
20:64	*Reicher Herbst, ihr kühlen Lüfte*, for t, vn, bc
20:65	*Ruht itzt sanft, ihr zarten Glieder*, for s, bc
20:66	*Sagt, ihr allerschönsten Lippen*, for b, bc
20:67	*Seufzen, Kummer, Angst und Tränen*, for a, bc
20:68	*So bald wird man das nicht vergessen*, for s, bc
20:69	*Soll die Marter meiner Seelen*, for s, bc
20:70	*Die Hoffnung des Wiedersehens* (*Süße Hoffnung, wenn ich frage*), for s, 2 bn, str, bc
20:71	*Unbestand ist das Gift verliebter Seelen*, for s, bc
20:72	*Unbestand ist das Gift verliebter Seelen*, for s, vn, bc
20:73	*Voglio amarti, o caro nume*, s, vn, bc
20:74	*Von geliebten Augen brennen*, for s, vn, bc
20:75	*In den Strahlen jener Sonne*, s, vn, bc; 1 aria extant
20:*deest*	*Cantata perdono*; 1 aria extant
20:*deest*	*Fortuna scherzosa* (lib. E. Neumeister), for t, bc
20:*deest*	*Himmel, laß mich doch erlangen*, for b, bc
20:*deest*	*Stirb nur armselges Hertz*, for b, ob, bc

17 Operas

TVWV	Title	Libretto	First perf./Comments
21:1	*Der lachende Democritus*	C.D. Lachs after N. Minato	Leipzig, New Year's fair, 1704; 1 aria extant
21:2	*Ferdinand und Isabella*		Leipzig, New Year's fair, 1703; lost
21:3	*Cajus Caligula*	C.D. Lachs	Leipzig, Easter fair, 1704; lost
21:*deest*	*Germanicus*	C.D. Lachs after G.C. Corradi	Leipzig, autumn fair, 1704; rev. 1710; 40 arias extant
21:4	*Adonis*	G.C. Lehms after C.H. Postel	Leipzig, Easter fair, 1708; one aria extant
21:5	*Narcissus*	G.C. Lehms after A. Zeno	Leipzig, New Year's fair, 1709; 3 arias extant
21:6	*Mario*	Telemann after S. Stampiglia	Leipzig, Easter fair, 1709; collaboration with P. Hebenstreit; 4 arias extant
21:7	*Der Unglückliche Alcmeon, oder Jupiter und Semele*	Telemann? after J.P. Förtsch	Leipzig, Easter fair, 1711; 4 arias extant
21:*deest*	*Die Syrische Unruh*	C.D. Lachs? after B. Feind	Leipzig, autumn fair, 1711; 11 arias extant
21:*deest*	*Ariadne*	Telemann? after C.H. Postel	Leipzig, New Year's Fair, 1712; lost
21:*deest*	*Die königliche Schäferin Margenis*	Telemann?	Leipzig, 1715; 1 aria extant
21:8	*Die Satyren in Arcadien;* rev. as *Der neumodische Liebhaber Damon*	Telemann after P. Pariati	Leipzig, 1718 or 1719; rev. version Hamburg, 30 Aug. 1724
21:9	*Der geduldige Socrates*	J.U. König after N. Minato	Hamburg, 5 Feb. 1721
21:10	*Sieg der Schönheit;* rev. as *Der Grosse König der Africanischen Wenden Gensericus, als Rom- und Carthagens Ueberwinder*	Telemann after C.H. Postel	Hamburg, 13 July 1722; rev. version Brunswick, 1725
21:11	*Das Ende der babylonischen Gefangenschaft oder Belsazar*	J. Beccau	Hamburg, 19 and 22 September 1723; 3 arias extant

21:12	*Alarich oder Die Straf-Ruthe des verfallenen Roms*		Bayreuth, 2 August 1723; lost
21:13	*Il Capitano*	Schwemschuh	Hamburg, 21 February 1724; third part of *Beschluß des Carnevals*; lost
21:14	*Omphale*	Telemann after H. de la Motte	Hamburg, 1724; 1 aria and several dances (in TWV 55:e8) extant
21:15	*Pimpinone oder Die ungleiche Heyrath*	J.P. Praetorius after P. Pariati	intermezzo; Hamburg, 27 September 1725; pub. as *Pimpinone* (Hamburg, 1728)
21:16	*La Capricciosa e il Credulo auch Die geliebte Eigensinnige und der leichtgläubige Liebhaber*	J.P. Praetorius	intermezzo; Hamburg, August/September 1725; 4 arias extant
21:17	*Adelheid oder die ungezwungene Liebe*	J.P. Praetorius after J.C. Hallmann	Bayreuth, 1724; 14 arias extant; 13 in *Lustige Arien aus der Opera Adelheid* (Hamburg, 1727)
21:18	*Die wunderbare Beständigkeit der Liebe, oder Orpheus;* rev. as *Die Rachbegierige Liebe, oder Orasia, verwittwete Königin in Thracien* (21:31)	Telemann after various	Hamburg, 9 March 1726; rev. version Hamburg, 15 Oct. 1736
21:19	*Calypso oder Sieg der Weisheit über die Liebe*		Hamburg, 12 May 1728; 1 chorus extant in *Der getreue Music-Meister* (1728–29)
21:20	*Sancio oder Die siegende Großmuth*	J.U. König after F. Silvani	Hamburg, 6 October 1727; 4 arias extant in *Der getreue Music-Meister* (1728–29)
21:21	*Buffonet und Alga*	C.G. Wend	intermezzo; Hamburg, 14 July 1727; lost
21:22	*Die Amours der Vespetta oder Der Galan in der Kiste*	C.W. Haken	intermezzo; Hamburg, 1 October 1727; lost
21:23	*Die verkehrte Welt*	J.P. Praetorius after R. le Sage	Hamburg, 10 February 1728; 1 aria extant in *Der getreue Music-Meister* (1728–29)
21:24	*Miriways*	J.S. Müller	Hamburg, 26 May 1728
21:25	*Die Last-tragende Liebe, oder Emma und Eginhard*	C.G. Wend	Hamburg, 22 November 1728

21:26	*Aesopus bei Hofe*	J. Mattheson after P. Pariati	Hamburg, 1729; 3 arias extant in *Der getreue Music-Meister* (1728–29)
21:27	*Flavius Bertaridus, König der Longobarden*	C.G. Wend after S. Ghigi	Hamburg, 23 November 1729
21:29	*Margaretha, Königen in Castilien*	J.G. Hamann	Hamburg, 10 August 1730; 1 aria extant as parody in TVWV 20:20?
21:30	*Der Weiseste in Sidon*	J.G. Hamann after S. Stampiglia	Hamburg, 4 February 1733; lost
21:32	*Don Quichotte auf der Hochzeit des Comacho*	D. Schiebeler	serenata; Hamburg, 5 November 1761

18 Music for operas by other composers

22:1 German duet for *Ulysses* by J.G. Vogler (Hamburg, 7 July 1721)
22:2 6 arias for *Tamerlano* by G.F. Handel (Hamburg, 1725)
22:3 14 arias for *Ottone* by G.F. Handel (Hamburg, 1726)
22:4 2 arias and a duet for *Syphax* by N. Porpora (Hamburg, 1727)
22:5 4 German arias for *Masagniello furioso* by R. Keiser (Hamburg, 1721, 1727 and 1729)
22:6 overture and 2 arias for *Nebukadnezar* by R. Keiser (Hamburg, 1728)
22:7 German aria for *Tempel des Janus* by R. Keiser (Hamburg, 10 October 1729)
22:8 14 German arias, 2 duets (lib. C.G. Wend), choruses and dances for *Riccardo Primo* by G.F. Handel (Hamburg, 3 February 1729)
22:9 Recitative for *Ernelinda* by G.M. Orlandini (Hamburg, 27 September 1730); music lost
22:10 Aria for *Der Streit der kindlichen Pflicht und Liebe oder Die Flucht des Aeneas nach Latien* by N. Porpora (Hamburg, 1731)
22:12 Recitative und 3 German arias (lib. J.G. Hamann) for the pasticcio *Judith, oder Die siegende Unschuld* (Hamburg, 7 January 1732)
22:13 Overture and 2 German arias for *Almira* by G.F. Handel (Hamburg, 1732)

19 Operatic prologues

All for Hamburg and music lost, unless otherwise indicated.

23:1 *Bey der höchst-glücklichen Verbindung* (lib. J.P. Praetorius), for the wedding of King Louis XV of France (17 September 1725)
23:2 *Prologus bey Gelegenheit einer neuen Einrichtung des Opern-Wesens* (lib. Telemann), before the opera *Arsace* by Orlandini and Amadei (24 April 1727)
23:3 *Der Briten Freude und Glückseligkeit* (lib. C.G. Wend), for the sixty-seventh birthday of King George I of England, before the opera *Giulio Cesare* by G.F. Handel (9 June 1727)
23:4 *Als Seiner Allerchristlichen Majestät* (lib. C.W. Haken), for the birth of the twin daughters of King Louis XV of France (9 September 1727)
23:5 *Das jauchzende Gross-Brittannien* (lib. J.P. Praetorius), for the coronation of King George II of England (21 October 1727)
23:6 *Die Kronen-würdige Jugend* (lib. C.G. Wend), for the coronation of Tsar Peter II of Russia, before *Calypso* (21:19) by Telemann (12 May 1728)
23:7 *Die aus der Einsamkeit in die Welt zurückgekehrte Opera* (lib. C.G. Wend), for the re-opening of the Gänsemarkt Opera, before *Tempel des Janus* by R. Keiser (10 October 1729)

23:8 *Das Neu-beglückte Sachsen* (lib. J.U. von König), for the birth of an electoral Saxon prince, before *Sancio* (21:20) by Telemann (30 October 1730)

23:9 *Die Glückseligkeit des Rußischen Kayserthums* (lib. J.G. Hamann), for the coronation of Tsarina Anna Ivanova, before *Margaretha* (21:29) by Telemann (10 August 1730); = 21:28

23:10 self-contained sequel to 23:8 (20 November 1730)

23:11 *Herr Fändrich Nothdurfft aus dem Lager bei Mühlberg* (lib. J.U von König), comic epilogue to 23:8 and 10 (9 February 1731)

23:12 *Das Lob der Musen* for the re-opening of the Gänsemarkt Opera (30 September 1730); recitatives and arias extant

20 Secular oratorios and serenatas

24:1 *Unschätzbarer Vorwurf erkenntlicher Sinnen*, for the Hamburg Admiralty on 6 April 1723 (lib. M. Richey), for SATB, 3 rec, 2 fl, 2 ob, ob d'am, 2 bn, 3 cor, 3 tr, timp

24:2 *Hamburg steht und blüht im Segen* (lib. C.F. Weichmann), for Hamburg's Petri-Mahl on 21 and 25 February 1724; music lost

24:3 *Freuet euch, ihr Ober-Alten, Gott hat diese Stadt erhalten* (oratorio) and *Das angenehme Nieder-Sachsen trägt itzt ein buntes Kleid* (serenata), lib. by J. Hübner, for the centennial celebration of Hamburg's Oberalten Collegium, 27 May 1728; music lost

24:4 Serenata for the centennial celebration of Hamburg's commerce deputation, 19 January 1765; only keyboard reduction extant as *Symphonie zur Serenate auf die erste hundertjährige Jubelfeyer der Hamburgischen Löblichen Handlungs-Deputation* (Hamburg, 1765), TWV Anh. 50:1

24:5 Work for 'merchants', 1 aria extant

21 Songs and odes

25:1–36 *Singende Geographie* (Hildesheim, 1708), 36 songs for v and bc to texts by J.C. Losius; probably spurious

25:37–38 'Das Frauenzimmer verstimmt sich immer' (text: M. Richey; originally for 11:6) and 'Säume nicht, geliebte Schöne', both for s, fl, vn, bc, both pub. in *Der getreue Music-Meister* (Hamburg, 1728–29)

25:39–85 *Singe-, Spiel- und Generalbass-Übungen* (Hamburg, 1733–34), 46 songs for v and bc to texts by various authors, with written-out continuo realisations and commentaries

25:86–109 *Vier und zwanzig, theils ernsthafte, theils scherzende, Oden, mit leichten und fast für alle Hälse bequehmen Melodien versehen* (Hamburg, 1741), 24 odes for v and bc to texts by various authors

25:110–12 'Muffel singt zu ganzen Tagen', 'Heraclid gleicht stumpfen Greisen' and 'Zmor sagt zu Cythere', all for s, bc in *Oden mit Melodien* (Berlin, 1753)

25:113 'Bartholomeus', quodlibet for ATB, bc

25:114	Untexted six-voice canon in the Schmid family album in Lüneburg, 23 June 1735

22 Keyboard and lute music

30:1–20	*XX kleine Fugen . . . nach besonderen Modis verfasset* (Hamburg: Telemann, 1731), org/hpd
30:21–26	*Fugues légères et petits jeux* (Hamburg, 1738–39), hpd
30:27–28	2 fughettas (F, D)
30:29	Fugue in E minor, incompl
30:*deest*	Praeludium (to 30:29)
31:1–48	*Fugirende und veraendernde Choraele* (Hamburg, 1735), org/hpd
31:49	chorale prelude, *Nun komm' der Heiden Heiland*
31:50	chorale prelude, *Befiehl du deine Wege*
31:51–52	chorale preludes, *Nun freut euch, lieben Christen g'mein*
32:1–2	Partia à cembalo solo, G; Ouverture à la Polonoise, d: both in *Der getreue Music-Meister* (Hamburg, 1728–29), lections 1–3 and 18–22
32:3–4	2 suites (C, F), hpd, in *Essercizii musici* (Hamburg, 1726)
32:5–10	*VI Ouverturen nebst zween Folgesätzen* (Nuremberg, 1745)
32:11	Suite in C major
32:12	Suite in A minor, by 1719
32:12a	Suite in A minor
32:13	Suite in G major (Courante = BWV 840)
32:14	Suite in A major, by 1720 (= BWV 824)
32:15	Suite in A major
32:16	Suite in A major (movts 4, 6 and 7 arr. of TWV 55:A10)
32:17	Suite in C major
32:18	Suite in A major (= BWV 832)
33:1–36	*Fantaisies pour le clavessin* (Hamburg, 1732–33)
33:37	Sonata in E minor, hpd, by 1744
34:1–50	*Sept fois sept et un menuet* (Hamburg, 1728)
34:51–100	*Zweytes sieben mal sieben und ein Menuet* (Hamburg, 1730)
35:1–2	Marche pour M. le Capitaine Weber (F), Retraite (F), La poste (B♭): all in *Der getreue Music-Meister*, lections 6 and 14
35:3–7	Menuet (G), Amoroso (A), Gigue (d), Menuet (D), Air en Gavotte (F)
37	*Lustiger Mischmasch oder scotländische Stücke* (Hamburg, 1734–35), kbd, other instruments, lost
39:1	Partie Polonoise in B-flat, 2 lutes (arr. of lost suite for 2 vadg, bc)
39:2	Suite in G minor for 2 lutes (= arr. of 55:a7)

23 *Music for one to four instruments without continuo*

40:1	Sonata (D), vadg, in *Der getreue Music-Meister* (Hamburg, 1728–29)
40:2–13	*12 Fantaisies à travers. sans basse* (Hamburg, 1731), fl
40:14–25	*XII Fantasie per il violino senza basso* (Hamburg, 1735), vn
40:26–37	[12] *Fantaisies pour la basse de violle* (Hamburg, 1735), vadg
40:101–06	*Sonates sans basse* (Hamburg, 1726), 2 fl/vn/rec
40:107–11	Sonata (B flat), 2 rec/fl/vadg; Intrada, nebst burlesquer Suite (D), 2 vn; Carillon (F), 2 chal or fl/rec (b); Menuet, 2 cor; Sonata (B flat/G/A), 2 instruments: all in *Der getreue Music-Meister*
40:112–17	*Duos à travers. et violoncell* (Hamburg, 1735 or 1736), fl, vc; lost
40:118–23	*XIIX* [12] *Canons mélodieux, ou VI sonates en duo* (Paris, 1738), 2 fl/vn/vadg
40:124–29	*Second livre de duo* (Paris, 1752), 2 vn/fl/ob
40:130–35	Sei duetti, 2 fl
40:141–49	9 duets, 2 fl; Nos. 7–9 doubtful
40:150–52	3 sonatas (D, e, b) in *Sonates en trio* (Paris, 1738–42), 3 fl/vn; only 1 instrumental part extant
40:200	See section 26
40:201–03	Concertos (G, D, C) for four violins

24 *Music for one instrument and continuo (solos)*

Abbreviations for Telemann's publications containing solos:

SixSon	*Six sonates à violon seul* (Frankfurt, 1715; 2nd edn, Hamburg, 1727/28)
KCM	*Die Kleine Cammer-Music* (Frankfurt, 1716; 2nd edn, as *La petite musique de chambre*, Hamburg, 1728)
SeiSuo	*Sei Suonatine* (Frankfurt, 1718)
EM	*Essercizii musici* (Hamburg, 1726)
SonMet	*Sonate metodiche* (Hamburg, 1728)
GMM	*Der getreue Music-Meister* (Hamburg, 1728–29)
NouSon	*Nouvelles sonatines* (Hamburg, 1730/31)
ConSon	*Continuation des sonates méthodiques* (Hamburg, 1732)
MDT	*Musique de table* (Hamburg, 1733)
DouSol	*XII Solos à violon ou traversière* (Hamburg, 1734)

TWV 41:	*Solo instrument*	*Publication/comments*
C1	tr	'Air'; GMM
C2	rec	GMM
C3	fl/vn	ConSon
C4	fl/vn	DouSol
C5	rec	EM

C6	vn	
C7	vn	
c1	ob/fl/vn	KCM
c2	rec/bn/vc	NouSon
c3	fl/vn	ConSon
c5	vn	
c6	vn/ob	
D1	vn	SixSon
D2	vn	SeiSuo
D3	fl/vn	SonMet
D4	fl/vn	'Polonoise'; GMM
D5	various	'Pastourelle'; GMM
D6	vc	GMM
D7	vn/fl	NouSon; incompl
D8	fl/vn	DouSol
D9	fl	EM
D10	fl	
d1	various	'L'hiver'; GMM
d2	fl/vn	ConSon
d3	fl/vn	DouSol
d4	rec	EM
d6	vn	
d7	vn	
Es1	ob/fl/vn	KCM
E1	vn	SeiSuo
E2	various	'Niaise'; GMM
E3	fl etc.	'Pastorale'; GMM
E4	vn/fl	NouSon; incompl
E5	fl/vn	ConSon
E6	fl/vn	DouSol
e1	ob/fl/vn	KCM
e2	fl/vn	SonMet
e3	vn/fl	NouSon; incompl
e4	fl/vn	DouSol
e5	vadg	EM
e6	ob	GMM
e8	vn	
e9	fl	
e10	fl	

e11	fl	
F1	vn	SeiSuo
F2	rec	GMM
F3	fl/vn	DouSol
F4	vn	EM
f1	bn/rec	GMM
f2	rec	
fis1	fl/vn	DouSol
fis2	vn	
G1	vn	SixSon
G2	ob/fl/vn	KCM
G3	vn	SeiSuo
G4	fl/vn	SonMet
G5	fl	'Capriccio'; GMM
G6	treble vadg	GMM
G7	vn/fl	NouSon; incompl
G8	fl/vn	DouSol
G9	fl	EM
G10	vn	
G11	fl	
G12	fl	
g1	vn	SixSon
g2	ob/fl/vn	KCM
g3	fl/vn	SonMet
g4	vn/ob	GMM
g5	fl/ob/vn	'Sonata di Chiesa'; GMM
g6	ob	MDT
g7	fl/vn	DouSol
g9	vn	
g10	ob	
g11	vn	
g12	ob	
A1	vn	SixSon
A2	vn	SeiSuo
A3	fl/vn	SonMet
A4	vn	MDT
A5	fl/vn	DouSol
A6	vn	EM
A7	vn	

a1	vn	SixSon
a2	fl/vn	SonMet
a3	ob	GMM
a4	rec/bn/vc	NouSon
a5	fl/vn	DouSol
a6	vadg	EM
a8	fl	
a9	fl	
B1	ob/fl/vn	KCM
B2	vn	SeiSuo
B3	va/vadg	also for rec, va/vadg without bc, or in A major for fl/vn and va/vadg without bc; GMM
B4	ob d'am etc.	'Napolitana'; GMM
B5	fl/vn	ConSon
B6	ob	EM
B8	vn	
h1	vn	SixSon
h2	fl	GMM
h3	fl/vn	ConSon
h4	fl	MDT
h5	fl/vn	DouSol

25 *Music for two instruments and continuo (trios)*

Abbreviations for Telemann's publications containing trios:

SixTr	*Six trio* (Frankfurt, 1718)
EM	*Essercizii musici* (Hamburg, 1726)
GMM	*Der getreue Music-Meister* (Hamburg, 1728–29)
TriMet	*III Trietti methodichi e III scherzi* (Hamburg, 1731)
SixSon	*Six sonates en trio dans le goust italien* (Paris, 1731–33)
MDT	*Musique de table* (Hamburg, 1733)
SM	*Scherzi melodichi* (Hamburg, 1734)
SixCon	*Six concerts et six suites* (Hamburg, 1734)
SonCor	*Sonates corellisantes* (Hamburg, 1735)
SonTr	*Sonates en trio* (Paris, 1738–40), only one partbook extant

TWV 42:	*Solo instruments*	*Publication/comments*
C1	2 rec	GMM; alternative scoring in A major for 2 fl/vn
C2	rec, treble vadg	
C3	2 vn	
C4	vn, ob	lost
c1	2 fl/vn or fl/vn	SixSon
c2	rec, ob	EM
c3	treble vadg, ob	
c4	2 fl/ob/vn	
c5	ob, violetta	
c6	fl, vadg	
c7	rec, ob	
c8	2 vn	
D1	2 vn	SixTr
D2	2 fl/vn	TriMet
D3	2 fl/vn	TriMet
D4	2 fl/vn or fl/vn	SixSon
D5	2 fl	MDT
D6	fl, obbl kbd	SixCon; various alternative scorings with vn
D7	vn, va	SM
D8	2 fl/vn	SonCor
D9	vn, vadg	EM
D11	vn, va	
D12	2 vn	
D13	2 vn	
D14	2 vn	
D15	fl, vn in scordatura/va d'am	
D16	2 fl	
D18	vn, vadg	lost
D19	2 fl?	frag.
d1	2 fl/vn	TriMet
d2	2 fl/vn or fl/vn	SixSon
d3	fl, obbl hpd	SixCon; various alternative scorings with vn
d4	fl, ob	EM
d5	2 fl/vn	SonTr
d6	2 vn in scordatura	
d7	rec, treble vadg	

d8	2 vn	
d9	2 vn	
d10	rec, vn	doubtful
d11	2 fl	
Es1	2 vn	MDT
Es2	vn, va	SM
Es3	ob, obbl kbd	EM
E1	2 fl/vn	TriMet
E2	fl, obbl hpd	SixCon; various alternative scorings with vn
E3	2 vn/fl	SonCor
E4	fl, vn	EM
E5	2 vn	
E6	vn, vadg	
E7	vn, vadg	
e1	2 fl/vn or fl/vn	SixSon
e2	fl, ob	MDT
e3	fl, obbl hpd	SixCon; various alternative scorings with vn
e4	vn, va	SM
e5	ob, treble vadg	
e6	fl, ob	
e7	fl, vn	
e8	2 vn	version in G minor for 2 rec
e9	fl, ob	
e10	fl, vn	
e11	2 fl/vn	
e12	2 vn	
e14	2 fl	lost
F1	vn, bn/vc	SixTr
F2	2 vn/fl	SonCor
F3	rec, vadg	EM
F4	ob, vn	
F5	fl, vadg	
F6	fl, treble vadg	
F7	2 rec	
F8	fl, vn	
F9	fl, ob	
F10	vn, vadg	
F11	2 vn	2 movts extant

F12	ob, vn	
F13	ob, vn	
F14	rec, cor	
F15	rec, ob	
F17	vn, ob	lost
f1	2 fl/vn	SonTr
f2	rec, vn	
G1	fl, vn	SixTr
G2	2 fl/vn	TriMet
G3	2 fl/vn or fl/vn	
G4	fl, obbl hpd	SixCon; various alternative scorings with vn
G5	vn, va	SM
G6	vadg, obbl hpd	EM
G7	vn, vc	
G8	ob, treble vadg	
G9	2 vn	
G10	vn, vadg	
G11	2 vn	
G12	2 fl/vn or fl/vn	SixSon
G13	fl, ob/vn	
G14	vn, vadg	lost
[G15]	2 vn	
g1	v, vadg	SixTr
g2	fl, obbl hpd	SixCon; various alternative scorings with vn
g3	vn, va	SM
g4	2 vn/fl	SonCor
g5	ob, vn	EM
g6	ob, treble vadg	
g7	fl, vadg	
g8	ob, vn	
g9	rec, treble vadg	
g10	vn, vadg	
g11	vn, vadg	
g12	ob, vn	
g13	fl, vn or 2 vn	
g14	ob, vn	
g15	fl, vadg	
A1	2 fl/vn	TriMet

A2	2 fl/vn or fl/vn	SixSon
A3	fl, obbl hpd	SixCon; various alternative scorings with vn
A4	vn, va	SM
A5	2 vn/fl	SonCor
A6	fl, obbl hpd	EM
A7	2 fl/vn	SonTr
A8	2 vn	
A9	fl, vn/ob d'am	
A10	ob, treble vadg	
A11	2 vn	
A12	2 vn	1 movt extant
A13	2 vn	
A14	ob d'am, vn	
A16	2 fl	frag.
[A17]	2 vn	incompl
a1	rec, vn	SixTr
a2	fl, obbl hpd	SixCon; various alternative scorings with vn
a3	fl, obbl hpd	SixCon; various alternative scorings with vn
a4	rec, vn	EM
a5	2 vn	
a6	rec, ob	
a7	fl, vadg	
a8	vn, va	
B1	ob, vn	SixTr
B2	fl, obbl hpd	SixCon; various alternative scorings with vn
B3	vn, va	SM
B4	rec, obbl hpd	EM
B5	vn, bn	
B6	2 vn	
h1	fl, obbl hpd	SixCon; various alternative scorings with vn
h2	fl, obbl hpd	SixCon; various alternative scorings with vn
h3	2 vn/fl	SonCor
h4	fl, vadg	EM
h5	2 fl/vn	
h6	vn, vadg	
h7	2 vn	

26 Music for three instruments and continuo (quartets and ripieno concertos)

Abbreviations for Telemann's publications containing quartets:

Quad *Quadri* (Hamburg, 1730)
MDT *Musique de table* (Hamburg, 1733)
QuTr *Six quatuors ou trios* (Hamburg, 1733)
NouQ *Nouveaux quatuors en six suites* (Paris, 1738)
Quat *Quatrième livre de quatuors* (Paris, 1752–60)

TWV 43:	*Solo instruments*	*Publication/comments*
C1	2 vn, va	Quat; arr. for fl, vn, va
C2	fl, vadg, bn	
D1	fl, vn, vadg/vc	Quad
D2	2fl/vn, vc/bn and optional vc/bn/hpd	QuTr
D3	fl, vn, vadg/vc	NouQ
D4	2 vn, va	Quat; arr. for fl, vn, va
D5	2 vn, va	ripieno concerto
D6	fl, vn, bn/vc	
D7	2 ob, tr	
D10	fl, ob, vadg	lost
44:1	2 vn, va	ripieno concerto; part for 'Tromba se piace'
d1	2 fl, rec/bn/vc	MDT
d2	2 vn, va	Quat; arr. for fl, vn, va
d3	fl, vn, bn/vc	
Es1	2 vn, va	ripieno concerto
E1	2fl/vn, vc/bn and optional vc/bn/hpd	QuTr
E2	2 vn, va	ripieno concerto
e1	fl, vn, vadg/vc	Quad
e2	fl, vn, vc	MDT
e3	2 fl/vn, vc/bn and optional vc/bn/hpd	QuTr
e4	fl, vn, vadg/vc	NouQ
e5	2 vn, va	ripieno concerto
F1	2 vn, va	Quat; arr. for fl, vn, va
F2	2 chal, vn	
F3	2 vn, va	ripieno concerto
F4	2 vn, va	ripieno concerto

F5	2 vn, va	ripieno concerto
F6	vn, cor, vc	
G1	fl, vn, vadg/vc	Quad
G2	fl, ob, vn	MDT
G3	2 fl/vn, vc/bn and optional vc/bn/hpd	QuTr
G4	fl, vn, vadg/vc	NouQ
G5	2 vn, va	Quat; arr. for fl, vn, va
G6	rec, ob, vn	
G7	2 vn, va	ripieno concerto; 'Concerto alla Polonese'
G8	2 vn, va	ripieno concerto
G9	2 vn, va	ripieno concerto
G10	fl, 2 vadg	
G11	fl, vn, bn	
G12	fl, 2 vadg	arr. with 2 vn replacing vadg
G13	fl, vn, ob d'am	incompl
g1	fl, vn, vadg/vc	Quad
g2	ob, vn, vadg	
g3	rec, 2 vn	'Concerto di camera'
g4	rec, vn, va	
g5	ob, vn, va	lost
A1	fl, vn, vadg/vc	Quad
A2	2 fl/vn, vc/bn and optional vc/bn/hpd	QuTr
A3	fl, vn, vadg/vc	NouQ
A4	2 vn, va	Quat; arr. for fl, vn, va
A5	2 vn, va	ripieno concerto
A6	2 vn, va	ripieno concerto
40:200	2 vn, va	ripieno concerto
a1	2 fl/vn, vc/bn and optional vc/bn/hpd	QuTr
a2	fl, vn, vadg/vc	NouQ
a3	rec, ob, vn	'Concerto'
a4	2 vn, va	ripieno concerto
a5	2 vn, va	ripieno concerto
a6	2 vn, va	lost
B1	2 vn, va	ripieno concerto
B2	2 vn, va	ripieno concerto
B3	2 vn, va	ripieno concerto; 'Concerto Polonoise'

h1	fl, vn, vadg/vc	Quad
h2	fl, vn, vadg/vc	NouQ
h3	fl, vadg, bn	'Concerto'

27 Music for four to six instruments and continuo

TWV	*Key*	*Scoring (+ bc)*	*Comments*
44:3	D	2 ob, 2 cor	overture-suite; = 55:D24
44:4	D	2 ob da'm, 2 va	'Concerto'; lost
44:5	e	2 vn, 2 va	
44:6	F	2 chal, 2 violette	overture-suite; = 55:F2
44:7	F	2 vn, 2 cor	overture-suite; = 55:F4
44:8	F	2 ob/vn, 2 cor	overture-suite; = 55:F5
44:9	F	2 ob, 2 cor	overture-suite; = 55:F8
44:10	F	2 ob, 2 cor	overture-suite; = 55:F9
44:11	F	2 vn, 2 va	
44:12	F	2 ob, 2 cor	overture-suite; = 55:F15
44:13	F	2 ob, 2 cor	suite
44:14	F	2 ob d'am, 2 cor	overture-suite; = 55:F18
44:16	F	2 ob, 2 cor	overture-suite; bass part for bn
44:17	a	2 ob d'am, 2 vn	lost
44:32	f	2 vn, 2 va	
44:33	g	2 vn, 2 va	
44:34	B-flat	2 vn, 2 va	
[44:35]	A	2 vn, 2 va	
44:41	F	2 rec, 2 ob, 2 vn	
44:42	a	2 rec, 2 ob, 2 vn	
44:43	B-flat	3 ob, 3 vn	

28 Sinfonias, divertimentos and marches

TWV 50:	*Key*	*Scoring (+ bc)*	*Comments*
1	G	fl, picc, ob, chal, str, 2 concertante double basses	'Grillen-Symphonie'
2	C	2 ob, str	'Sinfonia melodica'
3	F	rec, vadg, 2 ob, corn, 3 trb, str	'Sinfonia'
4	e	2 ob, 2 vn, 2 va	'Sonata'
5	e	2 fl, 2 ob, bn, str	'Sinfonia'; only 2 movts
6	B-flat	?	'Sinfonia'; incompl

7	F		'Sinfonia'; incompl
8			'scherzende Symphonie auf das Modelied von Pere Barnabas', Paris, 1737/38; lost
9	D	ob, tr, str	'Conclusion'; pub. in *Musique de table* (Hamburg, 1733)
10	B-flat	2 ob, str	'Conclusion'; pub. in *Musique de table* (Hamburg, 1733)
21	E-flat	2 fl, 2 cor, str	'Divertimento', for Landgrave Ludwig VIII of Hessen-Darmstadt, c. 1763–66
22	A	str	'Divertimento', 'sinfonia graciosamente pomposa', for Landgrave Ludwig VIII of Hessen-Darmstadt, c. 1763–66
23	B-flat	str	'Divertimento', for Landgrave Ludwig VIII of Hessen-Darmstadt, c. 1763–66
31–42		[2 ob/vn, 2 cor, tr]	*Musique héroique ou XII marches* (Hamburg, 1728); lost
43	F	3 ob, 2 cor, bn	march, 1716?
44	D	2 fl, cor, str	'Fanfare', for Landgrave Ludwig VIII of Hessen-Darmstadt, c. 1763–66

29 *Concertos for one solo instrument*

Accompaniment consists of str, bc, unless otherwise indicated

TWV 51:	*Solo instrument*	*Comments*
C1	rec	
C2	vn	
C3	vn	overture to *Der neumodische Liebhaber Damon* (1724), 21:8
c1	ob	c. 1708–15
c2	ob	c. 1708–15
D1	fl	
D2	fl	

D3	fl	'Concerto Polonaise'
D4	fl	
D5	ob	
D6	ob	str = vn, va
D7	tp	str = 2 vn; c. 1708–15
D8	cor	with ob, vn, 2 va; c. 1708–15
D9	vn	
D10	vn	c. 1708–15
d1	ob	c. 1708–15
d2	ob	incompl
E1	fl	
E2	vn	
E3	vn	c. 1708–15
e1	ob	comp. for Johann Christian Richter
e2	ob d'am	
e3	vn	
F1	rec	
F2	vn	str = 2 va
F3	vn	str = vns in unison; c. 1708–15
F4	vn, 2 fl, 2 ob, 2 cor	concerto-suite, c. 1745–55, for J.G. Pisendel?
f1	ob	
f2	ob	str = vns in unison, va
fis1	vn	
G1	fl	'Concerto en Polonosse'; str = 2 vn
G2	ob/fl	
G3	ob d'am	
G4	vn	
G5	vn	c. 1708–15
G6	vn	str = vns in unison
G7	vn	str = 2 vn/violettas
G8	vn	ca. 1708–15
G9	va	str = 2 vn
g1	vn	transcribed for hpd by J.S. Bach (BWV 985); c. 1708–15
A1	fl d'am	lost
A2	ob d'am	
A3	vn	
A5	vadg	str = 2 vn
a1	vn	originally for oboe?; c. 1708–15

a2	vn	overture to *Die Last-tragende Liebe oder Emma und Eginhard* (1728), 21:25
B1	vn	'Concerto grosso', Dresden, 14 September 1719; for J.G. Pisendel
B2	vn	transcribed for organ by J.G. Walther (Anh. 33:6); c. 1705–06
h1	fl	
h2	vn	c. 1708–15
h3	vn	Lost; known only from anon. transcription for hpd (Anh. 33:1)

30 Concertos for two to four solo instruments

Accompaniment consists of str, bc, unless otherwise indicated

TWV	*Solo instrument*	*Comments*
52:C1	2 chal	with 2 bn, vn, va
52:C2	2 vn	c. 1708–15
52:c1	ob, vn	Transcribed for org by J.G. Walther (Anh. 33:2); c. 1708–15
52:D1	2 cor	
52:D2	2 cor	c. 1708–15
52:D3	2 vn	c. 1708–15
52:d1	2 chal	
52:Es1	2 cor	
52:e1	rec, fl	
52:e2	2 fl	c. 1718–19
52:e3	fl, vn	str = vn, 2 va
52:e4	2 vn	c. 1708–11
52:F1	rec, bn	
52:F2	ob, vn	incompl
52:F3	2 cor	
52:F4	2 cor	c. 1708–15
52:F5	2 bagpipes?	str = vns; lost
52:G1	2 vn	str = vn, 2 va; c. 1708–15
52:G2	2 vn	c. 1708–09
52:G3	2 violettas	
52:g1	2 vn	c. 1708–15
52:A1	2 ob d'am	
52:A2	2 vn	c. 1708–15
52:A3	2 va	lost
52:a1	rec, vadg	str = vn, va

52:a2	2 rec	c. 1718–19
52:B1	2 rec	c. 1718–19
52:B2	2 vn	c. 1708–15
53:C1	2 ob	'Concerto à la francese'; c. 1718–19
53:D1	2 fl	c. 1718–19
53:D2	tr, 2 ob	
53:D3	2 ob d'am, vc	str = vns in unison, va; overture to *Das Ende der babylonischen Gefangenschaft oder Belsazar* (1723), 21:11
53:D4	2 vn, bn	str = vns in unison, 2 va
53:D5	vn, vc, tr	
53:d1	2 ob, bn	
53:E1	fl, ob d'am, va d'am	
53:e1	2 fl, vn	c. 1718–19
53:e2	2 ob, vn	
53:F1	3 vn	str = vn, va; pub. in *Musique de table* (Hamburg, 1733)
53:G1	2 fl	c. 1718–19
53:g1	2 ob	str = 2 vn, 2 va
53:A1	2 fl	c. 1718–19
53:A2	fl, vn, vc	pub. in *Musique de table* (Hamburg, 1733)
53:a1	2 fl	c. 1718–19
53:h1	2 fl	c. 1718–19
54:D1	2 fl, vn, vc	
54:D2	3 cor, vn	str = vn, 2 va
54:D3	2 ob, 3 tr, tim	= introduction to serenata *Teutschland grünt und blüht im Frieden*, 12:1c (1716)
54:D4	3 tr, tim	
54:Es1	2 cor, 2 vn	pub. in *Musique de table* (Hamburg, 1733)
54:F1	rec, ob, vn, 2 cor	concerto-suite
54:A1	2 vn	c. 1708–15
54:B1	2 fl, ob, vn	str = vn, 2 va
54:B2	2 rec, 2 ob	str = vn, 2 va

31 Overture-suites

For str, with additional instruments listed under 'Scoring'

Abbreviations for Telemann's publications containing overture-suites:

MDT *Musique de table* (Hamburg, 1733)
Ouv *VI Ouvertures à 4 ou 6* (Hamburg, 1736)

TWV 55:	*Scoring*	*Comments*
C1	3 vn	
C2	ob	
C3	2 rec, 2 ob, bn	'Wasser-Ouverture', 'Hamburger Ebb und Fluht', 'Musica maritima', 'Ouverture à 7, qui réprésente L'eau avec ses divinités et le commerce de la mere'
C4	2 ob, bn	
C5		'La Bouffonne'
C6	3 ob	
C7		
c1	2 ob, bn	
c2	2 ob	
c3		Telemann's arr. (with new ouverture) of partia from *Die Kleine Cammer-Music* (Frankfurt, 1716)
c4	vn, 2 ob	only overture extant
D1	ob, tr	MDT
D2	2 cor ad lib.	Ouv
D3	2 ob, bn	
D4	2 ob, bn	
D5		'La Galante'
D6	solo vadg	
D7	tr	
D8	tr	
D9		
D10		movt 1 is overture to *Sieg der Schönheit* (1722), 21:10
D11		
D12		
D13		'La Gaillarde'
D14	solo vn	
D15	3 ob	
D16		
D17	2 cor	
D18	2 tr, tim	
D19	2 cor	
D20		only 3 movts extant
D21	2 ob, 2 cor	for Landgrave Ludwig VIII of Hessen-Darmstadt, 1765
D22	3 tr, tim	'Ouverture, jointes d'une suite tragi-comique', for Landgrave Ludwig VIII of Hessen-Darmstadt, c. 1763–66

D23	2 fl, bn	for Landgrave Ludwig VIII of Hessen-Darmstadt, 1763
D26	fl, vn, 3 tr, tim	lost
d1		
d2		
d3	3 ob, bn	
Es1	2 cor ad lib.	Ouv
Es2	solo fl	solo instrument 'Flûte Pastorelle'
Es3		'La Lyra'
Es4		arr. for kbd by Johann Christoph Bach in the Andreas Bach Book, ca. 1708–18 (Anh. 32:1)
Es5	2 ob	Telemann's arr. (with new ouverture) of partia from *Die Kleine Cammer-Music* (Frankfurt, 1716)
E1		
E2	ob d'am	arr. for org by J.G. Walther (Anh. 32:5)
E3	solo vn	
E4		
e1	2 fl	MDT
e3	2 fl, 2 ob, bn, 2 vn	
e4		
e5	ob, bn	
e6	2 ob	Telemann's arr. (with new ouverture) of partia from *Die Kleine Cammer-Music* (Frankfurt, 1716)
e7		
e8		'L'Omphale'; contains movts from *Omphale* (1724), 21:14
e9		
e10	solo ob/fl	
F1	2 cor ad lib.	Ouv
F3	2 ob, 2 cor, bn	
F6		
F7		'Ouverture à la pastorelle'
F10		'Ouverture à la burlesque'
F11	2 ob, 2 vn, 4 cor	known in modern times as the 'Alster-Ouverture'
F12	2 cor	
F13	solo vn	
F14		
F16	2 cor, bn	for Landgrave Ludwig VIII of Hessen-Darmstadt, c. 1763–66

f1	2 rec	
fis1		
G1	2 ob	
G2		‘La Bizarre’
G3		
G4		‘Ouverture des nations ancien[ne]s et modernes’; movt 1 used as overture to *Der geduldige Socrates* (1721), 21:9
G5	2 ob, bn	
G6	solo vn	= G13
G7	solo vn, 2 ob	str = 2 vn, 2 va
G8		‘La Querelleuse’
G9		str = 2 vn, 2 va
G10		‘Ouverture burlesque de Quixotte’
G11	2 ob	Telemann’s arr. (with new ouverture) of partia from *Die Kleine Cammer-Music* (Frankfurt, 1716)
G12		‘Ouverture avec la suite burlesque’
g1	2 cor ad lib.	Ouv
g2		‘La Changeante’
g3	2 ob, bn	Telemann’s arr. (with new ouverture) of partia from *Die Kleine Cammer-Music* (Frankfurt, 1716)
g4	3 ob, bn	
g5		
g6		
g7	solo vn	
g8	2 solo vn	str = 2 vn
g9	2 ob, bn	for Landgrave Ludwig VIII of Hessen-Darmstadt, c. 1763–66
A1	2 cor ad lib.	Ouv
A2		
A3		
A7	solo vn	
A8		
A9		lost
A10		movts 4, 6 and 7 arr. for kbd (32:16)
a1	2 cor ad lib.	Ouv
a2	sol rec	
a3	2 ob, bn	
a4	2 rec, 2 ob	
a5		

a4	2 ob	
a7		arr. for two lutes = 39:2
B1	2 ob	MDT
B2		Telemann's arr. (with new ouverture) of partia from *Die Kleine Cammer-Music* (Frankfurt, 1716)
B3		
B4		
B5		known in modern times as the 'Völker-Ouverture'
B6	fl, 2 rec, 2 ob, bn	arr. of vocal arias?
B7	2 ob, bn	
B8		'Ouverture burlesque'
B9		'Ouverture avec des airs'
B10	3 ob, bn	
B11	2 ob	c. 1719–20
B12		
B13	2 ob	
B14		lost
h1	2 vn, 2 ob, 2 bn	
h2		
h3		
h4	solo vn	

Bibliography

AllQua Ingeborg Allihn, *Georg Philipp Telemann und Johann Joachim Quantz: Der Einfluß einiger Kammermusikwerke Georg Philipp Telemanns auf das Lehrwerk des Johann Joachim Quantz "Versuch einer Anweisung die Flöte traversiere zu spielen"* (Magdeburg: Arbeitskreis Georg Philipp Telemann, 1971).

AndOst Greger Andersson, 'Zur Telemann-Überlieferung im Ostseeraum', in Ekkehard Ochs, Nico Schüler and Lutz Winkler (eds.), *Musica Baltica: Interregionale musikkulturelle Beziehungen im Ostseeraum: Konferenzbericht Greifswald-Gdansk, 28. November bis 3. Dezember 1993* (St Augustin: Academia, 1996), 35–45.

AnsViv Peter Ansehl, 'Bemerkungen zur Vivaldi-Rezeption bei Georg Philipp Telemann', in *FleBed*, 2:110–16.

Bach *Bach: Journal of the Riemenschneider Bach Institute, Baldwin Wallace University*

BasBez Bernd Baselt, 'Schöpferische Beziehungen zwischen G. Ph. Telemann und G. F. Händel: G. Ph. Telemanns "Harmonischer Gottesdienst" als Quelle für Händel', in *FleBed*, 2:4–14.

BasDon Bernd Baselt, 'Georg Philipp Telemanns Serenade "Don Quichotte auf der Hochzeit des Comacho": Beiträge zur Entstehungs-Geschichte von Telemanns letztem Hamburg Bühnenwerk', in Constantin Floros, Hans Joachim Marx and Peter Petersen (eds.), *Studien zur Barockoper, Hamburg Jahrbuch für Musikwissenschaft* 3 (Hamburg: Wagner, 1978), 85–100.

BasFre Bernd Baselt, Günter Fleischhauer, Wolf Hobohm, Ute Poetzsch and Walther Siegmund-Schultze (eds.), *Telemann und seine Freunde: Kontakte, Einflüsse, Auswirkungen: Bericht über die International Wissenschaftliche Konferenz anläßlich der 8. Telemann-Festtage der DDR, Magdeburg 15. und 16. März 1984*. 2 vols (Magdeburg: Zentrum für Telemann-Pflege und -Forschung, 1986).

BasHän Bernd Baselt, 'G. Ph. Telemann und G. F. Händel: Eine Kunstlerfreundschaft', in *BasFre*, 1:27–33.

BasVor Bernd Baselt, 'Deutsche Vortragsbezeichnungen bei Georg Philipp Telemann', in *ThoAuf*, 86–93.

BecCha Heinz Becker, 'Das Chalumeau bei Telemann', in *FleAuf*, 2:68–76.

BeiHam Arnd Beise, '". . . indem eine Opera keine Philosophische Geschichte ist": Johann Georg Hamanns musikdramatische Aufklärung', in *SteMet*, 867–76.

BeiBri Arnd Beise, 'Georg Philipp Telemann als Briefschreiber', in *JahExt*, 127–38.

BibLeb *Bibliographie zu Leben und Werk Georg Philipp Telemanns*, Zentrum für Telemann-Pflege und -Forschung Magdeburg: www.telemann.org/telemann-zentrum/bibliographie/bibliographie.html

BigLes Michelle Biget-Mainfroy and Rainer Schmusch (eds.), *"L'esprit français" und die Musik Europas: Entstehung, Einfluss und Grenzen einer ästhetischen Doktrin / "L'esprit français" et la musique en Europe: Émergence, influence et limites d'une doctrine esthétique: Festschrift für Herbert Schneider* (Hildesheim: Olms, 2007).

BilGra Oswald Bill, 'Telemann und Graupner', in *BasFre*, 2:27–35.

BolBeg Norbert Bolin, 'Nun lasset uns den Leib begraben: Georg Philipp Telemanns Begräbniskompositionen für hamburgische Bürgermeister', *Augsburger Jahrbuch für Musikwissenschaft* 6 (1989), 69–104.

BönPub Holger Böning, 'Publizistik und Musik im Hamburg Telemanns und Bachs', in *LanImp*, 18–40.

BraRhe Zöe Bragg, 'Rhetoric and Affekt, and Their Influence on Telemann's Fantasie für Flöte Solo No. 1', *The Consort* 60 (2004), 48–59.

BruAro Friedhelm Brusniak, 'Zur Pflege der Musik Georg Philipp Telemanns am Fürstlich Waldeckschen Hofe zu Arolsen', in *HobWer*, 2:95–108.

BruNun Friedhelm Brusniak (ed.), *"Nun bringt ein polnisch Lied die gantze Welt zum springen": Telemann und Andere in der Musiklandschaft Sachsens und Polens* (Sinzig: Studio, 1998).

BruFra Friedhelm Brusniak and Annemarie Clostermann (eds.), *Französische Einflüsse auf deutsche Musiker im 18. Jahrhundert* (Cologne: Studio, 1996).

BütKon Horst Büttner, *Das Konzert in den Orchestersuiten Georg Philipp Telemanns* (Wolfenbüttel: Kallmeyer, 1935).

CahFra Peter Cahn (ed.), *Telemann in Frankfurt: Bericht über das Symposium, Frankfurt am Main, 26./27. April 1996* (Mainz: Schott, 2000).

CalRez Michele Calella, 'Graun, Telemann und die Rezeption des französischen Rezitativs', *Basler Jahrbuch für historische Musikpraxis* 28 (2004), 95–109.

CarPas 'Anmerkungen zu Georg Philipp Telemanns Passionsoratorien im frühen bürgerlichen Konzertleben des 18. Jahrhunderts', in *CarSpa*, 278–94.

CarSpa Carsten Lange and Brit Reipsch (eds.), *Komponisten im Spannungsfeld von höfischer und städtischer Musikkultur: Bericht über die Internationale Wissenschaftliche Konferenz, Magdeburg, 18. bis 19. März 2010, anlässlich der 20. Magdeburger Telemann-Festtage* (Hildesheim: Olms, 2014).

ChaCou Keith Chapin, 'Counterpoint: From the Bees or for the Birds? Telemann and Early Eighteenth-Century Quarrels with Tradition', *Music & Letters* 92/3 (2011): 377–409.

ClaLet Stephen L. Clark, 'The Letters from Carl Philipp Emanuel Bach to Georg Michael Telemann', *Journal of Musicology* 3/2 (1984), 177–95.

CloHam Annemarie Clostermann, *Das Hamburger Musikleben und Georg*

Philipp Telemanns Wirken in den Jahren 1721 bis 1730 (Reinbek: Clostermann, 2000).

CloMis Annemarke Clostermann, 'Die "Missen" des Georg Philipp Telemann (1681–1767): Anmerkungen zum Werkbestand TWV 9', in Heribert Klein, Klaus Wolfgang Niemöller and Jürgen Schaarwächter (eds), *Kirchenmusik in Geschichte und Gegenwart: Festschrift Hans Schmidt zum 65. Geburtstag* (Cologne-Rheinkassel: Dohr, 1998), 217–236.

CloRat Annemarie Clostermann, 'Der Ratsbuchdrucker-Streit: Neue Materialen zu einer "Hamburgischen Affaire" Georg Philipp Telemanns', in *GutTel*, 92–99.

CloTon Annemarie Clostermann, 'Georg Philipp Telemanns Tonarten-Wahl und der französische Einfluß, dargestellt an Arien an den Opern *Der geduldige Sokrates* (1721), *Orpheus* (1726) und *Miriways* (1728)', in *BruFra*, 93–113.

CorWol Paul Corneilson and Peter Wollny (eds.), *Er ist der Vater, wir sind die Bub'n: Essays in Honor of Christoph Wolff* (Ann Arbor: Steglein, 2010).

CumHän Graham Cummings, 'Händel, Telemann and Metastasio, and the Hamburg *Cleofida'*, *Händel-Jahrbuch* 46 (2000), 335–73.

CzoGra Peter Czornyj, 'Georg Philipp Telemann (1681–1767): His Relationship to Carl Heinrich Graun and the Berlin Circle', PhD dissertation, University of Hull, 1988.

CzoTod Peter Czornyj, '*Der Tod Jesu* (1755): Ein Gelegenheitswerk mit Zukunft: Versuch einer Darstellung der Entstehung und frühen Aufführungstradition der Passionsvertonung Telemanns in Beziehung zur gleichnamigen Vertonung Carl Heinrich Grauns', in *HobAuf*, 152–58.

DelGal Louis Delpech, 'Zwischen Galanterie und Frühaufklärung: Telemann und die Rezeption französischer Opern in Hamburg um 1725', in *TadUrb*, 53–74.

DerHan Ellwood Derr, 'Handel's Procedures for Composing with Materials from Telemann's "Harmonischer Gottes-Dienst" in "Solomon"', in *Göttinger Händel-Beiträge* 1 (1984), 116–46.

DraHan Hansjörg Drauschke, 'Händels Opern in Hamburg: Aspekte der Bearbeitung und Anverwandlung', *Händel-Jahrbuch* 57 (2011), 147–73.

DraLin Hansjörg Drauschke, 'Telemanns zweiter Jahrgang auf Texte Hermann Ulrich von Lingens von 1728/29', in *JahExt*, 249–80.

DruCon Pippa Drummond, *The German Concerto: Five Eighteenth-Century Studies* (Oxford: Oxford University Press, 1980).

EbeKon Kathrin Eberl and Wolfgang Ruf (eds.), *Musikkonzepte – Konzepte der Musikwissenschaft: Bericht über den internationalen Kongreß der Gesellschaft für Musikforschung Halle (Saale) 1998*, 2 vols (Kassel: Bärenreiter, 2000).

EdlHer Arnfried Edler, 'Telemann und Johann Friedrich Hertel: Eine Musikerfreundschaft', in *BasFre*, 1:87–94.

EicInn Nina Eichholz, 'Innovation und Geschäftssinn im geistlichen Kantatenschaffen Georg Philipp Telemanns', in *JahExt*, 299–315.

EicKan Nina Eichholz, *Georg Philipp Telemanns Kantatenjahrgang auf Dichtungen von Gottfried Behrndt* (Hildesheim: Olms, 2015).

EicSpä Nina Eichholz, 'Vor und nach der Paris-Reise: Die Jahrgänge der späten 1730er und 1740er Jahre', *Die Tonkunst* 11/4 (2017), 491–500.

EppFan Sigrid, Eppinger, 'Georg Philipp Telemann: 12 Fantasien für Flöte solo', *Tibia* 9/2–3 (1984), 86–99 and 172–79.

EveEng Timo Evers, 'Georg Philipp Telemann und Carl Philipp Emanuel Bach im Spiegel englischer Musikerbiographik zwischen 1773 und 1835', in *LanImp*, 344–84.

ExnGod Ellen Exner, 'The Godfather: Georg Philipp Telemann, Carl Philipp Emanuel Bach, and the Family Business', *Bach* 47/1 (2016), 1–20.

FabWit Sarah-Denise Fabian, '"aufgeweckte Einfälle" und "sinnreiche Gedanken": Witz und Humor in Ouvertürensuiten Georg Philipp Telemanns', PhD dissertation, Heidelberg University, 2015.

FalRis Martina Faletta, 'Telemanns Kompositionen aus dem Blickwinkel neuer, durch das RISM-Projekt erschlossener Quellen', in *LanKir*, 178–207.

FalSel Martina Faletta, Annette Mehlhorn and Ulrich Siegele (eds.), *Georg Philipp Telemanns Passionsoratorium 'Seliges Erwägen' zwischen lutherischer Orthodoxie und Aufklärung: Theologie und Musikwissschaft im Gespräch* (Frankfurt am Main: Haag + Herchen, 2005).

FalStu Martina Faletta, 'Georg Philipp Telemann zu Besuch in Stuttgart', *Musik in Baden-Württemberg Jahrbuch* 18 (2011), 129–35.

FalTra Martina Falletta, Eric F. Fiedler and Adolf Nowak (eds.), *Trauermusik von Telemann: Ästhetische, religiöse, gesellschaftliche Aspekte* (Beeskow: Ortus, 2015).

FavNet Thierry Favier, 'Aufgeklärte Netzwerke? Telemann und seine französischen Liebhaber', in *TadUrb*, 110–69.

FecDan Manfred Fechner, 'Eine Auswirkung freundschaftlicher Beziehungen: Telemanns Danziger Choralpassion (nach Matthäus) von 1754', in *BasFre*, 2:82–98.

FecPis Manfred Fechner, 'Johann Georg Pisendel als Überlieferer und Bearbeiter Telemannscher Werke', in *RufKla*, 33–47.

FecStu Manfred Fechner, *Studien zur Dresdner Überlieferung von Instrumentalkonzerten deutscher Komponisten des 18. Jahrhunderts: Die Dresdner Konzert-Manuskripte von Georg Philipp Telemann, Johann David Heinichen, Johann Georg Pisendel, Johann Friedrich Fasch, Gottfried Heinrich Stölzel, Johann Joachim Quantz und Johann Gottlieb Graun: Untersuchungen an den Quellen und thematischer Katalog* (Laaber: Laaber, 1999).

FieTra Eric F. Fiedler, '"Nun, noch einmal: Gute Nacht": Telemanns Trauermusik für Hamburger Bürgermeister', in *FalTra*, 87–110.

FieWie Eric Fiedler, 'Telemann in Wien: Zur Wiederentdeckung von sieben als verschollen geltenden Kantaten aus Telemanns "Zweitem Lingen'schen Jahrgang" in der Österreichischen Nationalbibliothek', *Die Musikforschung* 61/3 (2008), 205–21.

FinAng Ludwig Finscher, 'Der angepaßte Komponist: Notizen zur sozialgeschichtlichen Stellung Telemanns', *Musica* 23 (1969), 549–54.

FinCor Ludwig Finscher, 'Corelli und die "Corellisierenden Sonaten" Telemanns', in *Studi Corelliani: Atti del primo Congresso internazionale, Fusignano, 5–8 settembre 1968* (Florence: Olschki, 1972), 75–95.

FisDok Roman Fischer, *Frankfurter Telemann-Dokumente*, ed. Brit Reipsch and Wolf Hobohm (Hildesheim: Olms, 1999).

FleAna Günter Fleischhauer, 'Analytische Bemerkungen zum Suiten-Konzert F-Dur für Violine und Orchester von Georg Philipp Telemann', in Eitelfriedrich Thom and Renate Bormann (eds.), *Die Saiteninstrumente in der ersten Hälfte des 18. Jahrhunderts und unserer heutigen Besetzungsmöglichkeiten: Konferenzbericht der 6. Wissenschaftliche Arbeitstagung, Blankenburg/Harz, 23. bis 25. Juni 1978* (Blankenburg/Harz: Die Kultur- und Forschungseinrichtung Michaelstein, 1979), 81–102.

FleAnn Günter Fleischhauer, *Annotationen zu Georg Philipp Telemann: Ausgewählte Schriften*, ed. Carsten Lange (Hildesheim: Olms, 2007).

FleAuf Günter Fleischhauer and Walther Siegmund-Schultze (eds.), *Georg Philipp Telemann: Ein bedeutender Meister der Aufklärungsepoche: Konferenzbericht der 3. Magdeburger Telemann-Festtage vom 22. bis 26. Juni 1967*, 2 vols (Magdeburg: Rat der Stadt Magdeburg, 1969).

FleBed Günter Fleischhauer, Wolf Hobohm and Walther Siegmund-Schultze (eds.), *Die Bedeutung Georg Philipp Telemanns für die Entwicklung der europäischen Musikkultur im 18. Jahrhunderts: Bericht über die International Wissenschaftliche Konferenz anläßlich der Georg-Philipp-Telemann-Ehrung der DDR, Magdeburg 12. bis 18. März 1981*, 3 vols (Magdeburg: Zentrum für Telemann-Pflege und -Forschung, 1983).

FleBre Günter Fleischhauer, 'Annotationen zu Werken Telemanns in den Katalogen des Verlagshauses Breitkopf in Leipzig (1760–1787)', in *HobWer*, 1:49–56. Reprinted in *FleAnn*, 257–66.

FleDic Günter Fleischhauer and Walther Siegmund-Schultze (eds.), *Telemann und seine Dichter: Konferenzbericht der 6. Magdeburger Telemann-Festtage vom 9. bis 12. Juni 1977*, 2 vols (Magdeburg: Rat der Stadt Magdeburg, 1978).

FleGet Günter Fleischhauer, 'Telemanns Journal "Der getreue Music-Meister" (1728–1729) unter musikpädagogischen Aspekten', in *FleMus*, 43–59.

FleIns Günter Fleischhauer, 'Einige Gedanken zur Instrumentation Telemanns', in *FleAuf*, 2: 40–67. Reprinted in *FleAnn*, 96–199.

FleMar Günter Fleischhauer, 'Die "galante" und kontrapunktische Schreibart Telemanns im Urteil Friedrich Wilhelm Marpurg', in *BasFre*, 2:71–81.

FleMay Günter Fleischhauer, 'Karl Wilhelm Ramlers musikalische Idylle "Der May" in der Vertonung Georg Philipp Telemanns', in *FleBed* 3: 82–93. Reprinted in *FleAnn*, 198–208.

FleMes Günter Fleischhauer, '*Annotationen zum Wort-Ton-Verhältnis in Georg Philipp Telemanns "Messias" (TVWV 6:4)'*, in *Georg Friedrich Händel: Ein Lebensinhalt: Gedenkschrift für Bernd Baselt (1934–1993)*, ed. Klaus Hortschansky and Konstanze Musketa (Halle an der Saale: Händel-Haus; Kassel: Bärenreiter, 1995), 381–93. Reprinted in *FleAnn*, 322–32.

FleMor Günter Fleischhauer, 'Georg Philipp Telemanns Zyklen "VI Moralische Cantaten" (TVWV 20:23–28 und 29–34) im Urteil Johann Adolph Scheibes', in *Musica Privata: Die Rolle der Musik im privaten Leben: Festschrift zum 65. Geburtstag von Walter Salmen*, ed. Monika Fink, Rainer Gstrein and Günter Mössmer (Innsbruck: Helbling, 1991, 315–38. Reprinted in *FleAnn*, 267–90.

FleMus Günter Fleischhauer and Walther Siegmund-Schultze (eds.), *Telemann und die Musikerziehung: Konferenzbericht der 5. Magdeburger Telemann-Festtage vom 19. bis 27. Mai 1973* (Magdeburg: Rat der Stadt Magdeburg, 1975).

FleRen Günter Fleischhauer, Wolf Hobohm and Willi Maertens (eds.), *Telemann-Renaissance: Werk und Wiedergabe: Bericht über die Wissenschaftliche Arbeitstagung aus Anlass des 20. Jahrestages des Telemann-Kammerorchesters Sitz Blankenburg/Harz* (Magdeburg: Arbeitskreis Georg Philipp Telemann im Kulturbund der DDR, 1973).

FleTod Günter Fleischhauer, Wolfgang Ruf, Bert Siegmund and Frieder Zschoch (eds.), *Tod und Musik im 17. und 18. Jahrhundert: XXVI. Internationale wissenschaftliche Arbeitstagung Michaelstein, 12. bis 14. Juni 1998* (Michaelstein: Stiftung Kloster Michaelstein, 2001).

FleUrt Günter Fleischhauer, 'Die Musik Georg Philipp Telemanns im Urteil seiner Zeit', *Händel-Jahrbuch* 13–14 (1967–68), 173–205 and 15–16 (1969–70), 23–73. Reprinted in *FleAnn*, 38–95.

FloFrü Constantin Floros, Hans Joachim Marx and Peter Petersen (eds.), *Die frühdeutsche Oper und ihre Beziehungen zu Italien, England und Frankreich; Mozart und die Oper seiner Zeit, Hamburger Jahrbuch für Musikwissenschaft* 5 (Laaber: Laaber Verlag, 1981).

FreBro Henning Fredrichs, *Das Verhältnis von Text und Musik in den Brockespassionen Keisers, Händels, Telemanns und Matthesons: Mit einer Einführung in ihre Entstehungs- und Rezeptionsgeschichte sowie den Bestand ihrer literarischen und musikalischen Quellen* (Munich: Katzbichler, 1975).

GiuGre Matteo Giuggioli, 'Die Grenze erforschen: Zur Ausdrucks- und Kommunikationsweise der Hamburger und Pariser Quartette Telemanns', in *TadUrb*, 170–89.

GlöKuh Andreas Glöckner, 'Johann Kuhnau und Georg Philipp Telemann', in *BasFre*, 1:21–26.

GlöLei Andreas Glöckner, 'Frühe Leipziger Telemann-Quellen', in *HobWer*, 1:57–71.

GlöNeu Andreas Glöckner, *Die Musikpflege an der Leipziger Neukirche zur Zeit Johann Sebastian Bachs* (Leipzig: Nationale Forschungs- und Gedenkstätten Johann Sebastian Bach, 1990).

GodMes Günter Godehart, 'Telemanns "Messias"', *Die Musikforschung* 14 (1961), 139–55.

GraCho Jason Grant, 'Chorale Arrangements in the Late Liturgical Passions of Georg Philipp Telemann', in *Genre in Eighteenth-Century Music*, ed. Anthony R. DelDonna (Ann Arbor: Steglein, 2008), 228–55.

GraPas Jason Benjamin Grant, 'The Rise of Lyricism and the Decline of Biblical Narration in the Late Liturgical Passions of Georg Philipp Telemann', PhD dissertation, University of Pittsburgh, 2005.

GreBio Karl Grebe, *Georg Philipp Telemann in Selbstzeugnissen und Bilddokumenten* (Reinbek bei Hamburg: Rowohlt, 1970).

GutAuf Dieter Gutknecht, Wolf Hobohm and Brit Reipsch (eds.), *Freiheit oder Gesetz?: Aufführungspraktische Erkenntnisse aus Telemanns Handschriften, zeitgenössischen Abschriften, musiktheoretischen Publikationen und ihre Anwendung: Bericht über die Internationale Wissenschaftliche Konferenz, Magdeburg*, 15. bis 17. März 2000, anläßlich der 15. Magdeburger Telemann-Festtage (Hildesheim: Olms, 2007).

GutTel Dieter Gutknecht, Hartmut Krones and Frieder Zschoch (eds.), *Telemanniana et alia musicologica: Festschrift für Günter Fleischhauer zum 65. Geburtstag* (Oschersleben: Ziethen, 1995).

HarGri Andrea Hartmann, compiler, *Katalog der Musikhandschriften der Fürstenschule Grimma* (Dresden: Qucosa, 2009): www.qucosa.de/fileadmin/data/qucosa/documents/2484/Grimma_Katalog.pdf

HarMag Clemens Harasim, 'Das Magnificat als frühes kirchenmusikalisches Opus summum bei Georg Philipp Telemann und Carl Philipp Emanuel Bach', in *LanImp*, 254–63.

HarRic Klaus Harnisch, 'Telemann als Bearbeiter von Händels Oper "Riccardo I." (Hamburg 1729)', in *FleBed*, 1:114–20.

HauSto Eberhard Haufe, 'Daniel Stoppe als Textdichter Telemanns', in *FleDic*, 1:75–86.

HayKle Bruce Haynes, 'Telemann's Kleine Cammer-Music and the Four Oboists to whom It was Dedicated', *Journal of the International Double Reed Society* 15 (1987), 27–32.

HelRom Eva Helenius, 'Johan Helmich Roman und Europa: Zu Dreiecksbeziehungen zwischen Stockholm, London und Hamburg', in *LanHän*, 257–76.

HenSin — Christoph Henzel, 'Telemann-Überlieferung im Spiegel des Notenarchivs der Sing-Akademie zu Berlin', in *LanMal*, 364–411.

HerFra — Martin Hertel, 'Der Französische Jahrgang von Georg Philipp Telemann zwischen Gebrauchsmusik und zyklischem Kunstwerk', in *NowVok*, 199–227.

HirAlt — Wolfgang Hirschmann, 'Georg Philipp Telemanns Festmusik zur Altareinweihung an der St Getrudkirche (Hamburg 1742): Liturgische Integration und politische Funktion', in *ThoAuf*, 59–68.

HirAri — Wolfgang Hirschmann, '"Rufst du, süße Hirtenstimme?": Analytischer Versuch über eine Arie aus Telemanns Arienjahrgang von 1727', in *Aria: Eine Festschrift für Wolfgang Ruf* (Hildesheim: Olms, 2011), 373–87.

HirCon — Wolfgang Hirschmann, *Studien zum Konzertschaffen von Georg Philipp Telemann*, 2 vols (Kassel: Bärenreiter, 1986).

HirFes — Wolfgang Hirschmann, 'Georg Philipp Telemanns Festmusiken zu Kircheneinweihungen: Einige Präzisierungen', *Neues Musikwissenschaftliches Jahrbuch* 6 (1997), 109–20.

HirFra — Wolfgang Hirschmann, 'Telemanns Frankfurter Konzertschaffen: Quellen- und stilkritische Bemerkungen zur Datierungsproblematik', in *CahFra*, 208–39.

HirHän — Wolfgang Hirschmann, 'Händels und Telemanns Konzertschaffen: Gemeinsamkeiten, Beziehungen, Unterschiede', in *LanHän*, 28–44.

HirHei — Wolfgang Hirschmann, 'Zweimal Heilig: Bach in Hamburg und das Vorbild Telemanns', in *JanGen*, 85–97.

HirHör — Wolfgang Hirschmann, 'Die Wiederaufführungen von Telemanns Johannespassion 1741/49 unter Hans Hörner in den Jahren 1932 und 1934', in *LanUmg*, 185–218.

HirInd — Wolfgang Hirschmann, '"He Liked to Hear the Music of Others": Individuality and Variety in the Works of Bach and His German Contemporaries', in *TalBac*, 1–23.

HirInn — Wolfgang Hirschmann, '"Toute innovation dans les Arts est dangereuse": Telemanns 71. Psalm, sein "Neues musikalisches System" und die ramistische Ästhetik', in *BigLes*, 373–85.

HirIno — Wolfgang Hirschmann, 'Christian Gottfried Krauses Bearbeitung der *Ino*-Kantate von Georg Philipp Telemann', in *NowVok*, 323–52.

HirJoh — Wolfgang Hirschmann, '"Gluck zu, o Erlöser, du hast es vollbracht": Quellenphilologische und analytisch-interpretatorische Bemerkungen zur Johannespassion 1745 von Georg Philipp Telemann und Joachim Johann Daniel Zimmermann', in *HirSpu*, 36–66.

HirKan — Wolfgang Hirschmann and Dirk Rose (eds.), *Die Kantate als Katalysator: Zur Karriere eines musikalisch-literarischen Strukturtypus um und nach 1700* (Berlin: De Gruyter, 2018).

HirKom — Wolfgang Hirschmann, 'Kompilation als Emanzipation: Bachs Johannespassion von 1772 und ihr Modell', in *LanImp*, 264–73.

HirMic Wolfgang Hirschmann, 'Die Stadt als soziales Gefüge und Spannungsfeld: Telemanns Festmusik zur Einweihung der Großen St Michaelis-Kirche (Hamburg 1762)', in *CarSpa*, 210–26.

HirNeu Wolfgang Hirschmann, '"Aber es klinget doch süß": Mikrointervallik als theoretisches, ästhetisches und kompositorisches Problem in Telemanns Neuem Musikalischem System', in *MooAuf*, 82–95.

HirPol Wolfgang Hirschmann, 'Polyphonie der Stile und aufgeklärt-emanzipatorisches Denken in Telemanns Oper "Die Last-tragende Liebe, oder Emma und Eginhard"', in *HobVol*, 305–12.

HirPas Wolfgang Hirschmann, 'Aufklärung und ästhetische Autonomie: Zu Telemanns frühen Passionsoratorien', in *FalSel*, 19–32.

HirPsa Wolfgang Hirschmann, 'Der 71. Psalm in den Vertonungen von André Campra, Charles-Hubert Gervais und Georg Philipp Telemann', in *HobVol*, 52–76.

HirPol Wolfgang Hirschmann, '"Deutschland grunt und blüht im Friede" – nach polnischer Art: Telemanns Frankfurter Serenata von 1716 und der polnische Stil', in Stefan Keym and Stephan Wünsche (eds.), *Musikgeschichte zwischen Ost und West: von der 'musica sacra' bis zur Kunstreligion: Festschrift für Helmut Loos zum 65. Geburtstag* (Leipzig, 2015), 451–60.

HirRez Wolfgang Hirschmann, 'Französische Elemente in Telemanns Passionsrezitativ', in *BruFra*, 149–68.

HirSch Wolfgang Hirschmann, 'Auf den Schultern des Riesen: Kompositionen von Georg Philipp Telemann in der Bearbeitung des Enkels Georg Michael', *Concerto*, No. 55 (1990), 9–14.

HirSer Wolfgang Hirschmann, 'Musikalische Festkultur im politisch-sozialen und liturgisch-religiösen Kontext: Telemanns Serenata und Kirchenmusik zur Geburt des Erzherzogs Leopold (Frankfurt 1716)', in *CahFra*, 163–95.

HirSpä Wolfgang Hirschmann, 'Wege ins Spätwerk: Telemann in den 1740er Jahren', in *EbeKon*, 2:337–61.

HirSpu Wolfgang Hirschmann (ed.), *Auf der gezeigten Spur: Beiträge zur Telemannforschung: Festgabe Martin Ruhnke zum 70. Geburtstag am 14. Juni 1991* (Oschersleben: Ziethen, 1994).

HirVer Wolfgang Hirschmann, 'Le monde renversé – Die verkehrte Welt: Zur Adaption und Transformation der Opéra comique auf deutschen Bühnen des frühen 18. Jahrhunderts', in *LanFra*, 238–66.

HirWil Wolfgang Hirschmann and Peter Wollny (eds.), *Wilhelm Friedemann Bach und die protestantische Kirchenkantate nach 1750* (Beeskow, 2012).

HobAdh Wolf Hobohm, 'Telemanns Bayreuther Oper "Adelheid"', in Friedhelm Brusniak (ed.), *Musiktheatralische Formen in kleinen Residenzen: 7. Arolser Barock-Festpiele 1992, Tagungsbericht* (Cologne: Studio, 1993), 102–21.

HobAuf Wolf Hobohm, Carsten Lange and Brit Reipsch (eds.), *Telemanns Auftrags- und Gelegenheitswerke: Funktion, Wert und Bedeutung: Bericht über die Internationale Wissenschaftliche Konferenz anläßlich der 10. Magdeburger Telemann-Festtage, Magdeburg, 14. bis 16. März 1990* (Oschersleben: Ziethen, 1997).

HobBei Wolf Hobohm and Brit Reipsch (eds.), *Telemann-Beiträge 3* (Oschersleben: Ziethen, 1997).

HobBem Wolf Hobohm, 'Bemerkungen zum Konvolut T6 der Deutschen Staatsbibliothek zu Berlin (DDR)', in *LanBei*, 2:4–13.

HobBer Wolf Hobohm, 'Berührungspunkte in den Biographen Georg Philipp Telemanns und Johann Sebastian Bachs sowie ihrer Familien', in *ReiBac*, 11–23.

HobBib Wolf Hobohm, 'Verzeichnis des Telemann-Schrifttums', in *NeuBil*, 83–95.

HobBio Wolf Hobohm, 'Zwei Biographen aus dem Umkreis Telemanns', in *LanBei*, 1:11–20.

HobBog Wolf Hobohm, 'Der Telemannische Bogen', in Günter Fleischhauer, Walther Siegmund-Schultze and Eitelfriedrich Thom (eds.), *Generalbaßspiel im 17. und 18. Jahrhundert: Editionsfragen aus der Sicht vorliegender Ausgaben zum Jubiläumsjahr 1985: Konferenzbericht der XIV. wissenschaftlichen Arbeitstagung Blankenburg/Harz, 13. Juni bis 15. Juni 1986* (Magdeburg: Rat des Bezirkes; Michaelstein: Kultur- und Forschungsstätte, 1987), 32–35.

HobBri Wolf Hobohm, 'Ein unbekannter Brief aus dem Alltag des Kapellmeisters Telemann', in Wolf Hobohm (ed.), *Kleine Beiträge zur Telemann Forschung* (Magdeburg: Zentrum für Telemann-Pflege und -Forschung, 1983), 29–35.

HobDok Wolf Hobohm (ed.), *. . . aus diesem Ursprunge: Dokumente, Materialien, Kommentare zur Familiengeschichte Georg Philipp Telemanns* (Magdeburg: Zentrum für Telemann-Pflege und -Forschung, 1988).

HobDru Wolf Hobohm (ed.), *Georg Philipp Telemann, Drucke aus dem Verlag Balthasar Schmid in Nürnberg: Porträt – Deutsch-Französischer Lebenslauf – Vorbericht – Kantate zum 1. Advent* (Oschersleben: Ziethen, 1998).

HobEmm Wolf Hobohm, 'Die Briefszenen in Telemanns Oper Emma und Eginhard', in *RufKla*, 58–69.

HobErb Wolf Hobohm, 'Georg Michael Telemann als "Sachwalter" des großväterlichen Erbes', in *EbeKon*, 2:346–54.

HobGru Wolf Hobohm, 'Grundzüge der Telemann-Überlieferung', in *HobWer*, 1:5–18.

HobHau Wolf Hobohm, 'Telemanns Musik für Hautboisten-Ensembles', in *SchHar*, 69–81.

HobHer Wolf Hobohm, 'G. Ph. Telemann als Herausgeber', in *FleRen*, 47–61.

HobJah Wolf Hobohm, 'Telemann als Kantatenkomponist: Versuch einer Ordnung und Typologie seiner Jahrgänge', in *BruNun*, 29–52.

HobKan Wolf Hobohm, 'Telemann als Kantatenkomponist zwischen 1710 und 1730', in *CahFra*, 55–73.

HobKle Wolf Hobohm, 'Pädagogische Grundsätze und ästhetische Anschauungen Telemanns in der "Kleinen Kammermusik" (1716)', in *FleMus*, 30–42.

HobLei Wolf Hobohm, 'Georg Philipp Telemann und die bürgerliche Oper in Leipzig', *Händel-Jahrbuch* 36 (1990), 49–61.

HobLom Wolf Hobohm, 'Zum lombardischen Rhythmus bei Telemann', in *FleBed* 3:4–22.

HobMar Wolf Hobohm, 'Telemann und Marcello', in *BasFre*, 1:57–73.

HobMis Wolf Hobohm, 'Drei Telemann-Miszellen', *Beiträge zur Musikwissenschaft* 14 (1972), 237–40.

HobNeu Wolf Hobohm, 'Telemanns Kantatenjahrgänge nach Neumeister-Texten: Datierungen, Auftraggeber, Gestaltung', in Henrike Rucker (ed.), *Erdmann Neumeister (1671–1756): Wegbereiter der evangelischen Kirchenkantate* (Rudolstadt: Hain, 2000), 111–34.

HobRam Wolf Hobohm, 'Telemann und Ramler', in *FleDic*, 2:61–80.

HobRei Wolf Hobohm, 'Elias Caspar Reichard (1714–1791), ein Gelegenheitsdichter Georg Philipp Telemanns und Johann Heinrich Rolles', in *HobAuf*, 231–43.

HobSch Wolf Hobohm, 'Georg Philipp Telemann und seine Schüler', in *Bericht über den internationalen musikwissenschaftlichen Kongreß Leipzig 1966* (Kassel: Bärenreiter, 1970), 260–65.

HobTom Wolf Hobohm, 'Georg Philipp Telemanns "Tombeau" für Georg Friedrich Händel', in *FleTod*, 233–34.

HobTod Wolf Hobohm, 'Karl Wilhelm Ramlers zweite Fassung seines "Tod Jesu" in der musikalischen Bearbeitung von Christian Gottfried Krause', in *LanMal*, 423–52.

HobÜbe Wolf Hobohm, 'Überlegungen zu einer Telemann-Biographie', in *KreBio*, 193–207.

HobVer Wolf Hobohm, 'Neues aus dem Telemannischen Verlag', in *GutTel*, 83–91.

HobVol Wolf Hobohm and Brit Reipsch (eds.), *Volksmusik und nationale Stile in Telemanns Werk: Bericht über die Internationale Wissenschaftliche Konferenz anläßlich der 12. Magdeburger Telemann-Festtage, Magdeburg, 10. bis 14. März 1994 / Der Opernkomponist Georg Philipp Telemann: Neue Erkenntnisse und Erfahrungen: Bericht über die Internationale Wissenschaftliche Konferenz anläßlich der 13. Magdeburger Telemann-Festtage, Magdeburg, 14. bis 15. März 1996* (Hildesheim: Olms, 2006).

HobWer Wolf Hobohm and Carsten Lange (eds.), *Georg Philipp Telemann: Werküberlieferung, Editions- und Interpretationsfragen: Bericht über die Internationale Wissenschaftliche Konferenz anläßlich der 9.*

Telemann-Festtage der DDR, Magdeburg 12. bis 14. März 1987, 3 vols in 1 (Cologne: Studio, 1991).

HofHar Achim Hofer, 'Geburtsmomente der Harmoniemusik: Beispiele – Perspektiven', in *SchHar*, 37–52.

HofKon Adolf Hoffmann, *Die Orchestersuiten Georg Philipp Telemanns: TWV 55* (Wolfenbüttel: Möseler, 1969).

HofSin Adolf Hoffmann, *Die Lieder der Singenden Geographie von Losius-Telemann: Zugleich ein Beitrag zur Deutung der Umwelt Georg Philipp Telemanns während seiner Schulzeit in Hildesheim um 1700* (Hildesheim: Lax, 1962).

HörPas Hans Hörner, *Gg. Ph. Telemanns Passionsmusiken: Ein Beitrag zur Geschichte der Passionsmusik in Hamburg* (Borna-Leipzig: Noske, 1933).

HotEin Katharina Hottmann, 'Liedminiaturen: Telemanns Experimente mit der Einstrophigkeit', in *JahExt*, 45–70.

HotKon Katharina Hottmann, 'Kontinuität und Diskontinuität: Dichter-Generationen in weltlichen Liedern zwischen 1730 und 1780', in *LanImp*, 160–92.

HotLie Katharina Hottmann, *'Auf! stimmt ein freies Scherzlied ein': Weltliche Liedkultur im Hamburg der Aufklärung* (Stuttgart: Metzler, 2017).

HutFra Peter Huth, 'Telemanns Hamburger Opern nach französischen Vorbildern', in *BruFra*, 115–48.

HutSui Peter Huth, 'Ein weiteres Suitenkonzert in F-Dur', in *FleBed*, 2:96–109.

HutTod Peter Huth, 'Tod und Todesnähe in den Opern von Georg Philipp Telemann', in *FleTod*, 253–75.

JaeAut Joachim Jaenecke, *Georg Philipp Telemann: Autographe und Abschriften*. Staatsbibliothek zu Berlin- Preussischer Kulturbesitz: Kataloge der Musikabteilung, series 1, vol. 7 (Munich: Henle, 1993).

JahDon Bernhard Jahn, 'Die Musik zum Roman: Daniel Schiebelers und Georg Philipp Telemanns Gattungsexperiment Don Quichotte auf der Hochzeit des Comacho', in Ute Jung-Kaiser and Annette Simonis (eds.), *'Poesie in reinstes Gold verwandeln. . .': Cervantes' Don Quijote in Literatur, Kunst, Musik und Philosophie* (Hildesheim: Olms, 2016), 97–114.

JahExt Bernhard Jahn and Ivana Rentsch (eds.), *Extravaganz und Geschäftssinn: Telemanns Hamburger Innovationen*, Hamburg Yearbook of Musicology 1 (Münster: Waxmann, 2019).

JanGed Martina Janitzek, '"Ihr Männer, lernet nur beizeit' geduldig sein!": *Der Geduldige Socrates* von Georg Philipp Telemann', in *CahFra*, 260–83.

JanGen Tobias Janz, Kathrin Kirsch and Ivana Rentsch (eds.), *C. P. E. Bach und Hamburg: Generationenfolgen in der Musik* (Hildesheim: Olms, 2017).

JanPol Martina Janitzek, 'Die Arolser Hofsängerin und Telemann-Interpretin Maria Domenica Polon', in Friedhelm Brusniak (ed.), *Italienische Musiker und Musikpflege an deutschen Höfen der Barockzeit: 9. Arolser Barock-Festspiele 1994, Tagungsbericht* (Cologne: Studio, 1995), 53–72.

JunKan Christiane Jungius, *Telemanns Frankfurter Kantatenzyklen* (Kassel: Bärenreiter, 2008).

JunMiz Hans Rudolf Jung, 'Telemann und die Mizlersche "Societät der musikalischen Wissenschaften"', in *FleAuf*, 2:84–97.

KeiDan Klaus Keil, 'Georg Philipp Telemanns Kantaten für Danzig', in Janusz Krassowski (ed.), *Musica Baltica: Danzig und die Musikkultur Europas* (Gdańsk: Akademia Muzyczna im. Stanislawa Moniuszki w Gdansku, 2000), 314–21.

KerKan Ann Kersting-Meuleman, 'Die Telemann-Kantatensammlung in der Universitätsbibliothek Johann Christian Senckenberg in Frankfurt am Main: Jahrgangscharakteristik und -chronologie anhand der Schreiber, Papiere und Textbücher', in *NowVok*, 391–424.

KerQue Ann Kersting-Meuleman, 'Einigen grundsätzliche Überlegungen zur Quellenkunde der in Frankfurt aufbewahrten Telemann-Kantatenhandschriften, dargestellt am Beispiel der Advents- und Weinachtskantaten des Französischen Jahrgangs', in *ReiZwi*, 159–93.

KerRez Ann Kersting-Meuleman, 'Zwischen Hamburg und Frankfurt: Zur Rezeption der Vokalwerke Telemanns in Frankfurt 1722 bis 1767', in *JahExt*, 281–98.

KirErh Kathrin Kirsch, 'Dramaturgien des Erhabenen: Telemanns "Donner-Ode" und Carl Philipp Emanuel Bachs "Morgengesang am Schöpfungsfeste"', in *LanImp*, 89–111.

KiuFra Birgit Kiupel, 'Zu den Frauengestalten in den Opern Telemanns', in *HobVol*, 272–82.

KleDok Christine Klein, *Dokumente zur Telemann-Rezeption, 1767 bis 1907* (Oschersleben: Ziethen, 1998).

KleSch Christine Klein, 'Zwischen "konventionellem Phrasenwerk" und "unerschöpflicher Phantasie": Telemanns Instrumentalkonzert im Urteil Arnold Scherings', in *LanUmg*, 120–49.

KleHam Eckart Kleßmann, *Telemann in Hamburg, 1721–1767* (Hamburg: Hoffmann und Campe, 1980).

KleTel Eckart Kleßmann, *Georg Philipp Telemann* (Hamburg: Ellert & Richter, 2004).

KliCas Regine Klingsporn, 'Französisches "Hunde Geheule" versus deutsche "Rhetoric": Zu Telemanns Rezeption von Rameaus "Castor et Pollux"', in *LanFra*, 74–81.

KnoHam Mark W. Knoll, 'Carl Philipp Emanuel Bachs Osterkantate "Gott hat den Herrn auferwecket" Wq 244 und Ihre Hamburger Fassung', in *LanImp*, 314–20.

KocHän Annerose Koch, 'Telemanns Auseinandersetzung mit Charakterisierungskunst und Wort-Ton-Verhältnis im Opernschaffen Händels', in *BasFre*, 2:15–26.

KocKei Klaus-Peter Koch, 'Reinhard Keiser und Georg Philipp Telemann: Bemerkungen zu ihren Beziehungen untereinander', in *HirSpu*, 67–86.

KocOtt Annerose Koch, 'Telemanns Bearbeitung der Händel-Oper "Ottone" in bezug auf Sujet, Libretto und Rezitativstil', in *FleDic*, 1:58–67.

KocPim Klaus-Peter Koch, 'Keisers "Hamburger Jahrmarkt" und Telemanns "Pimpinone"? Bemerkungen zu den Beziehungen Keiser – Telemann', in *HobVol*, 295–304.

KocPol Klaus-Peter Koch, *Die Polnische und Hanakische Musik in Telemann's Werk*, 2 vols (Magdeburg: Zentrum für Telemann-Pflege und -Forschung, 1982 and 1985).

KocRez Klaus-Peter Koch, 'Zur Rezeption von Telemann-Vokalwerken nach 1767 bis zur Mitte des 19. Jahrhunderts: Fakten, Indizien, Hintergründe', in *LanUmg*, 67–83.

KocRig Klaus-Peter Koch, 'Telemann, Riga und die 1730er Jahre', in *ReiZwi*, 257–69.

KocSor Klaus-Peter Koch, 'Telemann als Sorauer Hofkapellmeister und Nachwirkungen in Sorau im 18. Jahrhundert', in *CarSpa*, 45–82.

KocSto Klaus-Peter Koch, 'Der Komponist Georg Philipp Telemann und sein schlesischer Textdichter Daniel Stoppe (1697–1747)', in Wojciech Kunicki (ed.), *Aufklärung in Schlesien im europäischen Spannungsfeld: Tradition – Diskurse – Wirkungen*, 2 vols (Wrocław: Wydawnictwo Uniwersytetu Wrocławskiego, 1996), 161–76.

KreBio Joachim Kremer, Wolf Hobohm and Wolfgang Ruf (eds.), *Biographie und Kunst als historiographisches Problem: Bericht über die Internationale Wissenschaftliche Konferenz anläßlich der 16. Magdeburger Telemann-Festage, Magdeburg, 13. bis 15. März 2002* (Hildesheim: Olms, 2004).

KreCan Joachim Kremer, *Das norddeutsche Kantorat im 18. Jahrhundert* (Kassel: Bärenreiter, 1995).

KreFre Joachim Kremer, 'Freylinghausens Geist=reiches Gesang=Buch und Telemanns Liederbuch von 1730 im Vergleich: Anmerkungen zum Liedbestand', in *MieFre*, 349–72.

KreHän Joachim Kremer, 'Telemann und Händel: Freundschaft, "Gleichheit der Gemüther" und die Musik in der ersten Hälfte des 18. Jahrhunderts', in *LanHän*, 9–27.

KreLie Joachim Kremer, 'Telemanns Liederbuch (1730): Musikgeschichte des protestantischen Choralgesangs oder im Dienste aktueller Anwendung?', *Die Tonkunst* 11/4 (2017), 486–90.

KreMem Joachim Kremer (ed.), *Georg Philipp Telemanns Memorial an das Collegium Scholarchale vom 15. Oktober 1722* (Hamburg: Hamburger Telemann-Gesellschaft, 1993).

KreRol Joachim Kremer, 'Johann Sebastian Bach und sein "glücklicher Rivale": Zu Romain Rollands Telemannbild', in *ReiBac*, 34–53.

KreTra Joachim Kremer, 'Telemanns frühe und undatierte Trauermusiken:

Musikalische Innovation zu Beginn des 18. Jahrhunderts', in *FalTra*, 65–85.

KroCon Siegfried Kross, *Das Instrumentalkonzert bei Georg Philipp Telemann* (Tutzing: Schneider, 1969).

KroLie Siegfried Kross, 'Telemann und die Liedästhetik seiner Zeit', in *FleBed*, 2:31–46.

KruPle Jan Kruczek, 'Georg Philipp Telemann in Pless und die Plesser Hofkapelle des Hauses Anhalt', in *LanSch*, 39–51.

KrüRos Ekkehard Krüger, *Die Musikaliensammlungen des Erprinzen Friedrich Ludwig von Württemberg-Stuttgart und der Herzogin Luise Friederike von Mecklenburg-Schwerin in der Universitätsbibliothek Rostock*, 3 vols (Beeskow: Ortus, 2006).

KühAri Jana Kühnrich, 'Ein Arienjahrgang von Georg Philipp Telemann (1727) für Haus- und Privatandachten', in Christian Philipsen and Ute Omonsky (eds.), *Hausmusik im 17. und 18. Jahrhundert: XXXIX. Wissenschaftliche Arbeitstagung, Michaelstein, 23. bis 25. November 2012* (Augsburg: Wissner, 2016), 187–95.

LalPar Lionel de La Laurencie, 'G. Ph. Telemann à Paris', *Revue de musicologie* 16/2 (1932), 75–85.

LanAlt Carsten Lange, 'Telemanns Verbindungen zur französisch-reformierten Gemeinde in Altona: Eine Spurensuche', in *JahExt*, 175–93.

LanBac Carsten Lange, '"Der Herr ist König": Eine weitere Telemann-Kantate aus Bachs Notenschrank', in *LanBei*, 2:14–21.

LanBei Carsten Lange (ed.), *Telemann-Beiträge*, 2 vols (Magdeburg: Zentrum für Telemann-Pflege und -Forschung, 1987 and 1989).

LanBro Carsten Lange, 'Zur Aufführung von Telemanns Brockes-Passionsoratorium in Frankfurt am Main', in *CahFra*, 142–62.

LanDan Carsten Lange, 'Georg Philipp Telemanns Beziehungen zu Danzig, dargelegt am Beispiel der Matthäuspassion von 1754 ("Danziger Passion")', in *LanSch*, 87–104.

LanFra Carsten Lange, Brit Reipsch and Wolf Hobohm (eds.), *Telemann und Frankreich / Frankreich und Telemann: Bericht über die International Wissenschaftliche Konferenz, Magdeburg, 12. bis 14. März 1998, anläßlich der 14. Magdeburger Telemann-Festtage* (Hildesheim: Olms, 2009).

LanHän Carsten Lange and Brit Reipsch (eds.), *Telemann und Händel: Musikerbeziehungen im 18. Jahrhundert: Bericht über die Internationale Wissenschaftliche Konferenz, Magdeburg, 12. bis 14. März 2008, anlässlich der 19. Magdeburger Telemann-Festtage* (Hildesheim: Olms, 2013).

LanHer Carsten Lange, 'Der Herr ist König: Eine weitere Telemann-Kantate aus Bachs Notenschrank', in *LanBei*, 2:14–21.

LanImp Carsten Lange, Brit Reipsch and Ralph-Jürgen Reipsch (eds.), *Impulse – Transformationen – Kontraste: Georg Philipp Telemann und Carl Philipp Emanuel Bach: Bericht über die Internationale Wissenschaftliche Konferenz, Magdeburg, 17. und 18. März 2014, anlässlich der 22. Magdeburger Telemann-Festtage* (Hildesheim: Olms, 2018).

LanKir Carsten Lange and Brit Reipsch (eds.), *Telemann und Die Kirchenmusik: Bericht über die Internationale Wissenschaftliche Konferenz, Magdeburg, 15. bis 17. März 2006, anlässlich der 18. Magdeburger Telemann-Festtage* (Hildesheim: Olms, 2011).

LanMal Carsten Lange and Brit Reipsch (eds.), *Telemann, der musikalische Maler / Telemann-Kompositionen im Notenarchiv der Sing-Akademie zu Berlin: Bericht über die Internationale Wissenschaftliche Konferenz, Magdeburg, 10. bis 12. März 2004, anlässlich der 17. Magdeburger Telemann-Festtage* (Hildesheim: Olms, 2010).

LanNot Ortrun Landmann, 'Die Dresdner Hofnotisten von ca. 1720 bis ca. 1850. Neue Ermittlungen samt einem Überblick über die bisherigen Untersuchungsergebnisse', in Landmann, *Über das Musikerbe der Sächsischen Staatskapelle: Drei Studien zur Geschichte der Dresdner Hofkapelle und Hofoper anhand ihrer Quellenüberlieferung in der SLUB Dresden*, 2nd edn (Dresden: Qucosa, 2010), nbn-resolving.de/urn:nbn:de:bsz:14-qucosa-38515

LanNou Carsten Lange, 'Georg Philipp Telemanns "Nouveaux Quatuors en Six Suites" (Paris 1738): Eine Sammlung mit Modellcharakter', in *LanFra*, 275–87.

LanPas Carsten Lange, '"Eingemischte Poesien in Telemanns gottesdienstlichen Passionen der 1720er Jahre', in *LanKir*, 416–36.

LanQue Ortrun Landmann, *Die Telemann-Quellen der Sächsischen Landesbibliothek: Handschriften und zeitgenössische Druckausgaben seiner Werke* (Dresden: Sächsische Landesbibliothek, 1983).

LanSch Carsten Lange and Wolf Hobohm (eds.), *Musikkultur in Schlesien zur Zeit von Telemann und Dittersdorf: Berichte der musikwissenschaftlichen Konferenzen in Pszczyna/Pless und Opava/Troppau 1993* (Sinzig: Studio, 2001).

LanSoc Carsten Lange, '"Der geduldige Socrates": Eine Telemann-Oper auf dem Weg zum Repertoirestück', in *LanUmg*, 250–78.

LanTra Carsten Lange, 'Der Affekt der Trauer in Oratorien und Passionen Georg Philipp Telemanns', in *FalTra*, 143–71.

LanUmg Carsten Lange and Brit Reipsch (eds.), *Vom Umgang mit Telemanns Werk einst und jetzt: Telemannrezeption in drei Jahrhunderten: Bericht über die Internationale Wissenschaftliche Konferenz, Magdeburg, 15. und 16. März 2012, anlässlich der 21. Magdeburger Telemann-Festtage* (Hildesheim: Olms, 2017).

LauAri Helmut Lauterwasser, '"Mein Herz ist viel zu schwach, euch zu verlassen": Eine neu entdeckte Arie von Georg Philipp Telemann', *Concerto*, No. 277 (2018), 22–25.

LawCha Colin Lawson, 'Telemann and the Chalumeau', *Early Music* 9/3 (1981), 312–19.

LebCan Ann Le Bar, '"The Public would surely welcome such a work": Telemann and the Career of the Cantata as a Consumer Good', in *HirKan*, 288–308.

LebDom Ann Le Bar, 'The Domestication of Vocal Music in Enlightenment Hamburg', *Journal of Musicological Research* 19/2 (2000), 97–134.

LeiTra Ulrich Leisinger, 'Georg Philipp Telemanns "Trauer-Sinfonien"', in *FleTod*, 245–52.

LesCon Philippe Lecat, 'Georg Philipp Telemann im Concert spirituel', in *LanFra*, 57–73.

LölTod Herbert Lölkes, *Ramlers "Der Tod Jesu" in den Vertonungen von Graun und Telemann: Kontext, Werkgestalt, Rezeption* (Kassel: Bärenreiter, 1999).

LütDon Laurenz Lütteken, 'Sprachverlust und Sprachfindung: Die Donnerode und Telemanns Spätwerk', in Annegrit Laubenthal and Kara Kusan-Windweh (eds.), *Studien zur Musikgeschichte: Eine Festschrift für Ludwig Finscher* (Kassel: Bärenreiter, 1995), 206–21.

LütMon Laurenz Lütteken, *Das Monologische als Denkform in der Musik zwischen 1760 und 1785* (Tübingen: Niemeyer, 1998).

LynOpe Robert D. Lynch, 'Opera in Hamburg 1718–1738: A Study of the Libretto and Musical Style', PhD dissertation, New York University, 1979.

LynOtt Robert D. Lynch, 'Händels "Ottone": Telemanns Hamburger Bearbeitung', *Händel-Jahrbuch* 27 (1981), 117–39.

MaeAdm Willi Maertens, 'Georg Philipp Telemanns Hamburger "Admiralitätsmusik" 1723', in *FleAuf*, 1:106–24.

MaeEng Willi Maertens, 'G. Ph. Telemanns "englische Trauermusik" auf den Tod König Georgs II. Von Grossbritannien', *Ars musica* 5 (1992), 18–25.

MaeHam Willi Maertens, 'Johann Georg Hamann der Ältere (1697–1733): Der Typ des Literaten-Journalisten als Gelegenheitsdichter Telemanns', in *HobAuf*, 205–30.

MaeInt Willi Maertens, 'Georg Philipp Telemann und seine Interpreten Margaretha Susanna und Joachim Kayser', in *FleRen*, 68–85.

MaeKap Willi Maertens, *Georg Philipp Telemanns sogenannte Hamburgische Kapitainsmusiken (1723–1765)* (Wilhelmshaven: Noetzel, 1988).

MaeMar Willi Maertens, 'Marginalien zu Georg Philipp Telemanns "Kapitainsmusiken"', in *HirSpu*, 13–25.

MaeOrc Willi Maertens, 'Georg Philipp Telemanns Orchester-Suite mit Hornquartett: Zu ihrer Deutung und Bedeutung', in *NeuBil*, 64–80.

MaePlä Willi Maertens, '"Ich hoffete aufs Licht": Pläyoder für eine Gelegenheitsmusik G. Ph. Telemanns', in *Festschrift Martin Ruhnke zum 65. Geburtstag* (Neuhausen-Stuttgart: Hänssler, 1986), 235–54.

MaeZel Willi Maertens, 'Georg Philipp Telemann und Jan Dismas Zelenka', in *BasFre*, 1:46–56.

MahPar Christoph-Hellmut Mahling, 'Telemann und Paris', in *BasFre*, 2:61–70.

MarMat Hans Joachim Marx, 'Telemann aus der Sicht Matthesons', in *BasFre*, 2:36–42.

MauAlm Michael Maul, 'Telemann oder Hoffmann? Überlegungen zur Leipziger Almira-Oper', in *LanHän*, 147–62.

MauLei Michael Maul, *Barockoper in Leipzig (1693–1720)*, 2 vols (Freiburg im Breisgau: Rombach, 2009).

MauTho Michael Maul, '"alle 14. Tage ein Stück" für die Thomaskirche: Überlegungen zu Telemanns Leipziger Jahren', in *Die Tonkunst* 11/4 (2017), 441–48.

MauNar Michael Maul, 'Vom Ansbacher Hof ins Leipziger Opernhaus: Telemanns Leipziger "Narcissus" (1709): Eine Fallstudie zur "bürgerlichen" Bearbeitungspraxis höfischer Libretti', in *CarSpa*, 83–100.

MenBil Werner Menke, *Georg Philipp Telemann: Leben, Werk und Umwelt in Bilddokumenten* (Wilhelmshaven: Florian Noetzel, 1987).

MenFac Werner Menke, 'Telemann als Verfechter deutscher übersetzung der italienischen musikalischen Fachausdrücke', in *Zeitschrift für Musik* 108/7 (1941), 441–42.

MenRic Werner Menke, 'Michel Richey und Telemann', in *BasFre*, 2:43–52.

MenVok Werner Menke, *Das Vokalwerk Georg Philipp Telemanns: Überlieferung und Zeitfolge* (Kassel: Bärenreiter, 1942).

MieFre Wolfgang Miersemann and Gudrun Busch (eds.), "Sing dem Herrn nah und fern": 300 Jahre Freylinghausensches Gesangbuch (Tübingen, 2008).

MitBla Mitteilungsblatt der Internationalen Telemann-Gesellschaft e.V. (newsletter of the International Telemann Society).

MooAuf Silvan Moosmüller, Boris Previšić and Laure Spaltenstein (eds.), *Stimmungen und Vielstimmigkeit der Aufklärung* (Göttingen: Wallstein, 2017).

NeuBil *Beiträge zu einem neuen Telemannbild: Konferenzbericht der 1. Magdeburger Telemann-Festtage vom 3. bis 5. November 1962* (Magdeburg: Arbeitskreis 'Georg Philipp Telemann' im deutschen Kulturbund Magdeburg, 1963).

NeuBot Jürgen Neubacher, 'Göttinger Botanik und Hamburgs "Gahrtenlust": Ein unbekannter Telemann-Brief der Bayerischen Staatsbibliothek aus dem Füllhorn der Kalliope', *Auskunft: Zeitschrift für Bibliothek, Archiv und Information in Norddeutschland* 23/2–3 (2003), 172–80.

NeuEng Jürgen Neubacher, 'Zur Aufführung von Telemanns Engel-Jahrgang und zu Zensurbestrebungen für kirchenmusikalische Texte in Hamburg', in *ReiBac*, 144– 57.

NeuKir Jürgen Neubacher, *Georg Philipp Telemanns Hamburger Kirchenmusik und ihre Aufführungsbedingungen (1721–1767)* (Hildesheim: Olms, 2009).

NeuLie Jürgen Neubacher, 'Zwischen Choralkantate und Odenkomposition: Telemanns Hamburger *Lieder-Andachten-Jahrgang* von 1743/44', in *NowVok*, 229–51.

NeuQue Jürgen Neubacher, 'Eine neue Quelle und neue Überlegungen zur Datierung von Telemanns Lied-Jahrgang', in *MitBla* 29 (2015), 18–22.

NeuTra Jürgen Neubacher, 'Telemanns Hamburger Trauermusiken für römisch-deutsche Kaiser aus den Jahren 1740, 1745 und 1765 (TVWV 4:10, 4:13 und 4:16)', in *FalTra*, 111–42.

NoaDar Elisabeth Noack, 'G. Ph. Telemanns Beziehungen zu Darmstädter Musikern', in *FleAuf*, 2:13–17.

NowVok Adolf Nowak and Andreas Eichhorn (eds.), *Telemanns Vokalmusik: Über Texte, Formen und Werke* (Hildesheim: Olms, 2008).

OefEis Claus Oefner, *Telemann in Eisenach: Die Eisenacher Musikpflege im frühen 18. Jahrhundert* (Eisenach: Kreiskommission zur Erforschung der Geschichte, 1980).

OefTex Claus Oefner, 'Johann Friedrich Helbig und Hermann Ulrich von Lingen: Zwei Eisenacher Textdichter Telemanns', in Günter Fleischhauer, Wolf Hobohm and Willi Maertens (eds.), *Telemann und Eisenach: Drei Studien* (Magdeburg: Arbeitskreis Georg Philipp Telemann im Kulturbund der DDR, 1976), 17–59.

OrtEre Daniel Ortuño-Stühring, 'Musik als soziales Ereignis: Zur Identitätskonstruktion in freien Reichsstädten des 18. Jahrhunderts am Beispiel von Georg Philipp Telemanns Einweihungsmusik für die "neue große St. Michaeliskirche" (Hamburg 1762)', *Die Musikforschung* 66/4 (2013), 339–61.

PayBac Ian Payne, 'Telemann's Musical Style c. 1709–c. 1730 and J. S. Bach: The Evidence of Borrowing', *Bach* 30/1 (1999), 42–64.

PayCap Ian Payne, 'Capital Gains: Another Händel Borrowing from Telemann?', *The Musical Times* 142, No. 1874 (2001), 33–42.

PayFra Ian Payne, 'Telemann's Fragmentary Ensemble Version of Keyboard Ouverture TWV 32:16 and the "Consort" Element in pre-c. 1730 Keyboard Suites', *Bach* 32/1 (2001), 44–72.

PayFre Ian Payne, 'Telemann and the French Style Revisited: Transformative Imitation in the Ensemble Suites (TWV 55)', *Bach* 37/2 (2006), 45–80.

PayOve Ian Payne, 'Telemann's Fragmentary Overture-Suites (TWV 55): Some Problems of Transmission and Reconstruction', in *ReiBac*, 214–42.

PecOpe Mary Adelaide Peckham, 'The Operas of Georg Philipp Telemann', PhD dissertation, Columbia University, 1972.

PegDam Rashid-S. Pegah, '"Weg, weg du Cerberus": Die beiden Fassungen des Telemannschen "Damon" im Vergleich', in *LanFra*, 196–209.

PegOrp Raschid-Sascha Pegah, '"Die wunderbare Beständigkeit der Liebe" oder Von Paris nach Berlin: Zur Rezeption des Orphée-Librettos von Michel du Boulay in Deutschland', in *ReiBac*, 158–91.

PegPas Rashid-S. Pegah, '"Pastorelle en Musique" von Telemann und seine Textvorlage von Molière', in *LanMal*, 453–64.

PegUff Rashid-S. Pegah, '"Archi-phonascus noster Telemannus": Zur Telemann-Rezeption der Gebrüder v. Uffenbach', in *LanUmg*, 9–22.

PetBio Richard Petzoldt, *Georg Philipp Telemann: Leben und Werk* (Leipzig: Deutscher Verlag für Musik, 1967). English trans. by Horace Fitzpatrick as *Georg Philipp Telemann* (London: Benn, 1974).

PfaLie Marc-Roderich Pfau, 'Kritische Überlegungen zu Jürgen Neubachers Neudatierung von Telemanns *Lied-Jahrgang*', in *MitBla* 30 (2016), 18–20.

PfaNeu Marc-Roderich Pfau, 'Telemann in der Neuen Welt: Das Kirchweihfest in Lancaster/Pennsylvania im Jahr 1766', in *MitBla* 29 (2015), 23–31.

PfaPro Marc-Roderich Pfau, 'Telemanns Probe-Music für das Leipziger Thomaskantorat im Jahre 1722', *Bach-Jahrbuch* 104 (2018), 95–111.

PfaSto Marc-Roderich Pfau, 'Zum Stolbergischen Jahrgang Telemanns (1736/37)', in *MitBla* 30 (2016), 21–36.

PfaTex Marc-Roderich Pfau, 'Neue Textquellen zu Kirchenjahrgängen Telemanns', in *MitBla* 24 (2010), 26–28.

PfeFas Rüdiger Pfeiffer, 'Fasch und Telemann: Zu einem Musikerverhältnis', in *LanBei*, 2:28–33.

PhiPro Michael Philipp, *Läppische Schildereyen? Untersuchungen zur Konzeption von Programmusik im 18. Jahrhundert* (Frankfurt am Main: Peter Lang, 1998).

PisFra Danièle Pistone, 'Telemann und Frankreich im 19. und 20. Jahrhundert', in *LanFra*, 210–21.

PoeBeh Ute Poetzsch, '"Ein gelehrter Amtmann zu Eichenbarleben": Gottfried Behrndt als Dichter für Georg Philipp Telemann', in *ReiZwi*, 99–136.

PoeBro Ute Poetzsch, '"Teure Freunde": Georg Philipp Telemann und Barthold Heinrich Brockes', in *Göttinger Händel-Beiträge* 19 (2018), 65–76.

PoeEdi Ute Poetzsch, 'Die Editionen der Werke Georg Philipp Telemanns', in Reinmar Emans and Ulrich Krämer (eds.), *Musikeditionen im Wandel der Geschichte* (Berlin/Boston: De Gruyter, 2015), 178–96.

PoeFak Ute Poetzsch, 'Fakten zu Telemanns "Zellischem" oder "Großem oratorischen Jahrgang"', in *LanImp*, 321–27.

PoeFor Ute Poetzsch, '"Schrift-mäszige Gedanken" und "Gemüts-Bewegungen": Die Fortsetzung des Harmonischen Gottesdienstes', in *JahExt*, 235–48.

PoeGot Ute Poetzsch, 'Das Oratorium im Gottesdienst zwischen "Bestück" und Drama', in *SteMet*, 889–98.

PoeKir Ute Poetzsch-Seban, *Die Kirchenmusik von Georg Philipp Telemann und Erdmann Neumeister: Zur Geschichte der protestantischen*

Kirchenkantate in der ersten Hälfte des 18. Jahrhunderts (Beeskow: Ortus, 2006).

PoeOra Ute Poetzsch, 'Oratorien als Kirchenmusik', *Die Tonkunst* 11/4 (2017), 480–85.

PoeOrd Ute Poetzsch, 'Ordentliche Kirchenmusiken, genannt Oratorium: Telemanns oratorische Jahrgänge', in *EbeKon*, 2:317–24.

PoeSel Ute Poetzsch, 'Zur Aufführungsgeschichte von Telemanns Passionsoratorium "Seliges Erwägen', in *FalSel*, 108–24.

PoeSie Ute Poetzsch, 'Georg Philipp Telemanns Oper "Der Sieg der Schönheit" in Braunschweig', in Friedhelm Brusniak (ed.), *Barockes Musiktheater im mitteldeutschen Raum im 17. und 18. Jahrhundert: 8. Arolser Barock-Festspiele 1993, Tagungsbericht* (Cologne: Studio, 1994), 63–74.

PoeStr Ute Poetzsch, 'Der Streit um das Libretto zu Telemanns Oper "Sieg der Schönheit"', in *HobVol*, 392–409.

PoeTon Ute Poetzsch-Seban, 'In welcher Tonart dachte Telemann?: Transpositionsverhältnisse in Telemann-Autographen und anderen handschriftlichen Quellen seiner Kirchenmusik', in *GutAuf*, 143–53.

PoeZer 'Telemann-Werke in der Zerbster Concert-Stube', in Konstanze Musketa and Barbara Reul (eds.), *Johann Friedrich Fasch und sein Wirken für Zerbst: Bericht über die Internationale Wissenschaftliche Konferenz am 18. und 19. April 1997 im Rahmen der 5. Internationalen Fasch-Festtage in Zerbst* (Dessau: Anhaltische Verlagsgesellschaft, 1997), 71–82.

PohUrh Hansjörg Pohlmann, *Die Frühgeschichte des musikalischen Urheberrechts* (Kassel: Bärenreiter, 1962).

PolLus Eva Maria Pollerus, 'Lustiger Mischmasch? Ein frischer Blick auf Telemanns Musik für Tasteninstrumente', *Concerto*, No. 278 (2018), 20–25.

RacSin Werner Rackwitz (ed.), *Georg Philipp Telemann: Singen ist das Fundament zur Music in allen Dingen: Eine Dokumentensammlung* (Leipzig: Reclam, 1981).

RamBio Siegbert Rampe, *Georg Philipp Telemann und seine Zeit* (Laaber: Laaber, 2017).

RamHän Siegbert Rampe, 'Händels Verhältnis zu Telemann', in Siegbert Rampe (ed.), *Georg Friedrich Händel und seine Zeit* (Laaber: Laaber Verlag, 2009), 269–81.

RatAle Markus Rathey, 'Von Gerichtsposaunen und Erdbeben: Telemanns und Bachs Kompositionen nach Texten von Christian Wilhelm Alers', in *LanImp*, 193–213.

RatDon Markus Rathey, 'Carl Philipp Emanuel Bachs *Donnerode*', *Archiv für Musikwissenschaft* 66/4 (2009): 286–305.

RatRic Jürgen Rathje, '"Weil nur die Freyheit mir die Flügel rege macht": Michael Richeys Musikalische Gedichte', in *NowVok*, 85–102.

RatRom Markus Rathey, 'Georg Philipp Telemann als Kommissionär für Johan Helmich Romans Flötensonaten von 1727', *Die Musikforschung* 57 (2004), 133–40.

RatOmp Jürgen Rathje, 'Die rühmliche Liebes-Ueberwindung des Alcides: "Omphale" bei Antoine Houdar de La Motte und Georg Philipp Telemann', in *LanFra*, 222–37.

RatSon Jürgen Rathje, 'Telemanns "Sonnet auf weyland Herrn Capellmeister Bach"', in *ReiBac*, 24–33.

ReiAma Brit Reipsch, 'Telemann-Motetten im Sammelband Nr. 326 der Amalienbibliothek: Überlegungen zum Gattungsbegriff bei Telemann', in *ThoAuf*, 94–102.

ReiAnn Brit Reipsch, 'Annotationen zu Georg Philipp Telemann, Johann Friedrich Helbig und Johann Sebastian Bach', in *ReiBac*, 63–85.

ReiAuf Ralph-Jürgen Reipsch, 'Zu Aufführungen von Kirchenmusiken Georg Philipp Telemanns in den Jahren 1770 und 1771 in Hamburg', in *LanImp*, 294–313.

ReiBac Brit Reipsch and Wolf Hobohm (eds.), *Telemann und Bach; Telemann-Beiträge* (Hildesheim: Olms, 2005).

ReiBea Ralph-Jürgen Reipsch, 'Georg Philipp Telemanns Oratorium "Die Auferstehung und Himmelfahrt Jesu" (TVWV 6:6) in der Bearbeitung von Georg Michael Telemann', in *ThoAuf*, 137–54.

ReiBeo Ralph-Jürgen Reipsch, 'Beobachtungen an Telemanns Kirchenmusik nach 1750', in *HirWil*, 85–108.

ReiBib Brit Reipsch and Ralph-Jürgen Reipsch (compilers), *Bibliographische Handreichung zu Telemanns kirchenmusikalischen Jahrgängen (ab Erscheinungsjahr 1990)*, Zentrum für Telemann-Pflege und -Forschung Magdeburg: www.telemann.org/telemann-zentrum/bibliographie/spezialbibliographien.html

ReiBio Ralph-Jürgen Reipsch, 'Unbekannte Biographien Georg Philipp Telemanns: Eine autobiographische Skizze und ein zweiter deutsch-französischer Lebenslauf', *Die Musikforschung* 67/4 (2014), 318–40.

ReiBlu Ralph-Jürgen Reipsch, 'Telemanns "Bluhmen-Liebe"', in *LanBei*, 2:34–46.

ReiCal Ralph-Jürgen Reipsch, 'Calchedon/Calcedono: Generalbaßlauten in Werken Telemanns', in *GutAuf*, 197–217.

ReiCan Brit Reipsch, '"Cantaten in Telemanns Hamburger Kirchenmusik der 1720er Jahre: Zur Genese des "Brandenburg-Jahrgangs" und des "Harmonischen Gottes-Dienstes", in *LanKir*, 290–308.

ReiDan Brit Reipsch, 'Ende des Rätselratens: Georg Philipp Telemanns Trauermusik "Du aber, Daniel, gehe hin" neu gesichtet', *Concerto*, No. 191 (2004), 23–24.

ReiDie Brit Reipsch, '"Damit er von einem Meister, und nicht von allerley Pfuschern bestände": Neue Überlegungen zu Manuskripten Johann Caspar Dietels', in Rainer Kaiser (ed.), *Bach und seine mitteldeutschen Zeitgenossen: Bericht über das Internationale*

Musikwissenschaftliche Kolloquium, Erfurt und Arnstadt 13. bis 16. Januar 2000 (Eisenach: Wagner, 2001), 161–78.

ReiDok Ralph-Jürgen Reipsch, 'Dokumente zu Georg Philipp Telemanns "Bluhmen-Liebe", in Joachim Fischer, Dietrich Roth and Gabriele Werthmann (eds.), *Das Moller-Florilegium des Hans Simon Holtzbecker (2)* (Berlin: Kulturstiftung der Länder; Hamburg: Staats- und Universitätsbibliothek Hamburg Carl von Ossietzky, 2001), 60–79.

ReiEbe Brit Reipsch, '". . . nach Anleitung der Poesie zu sehr mit Mahlereyen überladen": Zu Christoph Daniel Ebelings Telemannbild', in *LanMal*, 126–45.

ReiFra Ralph-Jürgen Reipsch and Wolf Hobohm (eds.), *Telemann und Frankreich – Frankreich und Telemann* (Oschersleben: Ziethen, 1998).

ReiGed Ralph-Jürgen Reipsch, 'Telemanns Gedichte auf das "Lübecker Wunderkind" Christian Henrich Heineken', in *MitBla* 32 (2018), 37–47.

ReiHel Brit Reipsch, 'Musik für Hof und zum Privatgebrauch: Ein Jahrgang von Georg Philipp Telemann auf Texte von Johann Friedrich Helbig', in *CarSpa*, 136–53.

ReiJah Brit Reipsch, 'Zum "Jahrgangsdenken" Georg Philipp Telemanns – dargelegt an Beispielen geistlicher Kantaten Eisenacher Dichter', in *BruNun*, 63–76.

ReiKlo Ralph-Jürgen Reipsch, 'Telemann und Klopstock: Annotationen', in *HobBei*, 104–30.

ReiLin Brit Reipsch, 'Die Telemannquellen in Goldbach: Der "erste Lingensche Jahrgang"', in *HobBei*, 64–95.

ReiLob Brit Reipsch, '"Ueber etliche Teutsche Componisten": Nur ein kollegialer Lobspruch Telemanns?', in *LanHän*, 55–63.

ReiMag Ralph-Jürgen Reipsch, 'Telemann-Pflege in Magdeburg vom Ende der 1920er Jahre bis 1945', in *LanUmg*, 219–49.

ReiMes Ralph-Jürgen Reipsch, 'Zwischen Tradition und Innovation: Telemanns Vertonungen aus Klopstocks Messias TVWV 6:4a/b', in *JahExt*, 71–91.

ReiMir Brit Reipsch, 'Georg Philipp Telemanns Oper "Miriways": Bemerkungen zu Libretto und Partitur', in *HirSpu*, 26–35.

ReiMol Ralph-Jürgen Reipsch, 'Telemann und der "Junker von Moldenit": Die unbekannte Widmung der Hamburger *Quadri* von 1730', in *MitBla* 14 (2003), 23–28.

ReiMot Brit Reipsch, 'Bemerkungen zu Georg Philipp Telemanns Motetten', in *EbeKon*, 2:308–16.

ReiOde Ralph-Jürgen Reipsch, 'Strophische Textformen und ihre musikalische Umsetzung: Zwei geistliche Oden in Telemanns Kirchenmusik um 1760', in *NowVok*, 267–311.

ReiPar Ralph-Jürgen Reipsch, 'Die Arienparodien des Johann Friedrich

Armand von Uffenbach: Eine Bestandsaufnahme', in *HobVol*, 352–91.

ReiPas Ralph-Jürgen Reipsch, 'Notizen zur Überlieferungssituation der oratorischen Passionen Telemanns: Neues zur Markuspassion 1759 TVWV 5:44', in *LanHän*, 227–56.

ReiQua Ralph-Jürgen Reipsch, 'Zur Rezeption von Telemanns Kompositionen für Traversflöte im Umfeld von Quantz: Neues aus dem Notenarchiv der Sing-Akademie zu Berlin', in Boje E. Hans Schmuhl and Ute Omonsky (eds.), *Flötenmusik in Geschichte und Aufführungspraxis zwischen 1650 und 1850* (Augsburg: Wißner, 2009), 249–73.

ReiRec Ralph-Jürgen Reipsch, 'Telemanns "Jahrgang ohne Recitativ"', in *LanKir*, 340–68.

ReiRez Ralph-Jürgen Reipsch, 'Telemanns Rezitativtechnik: Untersuchungen am vokalen Spätwerk', in Hermann Danuser and Tobias Plebuch (eds.), *Musik als Text: Bericht über den International Kongreß der Gesellschaft für Musikforschung, Freiburg im Breisgau 1993*, 2 vols (Kassel: Bärenreiter, 1993), 2:283–94.

ReiSer Ralph-Jürgen Reipsch, 'Telemanns Serenata auf den Tod August des Starken: Eine "bürgerliche" Gedenkmusik?', in *CarSpa*, 192–209.

ReiSic Brit Reipsch, 'Anmerkungen zum sogenannten *Sicilianischen Jahrgang* von Georg Philipp Telemann', in *CahFra*, 74–92.

ReiSin Ralph-Jürgen Reipsch, 'Der Telemann-Bestand des Notenarchivs der Sing-Akademie zu Berlin: Ein Überblick', in *LanMal*, 275–363.

ReiSpä Ralph-Jürgen Reipsch, 'Neue Ufer: Die Kirchenmusik des Spätwerks', *Die Tonkunst* 11/4 (2017), 501–07.

ReiTag Brit Reipsch, '"Jubelnd und singend wir schreiten": Telemanns "Tageszeiten" im Kontext von sozialdemokratischer Arbeiterbewegung und volkstümlichem Konzert', in *LanUmg*, 169–84.

ReiUff Ralph-Jürgen Reipsch, 'Johann Friedrich Armand von Uffenbach als Dichter von Kantatenjahrgängen: Eine Untersuchung in Hinblick auf Telemanns Kantatenschaffen', in *CahFra*, 102–41.

ReiUnb Ralph-Jürgen Reipsch and Steven Zohn, 'Unbekannte Instrumentalmusik von Georg Philipp Telemann: Zur Vergabe neuer TWV-Nummern', *Die Musikforschung* 59 (2006), 366–69.

ReiVer Brit Reipsch, 'Vertriebsstrategien eines Musikverlags im 18. Jahrhundert am Beispiel ausgewählter Druckwerke Georg Philipp Telemanns', in *JahExt*, 317–32.

ReiWor Ingo Reimann, 'Wie Wormstedt seinen Telemann wieder entdeckte', in *MitBla* 18 (2005), 21–23.

ReiZus Ralph-Jürgen Reipsch, 'Telemann's "Zuschrift" der "Vier und zwanzig, theils ernsthaften, theils scherzenden, Oden" (Hamburg 1741) an Scheibe: Eine Satire auf Mizler?', in *KreBio*, 231–60.

ReiZwi Brit Reipsch and Carsten Lange (eds.), *Zwischen Musikwissenschaft und Musikleben: Festschrift für Wolf Hobohm zum 60. Geburtstag am 8. Januar 1998* (Hildesheim: Georg Olms, 2001).

RetTro Simon Rettelbach, *Trompeten, Hörner und Klarinetten in der in Frankfurt am Main überlieferten 'Ordentlichen Kirchenmusik' Georg Philipp Telemanns* (Tutzing: Schneider, 2008).

RicHag Lukas Richter, 'Telemanns Lieder nach Hagedorn', in *FleDic*, 1:87–97.

RobHan John H. Roberts, 'Handel's Borrowings from Telemann: An Inventory', in *Göttinger Händel-Beiträge* 1 (1984), 147–71.

RodRet R. Rodman, 'Retrospection and Reduction: Modal Middlegrounds and Foreground Elaborations in Telemann's "Zwanzig kleine Fugen"', *Indiana Theory Review* 15 (1994), 105–37.

RolFor Romain Rolland, 'L'Autobiographie d'un illustre oublié', in Rolland, *Voyage musical aux pays du passé* (Paris: Edouard-Joseph, 1919). English trans. as 'Telemann: A Forgotten Master' in David Ewen (ed.), *Romain Rolland's Essays on Music* (New York: Dover, 1959), 121–44.

RosRec Lois Rosow, 'French Baroque Recitative as an Expression of Tragic Declamation', *Early Music* 11/4 (1983), 468–79.

RübAut Elisabeth Rübcke, 'Die Autobiographie des Plöner Pastors Andreas Telemann aus dem Jahr 1745', in *ReiBac*, 129–43.

RufKla Wolfgang Ruf (ed.), *Musik als Klangrede: Festschrift zum 70. Geburtstag von Günter Fleischhauer* (Cologne: Böhlau, 2001).

RuhDon Martin Ruhnke, 'Telemanns Umarbeitung des Textes zur Serenade "Don Quichotte auf der Hochzeit des Camacho"', in Klaus Hortschansky and Konstanze Musketa (eds.), *Georg Friedrich Händel: Ein Lebensinhalt: Gedenkschrift für Bernd Baselt* (1934–1993) (Halle: Händel-Haus, 1995), 369–80.

RuhFin Martin Ruhnke, 'Zu Ludwig Finschers neuestem Telemann-Bild', *Musica* 24 (1970), 340–45.

RuhFug Martin Ruhnke, 'Zu Telemanns "Fugues légères et petits jeux"', in *GutTel*, 100–07.

RuhKom Martin Ruhnke, 'Komische Elemente in Telemanns Oper und Intermezzi', in Christoph-Hellmut Mahling and Sigrid Wiesmann (eds.), *Bericht über den internationalen musikwissenschaftlichen Kongreß Bayreuth 1981* (Kassel: Barenreiter, 1984), 94–107.

RuhOpe Martin Ruhnke, 'Telemanns Hamburger Opern und ihre französischen und italienischen Vorbilder', in *FloFrü*, 9–27.

RuhPar Martin Ruhnke, 'Die Pariser Telemann-Drucke und die Brüder Le Clerc', in Kurt Dorfmüller (ed.), *Quellenstudien zur Musik: Wolfgang Schmieder zum 70. Geburtstag* (Frankfurt: Peters, 1972), 149–60.

RuhPas Martin Ruhnke, 'Zu Telemanns Matthäuspassion 1746', in *RufKla*, 128–44.

RuhQua Martin Ruhnke, 'Telemanns Beiträge zu den Solfeggi von Quantz', in *ReiZwi*, 10–18.

RuhSel Martin Ruhnke, 'Telemann und seine selbstverfaßten Texte unter Berücksichtigung des Passionsoratoriums "Seliges Erwägen"', in *FleDic*, 2:27–40.

RuhUmt Martin Ruhnke, 'Zur Hamburger Umtextierung von Telemanns Passionsoratorium "Seliges Erwägen"', in Thomas Kohlhase and Volker Scherliess (eds.), *Festschrift Georg von Dadelsen zum 60. Geburtstag* (Neuhausen-Stuttgart: Hänssler, 1978), 255–69.

RuhVer Martin Ruhnke, 'Telemann als Musikverleger', in Richard Baum and Wolfgang Rehm (eds.), *Musik und Verlag: Karl Vötterle zum 65. Geburtstag am 12. April 1968* (Kassel: Bärenreiter, 1968), 502–17.

SatEss Kota Sato, 'Zur Datierung der "Essercizii Musici"', in *MitBla* 27 (2013), 24–30.

SatFra Kota Sato, 'Telemanns Rezitativ im vermischten Geschmack: Französische Elemente im *Französischen Jahrgang* und deren Wirkung', *Ongakugaku* 60 (2014), 30–51.

SatNot Kota Sato, 'Telemanns Notenstich und die Chronologie seiner Werke', in *LanUmg*, 58–66.

SatRez Kota Sato, 'Die Rezitative in Telemanns Lukaspassion 1760 und deren Bearbeitungen', in *LanImp*, 274–93.

SawKan Elena Sawtschenko, 'Die Rezeption der Kantatenzyklen Georg Philipp Telemanns am Zerbster Hof und ihre Auswirkungen auf das Kantatenschaffen von Johann Friedrich Fasch', in *NowVok*, 353–90.

SawSim Elena Sawtschenko, 'Gottfried Simonis als Dichter der "Concertjahrganges" von Georg Philipp Telemann: Überlegungen zur Biographie des Autors und zur theologischen Position der Texte', in *LanKir*, 208–27.

SchAuf Harald Schultze, 'Telemann und die fromme Aufklärung: Beobachtungen zu den Dichtungen "Die Donnerode" und "Der Tod Jesu"', in *FalSel*, 66–86.

SchBac Hans-Joachim Schulze, '"Fließende Leichtigkeit" und "arbeitsame Vollstimmigkeit": Georg Philipp Telemann und die Musikerfamile Bach', in *BasFre*, 1:34–40.

SchBro Klaus Schaefer, 'Aktuelle Aspekte in den durch Telemann vertonten Texten von Barthold Hinrich Brockes', in *FleDic*, 1:68–74.

SchBru Martin Schneider, 'Bruchlinien der Intergration: Konkurrierende Modelle politischer Gemeinschaft in den Libretti Telemanns Kapitänsmusiken', in *JahExt*, 159–73.

SchDen Peter Schmitz, 'Planmäßige Auswahl und Nationalangelegenheit? Bemerkungen zu den Telemann-Editionen im Rahmen der "Denkmäler deutscher Tonkunst"', in *LanUmg*, 150–68.

SchFra Herbert Schneider, 'Telemanns französischer Stil unter interkultureller Perspektive: Zum Stiltransfer und zur

Stiltransformation im "Hochzeit=Divertissement" und im "Orpheus"', in *LanFra*, 93–118.

SchGlo Dorothea Schröder, '"Die Hamburgischen Glockenspiele": Ein Satz aus Telemanns Alster-Ouvertüre als Dokument einer alten Hamburger Musiktradition', in *CarSpa*, 160–72.

SchHar Bernhard Schrammek (ed.), *Zur Geschichte und Aufführungspraxis der Harmoniemusik* (Augsburg: Wissner; Michaelstein: Stiftung Kloster Michaelstein, 2006).

SchKat Joachim Schlichte, *Thematischer Katalog der kirchlichen Musikhandschriften des 17. und 18. Jahrhunderts in der Stadt- und Universitätsbibliothek Frankfurt am Main* (Frankfurt am Main: Klostermann, 1979).

SchKla Käte Schaefer-Schmuck, *Georg Philipp Telemann als Klavierkomponist* (Borna-Leipzig: Noske, 1934).

SchSon David Schulenberg, 'The Sonate auf Concertenart: A Postmodern Invention?', in Gregory Butler (ed.), *J. S. Bach's Concerted Ensemble Music: The Concerto*, Bach Perspectives 7 (Champaign: University of Illinois Press, 2007), 55–96.

SchTel Hans-Joachim Schulze, 'Telemann–Pisendel–Bach: Zu einem unbekannten Bach-Autograph', in *FleBed*, 2:73–77.

SchTex Tatjana Schabalina, 'Textfunde in Sankt Petersburg: Unbekanntes Passionsoratorium von Telemann aus dem Jahr 1731', in *MitBla* 26 (2012), 25–35.

SeiBio Max Seiffert (ed.), *Georg Philipp Telemann: Der Tag des Gerichts, Ino*, Denkmäler Deutscher Tonkunst, vol. 28 (Leipzig: Breitkopf & Härtel, 1907).

SeiIno Wilhelm Seidel, 'Die Metamorphose der Ino: Ihr Mythos in Telemanns dramatischer Kantate', in *LanMal*, 11–32.

SeiMat Natalia Seifas, 'Mattheson und Telemann: Eine vergleichende Analyse ihrer ästhetischen Ansichten', in *FleBed*, 2:21–30.

SeiMus Max Seiffert, 'G. Ph. Telemann's "Musique de table" als Quelle für Händel', in *Bulletin de la société "Union Musicologique"* 4 (1924), 1–28. Revised in *Georg Philipp Telemann (1681–1767): Musique de table: Ausführungen zu Band LXI und LXII der Denkmäler deutscher Tonkunst, Erste Folge: Beihefte zu den Denkmälern deutscher Tonkunst II* (Leipzig: Breitkopf & Härtel, 1927; repr. Graz: Akademische Druck- und Verlagsanstalt, 1960).

SenHan Jiří Senhal, 'Hannakische Musik in der Zeit Georg Philipp Telemanns', in *FleBed*, 1:81–88.

SieLeb Ulrich Siegele, 'Im Blick von Bach auf Telemann: Arten, ein Leben zu betrachten. Mit einem Anhang von Roman Fischer und Ulrich Siegele: Maria Catharina Textor: Georg Philipp Telemanns zweite Frau und ihre Familie', in *KreBio*, 46–89.

SieSel Ulrich Siegele, 'Zum Aufbau von Telemanns Passionsoratorium "Seliges Erwägen"', in *FalSel*, 125–55.

SieTel Walther Siegmund-Schultze, *Georg Philipp Telemann* (Leipzig: VEB Bibliographisches Institut, 1980).

StaCha Susanne Staral, 'Chalumeau und Violetta im Vokalwerk von Georg Philipp Telemann: Überlegungen und Aufführungspraxis', in *ThoAuf*, 69–85.

SteFrü Wolfram Steude, 'Zum kirchenmusikalischen Frühschaffen Georg Philipp Telemanns', in *HobWer*, 1:35–47.

SteHam Brian Douglas Stewart, 'Georg Philipp Telemann in Hamburg: Social and Cultural Background and Its Musical Expression', PhD dissertation, Stanford University, 1985.

SteMet Johann Anselm Steiger and Sandra Richter (eds.), *Hamburg: Eine Metropolregion zwischen Früher Neuzeit und Aufklärung* (Berlin: Akademie, 2012).

StePol Zofia Stęszewska, 'Polnische Elemente in der Musik Georg Philipp Telemanns', in *FleBed*, 1:56–69.

SteSel Renate Steiger, 'Zum theologischen Verständnis von Telemanns Passionsoratorium "Seliges Erwägen"', in *FalSel*, 156–277.

SucTel Ernst Suchalla, 'Telemann: Ein großer Name – eine große Verpflichtung: Georg Michael Telemann und sein Werk "Unterricht im Generalbaßspielen"', in Thomas Ott and Heinz von Loesch (eds.), *Musik befragt, Musik vermittelt: Peter Rummenhöller zum 60. Geburtstag* (Augsburg: Wißner, 1996), 388–404.

SwaBib Jeanne Swack, 'Georg Philipp Telemann', *Oxford Bibliographies Online* (2013), www.oxfordbibliographies.com

SwaCho Jeanne Swack, 'Telemanns Chor': Aufführungspraxis und Stimmensätze in Telemanns Frankfurter Kantaten', in *GutAuf*, 295–314.

SwaErn Jeanne Swack, 'Johann Ernst von Sachsen-Weimar als Auftraggeber: Bemerkungen zum Stil der *Six Sonates à Violon Seul* (1715) von Georg Philipp Telemann', in *HobAuf*, 53–70.

SwaJud Jeanne Swack, 'Antijudaismus in Telemanns Kantate zum Sonntag Judica "Der Kern verdammter Sünder" TVWV 1:303', in *LanKir*, 256–78.

SwaOuv Jeanne Swack, 'A Comparison of Bach's and Telemann's Use of the Ouverture as Theological Signifier', in Gregory Butler (ed.), *J. S. Bach's Concerted Ensemble Music: The Ouverture*, Bach Perspectives 6 (Urbana: University of Illinois Press, 2007), 99–135.

SwaPer Jeanne Swack, 'Performing Forces in Telemann's Frankfurt Cantatas', *Die Tonkunst* 11/4 (2017), 456–62.

SwaRes Jeanne Swack, 'Telemann Research Since 1975', *Acta Musicologica* 64/2 (1992), 139–64.

SwaSol Jeanne Swack, 'The Solo Sonatas of Georg Philipp Telemann: A Study of the Sources and Musical Style', PhD dissertation, Yale University, 1988.

SwaSon Jeanne Swack, 'On the Origins of the *Sonate auf Concertenart*', *Journal of the American Musicological Society* 46/3 (1993): 369–414.

SwaWal Jeanne Swack, 'John Walsh's Publications of Telemann's Sonatas and the Authenticity of "Op. 2"', *Journal of the Royal Musical Association* 118/2 (1993), 223–45.

SynFri Thomas Synofzik, 'Personalstil und Instrumentalidiom: Flötensonaten von Georg Philipp Telemann aus dem Nachlaß Friedrich des Großen', in *SynFri*, 19–37.

SynGen Thomas Synofzik, 'Generalbaßspiel und Bezifferungspraxis bei Georg Philipp Telemann', in *GutAuf*, 337–53.

SzéLit András Székely, 'Literatur und Wahrheit: Erste Erfahrungen mit den Kantaten des Jahrgangs 1748/49 von Telemann', in *ReiZwi*, 89–98.

TadUrb Ulrich Tadday (ed.), *Telemann und die urbanen Milieus der Aufklärung* (Munich: edition text + kritik, 2017).

TalAlb Michael Talbot, 'Albinoni, Telemann and the *Sonata a cinque*', *The Consort* 72 (2016), 69–89.

TalBac Andrew Talle (ed.), *Bach and His German Contemporaries*, Bach Perspectives 9 (Chicago: University of Illinois Press, 2013).

TalViv Michael Talbot, 'Giovanni Battista Vivaldi Copies Music by Telemann: New Light on the Genesis of Antonio Vivaldi's Chamber Concertos', *Studi vivaldiani* 15 (2015), 55–72.

TayBac Nicholas E. Taylor, 'Members of the Bach Family and the Published Church Cantatas of Georg Philipp Telemann', in *LanImp*, 328–36.

TayCan Nicholas E. Taylor, 'The Published Church Cantatas of Georg Philipp Telemann', PhD dissertation, Indiana University, 2014.

TelBri Hans Grosse and Hans Rudolf Jung (eds.), *Georg Philipp Telemann, Briefwechsel* (Leipzig: VEB Deutscher Verlag für Musik, 1972).

ThoAuf Eitelfriedrich Thom and Frieder Zschoch (eds.), *Zur Aufführungspraxis und Interpretation der Vokalmusik Georg Philipp Telemanns: Ein Beitrag zum 225. Todestag: Konferenzbericht der XX. Wissenschaftlichen Arbeitstagung Michaelstein, 19. bis 21. Juni 1992* (Blankenburg/Michaelstein: Institut für Aufführungspraxis, 1995).

ThoPra Eitelfriedrich Thom, 'Telemann und Praetorius: Gedanken zum Wort-Ton-Verhältnis', in *FleDic*, 2:41–50.

TreQua Erich Tremmel, 'Die "Quartflöte", insbesondere in Werken Telemanns', in *ReiBac*, 243–62.

TVWV Werner Menke (ed.), *Thematisches Verzeichnis der Vokalwerke von Georg Philipp Telemann*, 2nd edn, 2 vols (Frankfurt: Klostermann, 1988 and 1995).

TWV Martin Ruhnke (ed.), *Georg Philipp Telemann: Thematisch-Systematisches Verzeichnis seiner Werke (TWV): Instrumentalwerke*, 3 vols (Kassel: Bärenreiter, 1984–99).

ValBio Erich Valentin, *Georg Philipp Telemann, 1681–1767: Eine Biographie*

(Burg bei Magdeburg: Hopfer, 1931; 2nd edn, Hameln: Seifert, 1947; 3rd edn, Kassel: Bärenreiter, 1952).

VieAut Vera Viehöver, 'Wege ins "irdische Paradieß": Erzählter Erfolg in Autobiographien von Georg Philipp Telemann und Zeitgenossen', in *JahExt*, 139–57.

VosDan '"Der aus der Löwengrube errettete Daniel": Eine unbekannte Hamburger Michaelismusik von Georg Philipp Telemann?', in *LanKir*, 369–83.

VosMiz Steffen Voss, '". . . sur les loix d'une certaine societé": Die Mizlersche Societät der musikalischen Wissenschaften im Urteil Georg Philipp Telemanns und Johann Matthesons', in *ReiBac*, 206–13.

WacDic Andreas Waczkat, 'Die "Dicta Biblica" TVWV 10:21–31: Aspekte einer apokryphen Sammlung', in *LanKir*, 309–27.

WacMes Andreas Waczkat, 'Georg Philipp Telemanns Messias', *Concerto*, No. 182 (2003), 21–25.

WacNat Andreas Waczkat, 'Telemann, Carl Philipp Emanuel Bach und die domestizierte Natur', in *LanImp*, 78–88.

WacNeu Andreas Waczkat, '"Grönländische Sätze": Telemanns *Neue Musikalisches System* und der unverstandene Versuch, eine Praxis theoretisch herzuleiten', in *JahExt*, 33–43.

WeiPap Wisso Weiss, 'Zu Papieren und Wasserzeichen Telemannischer Notenhandschriften', in *HobWer*, 1:19–34.

WerOde Dirk Werle, "Telemanns Vier und zwanzig Oden (1741) und die deutsche Lyrik," in *TadUrb*, 190–204.

WetBib Hermann Wettstein, *Georg Philipp Telemann: Bibliographischer Versuch zu seinem Leben und Werk 1681–1767* (Hamburg: Wagner, 1981).

WilBor Chanan Willner, 'Handel's Borrowings from Telemann: An Analytical View', in Allen Cadwallader (ed.), *Trends in Schenkerian Research* (New York: Schirmer, 1990), 145–68.

WilPol Krystyna Wilkowska-Chomińska, 'Telemanns Beziehungen zur polnischen Musik', in *NeuBil*, 23–37.

WolBes Hellmuth Christian Wolff, 'Telemanns Beschreibung einer Augen-Orgel (1739) und seine Stellungsnahme zur Musikästhetik', in *FleBed*, 2:47–51.

WolFle Peter Wollny, '"Fleißige, reine Arbeit" oder "Abglanz einer großen Schule"? Wilhelm Friedemann Bach und die protestantische Kirchenkantate nach 1750', in *HirWil*, 13–31.

WolOpe Hellmuth Christian Wolff, *Die Barockoper in Hamburg* (1678–1738) (Wolfenbüttel: Möseler, 1957).

WolPim Hellmut Christian Wolff, '"Pimpinone" von Albinoni und Telemann: Ein Vergleich', in *FloFrü*, 29–36.

WolOst Peter Wollny, 'C. P. E. Bach, Georg Philipp Telemann und die

Osterkantate "Gott hat den Herrn auferwecket" Wq 244', in *CorWol*, 78–94.

WolPas Uwe Wolf, 'Der Anteil Telemanns an den Hamburger Passionen Carl Philipp Emanuel Bachs', in *LanMal*, 412–22.

ZohAes Steven Zohn, 'Aesthetic Mediation and Tertiary Rhetoric in Telemann's *VI Ouvertures à 4 ou 6*', in *TalBac*, 24–49.

ZohEns Steven Zohn, 'The Ensemble Sonatas of Georg Philipp Telemann: Studies in Style, Genre, and Chronology', PhD dissertation, Cornell University, 1995.

ZohFai Steven Zohn, 'Morality and the "Fair-Sexing" of Telemann's Faithful Music Master', in *Consuming Music: Individuals, Institutions Communities, 1730–1830*, ed. Emily Green and Catherine Mayes (Rochester, NY: University of Rochester Press, 2017), 65–101.

ZohFan Steven Zohn, 'Telemann's *Fantaisies pour la basse violle* and His Fantasia Principle', in *JahExt*, 107–24.

ZohIma Steven Zohn, 'Images of Telemann: Narratives of Reception in the Composer's Anecdote, 1750–1830', *Journal of Musicology* 21/4 (2004), 459–86.

ZohImi Steven Zohn with Ian Payne, 'Bach, Telemann, and the Process of Transformative Imitation in BWV 1056/2 (156/1)', *Journal of Musicology* 17/4 (1999), 546–84.

ZohJob Steven Zohn, 'Naïve Questions and Laughable Answers: An Eighteenth-Century Job Interview', in *Coll'astuzia, col giudizio: Essays in Honor of Neal Zaslaw*, ed. Cliff Eisen (Ann Arbor, MI: Steglein, 2009), 62–92.

ZohMar Steven Zohn, 'Telemann in the Marketplace: The Composer as Self-Publisher', *Journal of the American Musicological Society* 58/2 (2005), 275–356.

ZohMix Steven Zohn, *Music for a Mixed Taste: Style, Genre, and Meaning in Telemann's Instrumental Works* (New York: Oxford University Press, 2008; revised paperback edition, 2015).

ZohMor Steven Zohn, '"Am besten bleib' ich in der Mitte": Telemann's Moral Publishing Project', in *HirKan*, 231–55.

ZohPap Steven Zohn, 'Music Paper at the Dresden Court and the Chronology of Telemann's Instrumental Music', in *Puzzles in Paper: Concepts in Historical Watermarks: Essays from the International Conference on the History, Function, and Study of Watermarks, Roanoke, Virginia*, ed. Daniel W. Mosser, Michael Saffle and Ernest W. Sullivan II (New Castle, DE: Oak Knoll Press; London: British Library, 2000), 125–68.

ZohSon Steven Zohn, 'The *Sonate auf Concertenart* and Conceptions of Genre in the Late Baroque', *Eighteenth-Century Music* 1/2 (2004), 205–47.

ZohQua Steven Zohn, 'New Light on Quantz's Advocacy of Telemann's Music', *Early Music* 25/3 (1997), 441–61.

ZohRec Steven Zohn, '"Of His Works, Nothing is Remembered": Toward a Reception History of Telemann in England and the United States, 1740–1940', in *Lan Umg*, 84–108.

ZohRef Steven Zohn, '"Die vornehmste Hof-Tugend": German Musicians' Reflections on Eighteenth-Century Court Life', in Samantha Owens, Barbara Reul and Janice Stockigt (eds.), *Music at German Courts, 1715–1760: Changing Artistic Priorities* (Rochester, NY: Boydell & Brewer, 2011), 413–25.

ZohTaf Steven Zohn, 'Telemann's *Musique de table* and the *Tafelmusik* Tradition', *Oxford Handbooks Online* (2016), www.oxfordhandbooks.com

ZohViv Steven Zohn, 'Telemann the Vivaldian', in Francesco Fanna and Michael Talbot (eds.), *Antonio Vivaldi, Passato e futuro* (Venice: Fondazione Giorgio Cini, 2009), 95–107, www.cini.it/publications/antonio-vivaldi-passato-e-futuro-it

www.ingramcontent.com/pod-product-compliance
Lightning Source LLC
LaVergne TN
LVHW020506100826
845148LV00003B/710
9781837653218